Approaches to *Gravity's Rainbow*

Edited by Charles Clerc

Approaches to

Gravity's Rainbow

Ohio State University Press : Columbus

Library of Congress Cataloging in Publication Data

Main entry under title:
Approaches to Gravity's rainbow.

   Includes index.
   Contents: Introduction / by Charles Clerc—
War as background in Gravity's rainbow / by Khachig Tololyan—
Science and technology / by Alan J. Friedman—[etc.]
   1. Pynchon, Thomas. Gravity's rainbow.
I. Clerc, Charles, date.
PS3566.Y55G732   813'.54   82–6500
ISBN 0–8142–0337–X   AACR2

Contents

Editor's Notes

Page references to *Gravity's Rainbow* are to two available editions: first, the Viking Press edition, published simultaneously in hardcover and paperback (1973); second, the Bantam paperback edition (1974).

Pynchon's stylistic use of ellipses throughout his novel poses a problem in distinguishing omissions in quotations on the part of authors of the essays in this text, and may require a second glance from readers: ellipses that appear in *Gravity's Rainbow* are here set closed up, without space between the points (...); authorial omissions are indicated by the usual spaced points (. . .).

Approaches to *Gravity's Rainbow*

Introduction

By Charles Clerc

The word *classic* is bandied so freely these days that it has become virtually meaningless. It is a favorite in the bloated repertoire of hype, and hype, as we all know of contemporary culture, almost never delivers the goods promised. Nevertheless, the word still must be taken seriously when the genuine article comes along. The important criterion for a novel, beyond its own aesthetic accomplishments, is that it will have enduring significance and worth, a work of art to be read and discussed and analyzed with ever renewing enjoyment, understanding, and enrichment by generations of readers.

In these respects, Thomas Pynchon's *Gravity's Rainbow* is destined to become a classic of literature. Edward Mendelson, writing in the *Yale Review* (Summer, 1973), minced no words about *Gravity's Rainbow* at its publication: "This is certainly the most important novel to be published in English in the past thirty years, and it bears all the lineaments of greatness." To Richard Poirier, in *Saturday Review of the Arts* (March, 1973), the novel brought to mind both *Moby Dick* and *Ulysses*; but Poirier considered that "*Gravity's Rainbow* marks an advance beyond either book in its treatment of cultural inheritances, an advance that a merely literary education and taste will either distort or find uncongenial." And he added, "Pynchon is willing and able, that is, to work from a range of perspectives infinitely wider, more difficult to manage, more learned than any to be found elsewhere in contemporary literature." Walter Clemons commented, in *Newsweek* (March 19, 1973): "It isn't plausible to call a novel great the week it's published, because the future will decide that. It isn't tactful, either, because it arouses resistance in readers. But *Gravity's Rainbow* is, at the very least, tremendous." Along with

3

his prediction that "this novel is going to change the shape of fiction, if only because its genius will depress all competitors," W. T. Lhamon, Jr., in the *New Republic* (April 14, 1973), made a special plea that the novel, like *Ulysses*, not be buried in "seminars all over the land." Since "*Gravity's Rainbow* comes cyclically out of people and people's culture and should return to Us and Ours, resonantly," Lhamon urged that "it should not be routed into a 'no return' solitary confinement among the tastes of academe. Read this novel: it's one of the finest ever."

Similar laudatory reviews—their slips of incomprehension sometimes showing—appeared in some two dozen other journals and national magazines. However, it would be misleading to suggest that the novel escaped intelligently expressed detraction, whether by way of mixed feelings about its length, structure, and control, or by way of dissent against its accomplishments. Richard Locke, in the *New York Times Book Review* (March 11, 1973), and David Thorburn, in *Commentary* (September, 1973), provide good examples of each position. Still, no critic or reviewer initially denied its stature as a major work of art.

Controversy about Pynchon's work intensified over the years since the appearance of *Gravity's Rainbow*. Roger Sale, in *On Not Being Good Enough: Writings of a Working Critic* (1979), ranked Pynchon among "imperial novelists," those "writers whose imaginations are powerful, inventive, conquering." They may "detest the American empire" but "were in fact also expressing it, and deriving some of their enormous energy from it." Pynchon's writing, in spite of its flaws, can be "stunning," impelled by "thrusts of energy through long and often magnificent flights and swoops."

However, John Gardner, in *On Moral Fiction* (1978), listed Pynchon among writers of "inflated reputations"—grouped with John Updike and John Barth, they will "die of intellectual blight, academic narrowness, or fakery." When Gardner criticized *Gravity's Rainbow* as subversive of moral values, he echoed the opinions of certain journalists who overruled a panel of distinguished judges for recommending the novel for the fifty-eighth annual Pulitzer Prize. The judges had reported: "No work of fiction published in 1973 begins to compare in scale, originality, and sustained interest with Mr. Pynchon's book." Nevertheless, some newspapermen on the board argued that the book was incomprehensible and turgid, pernicious and obscene, and they decided that no fiction prize should be awarded for the year.

Their decision aroused the ire of several critics, including John

Leonard ("The Last Word," *New York Times Book Review*, 19 May 1974). He accused the Pulitzer trustees and advisory group of "scandalous" behavior and said that they "should take a crash course in remedial reading or they should get out of the awards business altogether." He wrote: "Really, there is no ignoring *Gravity's Rainbow*. . . . It is there, like the Grand Canyon. . . . The other novels of the year—and there were many worthy ones— disappear into its huge ambition, its range, its spectacular effects. As an act of imagination and a feat of style, it is simply more and better than any other fiction of the year, and maybe the decade."

Another illustration of the novel's stature could be found in the placement of Lawrence O. Wolfley's lengthy lead article "Repression's Rainbow: The Presence of Norman O. Brown in Pynchon's Big Novel" in the October, 1977, issue of *PMLA*. This eminent journal rarely accords space to recent fiction. Wolfley wrote that *Gravity's Rainbow* "has attained a cult following which continues to grow," and he regarded it as "a novel that bids well to stand as one of the greatest of our time." A similarly lofty ranking was accorded the novel later in a survey entitled "Immortal Nominations" in the *New York Times Book Review* (June 3, 1979). Critic Denis Donaghue and playwright Lillian Hellman both listed *Gravity's Rainbow* among "Post World War II books which have already established themselves or may eventually establish themselves in a group of a hundred or so of the most important books of western literature."

Yet the next year two critics attacked Pynchon as writer and *Gravity's Rainbow* as novel for their serious deficiencies. In a survey of "The American Political Novel" (*New York Times Book Review*, 10 August 1980), Robert Alter ranked Pynchon among "adversary novelists." Their strategy is "to render what is conceived of as an American sickness unto death in a zany phantasmagoria of an apocalyptic cast." Pynchon's work (along with others') exhibited an "astonishing degree of puerility." Alter also inveighed against Pynchon's "sexual and scatological imaginings." He saw this kind of writing as providing "a clear sanction for adolescent outbursts as an appropriate response to politics." In his essay "The Enemies of Intimacy" (*Harper's Magazine*, July, 1980), a critique of pseudoculture, the late George P. Elliott expressed his concern for "the madness that best characterizes our time . . . paranoia, or, in dilution, paranoid tendencies." He argued that "an example is the enormous overvaluation of a novel like Pynchon's *Gravity's Rainbow*, which does not realistically portray complex characters who, among their other qualities, take a paranoid view of the world, nor does it, as Beckett does, perform astonishing arabesques in the narrow strand between lush paranoia and nothingness. Instead, it *projects* paranoia. . . ."

Such disputations over the worth of Pynchon's work are minimal when compared with the multiplicity of views about its meaning. It is not difficult to see why. Worldwide, Pynchon may be counted among a handful of writers since Joyce who challenge to their utmost the intellectual capabilities of scholars. Because he is so fascinating, invigorating, demanding, he has become the object of an amazing surge of critical interest. His fiction, especially *Gravity's Rainbow*, is rich, resonant, ambiguous—it therefore invites and generates varied interpretations. Within the last decade, Pynchon studies proliferated rapidly. Articles sprouted by the dozens, numerous dissertations were undertaken, eleven books and two booklets have already been published,* and the presses continue to receive manuscripts from Pynchon enthusiasts. The valuable journal *Pynchon Notes*, which began as a modest newsletter in 1979, maintains an international circulation, under the editorship of John M. Krafft and Khachig Tololyan.

The Pynchon industry has flourished with neither help nor hindrance from the writer himself. Ironically, Pynchon's celebrated reclusiveness (no interviews, no photographs, no anything) continues to make him all the more newsworthy. That Pynchon chooses to remain secluded is his business, so his desire for privacy and his avoidance of the gamesmanship of the literary marketplace need not be belabored. However, to set the record straight and to oblige readers who wish to know something about the artist, a few facts may prove helpful.

Thomas Ruggles Pynchon, Jr., was born May 8, 1937, in Glen Cove, Long Island, and grew up with a younger brother and sister in East Norwich. His ancestors go back to the beginnings of Amer-

---

*Thomas Pynchon, by Joseph W. Slade (Warner, 1974); *Mindful Pleasures: Essays on Thomas Pynchon*, ed. George Levine and David Leverenz (Little, Brown, 1976); *Pynchon: A Collection of Critical Essays*, ed. Edward Mendelson (Twentieth Century Views, Prentice-Hall, 1978); *Pynchon: Creative Paranoia in "Gravity's Rainbow,"* by Mark Richard Siegel (Kennikat Press, 1978); *The Grim Phoenix: Reconstructing Thomas Pynchon*, by William M. Plater (Indiana University Press, 1978); *Thomas Pynchon: The Art of Allusion*, by David Cowart (Southern Illinois University Press, 1980); *A Reader's Guide to "Gravity's Rainbow,"* by Douglas Fowler (Ardis, 1980); *Pynchon's Fictions: Thomas Pynchon and the Literature of Information*, by John O. Stark (Ohio University Press, 1980); *The Rainbow Quest of Thomas Pynchon*, by Douglas A. Mackey (booklet, Borgo Press, 1980); *Pynchon: The Voice of Ambiguity*, by Thomas Schaub (University of Illinois Press, 1981); *Critical Essays on Thomas Pynchon*, ed. Richard Pearce (G. K. Hall, 1981); *Ordnung und Entropie. Zum Romanwerk von Thomas Pynchon*, ed. Heinz Ickstadt ([Hamburg,] Rowalt, 1981); *Thomas Pynchon*, by Tony Tanner (booklet, Methuen, 1982).

ican history. The first Pynchon to settle in America, William, came to the Massachusetts Bay Colony from England in 1630. As a magistrate, he achieved some notoriety by presiding at a witchcraft trial. He later returned to England, where he wrote controversial treatises on religion. His son John stayed in America and became wealthy. (Incidentally, the Pynchon family was later to be described in *The House of Seven Gables* [as Pyncheon]—Hawthorne's correspondence to his publisher about resulting chastisement by family descendents is amusing.) Leaders of succeeding generations of Pynchons did well in the New World as merchants, ministers, physicians, and teachers. Pynchon's father served as town supervisor of Oyster Bay and became an industrial surveyor. After distinguishing himself at Oyster Bay High School, Pynchon went to Cornell University in 1953. His early training came in physics; later his interest turned to literature. Following the interruption of his studies by a hitch in the navy, he graduated from Cornell with distinction in 1959. He had already begun to write fiction in college; his first stories appeared in *Epoch, New World Writing, Kenyon Review,* and *Noble Savage* between 1959 and 1961. While working on his first novel *V.,* he lived in Greenwich Village, and then moved west where he worked for the Boeing Company in Seattle as a technical writer between 1960 and 1962. Afterward he lived, by choice obscurely, in California and Mexico. Aside from a few excerpts from his novels in various magazines and an article on Watts in the *New York Times Magazine* in 1966, his major published work consists of three novels: *V.* (1963); *The Crying of Lot 49* (1966); and *Gravity's Rainbow* (1973). These novels have won important awards, including a share of the National Book Award for fiction for *Gravity's Rainbow*. In 1975 Pynchon received the Howells Medal from the American Academy of Arts and Letters for having produced the most distinguished work of American fiction of the preceding five years. In keeping with his unyielding reclusiveness, he declined to accept it.

With those three works in a ten-year period before he reached the age of forty, Pynchon was vaulted into the front ranks of twentieth-century writers. Unless his career takes a drastic turn in the manner, say, of Steinbeck or Fitzgerald, there is every reason to believe that whatever follows in years to come can only serve to enhance a formidable place in American letters. Reportedly Pynchon has been at work for years on two novels, but at this writing early in 1982 neither is yet in print. In any case, the position of his third novel is already established. A few American novels—*Moby Dick, The Adventures of Huckleberry Finn, The Great Gatsby, The Sound and the Fury,*

Invisible Man—stand alone on their merits, regardless of what their authors may have written before or after them. Now *Gravity's Rainbow* joins this illustrious list.

Although singular in its achievement, *Gravity's Rainbow* should also be seen as part of an expanding metamorphic process going on in fiction within the past couple of decades. Increasingly, American writers are breaking loose to create new modes. Science fiction, autobiographical elements, and pasticcio have been combined by Kurt Vonnegut, Jr., in, for example, *Slaughterhouse-Five* (1969). "Creative reportage" (or any other such ill-chosen term as the new journalism, energized biography, or faction now in vogue for the application of novelistic techniques to true-life events) has been practiced by Truman Capote in *In Cold Blood* (1966), and Norman Mailer in *The Armies of the Night* (1968) and *The Executioner's Song* (1979). A fraternally related type of writing grew out of the admixture of fiction and factual history so that lines between the two became blurred, as in William Styron's *The Confessions of Nat Turner* (1966), E. L. Doctorow's *Ragtime* (1975), and Robert Coover's *The Public Burning* (1977). Absurdist humor made inroads after Joseph Heller's *Catch-22* (1961). Unusual combinations of the grotesque, the violent, and the comic ranged from one extreme, in Flannery O'Connor's *The Violent Bear It Away* (1960), to another, in John Irving's *The World According to Garp* (1978). Myths were reworked to make new stories out of the old in Donald Barthelme's *Snow White* (1967), and John Barth's *Chimera* (1972). Counterculture zaniness reached a new height in Tom Robbins's *Another Roadside Attraction* (1971). The incursions into surrealism by William Burroughs, John Hawkes, and Ishmael Reed could also be included, as well as the steadily evolved narrative virtuosity of Saul Bellow and the late Vladimir Nabokov.

There is a little of all these people in Thomas Pynchon, yet on his own he is pushing fictional boundaries even farther outward, or deeper in, as the case may be. An expeditious, if not simplistic, way to introduce the changes wrought by *Gravity's Rainbow* is to compare it briefly with a novel far removed in method and scope. *Pride and Prejudice* will do as an example of the tradition of unified linear narrative devoted to a single idea. Although Jane Austen peoples her novel with a good-sized cast of characters, she keeps tight control over its range. Were a large blackboard at hand, it could be readily filled with lists of subjects that the novel is *not* about. From the memorable opening line ("It is a truth universally acknowledged, that a single man in possession of a good fortune, must be in want of a wife") through some three hundred pages, Austen is primarily concerned with problems of social manners and courtship, of preoccupation with self and misinterpretation of others. Although a perceptive and enduring study, it is nevertheless a novel that keeps within precisely confined limitations. By contrast, many, perhaps even all, of the subjects on that blackboard would apply to what Pynchon's novel *is* about. It is an encyclopedic, panoramic, global, multinational novel that deliberately exploits many styles and modes.

It would be unreasonable to expect that any single novel could provide sufficient materials for a liberal education, but certainly *Gravity's Rainbow* comes closer to that goal than any other work of fiction produced in America. It is a dazzling pioneer work in its utilization of manifold subject matter: history, war, mythology, literature, film, culture (whether canonical or pop), religion, philosophy, the military-industrial complex (whether in peace or war), psychology, politics, geography, cybernetics, sex, death, comedy, scatology, music, international cartels, engineering, ballistics, mysticism, plastics, and many more. Further, some of these areas have their own subdivisions; for instance, science, which includes specific uses of chemistry, mathematics, biology, physics, and cosmology. As a multitopic novel, it thus makes many demands of its readership.

The intent of this book is to explain the multiple perspectives of the novel and their implications. The essays are designed to supplement the novel's artistry and to make its difficulties more accessible and comprehensible to students and general readers. Because all eight essays are original, covering specifically designated topics, they minimize the duplication of criticism that is common to casebooks on individual novels. Furthermore, they escape the fate of fragmentation common to collections that must excerpt longer articles.

Admittedly there is a danger in a book of this kind. *Gravity's Rainbow* should be experienced, in the best sense of the word. It is a novel to be enjoyed and endured, fought with and agonized over in the zone of intimacy between reader and page. Because it is functionally chaotic, convoluted, complex, any attempt to impose critical order upon it may well impair its effects and dilute the totality of its power. In short: better to leave it alone. As Witold Gombrowicz said about his novel *Ferdydurke*: "Come, come, be more sensuous, less cerebral, start dancing with the book instead of asking for meanings." There is considerable truth in this view, but it can hardly console those readers who may not know how to dance across 760 pages of a radically different novel, one that often masks itself as antinovelistic, antiliterary, and, by an even greater deceptiveness, antihumanistic. Some keys need to be provided to open outer doorways.

The striking opening line, "A screaming comes across the sky," announces the unseen appearance of the Rocket over London in World War II. Its parabola, etching that invisible scar of destruction and death, represents stark reality, as well as a mock covenant, a response to God above and the pull of earth below. The rainbow of gravity eventuates in its final descent as a mightier missile upon "everybody" at an apocalyptic moment of the present. The specific target, which is Los Angeles, becomes less important than the symbolic indeterminacy: the Rocket is falling during the whole course of the novel, and in the world at large the Rocket is poised to fall anywhere at any time. The main action of the novel occurs in 1944–45: the last nine months of the war and the immediate postwar period. From that span of a year, the "present" of the novel, time is freely manipulated in flashforwards and flashbacks. For instance, Pynchon jumps ahead to relate the information "Eventually Jack and Malcolm both got murdered," to interject an authorial recommendation of contemporary writers like Beal and Reed, to accommodate a personal statement ("Between two station-marks, yellow crayon through the years of grease and passage, 1966 and 1971, I tasted my first blood" [V739/B862]), or to take us directly into the modern freeway confusion of his parodically Nixonized Los Angeles.

More prevalent, however, are the many flashbacks of etiological nature: to biblical and medieval times, the seventeenth and nineteenth centuries, but mostly to formative events of the 1920s and 1930s. With side excursions to New England, Southwest Africa, Argentina, and the Russian Steppes, the bulk of the action takes place in England, France, Switzerland, Holland, and Germany. Although at the outset the novel appears to establish a realistic series of events in London and elsewhere, later readings may suggest other interpretations. For example, a psychoanalytic critic may regard the realism as a series of delusions projected by one character or another; Captain Pirate Prentice, the intelligence officer whose nightmare begins the novel, is a prime candidate for schizophrenia. A totally different perspective could be cinematographic, which is to say that at novel's end we take the events to have occurred on screen—we have been witness to a movie about

World War II and its aftermath, the movie itself representing a mixture of genres (perhaps even some mixed-up reels), with leanings
toward musical comedy.

The temptation to read *Gravity's Rainbow* as something generically
different from a novel is very real, as separate critics like Edward
Mendelson and Khachig Tololyan have shrewdly demonstrated by
linking it to the tradition of the encyclopedic narrative. At the risk
of oversimplifying, a brief sample of other views: Eliot Brahn and
John Stark have traced its kinship to Menippean satire; David
Cowart has shown its workings of the quest tradition; Mark Siegel
has inverted them into anti-quest patterns; and Douglas Fowler,
along with stressing its gothic elements, sees the novel as a great
poem and claims that it should be read essentially as poetry is read,
rather than for fulfillment of the usual novelistic expectations.

Whatever interpretations are brought to bear, there is no mistak-
ing the historical foundations upon which the novel is built.
Although wonderfully inventive and imaginative, it pays scrupu-
lous attention to verifiable factual details. As historical fiction, one
of its chief intentions is to reflect inheritance of the past in the
present. The major historical symbol that unifies the four parts of
the novel and many of its seventy-three unnumbered chapters and
that also resonates into multiple meanings for our own time is the
German A-4 rocket, known more commonly as the V-2. The
terrible reign of these flying bombs shattered Britain during the
latter stage of the war. The Rocket is a symbol that betokens
modern civilization's obsession with technology, whether devising,
building, or launching the weapon, or pursuing the secrets of its
mysterious potency. As a gigantic destructive phallus, it couples sex
and death and links to other related obsessions. We are told, moreover, that the Rocket "has to be many things" to many people,
among them "Manichaeans who sees two Rockets, good and
evil . . . a good Rocket to take us to the stars, an evil Rocket for the
World's suicide, the two perpetually in struggle" (V727/B847–48).
It is many other things: "Torah," "throne," pyre; God's hand, pointing an omniscient finger; the papal staff of the Tannhäuser legend,
invertedly bringing damnation rather than blooming salvation and
forgiveness; "Baby Jesus" ascending to the heavens, betrayed by the
Judas of gravity; an amalgam of construction and destruction, renewal and termination, order and disorder; the ambivalent epitome
of human achievement and failure. As broader metaphor for an age,
bringer of "new revelations," it may portend the future of a nuclear
holocaust. So the screaming that comes across the sky—bomb and

writer's voice—resounds from source to destination and reverberates for everyone under the parabola, alpha to omega.

Gravity's Rainbow is the kind of artistic work that needs to be read slowly, thoughtfully, and persistently in small chunks, without distraction, and then read again and again. Many of its passages are so extraordinary that they ought to be read aloud. Such suggestions may seem unwarranted, perhaps pointless, because the same can be said of any challenging literature. But in this case the advice is emphatically necessary because the reader must surmount obstacles that grow fiercer along the way. To complicate matters, the author puts on an intellectual light show of such erudition that its beams bedazzle rather than clarify. Thus the reader may often be prevented from knowing where he or she is going. The "mess" in Argentina described by Francisco Squalidozzi (V264/B307) serves as a rough parallel for the plight the novel puts the reader into. "Where before there was open plain and sky," there are now "labyrinths." As Squalidozzi longs for "unscribbled serenity," the reader may yearn for more sureness of direction and understanding, but the "complex" patterns beckon toward disorientation.

First, the novel's enormous cast is difficult to keep track of, especially in the moiling rush of their entries and exits. Some of the principal characters do not appear until the middle third of the novel. The unsuspecting reader may be thrown off by the initial twenty pages devoted to minor characters. Some incidental characters occupy long later passages; others will merely trip in and out of a paragraph or even a sentence. Furthermore, an important character may be dropped, not to reappear for hundreds of pages, or simply dissolve.

In connection with Pynchon's treatment of his characters, a vexing critical problem has arisen. It results from a twofold assumption: that Pynchon does not get inside his characters, and that the reader cannot "identify" with them in the usual sense. Although this critical cavil may have attained a certain popularity, it is erroneous. Close reading of *Gravity's Rainbow* will prove that Pynchon gets inside his characters as much as, if not sometimes more so than, other novelists. The complaint against him probably stems from his concern with exterior forces at work upon people, his abandonment of the realist tradition of handling character, and his elliptical method of offering very few clues to explain his characters' functions. Moreover, many dramatic and all sentimental strategies are avoided. For another reason, the characters' actions in many cases go unresolved—the reader may be left dissatisfied by such inconclusiveness. For yet another, characterization is made disjunctive by persistent uses of hyperbolic comedy and parody, which tend to distort banal realities. This does not mean, however, that Pynchon's characters are cartoonish. Often in the novel human consciousness is so centered upon technology and its crises that expected human emotions will seem to be either awry or missing. The unusual perspective of seeing many of the characters through their war-induced work contributes to making them appear one-sidedly obsessed. Interestingly, the novel is so grounded in contradictions that an all-consuming war ends by a casual few sentences. Again, contrary to some critical opinion, the novel is not "icy cold," nor does it lack "food and warmth." It is, in fact, often compassionate, often achingly tender toward people.

Thirteen characters may be considered important, besides the major one. Touching almost every principal character of four different nationalities is the American protagonist, Tyrone Slothrop, a comic but nevertheless affecting antihero. Product of a Puritan tradition, former Harvard student, unknowing victim of early sexual conditioning, he is in 1944 a chubby, insouciant lieutenant stationed in England. His numerous sexual "conquests," which are perhaps more fantasized than real, give evidence on a starred map of his foreknowledge of German A-4 rocket hits in London. Authorities at "'The White Visitation,' which houses a catchall agency known as PISCES—Psychological Intelligence Schemes for Expediting Surrender" (V34/B39)—try to find out the relationship between Slothrop's erections and the rocket hits. The worst schemer, Dr. Edward W. A. Pointsman, is an obsessed Pavlovian whose bent for determinism and control dialectically opposes the beliefs of statistician Roger Mexico. This young British lieutenant happens to be largely preoccupied with his tenuous love affair with the British Army girl Jessica Swanlake, who also has been manipulated by Pointsman.

Convinced that "They" are out to get him, Slothrop escapes into the chaotic randomness of central Europe's Zone. (Like the "Combine" of Kesey's *One Flew over the Cuckoo's Nest*, "They" can be any oppressive, controlling, or conspiratorial group, be it specifically leaders of PISCES or more generally the Firm or the Elect.) Slothrop's paranoiac flight is combined with his search for the mysterious "quintuple-zero" rocket and its facsimile, which the Firm also wants to find. Thus Slothrop becomes both "seeker and sought," both "baited and bait" (V490/B571). Under various disguises and aliases, notably as Raketemensch in green cape and hornless Wagnerian helmet, Slothrop makes contact with nearly every important male character. They are mostly connected with rocketry, like Franz Pökler, a passive German chemical engineer, or black marketeering, like the energetic German film director Gerhardt von Göll, who goes under the *nom de pègre* Der Springer. Excepting Jessica Swanlake, Slothrop is sexually intimate with every important female character: Katje Borgesius, a Dutch triple agent, whom he rescues from a trained octopus on the Riviera; Geli Tripping, "apprentice witch" and German girlfriend of Vaslav Tchitcherine, a Soviet intelligence officer; Margherita (Greta) Erdmann, an aging German film actress, as well as her young daughter; and Leni Pökler, a German Marxist and Franz's former wife who becomes the whore Solange.

An enigmatic figure links Slothrop to the major German side of the story. He is Dr. Laszlo Jamf, who sexually conditioned the infant Slothrop in America and who later in Europe developed Imipolex G, a polymer used in the Rocket. It insulated the Schwarzgerät, or S-Gerät, a mysterious propellant "hardware," which is also the object of varied searches. Ironically, in the climactic launch it turns out to be a human being. Obsession with rocketry is represented, at fanatical extreme, by Lieutenant, then Major, Weissmann, who under the SS code name of Captain Blicero ("white death") demonically commits himself to the launching of the final secret 00000. The replica of that rocket, 00001, is being assembled by the Schwarzkommando, Hereros exiled in Germany. They are under the command of Oberst Enzian, who as a boy in colonized Southwest Africa was the homosexual protégé of Weissmann. Also, because Enzian is a stigmatized black half-brother, Tchitcherine seeks to kill him.

These intricate relationships are further complicated by fourteen other fairly important minor characters, separated here for convenience's sake by categories. *The White Visitation*: Brigadier Ernest Pudding, the decrepit superior who eats shit (in a repugnant scene that continues as locus of critical controversy); and a key victim, Oliver "Tantivy" Mucker-Maffick, a likable young British officer whose strange disappearance and death prompt Slothrop to flee into the Zone; *black marketeering and drug dealing*: Seaman "Pig" Bodine, AWOL from an American destroyer (like several others, he appeared in Pynchon's *V.*); Emil ("Säure") Bummer, former cat burglar and exponent of Rossini music; and Blodgett Waxwing, oafish fan of American cowboy movies; *Hereros*: Josef Ombindi, as leader of a faction, the Empty Ones, this compatriot-opponent of

Enzian favors racial suicide; *exiles*: Francisco Squalidozzi, whose followers have stolen a submarine in Argentina and invertedly seek asylum in Germany; *German rocketry*: Gottfried, captive German youth and Blicero's homosexual lover who is launched in the 00000; Kurt Mondaugen, radio electronics specialist and friend of Pökler at Peenemünde; and Ilse, Pökler's daughter and/or her surrogates who visit him every summer "to create for him the moving image of a daughter"; the *Anubis*: boat of the damned whose passengers include Bianca, Greta's precocious nymphet daughter; and Greta's sadomasochistic husband Miklos Thanatz; and *intelligence*: Major Duane Marvy, a brutish American who partakes in the pursuit and becomes himself a victim of the castration intended for Slothrop; and Prentice, the British commando, who has the "odd talent for living the fantasies of others" (V620/B722), and who, like Katje and Slothrop, dissolves away.

Behind them crowd about three hundred incidental characters, often whackily named—a Pynchon trademark. Some are fictional and located in the past, like Slothrop's Puritan ancestors; many are historical personages, like the German organic chemist August Kekulé, the Scottish physicist James Clerk Maxwell, the German industrialist Hugo Stinnes, and the American gangster John Dillinger. Also, a cast of real people figure in the novel's present, ranging from actor Mickey Rooney to rocket expert Wernher von Braun to Nazi Munitions Minister Albert Speer. In most instances the actual people are woven into the background—they do not play important roles in the narrative.

Besides the difficulty of keeping all the characters straight, the reader encounters difficulty following the lines of action. Just as Pynchon abandoned some traditional notions of characterization, he also dispenses with some of the standard and familiar guidelines for constructing plots. In a novel filled with schemes, conspiracies, spying, networks, conglomerates, the plotting cannot be disentangled with any ease, nor should it be. The same holds true for the intricate path-crossings of individuals, all in search of something or other: a rocket, relatives, lovers, power, secrets, drugs, kicks, or their own identity. The main threads, however, are the pursuit of Slothrop and his own "grail quest," the dissipative later attempts of the Counterforce to help him, the making and firing of the 00000 by Blicero and the building of its facsimile by Enzian's Schwarzkommando, the devotion of Pökler to rocket development and (in the clearest, least-interrupted story line) his obsessive reunions with his daughter(s), Tchitcherine's search for his half-brother, and the futile love affair between Roger and Jessica. On the one hand, the strands seem quite lax. Varied plots, major and minor, result in anticlimax, they get nowhere, they fizzle out. On the other hand, for all their open-endedness and lack of resolution, the multiple plots also show that "everything is connected"—at their most formidable level by an international rocket cartel that has been enormously influential in shaping the history of modern Europe. In this respect, whether by individual confluences, acronymous bureaucracies, or powerful shadowy corporations, the novel spins out webs of interrelated systems.

Although treatment of characters and plot may seem initially overwhelming, like a parody of an internationalized soap opera (and surely in the telling as absurd as the summary of *The Courier's Tragedy* in *The Crying of Lot 49*), the two problems can be surmounted. Many novels of the past—typical social novels or family sagas from Russia, Britain, Scandinavia—have had huge casts and multiple story lines. But Pynchon's ways of telling his story require some readjustment by even the most practiced readers. His narrative methodology confirms that the timeworn critical tactic of affixing convenient plot, characterization, motives, and so on may be in large measure an inappropriate enterprise. The episodic, discontinuous structure manages to work effectively for conveying varied modes of experience, and, in turn, for reflecting the chaos of fragmenting cultures. The swift movie-cutting, the mixture of styles, the picaresque movement, the sporadic pacing, the emphasis on poetic evocation, the crazy quilt of subject matter, historicity, and the outright subversion of that same historicity by comedy and surrealism, amply reveal that the reader who is used to the staples of consistency, causality, credibility, and unity of effect is in for many surprises.

One of them is digressiveness, which allows Pynchon to pursue any tangent, whether a scientific discourse or the history of generations behind a character. The reader must adjust to supplementary set pieces on, for example, the extermination of dodoes by one of Katje's ancestors on Mauritius, Tchitcherine's winter of alphabet politics in Central Asia, a rescue of the Radiant Hour in a fantasized future Rocket City (the Raketen-Stadt), the properties of polymers, the Masonic mysticism of Lyle Bland, the derivation of phrases like "Ass Backwards" or "Shit 'n' Shinola," the details of a toiletship (the *Rücksichtslos*), the shenanigans of a pair of kamikaze pilots in the Pacific. Unquestionably, some of the detours are long and self-indulgent. Creative genius may on occasion give way to excess, particularly when the artist is a put-inner, like Pynchon, rather than a take-outer. Once begun, the putting-in process becomes difficult to stop, a problem clearly evident in, say, Joyce's later fiction, in Jean-Luc Godard films, in the music of Stravinsky. Although this novel might have profited from greater selectivity in places, the detours eventually come to be regarded as within the itinerary. In fact, upon reflection most are found to be integral, and a few are positively brilliant, like the hilarious story of Byron, the immortal light bulb (beginning V647/B754), Kekulé's discovery of the benzene ring and the implications of his dream of the great serpent with its tail in its mouth (V410/B478), the briefer sections on the Mother Conspiracy (V505/B589), the Titans (V720/B839), the death of John Dillinger (V516/B601). Overall, the digressions contribute rather than detract, so that in the end—to use Pynchon's words from another context—"It was worth the trip, just to see this shining. . . ."

The narrative voice is extremely flexible. Of indeterminate gender, it often stays detached to maintain an objective third-person point of view, but it also rises in protean ways to become involved, intimate, even paranoid. It speaks pointedly to the reader ("You will want cause and effect. All right."), makes frequent other uses of second person ("You have to be on your toes for this: you trade four-line stanzas. . . ."), and on rare occasions gives parenthetic advice, like its recommendation that the reader check out Ishmael Reed. During an intimate scene between Roger and Jessica when Pynchon flouts a cliché of personification about a room Heaving a Sigh, he playfully inserts "oh me I'm hopeless, born a joker never change" (V122/B142). The voice is chameleonic enough to become editorial, as in "we would also have to show" or "some of us," to stutter hesitantly, to comment by "sure," "hmm," "hell," "you know," to question and answer itself: "What's this, is he actually, yes, he's skipping," to provide choice: "Is the baby smiling or is it just gas? Which do you want it to be?" Whenever objectivity is set aside, the flexibility of the voice makes possible various uses. Among examples, it can be didactic to settle a score (although Pynchon almost never delivers overt messages); it can be lyrical to convey emotions; it can be deeply concerned, in which case Pynchon may skirt character to address the reader directly, sometimes seeming to embrace humanity as he does so; it can be ambiguous, provoking diverse streams of thought in the reader. In these shifts the voice may give the impression of being many and haphazard, but it is singular and quite in control. Even punctuation becomes a manipulative instrument. Ellipses are liberally used to suspend action, to pause, to suggest prolonged continuance or repetition, to trail off, to interpolate, and conversely to join, ideas. And undercutting is achieved by glibly nimble phonetic shortenings, such as *sez* for *says*.

Like the mercurial voice, the tone also refuses categorization. It can be tender and compassionate, hard and ruthless, witty, sensitive, jolly, obscene. It can dynamically shift from straightforward scholarly data to jaunty hyperbolic cartooning, from graphic realism to sophomoric tomfoolery to elegiac beauty. Scant pages separate the farce of Pointsman's foot stuck in a toilet bowl during a dog chase, Blicero's orgiastic sexual perversions near a rocket site, and a lyrically evocative visit to a Kentish church at Christmastime. These tonal and stylistic shifts are also geared to accommodate cultural stereotyping too. A breezy informal style is used when dealing with Americans, in particular, Slothrop; in its treatment of Germans, it becomes more formal and serious. Such rendering is not always mimetically precise, but Pynchon stays close enough to suggest by speech patterns and decorum, by quirks and mannerisms, certain national characteristics, similarly attributable to an Englishman, a Japanese, an Argentine, a Russian.

Additional proof that Pynchon loves to play with mood, as he loves to play with language and ideas, may be seen in his use of interruptive-supportive songs and poems, which number close to a hundred and range in length from a couplet to some fifty lines. They cover a wide diversity of types: from macaronic to limerick to haiku, from cadenza to Broadway show tune; they come in varied languages, mostly English, but also German, Latin, Middle Dutch, Spanish, Japanese; their rhythms change from beguine to fox-trot to sea chanty, from rumba to jazz to Hawaiian beat. One beguine, "Pavlovia," is sung by laboratory rats and mice doing a Busby Berkeley dance routine. A few more are equally as silly. Others range from grave to raucous to delicate to vulgar. The lengthy "Aqyn's Song" on seeing the Kirghiz Light is as beautiful in its symbolic imagery as the song on the horse in Lorca's *Blood Wedding*. They work in a manner equivalent to songs in musical comedy, except that often their presence is oxymoronic. They are used to change mood and focus, to spoof, to extrapolate, to underscore action while at the same time achieving distance from it, to show a lighter underside to horror or ugliness or futility, to hint at the illusion behind the reality or vice versa. Notably, the songs, as if in spite of themselves, also lend support to an ironic affirmation. So many emendations must be made, so many items must be added to the "renunciation of the things of the world" in the song "Sold on Suicide" that suicide is "postponed indefinitely." Although most likely we may never finish the hymn, it is indeed significant that we are led at the end into singing to the bouncing ball as the Rocket comes down on our heads.

This juxtaposition of the apocalyptic and the comic is a sure sign of Pynchon's ambivalence. For all the novel's forbidding concerns with waste, fragmentation, destructiveness, victimization, and death, life is sustained. Much of that very sustenance derives from humor, the unquenchable human capacity to laugh at ourselves. *Gravity's Rainbow* is a very funny book, laden with sight gags, practical jokes, zany chases, and pratfalls. Its puns are deliberately egregious: "I Ching feet," "Unto thee I pledge my trough," "For De Mille, young fur-henchmen can't be rowing." At the opposite end of the scale, the choicest lines show true comic mastery, like Slothrop's immortal cry as he fights off two young hoods in front of the Chicago Bar in Berlin: "Fickt nicht mit der Raketemensch!"; the witty double entendre of the epigraph to part two, citing Merian C. Cooper to Fay Wray: "You will have the tallest, darkest leading man in Hollywood"; Säure Bummer, in defense of his favorite composer, assessing a renowned competitor: "A person feels *good* listening to Rossini. All you feel like listening to Beethoven is going out and invading Poland." Mirthful grotesquery appears in the form of Wernher, Geli's attack owl that eats Baby Ruth candy bars, the Polish undertaker out to get struck by lightning, or Lucifer Amp, the demobbed window crasher. Ribald surreal events include a trip down a toilet, vengeful pissing on conferees from a tabletop, and literal pie in the sky in a balloon-plane combat over the Harz.

Although one of the most serious novels ever written persistently attempts not to take itself too seriously, its seriousness is magnified—for the same reason that an image of giving the finger can be inverted and overblown to become an atomic bomb blast. So we are never able only to laugh, not with a book as concomitantly visceral and discomforting as this one. There is no way to avoid being moved by the homages to nature, by sadness for the passed-over Preterite, by pain of loss, especially of the young like Ilse or Bianca, because the author's sympathy for children comes through so genuinely. Nor is there any escape from the squirm of shock brought on by vivid details of sadomasochism and coprophilia. On the comic side of the spectrum, Slothrop falls naked through a tree using a purple bedsheet as a parachute; on the tragic side, Blicero sends Gottfried hurtling off to a fiery ritual suicide in the Rocket. It is not always easy to reconcile these disparities of low comedy and high tragedy. By the same token, Pynchon's narrative methodology is often so indirect and tortuous that the reader may be uncertain of what is going on. The fate of Blicero provides an example. It is possible that he immolated himself in the rocket's flame at the climactic scene. Yet the King of Cups in his tarot places him later in America, where he holds a "high" position. Like so much else in the novel we do not know exactly what happens. These difficulties come with the territory—surmounting them is less hazardous if we are willing to make allowances for the kind of writer who does not care about conventional dramatic effects yet who pulls out all stops to achieve the effects *he* is interested in.

Beams flashing the brightest in *Gravity's Rainbow* generate from Pynchon's own erudition. They cause us to blink and squint and grope because he knows so many subjects we may know little about: quantum mechanics, the Beveridge Proposal, the five positions on the launching switch of an A-4 rocket. His reconditeness encompasses tarot cards, the Cabala, mandala, Qlippoth, the Wheel of Fortune, delta-t, double integral, yin-yang, a mathematical equation for motion under yaw control. He dips into Orphic, Norse, and Teutonic myths, and divines with ease necessary detritus of pop culture: Wonderwoman, German movies, zoot suits, Plasticman, King Kong, the Wizard of Oz, Carmen Miranda's hats.

By authentic quotations and paraphrasing, Pynchon makes serious use of mathematicians, scientists, philosophers, sociopolitical thinkers like Leibniz, Kekulé, and Heisenberg, Max Weber, Wernher von Braun, and Teilhard de Chardin. He dredges up Patrick Maynard Stuart Blackett's buried remark that "the scientist can encourage numerical thinking on operational matters, and so can help to avoid running the war on gusts of emotion," which appeared in the obscure *Scientists at the Operational Level*, published in 1941 (see V12/B13). As is Pynchon's customary playfulness, these authoritative citations are counterbalanced by imaginative flights: his Proverbs for Paranoids, his excerpt from *Neil Nosepicker's Book of 50,000 Insults*, his fragment from the Gospel of Thomas: "Dear Mom, I put a couple of people in Hell today." A plethora of allusions from literature, art, opera, film, science, music, and scripture beckon the cataloger to Gilbert and Sullivan, Käthe Kollwitz, Conrad, *Moby Dick*, Tannhäuser, Prometheus, *The Waste Land*, Hänsel and Gretel and the Witch, Fritz Lang, the Bible, Elena Petrovna Blavatsky, the Niebelungen Saga, Jakob Ackeret. He authentically quotes Emily Dickinson on decay and death and parodically injects a monosyllabic "What?" from Richard Nixon. A mournful dirge is played by Rainer Maria Rilke's *Duino Elegies*, which recurs again and again.

The allusions have a way of reinforcing their new context and enlarging the situation. Moreover, they can be symbolic or analytical, and, most importantly, they can contribute by enriching thematic meaning. From among innumerable examples, a simple minor allusion to Phoebus may be chosen to illustrate. In the cartoonish "Byron the Bulb" sequence, Phoebus is an evil "international light bulb cartel," only one of a huge interlocking conspiracy of cartels dominating the world. Phoebus employs all its vast resources and wiles to get rid of any bulb extending beyond "mean operating life." In other words, in its coldly calculated system for planned obsolescence, no long-lasting bulb can be tolerated. The name Phoebus, from the Greek word *phoibos*, meaning bright or radiant, alludes to Apollo, the god of the sun, and is a poetic personification of the sun. By all rights, the victim Byron ought to be Phoebus. At a symbolic level, the sun betokens promise, renewal, source of life and energy, heroic image, active principle, masculine creativity. Obviously, the very opposites of these meanings apply to the cartel Phoebus, so now we see what Pynchon is up to: allusion is to be taken ironically in this case. To the public, the cartel wants to be associated with all those positive aspects of the sun. However, under the surface—the real world beyond the illusoriness of a sunny title—the actual negative aspects emerge: threat, death, menace, lack of passion, artificiality, underhandedness, darkness, repression. Thus Pynchonian concerns with paranoia, with conspiracies, with cabals, are heightened by our awareness of the ironic use of an allusion.

The keenest probe among the beams of erudition is historical: it emanates from Pynchon's sound knowledge of the organization of international cartels, life in London during the Blitz, inner workings of Peenemünde and Nordhausen, intricacies of the German black market. Down to the trivia of prison camp jargon, an American B movie, comic book action, radio shows, including who played what on the organ for the BBC, it is a brilliantly researched novel (overlooking a few minor errors), all the more remarkable because, as a child during World War II, Pynchon could bring no firsthand knowledge of the period to his book.

These ramifications of esoterica and research suggest that the reader be sufficiently literary and intellectual to want to pursue the references, the puzzles, the allusions, the concatenations. However, the appeal is not meant to be strictly elitist. A sensuous, unschooled vulnerability may be just as important as trained critical faculties. Put another way, the reader ought to be quite nonliterary too—open, responsive, amenable to radical form and diverse content. In either case, some powers of discernment are needed because Pynchon has a way of writing history as if it didn't happen, when it did—or vice versa. The reader is probably better off for knowing the difference. The same might be said of being able to distinguish between recorded actuality and fantasizing. Is there an orgy aboard the *Anubis* or isn't there? Does Pökler commit incest with Their Ilses or doesn't he? When does night watch merge into nightmare? Left without certainty, the reader is compelled to decide. Pynchon makes no concession to an audience to whom a more readable, clear-cut novel might otherwise appeal. Here, then, is a writer determined to go his own way, to present the universe as he sees it.

What is the nature of his vision in *Gravity's Rainbow*? The reader is forewarned on the very first page of "a progressive *knotting into*—." That entanglement becomes a cultural and historical emblem of Western traditions. The culmination of "knotting into" is the massive gargoyle of modern society malformed by war and political-industrial-technological chicaneries, all extensions of past malaise. Although authorial reach is necessarily vast, it is also selective in its fixations upon origins, values, hierarchies, upon superficialities, fantasies, and endings. Furthermore, the novel is tenaciously concerned with a mysterious supernatural world beyond the empirical ordinary one we know. This other world is always conspiring against us, and thus produces suspicion, fear, terror. That bifurcated way of seeing our existence also provides an impetus for writing. Flannery O'Connor once remarked that for the serious fiction writer "the real story" begins at an inexplicable depth and leaves over a "sense of Mystery which cannot be accounted for by any human formula." Her mystery was theological and brought inspiration and solace; Pynchon's is secular and induces paranoia and dread.

The complexity of Pynchon's vision is spun out by webs of motifs, images, and symbols each identifying with some theme or fragment of theme. The novel's major thematic subjects, only a dozen of which will have to do for now, give indication of its expansive perimeters: (1) the pervasiveness of paranoia, the temptation to seek "other orders behind the visible" (V188/B219); (2) the damages wrought by betrayal and conspiracy, whether by parents against their children or by bureaucracy against its individualized citizenry; (3) the ravages of waste, destructiveness, decay, communal annihilation; (4) the potentialities of transformation, either ameliorating by rebirth into new forms, or worsening by varied disintegrative processes; (5) the impelling but maybe never satisfiable need for quests and searches; (6) the contingencies of life, which demand a tolerance for uncertainty; (7) the power of survival, shored indirectly here as a manual on how to survive while still faced squarely upon the inexorability of death; (8) the necessity for disorder, to create purest freedom, especially by restoration of natural order; (9) the perils of obsessiveness, whether in the form of death wish, falsely romanticized love, overanalysis, superorganization, religious hysteria, or antipodes like emptiness, "leukemia of the soul," or "anti-paranoia, where nothing is connected to anything, a condition not many of us can bear for long" (V434/B506); (10), the factors that provoke loss of identity, the turning of people into things, and prevent personal salvation; (11) the consequences of any dominantly shaping force, such as repressiveness, of either individuals or cultures, or "routinization of charisma," especially when a pattern of control is established by systematized technology; and (12) the heedless entrapment of the powerless of the earth.

These and other thematic subjects emerge out of the brilliant conceptual stroke of creating a war novel that is less about war than it is about how a world was and is wrought. It fixes upon a moment in history when the world was poised at apparent teeter-totter balance—the past on one side, the future, including of course our own time, on the other. At a barely distinguishable fulcrum, a chaotic war ends, a chaotic peace begins, Europe is divided up, new allegiances are formed, and the dark, age-old magnetism points the weapons across the deadly playground all over again. Their firing must perforce follow the rainbow of gravity—if they fire. That basic tension is subjected to a series of interrelated dialectical tensions. (Perhaps Pynchon's pejorative term "bookish symmetries" could also serve for "dialectics.") Some are dramatic contrasts that do not necessarily provoke any authorial judgment: like German-American (or Russian-American, etc.), mind-body, cause-effect, war-peace.

The last duality reminds us again of the consistent unusualness of Pynchon's vision. In his view, there is virtually no difference in conditions of our existence in either peace or war. The teeter-totter hardly moved; nothing much happened at the fulcrum. Put another way, the same forces remain at work upon humanity when a war is over. This is one reason why almost no significance is attached in the novel to the ending of World War II.

Other tensions represent decidedly negative and positive poles:

control-freedom, rationality-fantasy, determinism-randomness, mundaneness-magic, supernature-nature, stasis-flux, repression-uninhibitedness, "modern analysis-savage innocences," frigid north-tropical climes, fragmentation-connectedness, white-black, Elect-Preterite, They-We. Pynchon's attraction to the positive poles in all these instances is clearly discernible. His sympathies go out to little people, clowns, rebels, children, endangered species (man or animals), victims, rapscallions who are endearing because they either resist the System or disdain it by their carefree attitudes. Some issues of the novel, such as uses of science and technology in the modern world or the relationship of man and machine, are not so easily settled because they tend to meld rather than to polarize. It is not an evasion to say that the novel is fraught with paradox and contradiction—some conclusions may not be reachable, let alone stand as infallible.

The resolution of one dispute will probably continue to remain tantalizing: ascertaining whether Pynchon is ultimately a diabolic prophet of doom or a humanistic visionary. At first, critical response to the novel seemed to favor the former, but in recent years the pendulum has swung toward more humanistic readings. Which is probably as it should be, since even in an apparent dead heat optimism will win out over pessimism. The writer, after all, is on hand to give alarm signals, not death knells. Otherwise, if the decline of civilization were irreversible, one must wonder the point of even writing about it. The issue merits continued debate. Meanwhile, artistry always matters more than polemics anyway, and we can be indebted to Pynchon for the richness of his created worlds and, we must hope, others to come.

The richness of *Gravity's Rainbow* is mined in this text by differing critical approaches to the lodes of subject matter. In their separate emphasis on war and history, on science and technology, on film, on psychology and religion, love and sex, on metaphorical systems, on philosophy and language and comedy, each provides a useful analysis of the novel. In their totality, they demonstrate the extent of Pynchon's accomplishments, and they try to suggest the import of his vision.

The central purpose of the lead essay by Khachig Tololyan is to describe the historical setting of *Gravity's Rainbow* and the ways in which Pynchon uses facts in order to make his fiction. Essential background information is given about World War II, especially the making and use of the V-2. After a brief introduction explaining his perspectives toward war as both thematic and formal imperative in the novel, Tololyan offers a listing that identifies dates and places of the action of every chapter. Readers will find it very helpful. The essay then focuses upon the following: (1) A discussion of the prewar mobilization of Germany's military and scientific resources in order to make terror weapons, the V-2 above all. (2) An analysis of Germany's mobilization of industry before the war, with emphasis on IG Farben, and the importance of the business-technology alliance to the German war effort. This material also has symbolic importance, chronicling as it does the human cost of technologies and the ways in which they facilitate victories of the Elect over the Preterite. (3) A discussion of the efforts by all the Allies during 1944–45 and the immediate postwar period to scour Germany for V-2 rockets, components, and scientists. These efforts are referred to and parodied in the attempts of Slothrop, Tchitcherine, and Enzian to locate the 00001. (4) A general discussion of war as thematic subject in the novel. (5) An examination of the paradoxes of war, particularly the use of destruction as a way of making a new world order, and a discussion of the formal implications that the theme of war has for encyclopedic fiction such as *Gravity's Rainbow*, which, like Tolstoy's *War and Peace* and Homer's *Iliad*, seeks to understand society and history by looking at a society when it is naked and exposed by mobilization for the total effort of war.

Armed with this background information, the reader can next face the challenge of Pynchon's treatment of science and technology. Physicist Alan J. Friedman contends that the universe of *Gravity's Rainbow* is dominated by two conflicting omnipresent states: order and chaos. Three metaphors from science illuminate the views that the novel's characters take of this puzzling co-existence. *Newtonian physics* imagined a universe of completely linked components, operating under rigid laws as deterministically as a clockwork. Apparent chaos was simply unseen mechanism. Nineteenth-century science developed *statistical physics* to cope with the immense complexity of this clockwork universe, but some of these statistical conveniences, like the second law of thermodynamics, suggested that the universe might not be so clearly mechanical after all. Twentieth-century *quantum theory* and its controversial "uncertainty principle" argue for the view that the universe itself has a fundamental disorder. Furthermore, Friedman shows how the technology of the V-2 rocket provides the novel's characters with concrete examples for each of these great paradigms from science. However, science is not a savior, as various views related to it become allied with paranoia or anti-paranoia. Functioning both as a guiding light and as a stylistic element, the science in *Gravity's Rainbow* demonstrates that our pursuits in both science and the humanities are common responses to our puzzling over the apparent requirement of life for both order and chaos.

The next essay is solely concerned with film. *Gravity's Rainbow* demonstrates the pervasive influence of movies throughout our culture, down to indelible effects upon individual sensibilities. Pynchon works film into the novel in at least seven ways: (1) by introducing fresh (but occasionally contradictory) perceptions about the relationships of film and life, especially as they reveal multisided realities; (2) by incorporating cinematic techniques into the texture itself so that the novel is like a movie; (3) by relying upon cinema as a source for metaphors, images, symbols, and associations; (4) by his means of revealing character, especially psychological states; (5) by dramatizing the literal power the film industry and movies exert in influencing people and shaping stituations; (6) by enforcing his other thematic concerns: the conflict between illusion and reality, modern man's need for entertainment, particularly humor, the robbing of true sensory response by vicarious experience, and the good and bad effects of the all-too-human bent for fantasizing; (7) by conveying a nostalgic mood for silent films and early movies. The last category is also historically instructive because Pynchon ranges from embryonic beginnings through the heyday of Hollywood up the the early 1940s, with emphasis in between upon the pre-Hitler Golden Age of German expressionism. *Gravity's Rainbow* spans the entire arc of cinema: from technical processes of invention to the writer's script to motion picture-making to final appreciation by an audience. In the course of tracing these developments and techniques, the essay attempts to explain why film is a crucial determinant in Pynchon's work.

Joseph W. Slade, who has previously written a book and other articles on Pynchon, has contributed a new wide-ranging essay. It deals with four separate but interrelated topics in *Gravity's Rainbow*: religion, psychology, sex, and love. Slade contends that in demystifying the world, Calvinism, à la Max Weber, has rationalized, linearized, and fragmented the universe for Western man. He argues that atrophied religious sensibility dictates the psychological aberrations to be found in modern life. One of his theories about Pynchon's work is that our loss of ability to perceive the world holistically has reduced our capacity for human love, community, and spiritual well-being. In *Gravity's Rainbow*, characters clutch at sexual perversion in their attempts to achieve love. They succumb to paranoia, a legacy of rationalization in their attempts to restore their spiritual well-being. Slade finds this lamentable situation ironic because twentieth-century science has demonstrated the validity of acausal relationships, and thus has made possible a unified view of the world. He says that modern technology, by its emphasis on information-gathering, has provided a basis for human community through communication. The results, however, are often dismal. Furthermore, twentieth-century psychology, specifically the work of Jung on synchronicity, has furnished a genuinely holistic, religious way of viewing creation. It provides a perspective of harmony that should foster love. But, as Slade says, love is a fragile shield in the armed camp of rationalism. Only on rare occasions does it survive. In addition to exploring Pynchon's uses of the ideas of Jung and Weber, Slade also sheds new light on the way Pynchon has applied the theories of Marshall McLuhan and Herbert Marcuse. Analyses of characters emphasize Enzian's faith in eternal recurrence, the essence of fascism in Blicero, the failure of Slothrop as a messiah. Among many topics that Slade explores are: the desacralization of nature, the power of language, exploitation of the Preterite by the Elect, concepts of death, the destructiveness of bureaucracies, parent-child conflicts, the significance of sadomasochism and homosexuality, the function of the iconic rocket, and human history as thermodynamic process.

Raymond M. Olderman approaches *Gravity's Rainbow* through Pynchon's exploration of the Freak world view as one expression of a new postwar consciousness. Olderman works from the basic premise that all systems of science, art, mathematics, religion, mythology, politics, economics—all systems of any kind in the novel—are metaphoric descriptions that participate in reality but are not reality in its entirety. Three interlocking areas of investigation in the essay are: (1) Pynchon's use of information organized into metaphoric systems, and the specific details of how these systems connect and relate to truth. (2) The process involved in getting beyond metaphor to comprehend the underlying structure of reality, including Pynchon's use of the parabola, the image of a turning face, his use of the rocket, revelation, paranoia, reversal, apocalyptics, multiple meanings, and his concept of universal consciousness. (3) The way the encounter between cultural "freak" and "straight" provides an interface between an old world view and an emerging new one. The interplay at varied levels (between individual freaks and straights, between freak and straight parts of individual consciousness, between freak and straight parts of universal consciousness) becomes metaphoric for the interplay of cosmic, sociopolitical, and psychospiritual forces.

In James Earl's view, *Gravity's Rainbow* is a philosophical novel. He shows that its major themes, the ideas from which its plots, characters, and symbols are generated, correspond to perennial problems of Western philosophy. Foremost among these is the problem of free will and determinism; and closely related to it is the problem of rational and intuitive knowledge. For Pynchon these two issues are not easily separated: rational analysis and determinism are natural allies, opposed to irrational intuition and freedom. Pynchon, of course, is an artist and not a systematic philosopher—his ideas are eclectic and do not belong to any definable school of thought. But Pynchon's philosophy is the product of a broad familiarity with contemporary ideas, and his vision is in harmony with them. Pynchon's attack on determinism, analysis, and behaviorism is actually in the mainstream of modern European philosophy, including the philosophy of science. In the course of tracing these themes, Earl makes use of theories of Bergson, Heisenberg, Norman O. Brown, Lévi-Strauss, and Husserl. In Earl's interpretation, the struggle between freedom and determinism is played out in Slothrop's progress: whether or not and how Slothrop can free himself from the control of Jamf, the IG, Pointsman, and the Firm. By the time Slothrop enters the Zone, our impression, and his, too, is that he is the totally conditioned man, programmed and monitored since infancy: he is a test case, the perfect "fox" for perfecting the theory of behavioral determinism. This condition also makes him the perfect test of the possibility of human freedom. Pynchon's theme, ultimately, Earl says, is that this freedom is possible, although only at the price of complete social alienation.

In the opinion of Charles Russell, language is the primary subject of fiction for Pynchon and many postmodern writers. Their self-reflexive works explore the relationship of literary language to the semiotic codes of our culture. The disruptive, comic surrealism of much of their writing is a rebellious response to the sensed oppressiveness of these codes. Russell finds this reaction clearly evident in *Gravity's Rainbow*, where Pynchon focuses on the nature of human-asserted meaning systems and urges their subversion. Pynchon shows how people strive to create a meaningful world through language and how they are inevitably oppressed by the results of their effort. Whether it is through technology, corporate economics, psychological analysis, or the workings of language upon which all these systems of ordering are based, humanity finds itself trapped within the destructive, artificial confines of its creations. Pynchon reveals two main tendencies of language: (1) the fragmentation of given experience by language and consciousness into discrete, abstract, and alienated entities; and (2) the attempted reformulation of the fragments into an alternative order that would take the place of the original experience. This new world consists of human dimensions, orientation, and control. Russell believes that control is the main goal, for fear of the given world is the primary emotion felt by Pynchon's characters. The greater their fear, the greater their rage for order and, ultimately, the more oppressive their systems of control. Both Pynchon and his fictional "Counterforce" recognize the inevitability of systemization but demand a constant process of self-conscious demystification and disruption of all systems. Although *Gravity's Rainbow* is an anarchic work of excess, parody, and comedy, it displays a marked nostalgia for a diminishing "human" reality. Overall, Russell observes, Pynchon's hope for the future is minimal.

The concluding essay by Roger B. Henkle explores the comic elements in *Gravity's Rainbow*. He argues that Pynchon uses comedy's power of metamorphosis to try to break the spell of obsession that traps modern men in their anxieties and paranoias. Comedy, as psychoanalysts such as Ernst Kris have suggested, often confronts symptoms of cultural angst by seeking to play with, and transfigure, those situations that we dread the most. But for Pynchon the powers of comic art to achieve real transformations of experience are limited. This is the case even where comedy seems to be the prevailing vision of Pynchon's world, as it is in the Zone—there the customary laws of experience no longer operate, and flux, anarchy, and unconstrained metamorphosis hold sway. Often in comic strip renditions, Pynchon illustrates the ways in which Western popular-culture clichés, such as the chase scene, the hero versus the villain, the idealization of the American dream-girl, have twisted themselves into grotesque self-parodies. As the novel progresses, it yields formally as well as thematically to the impulses of a comic vision, for ordered conventional narrative breaks down into a collage of techniques: spliced stories, film clips, skits, comic routines. Pynchon is illustrating the breakdown of assumptions about causality that had underlain so much of the war and international-conspiracy mentality. Similarly, Henkle says, the breakdown of assumptions about causality inspires our own search in the novel for connections. Thus comedy, with its stress on randomness and relentless metamorphosis, emerges as the mode appropriate to the final, shifting and dissolving vision of the book, but it remains, for Pynchon and his readers, a disquieting vision.

It is to be hoped that these eight essays make some worthwhile contribution to the growing storehouse of our knowledge about Pynchon's worlds. Since the novel is a veritable treasure, many more interpretations will of course follow. To that prospect one can only say: all to the good. As a seminal work of genius, the more *Gravity's Rainbow* can be read and discussed and written about, the greater will be the appreciation and dissemination of its remarkable artistry.

War as Background
in *Gravity's Rainbow*

By Khachig Tololyan

Gravity's Rainbow does not belong to the established narrative sub-genres of the historical novel or the war novel, yet a knowledge of the history of World War II is indispensable to a full and detailed understanding of the book. In one guise or another, war—and the diagnosis of the history of the twentieth century as an endless war waged by the Elect against the Preterite—has been important to most of Pynchon's fiction. Although the tangled events of *Gravity's Rainbow* cannot be rearranged into a single, clear, and unified plot by any means known to me, they do have a coherence that becomes more accessible when one constructs a chronology, a geography, and a chart of the combatants who are locked in the variety of struggles subsumed under the rubric of War.

We can construct such a chart by using internal evidence, which Pynchon provides; there are numerous details that seem cryptic but actually allude to historical events. Knowledge of such historical and geographical backdrops has proved useful in the study of other massive works, such as Joyce's *Ulysses*, which encompasses the events of only one day in one not-very-large city; by comparison, the range of Pynchon's fiction is almost global. *Gravity's Rainbow* is indeed not a novel in the usual sense of the word but a cosmography, that is, a fictional alternative to available historical versions of the real world, made up of fragments of reality welded together by an extraordinary imagination. The narrative that results is the greatest of our post-WAR books precisely because its author has thought through, in fictional terms, what World War II meant and heralded for our age.

Gravity's Rainbow is a new kind of war novel, then, that redefines not only the genre but our idea of war itself; it does so in the context of a fiction whose imagined characters and events are embedded in a scrupulously accurate historical context. My approach to the book will therefore try to encompass the literal and the figurative. I shall try to reconstruct historical time and geographical place as they are used in order to frame the narrative, and I shall then discuss both the historical reality and the symbolic value of the several wars that go on in *Gravity's Rainbow*. Clearly the book is not an infantryman's novel in the tradition of Hemingway, Mailer, or James Jones. Rather, it is Rocketman's book, and one of its earliest ascertainable dates is that of the V-2's first explosions over London.

When Pynchon wants to mark such a time and place exactly, the accuracy of his historical and scientific details can be nothing short of astonishing. As the book opens, London has already been under V-2 bombardment for some time. Slothrop recalls the first day, "last September when the rockets came. Them fucking rockets" (V21/B29), and elaborates on that day a few pages later. He recalls a

> Friday evening, last September . . . heading for the Bond Street Underground station . . . [when] suddenly in the sky, miles behind his back and up the river *memento mori* a sharp crack and a heavy explosion, rolling right behind, almost like a clap of thunder. But not quite. Seconds later, this time from in front of him, it happened again: loud and clear, all over the city. Bracketed. Not a buzzbomb, not that Luftwaffe. "Not thunder, either," he puzzled, out loud.
> "Some bloody gas main," a lady with a lunchbox [said]. (V25/B29)

The contents of this passage are almost a paraphrase of the description of the first V-2 explosions to be found in Calder's history of England under bombardment, *The People's War*:

> On the evening of September 8th, a mysterious shattering explosion was heard all over London, where everyone imagined that it had happened in his own borough. There was a thunderclap, followed by a noise like a faraway express train. A second explosion followed immediately. The areas affected were in fact Chiswick and Epping, at the western and eastern ends of the city. . . . Word was passed down official channels that these were to be treated as town gas explosions; but Londoners guessed from the flashes of white light through the sky that this was a new secret weapon, and sardonically talked about "flying gas mains."[1]

It is useful to dwell on a comparison of the two passages for a moment. Pynchon keeps the reference to "thunderclap" as "clap of thunder," not merely out of scrupulousness, but also because he can link the historian's description to his own invention of the design on Slothrop's ancestral tombstones, which shows God's hand emerging from the clouds, like a flash of lightning, presumably accompanied by thunder. In addition, Pynchon keeps Calder's reference to "flying gas mains," adapted in *Gravity's Rainbow* to "bloody gas mains." Here he has telescoped two items separated in time in the historical description into one fictional moment's chance remark. His accuracy about location is cartographic: Chiswick, the site of the first V-2 explosion, is about three miles to the west of Bond Street Underground station, where Pynchon chooses to situate Slothrop, and Epping, site of the second explosion, is nearly ten miles to the northeast. Thus the explosions can properly be said to "bracket" Slothrop.

Finally, there is a curious addition. Some paragraphs after the already cited description, Pynchon notes that the exact time was 6:43:16, British Double Summer Time (V26/B30). It is curious that he chooses to be so precise about the hour and yet never mentions the exact date, September eighth. Perhaps this partial precision is meant to be an ironic hint directed at readers and scholars, reminding us that the exact moment in which Slothrop has an erection—a fictional event that accompanies the first explosion—counts for much more than the exact history of V-2s or any related background of fact. We do well to keep such partial precisions in mind as we pursue the facts of his fiction.

Other dates and places can also be traced easily, if not always with such exactitude. Using the internal evidence available in *Gravity's Rainbow*, chronologies of the war, and maps, I have constructed the following table, which is as precise as the evidence permits. In many instances I have found it useful to explain briefly on what evidence the ascertainment of a date rests; when such explanations are missing, it is because the text contains an explicit reference. Since *Gravity's Rainbow* has no chapters, except for the four titled sections, I have numbered each sub-section separated by sprocket-squares as a "chapter." It seems to me inevitable that scholars will adopt some such system of reference, just as titles were once adopted for the untitled chapters of *Ulysses*.

	Time	*Place*
I.		
1.	Morning, date uncertain, but since Pirate seems already accustomed to V-2 bombardment, the date is some time after September 8, and before November 30, 1944.	London; Pirate's residence, near the Chelsea Embankment.

2.	Breakfast, same day.	Same.
3.	Probably same day, lunch-hour.	London; near Grosvenor Sq., Headquarters of ACHTUNG, a fictional organization similar to one that actually was headquartered at Grosvenor Square (see text).
4.	Early afternoon, same day.	London, at the Snipe and Shaft, a pub.
5.	Evening, same day.	A seance, somewhere in London.
6.	Night, same day.	Driving east across London.
7.	Same.	Bombed-out section, east London.
8.	Same.	London; St. Veronica's Hospital.
9.	Early morning, second day.	London, evacuated "stayaway" zone.
10.	Possibly same day, but could actually be any day before Christmas, 1944.	London, Abreaction Ward, St. Veronica's Hospital, Bonechapel Gate, E1. Extended flashback to Boston, 1938–39. References to Red, a black character figuring in Slothrop's hallucinations, who will later be identified as Malcolm X. Music played, "Cherokee" (V63–64/B73), was in fact a Roseland Ballroom favorite, according to Malcolm X's *Autobiography*.
11.	Probably second day. Pirate has papers recovered from rocket landed on previous day.	London.
12.	Another day, date uncertain, late 1944.	Ich Regis, White Visitation, near southeast coast of England.
13.	Same.	Same.
14.	Probably same day, but could be any other day in late 1944.	Chelsea, London. Pirate's place.
15.	Another day, late 1944	East End of London.
16.	After Advent and before Christmas, therefore between November 30, 1944, and December 24, 1944.	London, then somewhere in Kent.
17.	Two days after events described in section 15.	White Visitation.
18.	Same day.	Same.
19.	Flashback to Berlin, some time between 1936 and 1939.	Berlin, the Studentheim.
20.	Christmas Day, 1944.	White Visitation.

21.	Boxing Day, December 26, 1944.	London; at house of Jessica Swanlake's widowed sister.

II.

1.	Some time in January–February 1945. The War has "gone north" from the French Riviera, which was invaded on August 11, 1944, and completely conquered in the months following.	Near Cap d'Antibes, on French Riviera: The Casino Hermann Goering, and nearby beach.
2.	Evening of same day.	Casino-hotel.
3.	Several days later.	Same.
4.	Probably late February or early March, 1945.	England, White Visitation.
5.	Between March 12 and 23, 1945, probably March 21. (Von Braun broke his arm on 3/16/45, his birthday was 3/23), the vernal equinox is 3/21 (see V236–37/B275).	Casino Hermann Goering.
6.	Next day.	Same.
7.	Spring, 1945; probably April.	Nice, Zurich, Geneva.
8.	Whitsun, May 13, 1945, five days after V-E day and surrender of Germany.	Beach near White Visitation, England.

III.

1.	May 14, 1945. (Eis-Heiligen ends on May 13, 1945, and this is just after (see V284/B327).	Train in central Germany, on way to Nordhausen through Heiligenstadt (accompanying map names major sites marking Slothrop's journey in the Zone).
2.	A day or two later.	Mittelwerke (i.e., Central Works) in central Germany, Nordhausen. Underground factory for V-2, held by U.S. April 11 to June 1, 1945.
3.	Same day; also flashback to 1904–6 in Southwest Africa.	Bleicherode, village near Nordhausen, where technical personnel for manufacture and design of the V-2 had been quartered; most came there from Peenemünde.
4.	Nearly a month after May Day Eve, so late May, 1945 (see V329/B383).	The Brocken, in Harz mountains in Central Germany (see map). This is highest peak in Germany, 20 miles from Nordhausen. Linked to witch-

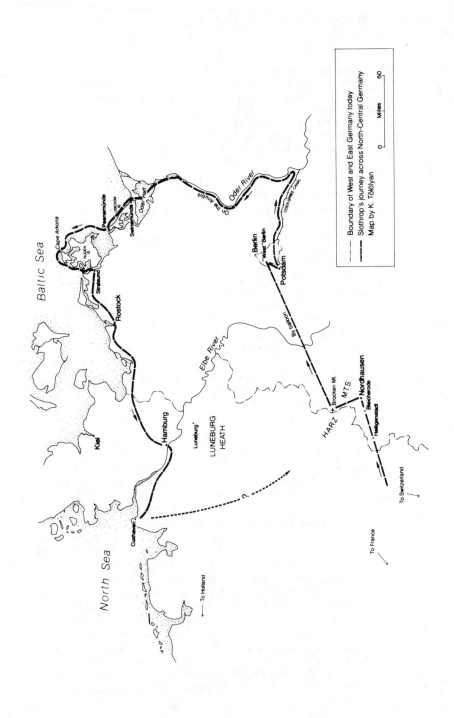

North Sea

Baltic Sea

Kiel

Hamburg

Lüneburg

LÜNEBURG
HEATH

Cuxhaven

Elbe River

Rostock

Stralsund

Cape Arkona

RÜGEN
IS.

Sassnitz

Peenemünde

USEDOM

Oder Haff

Swinemünde

On the Danube

Oder River

OBERSPREE CANAL

Berlin

West Berlin

Potsdam

By balloon

HARZ
MTS.

Brocken Mt.

Nordhausen

Bleicherode

Heiligenstadt

To Holland

To France

To Switzerland

Boundary of West and East Germany today

Slothrop's journey across North-Central Germany

Map by K. Tölölyan

0   50
      Miles

craft in German folk mythology and figures in Goethe's *Faust*. Brocken, May 1, and the Walpurgisnacht or Witches' Sabbath are all closely associated in German folklore and literature.

5. No real present, a series of flashbacks:

East-central Germany, zone conquered by Russians.

a. a brief moment in May, 1945

b. 1928–32. (Early days of Stalin's control and NTA imposition make late 1920s likeliest date.)

c. Moscow, before 1932. (IG Farben was forbidden to operate after that date in USSR; Wimpe works for this German chemical-pharmaceutical cartel.)

Moscow.

d. 1921–28; period of struggles over alphabet in the Soviet-held Caucasus.

Caucasus, especially Baku (Capital of Azerbaijan SSR, a Turkic-speaking area).

e. December, 1904.

SW Africa; now also known as Namibia. Refueling stop of Russian Tzarist fleet on its way to destruction; Enzian fathered by Russian sailor who is already Tchitcherine's father.

6. July, 1945, around the dates of the Potsdam conference (July 11–August 6, but more probably when President Harry Truman was actually present; therefore July 17–August 2).

Berlin.

7. Next day.

Potsdam, a few miles west of Berlin, in zone occupied by Russians (see map).

8. Late July or early August, 1945.

Submarine in North Sea near Cuxhaven, which is a German port on the southern tip of the estuary of Elbe River, northwest of Hamburg. Though in the British zone, it was

		under temporary American control; major supply base.
9.	Same general time period.	Potsdam.
10.	Same	Same.
11.	Early August, 1945. Anniversary of the times Pökler and his "daughter" took vacations in Zwölfkinder.	North Germany, Zwölfkinder, a kind of fictional Disneyland.
12.	Early August, 1945.	Berlin.
13.	Early August, 1945.	Near Kiel canal, North Germany (connects North to Baltic Sea).
14.	Next day.	Aboard the *Anubis*, traveling east on Spree-Oder canal, then north on Oder River, now border of East Germany and Poland, according to postwar boundaries (see map).
15.	Following day.	Same.
16.	Same.	Same.
17.	Same.	Same.
18.	Afternoon-night, same day.	Oder Haff; estuary of Oder River on Baltic Sea (see map).
19.	Following day	Swinemünde-Peenemünde, on island of Usedom in Oder estuary (see map).
20.	Same.	Peenemünde.
21.	Early August, 1945, exact day uncertain.	Hamburg.
22.	Same.	In the Baltic, traveling between islands and mainland coast of North Germany, from Usedom Island to Rugen Island. Cape Arkona, on latter island, is sighted, as is town of Stralsund opposite Rugen, on mainland (see map).
23.	Sometime in July or early August, 1945.	England; White Visitation and London.
24.	No specific time, but postwar is likely. A vision of modernity.	A labyrinth viewed as Hell; made up of offices of bureaucrats and committees (cf. also V402/B468): "Organization charts as prison cells."
25.	August, 1945.	North Germany, heading from the east (Stralsund) west toward Rostock, a town on the south shore of the Baltic. Heading away from the Russian zone of occupation toward the British zone.

26.	Night, same day.	Same. Just outside Rostock.
27	Same.	Same.
28.	Another day in August, 1945.	A fictional village on Baltic south shore, on day of its pig festival; also in Zwölfkinder, nearby (west of Rostock; see map).
29.	Later on in August, 1945; flashback to the 1930s.	Zwölfkinder.
30.	Just before August 6, 1945, the day the A-bomb was dropped on Hiroshima. Truman is said to have "his control-finger poised right on Miss Enola Gay's atomic clit" (V588/B685). Mostly, however, there is a flashback to 1930s.	Germany; mostly flashback to Boston.
31.	August, 1945.	Cuxhaven (see map).
32.	August, 1945.	London; also Luneburg Heath, SE of Hamburg, a region used as proving-ground of German heavy artillery and some rocket-like projectiles, though not the V-2 (see map).

IV.

1.	August, 1945.	North Germany, near Luneburg Heath and in the air over it.
2.	Fall, 1945.	North Germany, going toward Cuxhaven.
3.	Late fall, 1945 ("Winter is coming" V640/B746). Definitely after August 8, 1945: atomic bombs have been dropped (V642/B748).	Thuringia, a region of North-Central Germany
4.	Late August, 1945.	North Germany.
5.	Same.	Same.
6.	After atom bombs were dropped on August 6 and 8, 1945 (V693/B808), and "there are rumors of a War Crimes Tribunal in Nürnberg" (V681/B794), which began on November 20, 1945.	Raketen-Stadt, Rocket-city, a fantasized future-city.
7.	Earlier than above, August, 1945 (V700/B816).	Luneburg Heath.

8.	Some time during August 22–31, ("the brink of autumn," V706/B824), 1945.	Schleswig-Holstein, extreme north of Germany, near Danish border.
9.	Same period.	North Germany.
10.	Early fall, 1945.	Near Elbe River, North Germany.
11.	Same.	North Germany.
12.	Schwarzkommando in "September" (V735/B858) and firing of the 00000 in April (Eliot's cruelest month) or just before V-E day, May 8, 1945.	Luneburg Heath.

As we can see, the events of *Gravity's Rainbow*—barring cinematic flashbacks and flashforwards—occur in the year extending from September, 1944, to September, 1945. This decisive period at the end of World War II shaped the map of today's Europe, and was marked by the unveiling and use of a number of technological and military innovations, many of which are either alluded to or of central importance in *Gravity's Rainbow*.

The V-1, known to the Allies (and in *Gravity's Rainbow*) as the "doodlebug" or the "buzz bomb," was the first radically new weapon used by the Germans. The initial "V" stands for *Vergeltungswaffen* or "reprisal weapon," and this is an accurate description of its function. When the Allies landed in Normandy on June 6, 1944, the Germans were short of aircraft, and could not conduct bombing raids on England to avenge those massive air attacks that the Allies were directing at Germany. The unmanned V-1 rocket-bomb, which the Germans had been developing for several years, was their only answer. Each V-1 carried nearly one ton of explosive; each could—and sometimes did—kill a hundred or more people. Unlike aircraft the V-1 could attack by night or day, in fair weather or foul; it could also demoralize civilians with its unnerving noise. After June 12/13, 1944, V-1s fell on London with increasing frequency, sometimes a hundred in one day. The result was a "huge private evacuation of London."[2] Possibly memories of this evacuation provide some of the images of Pirate's nightmare in the opening section of *Gravity's Rainbow*.

The V-1, though frightful, was also erratic and vulnerable. Since it traveled at a top speed of 400 mph and at a ceiling of 7,000 feet, it could be—and often was—shot down by antiaircraft crews and fighter pilots. Having no built-in radio, it was not a true guided missile. This lack of communication with, and control from, base makes the V-1 a potentially less interesting object than the V-2 for Pynchon, whose interest in communication as a necessary prelude to control shapes much of his work.

In *Gravity's Rainbow* the V-1 helps define the special terror of the V-2. Like many actual English civilians, Slothrop takes comfort in their buzzing noise, which terrified but could also warn. By contrast, the V-2 outflies its own noise, and those who are killed by it never hear it. In the absurd world of the war, Pynchon suggests, the V-1 becomes an icon of normalcy, of the ordinary. Pointsman is quite explicit about this point. Spinning his orderly argument of stimulus and response, and puzzled by Slothrop's abnormality, he argues that his experimental subject should get an erection

> at any loud noise that's preceded by the same kind of ominous build-up. . . . That points to the V-1. . . . But oh, no. Slothrop only gets erections when this sequence happens *in reverse*. Explosion first, then the sound of approach: the V-2. (V86/B99)

It is one measure of Pynchon's imaginative and terrible irony that he can sketch a world in which the limits of normalcy are defined by, and include, an erection in response to an *ordinary* terror weapon.

In addition to the V-1, Pynchon briefly alludes to two other terror weapons that the German military-industrial complex worked on but never perfected. One is the Enzian; this is the German word for the gentian-flower, which recurs in Rilke's poetry and of which Blicero is so fond. The Enzian was a multi-booster, antiaircraft rocket, which was not yet perfected when the war ended. Only twenty-five were produced and test-fired. The second terror weapon was designed to emit a devastating "pulse" of sound. Pynchon refers to this as "the sonic death mirror" (V728/B850), which the Schwarzkommando stumble upon while searching for their rocket.

None of these weapons has been significant in the postwar history of mankind. Pynchon, whose intention is to use the last year of the war as a lens for viewing modern history, chooses to focus on the V-2, the first guided ballistic missile. The team of German scientists that designed it later became a "prize" of war, divided unevenly between the United States and the USSR, and went on to create the prototypes of all the major military and space-traveling rockets we have since known. The symbolic significance of the technology involved in the design and manufacture of the V-2 is a very complex issue deserving of lengthy consideration. Here I shall concentrate only on the bare minimum of necessary background detail that is directly connected to the war.

The V-2 was the product of a German "war effort" that began in peacetime: historians trace it back to the ill-advised Treaty of Versailles (1919). Signed less than a year after the end of World War I, this treaty sought to limit the rearmament of Germany and imposed conditions that the military aristocracy and industrial technocracy found humiliating. One of its provisions was that the German army, formerly the mightiest in the world, would not be allowed to enlist more than 100,000 men, and also would not be permitted most kinds of long-range artillery and aircraft. Rockets were not prohibited, however, for the simple reason that at that date no one could imagine their serious use in war. Although known to the medieval Chinese both as a weapon of war and as a form of entertaining fireworks, rocketry achieved prominence only in the nineteenth and early twentieth centuries. The British were early experts in the use of primitive rocket batteries, which they used against the United States in the War of 1812—hence the "rockets' red glare" in our national anthem. Later, rapid improvements in artillery made rockets seem less desirable. Theoreticians and dreamers adopted the rockets as a subject of study, focusing on the technical problems of yaw and control after firing, and on the possibilities of space travel.

Soon after the Treaty of Versailles was imposed, Germany's military-industrial complex began a search for ways of circumventing it. Such a search required secrecy, reorganization of the technocracies involved in order to camouflage the effort of rearmament, and a focus on promising secret weapons. Pynchon alludes to the decision to proceed in this manner when he refers to "Hjalmar Schacht's many bookkeeping dodges [needed] to keep official records clear of any hint of weapons procurement banned under the terms of Versailles" (V285/B331). Schacht was an industrial executive and Weimar minister who encouraged the development of the German army in the unconventional directions suggested by scientific and industrial organizations. German leaders recognized that successful armies of the future would be armed with products of modern technology; the traditionalist leaders of Allied armies did not recognize the inevitability of this trend as rapidly. As John Keegan has said of modern armies, their officers can no longer be warriors, or even gentlemen-administrators with little technological understanding. In the twentieth century, they must be technocrats, who create and serve costly, advanced new weapons. To assure this, military education and training change in order "to reduce the conduct of a war to a set of rules and a system of procedures

—and thereby to make ordinary and rational what is essentially chaotic and instinctive."[3] This paraphrases the seminal description of routinization by which bureaucracies perform. Clasically formulated by the German sociologist Max Weber, it is constantly echoed by Pynchon in *Gravity's Rainbow* (e.g., V325/B378; V464/B541). Routinization is the characteristic procedure of business, technological, and military organizations, all three of which the Germans succeeded in integrating in order to create the technocracy that would develop the V-2.

Between 1919 and 1930, technocratic integration went on through the good offices of the IG Farben Corporation (see pp. 53–58, below). After 1930 the German army established a separate rocket-research branch under the command of Major (later General) Dornberger. This able officer-engineer knew of the existence of an informal research organization whose members were scientists and civilian amateurs interested in the dream of developing rockets for space travel. Their original leader, Hermann Oberth, became one of the founders of modern rocketry and a technical adviser to the Ufa film company, but he is much less important to the development of the V-2 in *Gravity's Rainbow* than is his assistant Wernher von Braun.

Dornberger approached von Braun officially in 1932, a year before the Nazis achieved power in Germany.[4] At this time the members of the civilian research group were testing rocket engines at a site outside Berlin, which they called the Raketenflugplatz, "the Flight-Place of the Rocket." Dornberger was able to offer von Braun research funds and a post as his assistant, both of which he accepted. Doubtless the members of von Braun's group were motivated by dreams of space travel, but such dreams (in history and in *Gravity's Rainbow*) tend to be harnessed to the needs of military technology. So they were absorbed into the rocket-research branch of the German army, and were moved to Kummersdorf, near Berlin, in 1932. There the researchers began testing an engine for the first rocket of a series designated by the letter A.

The missile that we know as the V-2 was the fourth of this series, and so was designated the A-4; its design did not begin until 1937. Between 1932 and 1937, von Braun's group had tested three earlier models in the A-series, had acquired extra funds, and had been moved to Peenemünde, a research site on Usedom Island in the Baltic Sea. The group, now numbering 300 men, knew that for them the war had started, even if no formal declaration was to come for two more years.

By the time World War II began, in 1939, the research group was deemed an important part of the secret war effort in Germany, but as yet it had no priority over other influential groups. The A-4 still existed only in parts and on paper; it did not complete a full test flight until October 3, 1942. Ironically, funding for the A-4 program shrank in the first three years of the war because the extraordinary success of Hitler's Panzers made him think that peace would come soon and that expensive secret weapons would prove unnecessary. The paradoxical growth and shrinkage of the A-4 program out of phase with the success and failure of the German war effort recalls Pynchon's fiction of the schizophrenic held in the White Visitation, who thinks he *is* "the War." This man is "perked up" by the Normandy offensive, when casualties reach a new high, and by von Rundstedt's attack (the so-called Battle of the Bulge) in December, 1944:

> Whenever the rockets fall . . . he smiles. . . . He's to die on V-E Day. If he's not in fact the War then he's its child-surrogate, living high for a certain term, but come the ceremonial day, look out. The true king only dies a mock death. Remember. Any number of young men may be selected to die in his place while the real king, foxy old bastard, goes on. (V131/B152–53)

In the early years of World War II, it seemed the A-4 might die because German victory seemed assured. But by the end of the war, an ironic reversal had taken place, of the sort that Pynchon's fantasy of the schizoid prefigures. The Rocket and its technology, "the real King," synechdochically represent War itself, and live on when combat stops.

The major shift of research funds to the A-4 came in 1942, when the German armies were halted and then thrown back; a sense of urgency seized the Nazi government and the scientists at Peenemünde. The pace of design changed, testing and manufacture accelerated, and with the acceleration came new interagency battles within the military bureaucracies. The immense demand on German resources set the army (in charge of the A-4) at loggerheads with the air force (in charge of the V-1). Speer, the man who oversaw all German military-industrial production, and whose shadow looms over the arches of the Mittelwerke (V298, V411/B347, B480), became the champion of the A-4. Its terrible beauty and its elegance as a technological achievement appealed to this imaginative technocrat, so much so that he advocated granting it top priority, and persuaded a reluctant Hitler to do so. (Part of Hitler's reluctance was due to a dream in which he dreamed that the A-4's would never fly.)

Yet there were more rational reasons for opposing the A-4 as a weapon of war, and an examination of these suggests that once again in history a government at war made an expensive and irrational choice; this appeals to Pynchon's own vision of war as barely rationalized madness. The facts are eloquent. The German High Command could choose among four weapons that offered a hope of stopping the Allies. These were the A-4, the V-1, the Messerschmidt 163 (the world's first operational jet fighter), and the Wasserfall (the world's first guided antiaircraft missile). A good case can be made in favor of each, but especially for the V-1, which was fairly effective, inexpensive, and could be produced in large numbers without straining the German resources to the limit. Instead, Hitler and Speer eventually opted for the A-4, which required a staggering investment in research facilities and cost $143,000 apiece to produce (in 1981 dollars). It was "certainly not the cheapest way of delivering 1,620 pounds of conventional explosive to a maximum range of 200 miles."[5] True, no less an authority than General Eisenhower thought that had the V-2 been available earlier and in larger numbers, "the invasions of Europe would have proved exceedingly difficult, perhaps impossible."[6] But the rate of production needed to achieve such a volume of V-2 output was unattainable. All in all, 5,789 were produced and used (6,103 by another count), but the hopes the Nazis pinned on it were never realized.

England was struck by 1,115 V-2s, and Antwerp, the Belgian city that was a major supply port for the Allies, was hit by 1,265 more. In London the toll was 2,340 dead and 6,000 wounded. This figure, however dreadful in human terms, is less than half the casualties caused by the V-1, and shrinks into insignificance compared with the 130,000 people killed in one day in the Dresden raid by the Allies. (That event inspired Kurt Vonnegut's *Slaughterhouse-Five*.) In the end, the most accurate judgment is perhaps that of the British scientist who suggested that "the vast A-4 project had been conceived not out of military expediency but to quench the innate German thirst for romanticism."[7] Pynchon's vision is predicated on a similar judgment, so that the V-2 looms large in *Gravity's Rainbow* as the focal point of a grisly "romance" between men and technology. He evokes this romance not only by citing historical instances, such as the appeal of the A-4 to imaginative technocrats like Speer (V687/B801), but also by inventing others, such as the *Rücksichtslos* (III.13), which help him satirize the dream about which he shows the greatest ambivalence, that of transcendence achieved through technology. The Toiletship stands for all the absurd ideas that the war spawned and the laboratory proved useless, such as the Wehr-macht's work on sonic pulses, wind-generating weapons, and guns that shot around corners. Each of these enterprises drained men and resources from the A-4, itself a distorted dream of transcend-ence. It is typical of Pynchon's technique to anchor even the very fanciful notion of building a Toiletship in history as much as pos-sible. The steel needed for the Toiletship was "diverted clear out of the Navy over to the A-4 rocket program. Yes, that does seem un-usual, but Degenkolb was the man who was heading up the Rocket Committee by then, remember, and had both the power and the will to cut across all branches of the service" (V448/B522). Gerhard Degenkolb is a historical figure; he selected Nordhausen as the site of rocket manufacture, ran the production program, and gathered a great deal of bureaucratic power into his hands as the war went from bad to worse for the Germans and the A-4 became the last reed of hope for Hitler.

Long before the A-4 became operational as the V-2, the activity required to test and manufacture it was detected by the Allies, and this led to a specialized war-within-war, echoes of which abound in *Gravity's Rainbow*. At the beginning of the war, in 1939, a conscience-stricken German engineer notified the Allies in the so-called Oslo letter that work on a rocket was going on in Germany. But since no other reports reached Allied intelligence during 1940–42, the infor-mation was simply kept in an open file. Soon after the first success-ful flight of the A-4 on October 3, 1942, data began to trickle in to British intelligence about the work at Peenemünde. By April, 1943, Churchill was worried enough to appoint his son-in-law, Duncan Sandys, as head of a committee charged with the study of the threats posed by a long-range rocket. This committee was head-quartered in Shell Mex house (V251, V272/B292, B317). (Possibly it is this branch of Shell that suggested Roger Mexico's last name.) One of Shell Mex's scientists, Isaac Lubbock (V240/B279), had been involved since 1941 in an underfinanced attempt to create a motor for a liquid-fueled rocket. Given the limitations placed on the soli-tary scientist, he had done admirably, but because of bureaucratic rivalry his advice was not solicited until 1943. Eventually, his limited success convinced Sandys that the Germans might well do even better in creating a liquid-fueled rocket, and after much bureaucratic intrigue Churchill, too, was persuaded. British bombers were sent to devastate Peenemünde, and their bombing raid successfully delayed completion of the A-4 by some months. It also forced redistribution of the research and production facility to

Nordhausen and the nearby towns of Bleicherode and Kochel. This scattering, combined with the technical and administrative problems of producing a rocket containing 20,000 components, destroyed hopes for an effective V-2 program: it was never to be ready in time, and in sufficient numbers, to contribute significantly to the German war effort.

Yet that effort was too massive and important to be wholly crippled. The A-4 flight-tests were moved from the Baltic to Blizna, in southern Poland; Sarnaki, also in that region, became the target zone. Here von Braun and General Dornberger puzzled over the A-4's tendency to explode upon reentry and worked frantically, as the Russian troops advanced from the East, to correct the problem. Again Pynchon alludes to these sites; he places Pökler in the exact place and situation within the target area—Ground Zero—that a despairing von Braun actually occupied, hoping to observe the rocket's reentry and impact personally rather than through instrumental telemetry, and so to ascertain the nature of the problems plaguing the delayed rocket (V424/B496).

In Pynchon's references to Blizna, we again have an example of his combination of encyclopedic realism and imaginative control: the materials of history are made to serve his vision of the role of shit, which symbolizes decay and is taboo to the Elect, who seek to escape the organic by the Rocket. Casually, in describing Slothrop's cram-sessions with rocket-related material at the Casino Hermann Goering, Pynchon inserts this sentence:

> There is nothing specially erotic about reading manuals hastily translated from the German—brokenly mimeographed, even a few salvaged by the Polish underground from the latrines at the training site at Blizna, stained with genuine SS shit and piss. . . . (V211/B245–46)

From the author whose preoccupation with shit gives us Toiletships, this seems one more extravagance. In fact, however, every detail is historically accurate. General Kammler's SS troops (V424/B494) successfully defended the secrets of Blizna against the efforts of Allied intelligence until late 1944, when Russian troops occupied the area; they searched, but could find no rockets or documents relating to them. Despairing, they allowed a British captain, Geoffrey Gollin, assistant to Shell's Lubbock, to come and inspect the camp. Gollin thought a retreating enemy might shred and discard in the latrines the documents he had no time to burn and so had the SS latrines searched. There he found and pieced together the documents dealing with the rocket's fuel, a problem that had bedeviled

the Allies. It is those shit-stained documents that Slothrop holds in
the fiction. Gollin himself makes a cameo appearance in *Gravity's
Rainbow*, as a liaison officer reporting to the fictional Hilary Bounce
(V240/B279).[8]

By early 1945 the full potential of the V-2 was clear to the British,
American, and Soviet governments: postwar years would be unlike
what everyone had imagined because of military technology as well
as politics. The conferences of Teheran and Yalta (involving
Churchill, Stalin, and Roosevelt) had divided Central Europe into
spheres of influence, and the map of Europe would look different
for some generations to come; who would enforce adherence to
these boundaries would depend in part on possession of the new
rocket. This was a particularly serious issue by early 1945, when
Stalin and Churchill learned from Roosevelt that the atomic bomb
was in the making and realized that the V-2 would be the perfect
prototype of more sophisticated delivery systems for such a bomb.[9]
As a result, the three major Allies began to prepare for a new,
scavenger's war that, in turn, was destined to become the first of
those "bloodless" clashes that we later came to call the "cold war."

The Western Allies had already set up the Combined Intelligence
Objectives Subcommittee, or CIOS (V391/B455), in which cooperation was now replaced by emerging competition on a number of
matters, including the V-2 rockets. On the whole, the British were
outplayed by the Americans in this particular intelligence "game";
they contributed 90 percent of the relevant information and got far
less in return.

The British operation, code-named Backfire (V272, V277, V526/
B317, B322, B614), tried to obtain V-2s, either intact or assembled
from captured components (V709–10/B827); it also tried to capture
trained German personnel who would fire the rockets while British
scientists observed and obtained details on every aspect of the process. The British wanted to fire thirty of the V-2s out of Cuxhaven,
north over the North Sea parallel to the Danish coast. (It will be
remembered that north is a significant direction in *Gravity's Rainbow*.) With American help, the British eventually achieved their
limited objective. The units that helped accomplish the aims of
Operation Backfire mentioned in *Gravity's Rainbow* include: Technical Intelligence, or TI (V20, V24, V391/B22, B27, B455), and the
Special Projectiles Operation Group, or SPOG (V272, V277, V391,
V595, V605/B317, B322, B455, B694, B701).

The British search for rocket components and personnel was out-
matched by the U.S. and USSR efforts. There can be no doubt that

the Schwarzkommando's intentions—the search for the 00001 and their decision to fire it—offer an ironic fictional counterpart to this historical competition. Perhaps the Hereros' firing of the rocket is intended to be a symbol of the meager hope of liberation and transcendence through technology; yet it can only recall our postwar enslavement to the same technology. Pynchon, like his characters, rejects this enslavement, but not as an adherent to a back-to-nature, antitechnological ethos; instead he acknowledges the complex temptations and promises of the rocket, and of technology in general.

The United States devised the most successful approach to the problem of acquiring V-2s. In 1943 the army created its rocket branch, which in turn organized a group of "scavengers" commanded by Major Robert Staver. He was charged with the task of recovering what he could for American rocket-scientists. These scientists were not working directly for the government, however, because the army followed the time-honored American tradition of contracting out research, in this case to General Electric. The White Sands Proving Grounds in New Mexico became the laboratory for the GE Project, code-named Hermes (V287/B334).

Major Staver began by establishing himself at 27 Grosvenor Square in London. The fictional ACHTUNG's address near Grosvenor Square is probably an allusion to Staver's unit. From there, he obtained the CIOS-British information already mentioned. Traveling to the front lines in April, 1945, he captured a document known as the Osenberg List. Like the documents from Blizna, these were thrown by the retreating German troops into the toilet of a building whose toilets had malfunctioned because they were overworked in flushing away shredded documents. American soldiers salvaged the shreds of the list, and Staver's intelligence men reconstructed it. Osenberg, a middle-rank bureaucrat, had listed 15,000 rocket designers, engineers and technicians—virtually every German who had had prolonged contact with the V-2. He had also gathered references to their sexual predilections, vulnerabilities to alcohol, drugs, wife-beating, and so on. Although there is no reference to this list in *Gravity's Rainbow*, it was instrumental to the success of the American pursuit of the V-2 scientists, and it is interesting to observe the association of information with shit once again, along with the fact that both are linked to that passion for documentation which is itself an aspect of control.

Given the information on the Osenberg list, Staver compiled a secret or "black" list that specified every site and person he wanted to seize for the United States. He also organized task forces of support personnel and forward elements dubbed simply the T-forces (V588/B611). These were made up of soldiers with varied technical and language skills, who would secure and guard targets judged to be of interest to scientists. It is to one of these teams that Clayton "Bloody" Chiclitz is attached as a GE Project Hermes representative (V558–60, V566, V611/B650–51, B659, B712). Major Marvy is also a T-force man. This group was successful in obtaining a large number of intact V-2s because, after the British bombing of Peenemünde, manufacturing facilities for the V-2 had been relocated to Nordhausen, an area that was first overrun by U.S. troops. Ironically, the earlier Soviet capture of Peenemünde also served U.S. interests. The German scientists, carrying fourteen tons of documents, had been brought to Nordhausen and Bleicherode so as to escape the advancing Red Army, and were captured instead by the United States.

The Soviets were also active. Pynchon refers to all three agencies that participated in the Russian hunt for the V-2: VIAM (the Russian acronym for "All-Union Institute of Aviation Materials") (V273, V611/B317, B712), TsAgi (Central Aerodynamics and Hydrodynamics Institute) (V273, V337, V391, V706/B317, B392, B456, B823), and NISO (Scientific Research Institute for Airplane Equipment) (V273/B317). Tchitcherine reports to TsAgi, is detached from it briefly, and returns to it in disgrace when he fails to capture Slothrop, Enzian, or the Rocket. His failures are on one level symbolic of the generally unsuccessful Soviet efforts to capture scientists of stature and to obtain V-2s intact.

In November, 1944, the Allies agreed that when Germany's zones of occupation were taken over by their troops, nothing should be removed from the installations that were still standing. Less politely put, this meant that each Allied country felt entitled to loot all that had survived intact in its conquered zone.

Even before the Potsdam Conference in August, 1945, it was settled that Nordhausen would be in the Soviet zone. But American troops advanced faster than anticipated in that region, and the Russians more slowly, so Nordhausen was occupied by Americans during the period stretching from April 11 to June 1, 1945. On April 25 an Army ordnance officer, Colonel Holger Toftoy, was ordered by Staver to go to the Mittelwerke and to ship back at least 100 V-2 rockets for the Project Hermes scientists. The effort Toftoy then organized was called Special Mission V-2.

As usual, Pynchon is remarkably accurate in his use of this historical material. He describes the arrival of Slothrop-alias-Scuffling at the Mittelwerke when the hectic effort to gather up the enormous rockets is going on:

> Slothrop presents his sooper dooper SHAEF pass, signed off by Ike and even more authentic, by the colonel heading up the American "Special Mission V-2" out of Paris. A Waxwing specialty of the house. B Company, 47th Armored Infantry, 5th Armored Division appears to be up to something besides security for this place. (V298/B347)

It is worth lingering on this passage, whose intricacies are emblematic of Pynchon's technique through much of *Gravity's Rainbow*. Tonally, it takes root in the paranoia of Slothrop-disguised-as-Scuffling, and a reader accustomed to it but unaware of the history of World War II is quite free to proceed by assuming that Slothrop's suspicions are merely further examples of his paranoia. So they are, but, just as "even paranoids have real enemies," so also they often stumble upon plots not directed against them. Company B of the Forty-seventh Armored Infantry of the Fifth Armored Division was, historically, the unit assigned to secure Nordhausen for the Allies. The troops were sent to make sure that Colonel Toftoy's troops got the rockets out of there before the Russians came. This was in violation of the agreements between the United States and the USSR, but all was to be fair in the upcoming cold war. Thus, Slothrop is quite right in sensing a plot. It is worth noting that the man whose forged signature is on "Scuffling's" pass has the rank of colonel: this alludes to Colonel Toftoy, though his name itself never appears in *Gravity's Rainbow*.

The design, manufacture, use, and symbolic value of the Rocket ultimately displace Slothrop's search for his personal history as the central concern of the book. Such a complex role is not usually given to weapons of war in most novels; in this case, the Rocket's importance, combined with the encyclopedism of *Gravity's Rainbow*, points to the epic strain in the book. As Peter Conrad has written, "ever since Homer's account of the fashioning of Achilles's weapons, epic has been an image of industrial process, not only imitating the decorative surfaces of things, but, as Hegel insisted, dramatizing their manufacture."[10] The long account of the forging of Achilles's weapons in the *Iliad* includes the description of a shield that depicts pictorially, on its carved surface, a whole microcosm. Pynchon substitutes the Rocket for the shield in his fiction because he assumes that we can learn most about Western society in the middle of the twentieth century by seeing an image of it while at war, when all its structures are stripped to essentials and mobilized in order to enable it to focus on what it regards as a task of central significance. Pynchon "dramatizes the manufacture" of the Rocket because, as society builds it and makes war, so these activities shape society. Despite their enormous differences, the communities of major encyclopedic texts, like the *Iliad, War and Peace, Moby Dick,* and *Gravity's Rainbow,* are similar in this: in each, war or some other form of violent struggle is the organizing authority that drives men on, and in each we encounter a behemoth, a gigantic object capable of violence, that can be "read" as a text. In this context, the great white whale and the 00001 become analogous megatexts.

"Reading" the Rocket is a major part of the effort to understand War in *Gravity's Rainbow.* For individuals it may contain secret messages (Prentice), or be the vehicle of occult mysteries, or may hint at the secrets of a personal past (Slothrop); it may also point to needed changes in the perception of the scientists who must cope with the results of its use (Mexico, Pointsman). Readers begin by wanting to decipher the mystery of Slothrop's erections; by the end, it is the suspended Rocket and the ever-imminent war it symbolizes that become the dominating facts of the book.

Pynchon suggests that major cultures have always had a canonical text that they produce and interpret; in turn these cultures can be interpreted through the "texts" to which they commit themselves. The Jews called themselves People of the Book (the Old Testament), and the Greeks had the *Iliad.*[11] In our time, Pynchon claims, we are instead people of the Rocket; that is why the V-2 must not be seen as a specifically German object; it entices us all, and encroaches on every sphere of life. It is both a product and a symbol of the kind of activity that Western technological society idealizes. The Germans who make it and the Allies who seek to contain, counter, and eventually obtain it all share certain values. *Gravity's Rainbow* does not stress the most atypical or abhorrent aspects of Nazi Germany; it does not, for example, make the genocide of the Jews central, and deals instead with the colonial heritage of the "lesser" genocide of the Hereros, committed by Germans in Africa, in a way that is typical of the major Western powers. Pynchon wants us to see Germany as an embodiment of the most extreme tendencies of technological society: hence it is the Rocket, and not the Holocaust, that is central to his vision of World War II. For him, Western societies are defined by their willingness to focus all human and material resources on an object such as the Rocket.

In such cultures, as even Ernest Hemingway was forced to accept, "the Army is the biggest business . . . in the world."[12]

Germany invented that particular conjuncture of businessmen, scientists, and generals that we have come to call "the military-industrial complex." Pynchon devotes a large part of *Gravity's Rainbow* to a minutely detailed reconstruction of the way in which this complex developed and functioned during World Wars I and II, paying special attention to the roles of Rathenau and of I. G. Farben. In part this reflects the development of Pynchon's own vision and his coming-of-age during the cold war of the 1950s; it was President Eisenhower who popularized the term "military-industrial complex." Also, at that time, major American business-technocracies like General Electric began to play in the United States a role as large as that which I. G. Farben (henceforth to be cited as IG) had played in Germany.

Pynchon's concern with IG is particularly apt because the rise of this monopolistic cartel parallels the creation of the Prussian-German state. Both involved the consolidation of smaller units into larger ones, and were powered by a vision of economic and political life as skirmishes to be fought before the military showdown that would determine the victors. Politics and business were inextricably connected to the rise of scientific technology, and led to Germany's primacy in the field of organic chemistry in the nineteenth century. Richard Sasuly has said that "the story of the growth of IG is also the story of the development of organic chemistry."[13]

Gravity's Rainbow often alludes to, and sometimes discusses explicitly, these ties between German history, science, IG's technology, and the wars of Europe. It is worth noting that the company's acronym stands for Interessen Gemeinschaft Farbenindustrie Aktiengesellschaft, or Community of Interests in Dye Industries, Incorporated. Coincidentally, the dye industry's beginnings are emblematic of the economic wars fought by major industries, in which research played an essential part. Justus von Liebig (1803–73), the greatest chemist of his time, was the son of a dye manufacturer. He taught Kekulé (1829–96), among others. Both men are important to *Gravity's Rainbow*, representing as they do genius that has its roots in myth, symbol, and dream—this is especially true of Kekulé—but whose work is seized upon by technocracies like IG. Pökler, who represents the idealistic scientists and engineers devoted to the rocket, lives on the Liebigstrasse (Liebig Street), and the great chemist "had been one of his heroes, a hero of chemistry" (V161/B188). Pökler's "course in polymer theory was taught by Professor-Doctor Laszlo Jamf, who was latest in the true succession, Liebig to August Wilhelm von Hofmann, to Herbert Ganister to Laszlo Jamf, a direct chain, cause-and-effect" (V161/B188). The link between V-2 engineer Pökler and the chemists symbolizes the link between the Rocket and IG and, by implication, German business.

When von Hofmann (together with a British scientist) discovered techniques of isolating aniline from coal, and when Kekulé solved the twin mysteries of the tetravalency of carbon bonds in organic compounds (1858) and of the structure of the benzene ring (1865), a whole new industry became possible for Western Europe. Germany, which seized the leadership of the field, did so for three reasons: because (1) it routinized and institutionalized research most systematically; (2) it needed the industry most; and (3) it cartelized the chemical firms most successfully.

Part of the reason for Germany's success in the dye industry, and in the field of organic chemistry as a whole, was its desperate need for such an industry. Germany had no easy access to raw materials and captive markets, as the French and British did, possessing numerous colonies. All Germany had was coal and an abundance of human skills and organizational virtues. Having come to the Industrial Revolution rather late, Germany specialized, and the success of this approach encouraged a mania for the routinization of specialized tasks that made German armies and corporations highly efficient foes of the individual's claims to wholeness and integrity.

In the late nineteenth century, German chemical companies conspired to fix prices, divide up internal markets, and pool patents even as they stole the secrets of foreign industries that applied for manufacturing permits in Germany. Hypocritically, they cooperated with each other even while insisting on a pseudo-Darwinian metaphor of commercial competition as a war that had to be "exported" to the arena of international competition. By 1904 the first IG Cartel was formed by three of Germany's largest chemical companies. In the years following, this IG made a decision that was as much political and military as it was economic: Germany's dependence on foreign sources of supply could be disastrous in time of war, and would therefore have to be overcome through the inventive genius of synthetic organic chemistry. The Haber process for making fertilizer and explosives out of nitrogen achieved this end just before World War I, during which Haber also helped inspire the development of poison gas. IG obliged, making sure that its basic economic resource—dyes—also became the intermediate chemical stages for poison gas manufacture.[14]

During World War I, Walter Rathenau, president of the German General Electric Corporation (AEG), member of the board of 86 corporations,[15] was asked to lead the effort to preserve and distribute raw materials efficiently by integrating the efforts of scientists, businessmen, and generals. Single-handedly, Rathenau achieved in World War I what a reorganized IG would do in World War II. By my count, the names of both occur in *Gravity's Rainbow* over fifty times. Pynchon concentrates on them because the cartels they organized and represented gave modern war its peculiarly managerial character, and helped promote the view that peace is only a truce, during which foresighted technocrats prepare for the next war.

When the Treaty of Versailles curtailed the German army, limiting it to 100,000 men and to old weapons, businessmen and generals went to work to circumvent the terms of this treaty. In 1924–25, all German chemical companies entered the renewed cartel known as IG Farben. At the same time, Otto Gessler, an executive, observed that if the German army's General Staff was organized as a business company, it would be legal: "There is no clause in the Peace Treaty which forbids us to reconstitute the General Staff in the form of a corporation of limited liability."[16] This astute observation was followed by three-pronged action. First, IG provided camouflage for German officers who, disguised as researchers, prepared for the renaissance of a new army. At the same time, IG assisted certain nascent extremist parties, like Hitler's, with campaign funds, and did this so successfully that some historians have concluded that "the fascist state came into being as an alliance of Big Business, the Army, and the Nazi Party."[17] Finally, IG technocrats decided to free Germany completely from a dependence on imported raw materials (a procedure that Pynchon sees not only as a practical decision but also as a symbolic attempt to cut man off from Nature, its gifts, and the limitations it imposes).

Synthetic organic chemistry became more than a technique after this decision; it became a Saviour: "Germany had cracked up for lack of critical raw materials [in World War I]. It became above all the job of IG Farben to make Germany self-sufficient; it was the old question of *chemistry instead of colonies*."[18] IG became the crossroad where business, science, technology, and military skills met and conspired to create the Nazi state. Pynchon's focus on it, and his totally oblique approach to Hitler, who is hardly mentioned in *Gravity's Rainbow*, has seemed peculiar to many readers who have felt that an encyclopedic narrative that includes so much of the history of World War II must be shaped by a peculiar vision when it so steadfastly avoids Hitler and the Holocaust. The explanation for this lies in Pynchon's diagnosis: the real disease of our century, most clearly revealed in 1944–45, is best represented by Germany's creation of the military-industrial complex, whose main achievement during World War II was the V-2.

Before the war, IG "was willing to gamble its future on the coming of war."[19] In 1927 IG chemists achieved the synthesis of rubber. During World War I, a shortage of it, along with the resultant lack of tires for military trucks, had helped paralyze the German armies. More importantly, between 1926 and 1931 IG not only learned how to synthesize gasoline from coal tar but also invested an immense sum in building up factories that could produce 300,000 tons of synthetic gasoline per year. These investments could not be profitable in peacetime, since rubber and oil could be bought cheaply from colonies controlled by the West. IG thus developed a stake in war, during which shortages would raise the price of its products. Eventually, of the forty-three major products IG produced, twenty-eight were to be used by the Wehrmacht, ranging from lubricating oil to synthetic rubber, gasoline, nitrates, and, in the death camps, poison gas. In fact, the wartime record of IG was to furnish examples of every major war crime committed by the Nazis: looting of foreign plants, which were transported lock-stock-and-barrel into Germany; wholesale enslavement of millions of factory workers employed at places like the Mittelwerke; production of the gas used at Auschwitz and Maidanek, and eventually 95 percent of all poison gas. IG subsidiaries and related syndicates like Stickstoff (V580/B676) fixed nitrogen and produced fertilizer, liquid nitrogen, oxygen, and alcohol, the latter two being essential for the liquid-fueled V-2.

So great was IG's lead in industrial production, and so intimidated were Western corporations—and also, so greedy—that Cordell Hull, U.S. secretary of state during World War II, complained about the difficulty of stopping American companies from dealing indirectly with Germany and Italy. The latter had subsidiaries in neutral countries and through them purchased and supplied materials for IG. Sasuly quotes a memorandum from an unidentified Standard Oil executive, in the best Watergate tradition:

> [Just after] that agreement (concerning the catalytic cracking of oil) the war intervened. Because our grouping of interested parties included

Americans, British, Dutch, and Germans, the war introduced quite a number of complications. How we are going to make these belligerent parties lie down in the same bed isn't quite clear yet. We are now addressing ourselves to that phase of the problem and I hope we find some solution. *Technology* has to carry on—war or no war—so we must find some solution to these last problems.[20]

By obtaining the cooperation of major Western corporations, IG succeeded in undercutting the war effort of the Allies, and simultaneously became an even greater power in politics at home. Most IG executives were told to "stay clear of open government ties and exert pressure in secret conferences,"[21] and this they did admirably, even as they articulated their desires. As early as 1925, IG leader Duisberg, extolling Bismarck, had said: "We hope . . . [we] will find the strong man who will finally bring everyone under one umbrella . . . for he is always necessary for us Germans, as we have seen in the case of Bismarck."[22]

IG believed it could control the leader that was bound to emerge in Germany; this was the mistake other equally astute organizations made about Hitler. It is Duisberg's choice of words that is most significant. He speaks of bringing everyone under one umbrella, and indeed IG's own model of the ideal Germany was the cartel. Pynchon is aware of this; furthermore, he sees that post-War is likely to maintain what War has shown to be a flexible and efficient structure:

> Oh, Wimpe. Old V-Mann, were you right? Is your I.G. to be *the very model of nations?* . . . Oh, a State begins to take form in the stateless German night, a State that spans oceans and surface politics, sovereign as the International or the Church of Rome, and the Rocket is its soul. IG Raketen. (V566/B659–60)

IG prepared the foundations of the new corporate state by giving the Prussian officer class a home, just as many American manufacturers of arms today are an early-retirement haven for officers who keep close links with brother officers still on active service. Colonel Walter Nicolai, of the Wehrmacht General Staff, used an IG subsidiary, Chemnyco (V630/B734), as a cover for his industrial espionage operations, evaluating technical developments and resources in the world's armaments industry. He began to do this in 1928, five years *before* Hitler's rise to power. In an allusion to such major espionage activity, Pynchon mentions the fictional Wimpe's connection to Chemnyco, to whose New York City branch he is eventually transferred (V349/B406). It is here that for the first time Pynchon has a cartel man uttering the remarks that will later be heard from Bloody Chiclitz: "Our little chemical cartel," Wimpe says, "is the model for the very structure of nations" (V349/B406).

Pynchon is not alone in placing the responsibility for creating the cartelized war-state on IG. Sasuly emphasizes that the infrastructure for both Reich and V-2 rocket was prepared by it.

> After Hitler came to power in 1933, Germany went to war. It took six years before the first shots were fired. But the war had actually started long before that. It was quiet war: war by propaganda; war of spies; war for political advantage; and above all, war of economic aggression.[23]

In all these operations, the army and government found IG a willing ally. The IG's so-called Army Liaison Office, Vermittlungstelle Wehrmacht, is said by Pynchon to have been involved in the many-sided struggle "for the IG's intelligence machinery" (V630/B734), which of course is the one that had kept up surveillance on Slothrop in the interwar years. Historically, this organization was a front for an IG-army team of intelligence specialists who masqueraded under the title the "Statistical Department" of IG, operating from Berlin NW7, a camouflage office designation. It is to this office that Wimpe reports originally (V344/B400), and it was this Statistical Department that, under such flimsy covers as market research, collected maps of industrial and military installations and similar data. Maps and statistics, the domain of Roger Mexico's research, are central to much of *Gravity's Rainbow*.

Of the bureaucracies of war that play a major role in *Gravity's Rainbow*, those devoted to psychological warfare are the least known to historians, and hence to Pynchon. Since information on the activities of such Allied units was classified until 1975, two years after his book was published, Pynchon's source—if he used it—has to be Paul Linebarger's book on the topic, authorized by the U.S. government.[24]

"Black propaganda," that is, propaganda that attributes false quotations or ideas to enemy leaders in order to undermine the confidence of the enemy people in its own leadership, was the business of a U.S.-British group commanded by Lt. Col. Percy Black. Did Black and black propaganda have anything to do with inspiring the invention of the Schwarzkommando ("Black commando"), or had Pynchon been planning all along to carry on the story of the Herero from his first *V.* to the book of the V-2? It is significant that the group in charge of black propaganda is described as having "a most extraordinary coterie of odd personalities . . . socialist refugees, advertising men, psychologists, psychoanalysts . . . professional promoters, theatrical types, German professors, a commercial attaché, young men just out of college, oil executives, and popular authors"[25]—in other words, a group very much like that assembled at the White Visitation? It is likely that the link between history and the Schwarzkommando is no tighter than this, which makes the creation of the Schwarzkommando one of Pynchon's major innovations. The group incarnates the deepest fears of the colonialist West and especially of the Nazi adherents to the Aryan myth. Pynchon's special touch is to have von Göll and the psychological warfare people at the White Visitation invent black SS and Rocket troops (V112–13/B131) and then to give literary reality to that fantasy by creating the Schwarzkommando. It is a typical Pynchonian labyrinth of the real and the fantastic: the Political Warfare Executive (PWE) to which he refers was a real British agency, and Brendan Bracken, one of its chairmen, is mentioned in *Gravity's Rainbow* (V615/B717). In the end, the Schwarzkommando is the greatest of the many examples with which Pynchon drives home his point: we live in a dangerous age where our deepest fears and nightmares, expressed in filmic *or* linguistic image, threaten at any moment to become real:

> . . . just left behind with your heart, at the Stage Door Canteen, where they're counting the night's take, the NAAFI girls, the girls named Eileen, carefully sorting into refrigerated compartments the rubbery maroon organs with their yellow garnishes of fat—oh Linda come here feel this one, put your finger down in the ventricle here, isn't it swoony, it's still *going*.... (V134/B157)

Even as he spoofs the title of a popular American song of World War II, "I Left My Heart at the Stage Door Canteen," Pynchon also gives a grisly concreteness to the verbal cliché "leaving one's heart behind"; it becomes textually more "real," just as nightmare becomes historical fact. It is to a more theoretical consideration of this metamorphosis to which we must now turn, to see how the facts of World War II lead to that vision of imminent Apocalypse which dominates *Gravity's Rainbow*, from the first nightmare of evacuation to the last moment of Damoclean suspense, when the Rocket of the future hangs over the theater of the world.

The very scarcity of scenes of battle as we are taught to imagine them by war movies, or for that matter by a book like Mailer's *The Naked and the Dead*, is indicative of the kind of shaping imagination at work in Pynchon: modern war does not educate participants and victims by providing conflict that gives the characters a chance to make a new self, at the very least to leave behind the norms of civilian life. Instead, Pynchon's war exposes how deceptive the distinction between civilian and military life is, how entangling the norms of peace have been, and what kinds of violence are done to people in their enforcement. Pynchon, like Tolstoy in *War and Peace*, believes that the truths to be learned in wartime can and must be applied to peacetime. He writes as though to extend the Prussian general von Clausewitz's famous dictum that "war is the conduct of diplomacy by other means." In *Gravity's Rainbow* there is first the suggestion that war is the continuation of peace by other means, and then the reverse assertion that it is really peace that is the conduct of war by other means. Inherent in this extension-cum-reversal of the Clausewitzian notion is a blurring of those distinctions and contrasts that comfort and deceive: enemy/ally, peace/war, and so on.[26]

To achieve this reversal, Pynchon must show that continuity and separation are central issues, and that a sinister continuity enables a version of war to go on in the so-called peace. Concurrently, he must show that our belief in certain discontinuities, such as war/postwar, is invalid. In one way or another, much of the book addresses these issues of continuity and discontinuity, or order and disorder; but since to interrogate and interpret each fictional event that is concerned with such issues would result in a book as large as our text, it will be simpler to concentrate on the explicit declarations made by the narrator's many voices.

Pynchon's strategy is to assert the existence of connections where we have been taught to expect, and therefore frequently see, discontinuity. This is the formal imperative of his work as well as its thematic content. The solid connections are networks of power that continue beneath all superficial boundaries with which we are familiar. This in turn prepares us for a complex and multifaceted paradox: Pynchon will claim that war is used by the people who control these continuous structures of power in order to blind us to their own existence, and yet he will also claim that by its very nature war, which increases the rule of chance (of random events, in the statistical language of his text), inevitably opens up, for a brief historical moment, vistas of a world where there really are no secret networks of power and class, no barriers, no political boundaries and artificial discontinuities. Such a vista shows us a possible community of care, in which contact and touch transcend the barriers that separate by class, color, or nation. This, in turn, introduces the third aspect of the multifaceted problem of discontinuity: the people in power, by manipulating all that is small and frightened in the fictional characters, are able to separate men and women from each other, and achieve this successfully at several levels—on paper, in battle, in the bedroom. The most painful aspect of Pynchon's vision, and the one for which "humanist" critics blame him most, is that he seems to think a world without boundaries to be no more likely on the personal scale than on a public one. Only from May 8 to August 6, 1945, is the Zone without boundaries, providing a glimpse of all that can be; ironically, this vision is made possible only by the ravages of war.

What individual human contact is possible in Pynchon's Wartime? There is a great deal of it, *if* readers will accept Blicero and Katje and Gottfried together; or Pointsman and Maud in a closet, or Katje and Pudding, or the many encounters of Slothrop, including Bianca and Margherita. But precisely because these "perverted," fleeting, and doomed contacts are predominant, and because Roger and Jessica's affair begins with a calculatedly artificial "cute meet" from the movies and ends with the coming of post-War, many critics accuse Pynchon of coldness.

If Pynchon has any fault in the matter besides an unblinking fidelity to his own bleak vision for the chance that human contact has in the world, that fault lies in his attitude about human nature, which is to say, about the motivations he ascribes to his own characters. He is sometimes confused, and his assumptions range from the Calvinistic to Rousseauvian. I mean that even if his characters are not full of sweetness and light, they do manifest a tendency to illustrate freak-and-hip-culture "philosophies" of the sixties, for which Raymond Olderman has claimed him, and according to which man is inherently good but for the corrupting power of the systems in whose power he is held prisoner. In this scheme man is especially good when he is a "noble savage" close to his natural roots; note all the assertions of Herero goodness that would be condescending were they not masked by the complexity and manifold purpose inherent in Pynchon's use of the Schwarz-kommando.

The grim vision of life as war in *Gravity's Rainbow* is permeated with the statistical outlook at every level, including the psychological: the norm is human shipwreck. Some escape the norm because of their ability to achieve an odd form of human contact and continuity through sexual deviation. The exception is Roger Mexico, the most articulate diagnostician of the book and, not coincidentally, its statistician. He must learn to live between the zero and the one by virtue of his profession, and so finds the supposed gap between war and peace equally unconvincing. Jessica may think of the War as that "great struggle of good and evil the wireless reports everyday" (V54/B62), but Roger, despite his love for her, will eventually realize that Jessica needs to believe in such an absolute separation in order to be with Roger, to commit an adultery that she justifies by circumstances. By the same logic, she has to leave him when Peace comes (V628/B732). To Roger the War/Peace discontinuity merely serves to conceal: it is "theater"—a term that recurs from the first page of the book, when the Evacuation is described as theater (V3/B3) to the last movie theater (V760/B887).

Roger fantasizes a moment when They, satisfied with the new realignments of power, call off this costly distraction, this drama of War:

> . . . As you've seen . . . our optimum time is 8 May . . . giving us a few months' grace to get our Ruhr interests back on their feet—no, he [Roger] sees only the same flows of power, the same impoverishments he's been thrashing around in since '39. . . . There's *something* still on, don't call it a "war" if it makes you nervous, maybe the death rate's gone down a point or two, beer in cans is back at last and there *were* a lot of people in Trafalgar Square one night not so long ago...but Their enterprise goes on. (V628/B731)

Roger is convinced of this continuity partly because the demands of War and Peace seem so similar to him, the former merely intensifying them. He has seen for a long time "the rationalized power-ritual that will be the coming peace" (V177/B206), and he knows that it will continue to impoverish his life, just as the War has claimed much from him even while granting him his time with Jessica in recompense. That is why he thinks of her fiancé, Jeremy, as being identical with "every assertion the fucking War has ever made—that we are meant for work and government, for austerity: and these shall take priority over love, dreams, the spirit, the senses" (V177/B206). These are demands not so much for one's lifeblood, which wars are likely to ask of soldiers as a matter of course, but for things that peace also can and does demand.

Similarly, the narrator's voice, when it describes Roger and Jessica's visit to a church in Kent, repeats a litany of demands that wartime technology makes and that peacetime might make just as easily: "The War needs coal. . . . The War needs electricity . . ." (V133/B155). Also indicative of the continuity of wartime demands in peace is the Dracula-voice in which Pynchon's narrator intones the needs of the Elite, or They:

> . . . .*Dawn is nearly here, I need my night's blood, my funding, funding, ahh more, more....* The real crises were crises of allocation and priority, not among firms—it was only staged to look that way—but among the dif-

ferent Technologies, Plastics, Electronics, Aircraft, and their needs which are understood only by the ruling elite... (V521/B607)

It is worth noting that here, as elsewhere, Pynchon speaks of "staging," a term from the theater. It is his way of emphasizing that the story of military-industrial cartels, to which both he and this essay have devoted so much time, is a necessary means for "dramatically" or narratively representing what would otherwise require an analytical essay, namely, a discussion of the momentum of technologies and the elites that identify themselves with them. It is no accident, of course, that the technologies mentioned here all reach their acme after World War II, and do so by serving the Rocket itself.

Pynchon's elite is at war both in a literal and historical sense, but also figuratively because it hates and fears decay—hence the abhorrence of shit—and seeks to overcome both decay and life by promoting the survival of the inanimate, which in its mechanical forms is subject to obsolescence. This war for the preservation and advancement of the inanimate is a central process in Pynchon's work since *V.*, but he speaks of it with a special bitterness in the later parts of *Gravity's Rainbow*, both in his barely masked personal voice and in the narrative of Byron, the indestructible bulb—a semi-animate object that, by surviving too long, threatens the one thing that must survive longer, the producing technology itself. One passage told in the parodic narrative voice is particularly significant:

> Mister Information tonight is in a kind mood. He will show you Happyville. He will begin by reminding you of the 1937 Ford. Why is that dacoit-faced auto still on the roads? You said "the War," just as you rattled over the points onto the wrong track. The War *was* the set of points. Eh? Yesyes, Skippy, the truth is that the War is keeping things alive. *Things*. The Ford is only one of them. The Germans-and-Japs story was only one, rather surrealistic version of the real War. The real War is always there. The dying tapers off now and then, but the War is still killing lots and lots of people. (V645/B751)

Pynchon is unstinting in his efforts to remind us that killing is *not* the major aim of war. His narrative voice sometimes echoes Milo Minderbinder's claim in Heller's *Catch-22* about the importance of business to all America's efforts, even during wartime. One hears an echo of his words in Pynchon's:

> Don't forget the real business of the War is buying and selling. The murdering and the violence are self-policing, and can be entrusted to non-professionals. The mass nature of wartime death is useful in many ways. It serves as spectacle, as diversion from the real movements of the War. It provides raw material to be recorded into History . . . as sequences of violence, battle after battle. . . . The true war is a celebration of markets. . . . (V105/B122)

It is here, immediately after contrasting mass death (as distracting spectacle) and market-war (as real war) that Pynchon goes on to say, "So, Jews are negotiable" (V105/B123). He insists that we must not see the desire to inflict human suffering, no matter on how appalling the scale, as a *cause* of war. Blicero likes to cause pain, but what he does to Katje or Gottfried is harmless compared with what he does as a technocrat devoted to the perfecting of the V-2. It is mystical worship of the perfectibility of the inanimate that is the real enemy; human suffering is its epiphenomenon.

Once unleashed, military war can develop in directions that are not entirely planned and controlled by the elite. Roger, whose profession makes him most aware that even when an overall pattern of random events is determined the individual event is unpredictable, knows this. We too become aware of the temporary and accidental waning of the sovereignty of the elite when we compare two passages, one from the period when War's empire is still sovereign and another that comes after V-E day but before the closure of Potsdam. The first is part of the description of the soldiers gathered in a Norman church in Kent:

> The War, the Empire, will expedite such barriers between our lives. The War needs to divide this way, and to subdivide, though its propaganda will always stress unity, alliance, pulling together. The War does not appear to want a folk consciousness . . . it wants a machine of many separate parts, not oneness, but a complexity. (V130–31/B152)

We must note the emphasis on separation that distinguishes this from a passage marking Slothrop's movement into the Zone, the place of temporary freedoms and new visions of *continuity*. Traveling from Switzerland into Germany, Slothrop finds an absence of the boundaries he has been expecting:

> . . . Never a clear sense of nationality anywhere, nor even of belligerent sides, only the War, a single damaged landscape, in which "neutral Switzerland" is a rather stuffy convention, observed, but with as much sarcasm as "liberated France" or "totalitarian Germany," "Fascist Spain," and others....
> The War has been reconfiguring time and space in its own image. The track runs in different networks now. What appears to be destruction is really the shaping of railroad spaces to other purposes, intentions he can only . . . begin to feel the leading edges of.... (V257/B299)

The War is a force that shapes the landscape and the consciousness of the individuals roaming it. In a way it functions as an emblem of Pynchon's own creative, imaginative activity, which scans the landscape of literary forms, conventions, and genres. Both are at work "reconfiguring" their time and their space, although of course the War Pynchon mimes was all too real and painful, whereas the imaginative reconfiguration remains in part a hoped-for possibility, a model in fiction.

War marshals the men and women of the world, and we see them huddled together in armies, in bomb shelters and underground factories, in tunnels of nightmare and in Romanesque churches such as the one "somewhere in Kent" described in pages V127–36/B148–59. There, during Advent, we hear what Pynchon calls "the War's Evensong, the War's canonical hour;" we see the War and the Empire—not that of the British but of the Elect—collapsed into one. What Roger Sale has called Pynchon's imperialistic imagination is at work in such episodes, marshaling the information and detail of encyclopedic narrative just as the War collects Britons and Yanks, Italian POWs and Jamaicans, living and dead ghosts. The narrator's voice speaks of "the continuity, flesh to kindred metal, home to hedgeless sea, [that] has persisted," and of the bureaucracies that divide men: "It is not death that separates . . . but paper" (V130/B152). In the end, his anguished voice evokes "something . . . that could actually . . . destroy the boundaries between our lands, our bodies, our stories, all false" (V135/B158).

Collection and dispersal, continuity and separation—this is the nature and trajectory of human movement in modern, bureaucratized war, the shapes of which Pynchon parodies. The genres, styles, and conventions of modern art, from empirical narrative to fantasy, from funnies to film, are also mobilized. *Gravity's Rainbow* is a catalog writ large. Like most masters of encyclopedic narrative, Pynchon's purpose is to examine critically the pseudo-orders of culture, incarnate in its armies and catalogs, whose serried ranks mime the outward forms of a hoped-for order and unity while destroying its spirit. Originally, the epic catalog celebrates collectivity as well as collection; Pynchon mocks the latter and is frankly wary of most forms of the former. He looks back to the epigraph of E. M. Forster's *Howard's End*, "only connect," and shows us the paradoxical growth of networks of connection and the simultaneous impoverishment of their human content. In *Gravity's Rainbow*, where, Pynchon says, "the real and only fucking is done on paper" (V616/B718), the genuine connections of flesh and spirit are fleeting, illicit, often driven to sadomasochistic extremes.

War is both an occasion of such genuine connections and a demonstration of the abiding power of the inanimate. The bombing of Malta described by Fausto in *V.* perhaps marks the real inception of *Gravity's Rainbow*. It is there that the first distinction is made between war reality and war consciousness, on the one hand, and the exposed lies of peace, on the other. Fausto loses much to the War, but is educated by it. He waits out the German bombs with his wife and child, and speaks of the way in which, "when the bombs fall, . . . it's as if time were suspended" (*V.*, Bantam, 296). The configurations of time and space change more rapidly in *Gravity's Rainbow*, but the poised V-2 at its apocalyptic end is already prefigured in the first of our *V.*s. There, all false appearance of normalcy is dispelled after Fausto witnesses the disassembly of the bad priest. Writ large in *Gravity's Rainbow*, that event prefigures Slothrop's dispersal, an organic disassembly that is valorized by Pynchon in a stunning reversal of motif.

In the end, what makes Pynchon's discussion of war central to *Gravity's Rainbow* is his respect for tension between the planned and the unpredictable, a tension that the unleashed energies of wartime exacerbate. Pynchon celebrates the human form of many kinds of accident, of anarchic lusts and transient loves. The very form of his book is problematic because he uses it as a celebration of resistance against the forms that favor the Firm. In such a resistance, the War is a potent ally. Even the hapless anarchist Squalidozzi realizes this, and takes pleasure in it: "Decentralizing, back towards anarchism, needs extraordinary times...this War—this incredible War— just for the moment has wiped out the proliferation of little states that's prevailed in Germany for a thousand years. Wiped it clean. *Opened it*" (V265/B307–8). As we begin *Gravity's Rainbow*, we have to do so with the awareness that an understanding of war opens that difficult text for us.

I am indebted to the National Endowment for the Humanities, whose Summer Research Stipend enabled me to carry out the work essential to the completion of this essay; to Mr. Clay Leighton, who was my research assistant; to Patricia Camden, my typist; and to Ellen Rooney and Bernard Duyfhuizen, for their helpful criticism.

1. Angus Calder, *The People's War: Britain 1939–1945* (New York: Pantheon Books, 1969), p. 562.

2. Calder, p. 560.

3. John Keegan, *The Face of Battle* (New York: Viking, 1976), p. 20.

4. This date underscores the fact that the V-2 is the brainchild of technocracy, *not* of Hitler; this in turn is important because one of the intentions of Pynchon's fiction is to depict the demonic energies of technocracies and not those of any one leader, no matter how mad he may seem to us now.

5. David Irving, *The Mare's Nest* (Boston: Little, Brown, 1964), p. 314.

6. James McGovern, *Crossbow and Overcast* (New York: William Morrow & Co., 1964), p. 62.

7. Irving, p. 304.

8. Gollin's papers and reports about his mission are at the Imperial War Museum in London, and seem to be a major source for Irving's book *The Mare's Nest*.

9. Pynchon alludes to that fearsome symmetry of history that led the Allies to develop the atomic bomb just as the Germans were developing the perfect delivery system for it. Ensign Morituri and the references to Hiroshima serve as a vehicle for this topic (V480, V588, V693/B559, B685, B808), which may also have suggested Roger's last name, since the A-bomb tests were conducted in New Mexico.

10. Peter Conrad, "The Prince of Profligacy: [A Review of] Roland Aumini, *Scarlett, Rhett, and a Cast of Thousands*," *TLS*, September 10, 1976, p. 1094.

11. For an important discussion of the *Iliad*'s centrality to Greek culture, see Eric Havelock, *Preface to Plato* (Cambridge, Mass: Harvard University Press, 1963).

12. Ernest Hemingway, *Across the River and into the Trees* (New York: Charles Scribner's Sons, 1950), p. 238. Hemingway's hero, Cantwell, is describing a General Staff meeting in Eisenhower's command.

13. Richard Sasuly, *IG Farben* (New York: Bori & Gaer, 1947), pp. 19–20.

14. J. Borkin and C. Welsh, *Germany's Master Plan* (New York: Duell, Sloan & Pearce, 1943), pp. 26–28.

15. James Joll, *Intellectuals in Politics* (London: Weidenfeld & Nicolson, 1960), p. 73.

16. Sasuly, p. 77.

17. Sasuly, p. 131.

18. Sasuly, p. 39 (emphasis added).

19. Sasuly, p. 138.

20. Sasuly, p. 149 (emphasis added).

21. Sasuly, p. 67.

22. Sasuly, p. 65.

23. Sasuly, p. 89.

24. Paul Linebarger, *Psychological Warfare* (Washington: Infantry Journal Press, 1948).

25. Linebarger, p. 91.

26. Pynchon's theme has been taken up, belatedly, by Michel Foucault, the major figure of contemporary French thought: "Isn't power simply a form of *war*like domination? Shouldn't one therefore conceive all problems of power in terms of relations of *war*? Isn't power a sort of generalized war which assumes at particular moments the forms of peace and the state? Peace would then be a form of *war*, and the state a means of waging it" (*Power/Knowledge*, tr. Colin Gordon [N.Y.: Pantheon, 1980], p. 123).

Science and Technology

By Alan J. Friedman

Three Borrowed Visions

In science and in art, one time-honored way of explaining the behavior of elements of the universe has been to seek connections between elements and, through those connections, to find a cause behind every event. Poets and novelists, psychologists and sociologists, regarded the demonstration of causal links between man and society and the universe as a major goal and the paradigm of civilized thought.

In *Gravity's Rainbow* many characters seek causal explanations for their own conditions, and for the behavior of their fellows. But other characters suspect that this traditional quest is one not of rationality but of madness. "About the paranoia often noted under the drug, there is nothing remarkable. Like other sorts of paranoia, it is nothing less than the onset, the leading edge, of the discovery that *everything is connected*, everything in the Creation . . . " (V703/B820). The plot of the novel itself seems to support this denial of any encompassing patterns, as readers who have tried to summarize the novel have discovered.

A loss of linear plot and of deterministic causal connections is one hallmark of the postmodern novel, from Robbe-Grillet to Barth to Gaddis and most assuredly to Pynchon. Clear signs of the abandonment of the goal of demonstrating rigid links are evident in criticism and other aspects of the humanities as well.

The shift from viewing universal connectedness as a common mode of discourse to viewing it as paranoia is not simply the latest fashion of experimental fiction. That shift parallels a revolution in science, three hundred years in the making, from the "clockwork" universe inspired by Isaac Newton to our contemporary era of quantum physics and the "uncertainty principle."

Gravity's Rainbow ingeniously and explicitly demonstrates these parallel shifts in style, in function, and in physics. Understanding the metaphors, analogies, and images that connect this novel to science may help the reader decipher some of the book's more puzzling passages.[1] More subtly, this cross-cultural enterprise comprises one of the most effective devices in *Gravity's Rainbow* for entrapping the reader in the spirit of the novel. And finally, the accurate and convincing demonstration that the revolution in novelistic style parallels the most fundamental revolution in modern science cannot help but increase the power of *Gravity's Rainbow* as an important statement of the contemporary view of the human condition.

Characters, as well as plot style, illustrate the old and new attitudes of science. Pointsman, the Pavlovian, is the inheritor of the Newtonian view of a clockwork mechanical universe. Pointsman's followers and other determinists demonstrate their faith in man as machine. Roger Mexico is one of a rival assortment that figuratively as well as literally express the image today's scientists have (not ungrudgingly) taken, that God, if he exists at all, is a statistician, not a clockmaker.

This essay will explain *Gravity's Rainbow*'s pioneering uses of science from the eighteenth, nineteenth, and twentieth centuries. The major images and uses of these images in the structure of the novel will be examined by offering the nontechnical reader a self-contained introduction to the science itself. We know from the scant biographical data about Thomas Pynchon that he learned much science in all its mathematical majesty.[2] Yet the frequent references in Pynchon's fiction to real, excellent popularizations of science suggest that it is not necessary to learn the language of calculus to participate in the essential discussions of the importance of fundamental revolutions in science. As a physicist turned educator, I fully concur.

Three historical visions of the universe, borrowed from science, comprise the major topics for this essay. *Newtonian mechanism* is the oldest, but it is still a highly useful concept in science. Reaching the moon or predicting the flight of a V-2 rocket are exercises in Newtonian physics. Today the limitations of the method are understood to be fundamental as well as practical, but the concepts inspired by Newton's laws still represent, for us and for Pointsman's faction, a model for many endeavors.

In the nineteenth century, problems that were just too complex to be solved by straightforward applications of Newton's laws were found to yield to the conveniences known as *statistical physics*. Thermodynamics, one fascinating and highly useful ad hoc formulation, became an additional fundamental principle, and was eventually shown to be a direct analogue to the statistical approach. These theories provide some of the most effective imagery in *Gravity's Rainbow*—time reversal and Maxwell's Demon. The statistical laws happen also to fit many needs of twentieth-century physics, where they become not merely partial solutions but the only possible solutions for the microscopic world.

Finally, the vision of *quantum physics*, which accepts an irreducible uncertainty, a limit to possible knowledge, represents the extreme alternative to the universal linkage of a clockwork universe. In *Gravity's Rainbow* the world views associated with quantum physics are ultimately considered as an equal and opposite madness to the paranoia that threatened when all-encompassing linkages were the model for explanations of history. Characters who accept quantum physics' "uncertainty principle" as a guiding rule for human affairs are in danger of becoming "anti-paranoids" in *Gravity's Rainbow*.

Illuminating these three visions borrowed from science will not provide a final resolution of all the intriguing problems of reading *Gravity's Rainbow*. I hope this explication will help readers enjoy the fun of following the clever tricks *Gravity's Rainbow* plays with the gray eminence of Science. Unfortunately, the visions from science do not provide more hopeful guides away from the horrors *Gravity's Rainbow* reveals in life and death. Doctrinaire acceptance of any of these visions proves as sterile as the non-science-related images that obsess characters in *Gravity's Rainbow*. The tragedies of our times are even deepened when the philosophical offspring of science prove as deadly as some of its physical products. But the remarkable achievement of *Gravity's Rainbow* is to bring science within reach as a tool for the reader and for the novelist. Certainly, the scientists and technologists have already demonstrated their own range of possible uses of these tools. Perhaps novelists in the future will find new and more positive ways to make use of these visions offered by science.

Like Clockwork

The V-2 rocket, Vergeltungswaffe Zwei, was literally a vengeance weapon. Through a complex and inhumanly powerful machine, a bomb was thrown by remote control into the stratosphere to return to earth at supersonic speed over a metropolis.

Such a technological feat was possible because of the advances twentieth-century science and technology had made in metalurgy, chemistry, electronics, and mass production. But even before the twentieth century, we had the basic principles to teach us how to design and construct such a weapon. We could have confidence that it would work as predicted, even though it would have to function farther from the Earth than man had ever been, and at speeds faster than man had ever moved. Those principles had been announced by Isaac Newton more than two centuries before.[3]

The predicted path of the rocket could not be perfect—we shall have much to say about the limits of our ability to forecast its exact point of impact. But those predictions were a striking and gruesome example of the success of viewing the universe and its components as a machine. We shall see the dangers of trying to extend that vision to include absolute certainty, and to include man himself.

The Pointsman faction in *Gravity's Rainbow* sees life on a clockwork model, and their goal is to predict human behavior as reliably as the engineers predict the motion of the rocket. Examining just how the rocket flight can be analyzed will demonstrate the Newtonian principles, and touch on many of *Gravity's Rainbow*'s major images.

What follows may seem highly simplified. That simplification is one of the most reliable tricks that science has found. Many of the greatest breakthroughs have occurred when a vastly simpler approach to a problem has been found. Newton's laws of motion simplify the motion of any body by first considering any matter as a point of mass. Mass is a given property, and according to Newton's first law, any mass tends to remain at rest or in uniform motion. The rocket sits on the ground. Gravity pulls it down, but the atoms of the concrete launching pad are held together by other forces, electricity and magnetism, that push up enough to keep the rocket from obeying gravity and sinking into the earth. Thus the forces on the rocket, gravity pulling down and the concrete pushing up, balance, and the net force is zero. To make any mass change its motion, a net unbalanced force must be applied—the thrust of the rocket engines must exceed the force of gravity to start the rocket off. The rate of change in velocity that results is *acceleration*. Newton's second law relates the acceleration produced to the mass of the matter and the net force applied. Reasonably enough, the greater the force and the lower the mass, the more change. Mathematically, the relation between acceleration, force, and mass is: *Acceleration* equals *Force* divided by *Mass* ($A = F/M$, or equivalently, $F = M \times A$). With these mathematical tools, we can describe the motion of a V-2 rocket, a baseball thrown to a batter, atoms of air vibrating in a room, or the planet Earth traveling through space.

Predicting a path for the V-2 rocket is in principle simply a matter of applying this equation, $A = F/M$, to the rocket at every moment of its flight. We figure the net force (engine, gravity, air resistance), divided by the mass of the rocket, and get the acceleration, the change in velocity. We can first calculate the acceleration at the first moment of lift-off. That gives us the velocity at the start of the next moment. So we calculate the next acceleration, the resulting new velocity, and continue on for every moment into space and back down to earth. But how short is "a moment"? We could calculate the changes in motion at intervals of one minute, or one second, or 1/100th of a second. The accelerated motion is not constant: the rocket's engine changes its rate of fuel burn, for example. The rocket's motion is always changing in speed and direction. If we calculate every second and assume constant motion between calculations, we will have an *approximate* description of the path. The more frequently we recalculate the changing motion, the more accurately we will be able to predict the path; but we would need to do an infinite number of recalculations for each infinitesimal interval of time to get the most accurate prediction. Newton (and independently Leibnitz) developed a mathematical procedure, calculus, to assist in figuring motion without having to recalculate every "moment." In effect, calculus permits us to sum up the results to find a prediction of the rocket's motion at any instant we desire: the fatest speed, highest altitude, moment of impact. Calculus gives us the same results we would have gotten if we had done that infinite number of intermediate calculations. One symbol from calculus, the integral sign, plays a role in *Gravity's Rainbow* unrelated to its meaning, as we shall discuss later in this essay.

The image of recalculating for increasingly small intervals is a central one of *Gravity's Rainbow*. In the language of physics and technology, time is represented by the letter t, and the Greek Δ (delta) represents change. The task might be to calculate $A = F/M$ for every interval $\Delta t = 1$ sec. The smaller a Δt we choose, the more calculations would need to be done to reach any instant of the rocket's flight, but the more accurate the result. Calculus permits us to do a calculation in which, in effect, Δt approaches zero.[4]

Calculus is based on firm mathematical logic. But achieving the same effect that an impossible infinite number of calculations would achieve might seem like magic to the uninitiated. To many of *Gravity's Rainbow's* characters, approaching zero is magic. In science a mathematical scheme has enabled us to perform feats of calculation that were not possible before the scheme was invented. The dream of ideal, perfect calculation has been reached.

Leni Pökler uses the calculus image to try to explain her vision of impending perfect doom:

> She even tried, from what little calculus she'd picked up, to explain it to Franz as Δt approaching zero, eternally approaching, the slices of time growing thinner and thinner, a succession of rooms each with walls more silver, transparent, as the pure light of the zero comes nearer. . . . (V159/B185)

Franz Pökler is a "cause-and-effect man" (V159/B186), however, and cannot appreciate metaphors. That is unfortunate, since the literal analogy between Δt and the illusion of motion on film (where Δt = time between frames) is an excellent comparison, made twice in *Gravity's Rainbow* (V407/B474 and V567/B661).

Approaches to zero are metaphors throughout *Gravity's Rainbow* for approaching a destiny. Wartime London is a weird panorama of people going underground "to bring events to Absolute Zero" (V3/B4). Mondaugen sees Pökler's search for his destiny as approaching his zero-error true course, like the rocket (V406/B473), and Enzian, "closest to the zero" (V404/B471), leads a group of Hereros, one faction of which considers extermination (literal reduction to zero) as their destiny.

The calculation of a simple rocket's path is one ideal destiny that is calculable in the mathematical logic of Newtonian physics. But real rockets are more complex than we have described. Does this model of an ideal calculated destiny carry over to describe real rockets, or the destiny of real people, as some characters in *Gravity's Rainbow* assume?

Consider the motion of one real object, the rocket, in more detail. The initial mass of the rocket is easily determined, by weighing it. Once the fuel starts to burn and is exhausted from the nozzle, the rocket loses mass. This can be calculated from the rate of burn. In any event, when fuel burn is ended (*Brennschluss*), the rocket represents a constant mass for the rest of the flight.

The net force on the rocket is due to several factors. Physically and symbolically, gravity is the first force to consider. The force of gravity depends on the mass of the rocket, and so that force too will change until the fuel burn ends. The force of gravity can be calculated, thanks again to Newton. His law of universal gravitation tells us how to calculate the gravitation force that exists between any two masses (such as Earth and rocket). That force depends only on a universal constant factor, the amounts of the masses, and distance between them. The rocket takes off and quickly reaches high velocity because of a second major force, and the one produced by burning fuel. The hot expanding gas is forced out of the engine, and in return, a force is exerted on the rocket's engine pushing it away from the direction of the gas exhaust. Here we have used Newton's third, and final, law of motion: for every action there is an equal and opposite reaction. Air resistance is the third and only other important force on the rocket.

We have now described the four major laws of the Newtonian universe: three laws of motion, and the law of universal gravitation. That is all. In principle we can now describe the future behavior of not only a rocket but any mass in the universe from any known starting configuration.

Eighteenth- and nineteenth-century science could dream of devising mechanical models for everything, applying Newtonian laws, and then obtaining *perfect* predictions of behavior. That dream is not lost for many of *Gravity's Rainbow*'s characters. Even "the Rocket's terrible passage reduced, literally, to bourgeois terms, terms of an equation such as that elegant blend of philosophy and hardware, abstract change and hinged pivots of real metals which describes motion . . . " (V239/B278). The ultimate nineteenth-century image of the mechanization of the universe would be a clockwork man, realized in *Gravity's Rainbow* as Marcel the mechanical chessplayer (V675/B786), who would become indistinguishable from a biological man.

What is perfectible here in principle is impossible in practice. Certainly there is no complete description of the universe from which to start, or even a complete starting description of every atom of air that will exert force on a single rocket. Newton has given us rules for calculating only one force, gravity, and even calculating all gravitational forces would require knowledge of the whereabouts of every bit of matter in the universe. Gravity is, after all, universal: every bit of matter exerts a force on every other. Nineteenth-century physicists gave us rules for calculating other forces, magnetic and electric, and physicists today are working on the rules for nuclear forces of one or more kinds. But in practice no complete calculation of forces is ever possible.

The metaphor need not stop here, however. First, the principle is clear. Even if *we* cannot do a perfect calculation, it is possible. A god could establish the initial locations and motions of everything, and all the universe would then follow along predicted paths. The universe would operate like a gigantic clockwork—not as simple mechanical motion of gears and dials, but just as reliably. If humans are just complex assemblies of masses, biochemicals, and their thoughts are just fleeting electric currents in the brain, then human behavior too is predictable to this god.

In the practice of humankind, the universe as a whole or a human mind is far beyond our ability to calculate. But the behavior of a planet or moon, baseball or rocket, is not beyond a reasonable mathematical approximation. Returning to the rocket in more detail demonstrates how we can calculate a good approximation to its complete path despite these practical limitations in available data.

For gravity we need not consider every bit of mass in the universe. The Earth as a whole may be represented as one great mass, and once the rocket leaves the ground, all gravitational effects are those of a single point, at the center of the Earth with the mass of the entire globe, acting on another single point, the "center of gravity" of the rocket (Pökler had to worry about changing the center of gravity when Gottfield was installed in rocket number 00000). Another major force is the thrust created by the engine. We can calculate that from models, or estimate it from our knowledge of chemistry, or measure it using instruments on the rocket itself. Or we can ignore that force, which lasts for only a minute, and begin to calculate the path at the moment of burnout, with the rocket a measured distance above the surface of the earth, traveling at a measured speed. Finally, there are the forces of air molecules, striking the rocket—friction. Again, these can be measured, calculated from models, estimated from approximate formulas, or just ignored. Even starting with an approximate height, speed, and direction at burn-out, we can calculate the path of the rocket surprisingly well. We shall skip the mathematics here, but it is nearly as simple as Newton's $A = F/M$. A couple of equations, a few algebraic operations like squaring, and we can draw the approximate path of the rocket. It is like the path of a baseball, or some comets. A great, gentle arch. A curve like the entrance to the tunnel at Mittelwerke (V298/B347) or the arc of a rainbow. A parabola.

The rocket flies out to the stratosphere and back to earth, two hundred miles from its origin. We can predict the point of impact, using Newton's physics, within a few miles. Knowing where the rocket will land, with this small uncertainty, is a feat of Newtonian science. Choosing to launch a weapon at all and selecting a target are beyond the competence of this science.

This completes a sketch of Newtonian physics. A simple set of four rules in principle allows prediction of the behavior of the universe. In practice, perfect predictions are not possible for us, but small pieces of the universe, like planets, baseballs, and rockets, may in fact behave as predicted to a very fine approximation. Physics has succeeded to a remarkable degree, and for two hundred years Western civilization has had a model for understanding in all fields. Finding the mechanism, and then the simplifications that make it tractable to calculation, should lead to predictability as close as one has patience to achieve.

In *Gravity's Rainbow* Pavlov's experiments with dogs are seen as straightforward extensions of the Newtonian process from relatively simple mechanisms, like rockets, to more complex ones, like dogs. If the extension works, the behavior of the dogs can be described entirely in terms of forces (now physiological and psychological) and universal laws (such as conditioned reflex). According to Pointsman, Pavlov's disciple in *Gravity's Rainbow*,

> "Pavlov believed that the ideal, the end we all struggle toward in science, is the true mechanical explanation. He was realistic enough not to expect it in his lifetime. Or in several lifetimes more. But his hope was for a long chain of better and better approximations. His faith ultimately lay in a pure physiological basis for the life of the psyche. No effect without cause, and a clear train of linkages." (V89/B102)

For some characters in *Gravity's Rainbow*, the paradigm of searching for mechanism pervades all thinking. Everything must be explainable in mechanistic terms, even if the particular equations are not known, and if the builders of the mechanisms who established the initial conditions are only dimly suspected.

Pointsman is the leading determinist, but he has many followers. Webley Silvernail describes a determinism that admits no freedom from the universal rigid clockwork, for experimental animals or even their experimentors: "I would set you free, if I knew how. But it isn't free out here. All the animals, the plants, the minerals, even other kinds of men, are being broken and reassembled every day, to preserve an elite few, who are the loudest to theorize on freedom, but the least free of all" (V230/B268). We have already noted that Pökler is identified as the "cause-and-effect man." An American colonel wonders about the causes ordering the colors of the sunset, while Eddie Pensiero, his barber, considers all the mechanisms responsible for the arrangement of each hair on the colonel's head (V642–43/B748–49). Even the reader is accused of being rigidly deterministic: "You will want cause and effect" (V663/B772).

If the determinists' suspicions of universal mechanism are

correct, they could learn how the world works by studying individual effects. That model for learning served classical science well, although science looks at only the simplest cause-and-effect combinations. Information about the mechanisms of nature could be present in the path of the rocket or the hairs on a colonel's head.

Strictly speaking, paranoia is not just a suspicion of universal mechanisms and order. If it were, all nineteenth-century scientists would be classified paranoids. But in *Gravity's Rainbow*, the term suggests the smooth and invisible transition between accepting the sometimes useful paradigm of a clockwork universe, and unreasonably believing the mechanism has a conscious, personal purpose.

Statistics for Convenience

The use of entropy and thermodynamics in nearly all Pynchon's works has attracted much critical attention. Particular symbols from the physics of entropy, such as Maxwell's sorting demon, recur frequently. In *Gravity's Rainbow* not only do the familiar themes of entropy versus order occur but so does *statistical mechanics*, a branch of physics that was recognized at the end of the nineteenth century as the mathematical base to the entropy concept.[5]

Newtonian physics had presented the eighteenth century with a set of fundamental rules for understanding the behavior of matter. But as we have seen, exact application of these rules often was impossible in practice, although approximations and simplification could take us a long way. But what of the problems that we could not even approximate? For example, what will be the pressure inside a cylinder of gas, like a can of hair spray? The pressure will be the sum of all the forces exerted by the trillions of atoms inside against the walls. Those forces depend on the impacts of atom against atom, bouncing back and forth a trillion-trillion times a second. Applying Newton's laws directly is hopeless.

The goal of predicting the *exact* trajectory and striking point of a V-2 rocket is similarly hopeless. Pointsman, who believes in predictability for humans, has a hard time accepting uncertainty in something so relatively simple as a rocket: "Can't you...*tell*, . . . from your map here, which places would be safest to go into, safest from attack?" he asks Roger Mexico (V55/B64). Mexico tries to explain that at best we can get a good approximation and present the odds. Even good approximation, an uncertainty of a few hundred yards, would still be an uncertainty of life or death, as Mexico and his lover Jessica Swanlake know (V59/B69). The small deviations from the ideal path of a rocket are caused by air resistance, among other factors, and we are back to calculating trillions of collisions between atoms of air and the skin of the rocket.

Statistical mechanics allows us to handle these problems within the Newtonian scheme, although in the example of the rocket, the solution is not nearly as precise as we would like. We achieve statistical answers, convenient answers, but without the absolute certainty we would desire.

One classic example of these statistics of convenience is calculating the pressure on the wall of the cylinder of compressed gas. We cannot measure the exact path of even one single atom of the trillions in the cylinder, so how might we possibly be able to predict the pressure of the gas, which depends on the average impacts of all the atoms that strike the wall every second? Statistical mechanics allows us to predict the pressure, given the amount of gas and the temperature, for example, to a remarkable accuracy, within an infinitesimal fraction of a percent. How is this possible?

First, every atom is an identical unit. If we can compute a *typical* path, number of collisions per second, we can apply that typical figure to all other atoms. We do not expect any atoms to reproduce exactly the typical path. Some will collide more vigorously and frequently, and some much less. But the huge numbers—a trillion atoms in a volume the size of a can of hair spray—makes this typical result extremely valuable. If we think of individual atoms deviating at random from the average, the number of more vigorous actions will equal the number of less vigorous actions very precisely because of the huge number being averaged. The result of simple calculations of typical behavior (or average or "mean," depending on the mathematical language being used) will give an extremely accurate answer. The statistics are convenient, even if we can learn from them nothing at all about the path of a single individual atom.

Pynchon has used the straightforward images of statistical mechanics in earlier works. In *The Crying of Lot 49*, we have the image of the wild can of hair spray that bounces frantically between the walls of Oedipa Maas's motel bathroom. Oedipa recognizes the practical impossibility of calculating the path of a single particle represented by the can, but believes in principle in the power of classical mechanics ("God or a digital computer") to accomplish the task.[6]

Predictions of the rockets' actual striking pattern work the same way, although the numbers of rockets are in the hundreds, not the trillions. Individual rockets are very similar to each other. The chance fluctuations of wind and moment of burn-out will make some rockets go a bit farther, and others may reach shorter distances. The average will still be well defined, and if the flight of many rockets is considered, the impacts will make a roughly symmetrical scatter pattern around the predicted target center.

Statistical methods allow us to describe the pattern of strikes in even more detail. Of mortally serious interest to residents of a particular area—for example, a given square kilometer of a target city—is the likelihood of their square receiving one or more strikes. Using a mathematical formula, the Poisson distribution, we can predict the odds of strikes falling on a given area. Each specific distribution depends on the overall pattern width and the total number of rockets, but a typical pattern, graphed as a mathematical line or curve, could look like figure 1.

The curve gives us odds. Above each possible number of strikes is a dot on the curve. The height of the dot tells us the odds of that number of strikes occurring in any one square. In this case, there is a 5 percent chance of being lucky and receiving zero strikes, a 15 percent chance of receiving one strike, and a 22 percent chance of receiving two strikes. The curve does not tell us the exact number that actually will strike a given square, but if we study many squares, the odds become increasingly reliable. As more and more data come in, we will find the actual number of squares receiving no strikes approaches 5 percent, the number of squares receiving one strike approaches 15 percent, and so on.

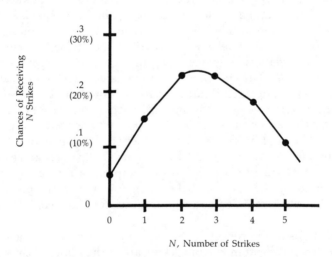

Figure 1. Chances of receiving N strikes on a square kilometer of the target. This is the Poisson distribution for a mean of 3 strikes per square.

These numbers sound precise enough. Does that not mean that statistical physics is giving us the complete predictions we desire? "Roger has tried to explain to her the V-bomb statistics: the difference between distribution, in angel's-eye view, over the map of England, and their own chances, as seen from down here. She's almost got it: nearly understands his Poisson equation, yet can't quite put the two together—put her own enforced calm day-to-day alongside the pure numbers, and keep them both in sight" (V54/B62).

Point 1. Even if our lives depended on it, we could not predict the path of a single rocket beyond saying that it is likely to fall within a few miles of the target center. Only when we have many examples do the statistics tell us something, and then it is only about the pattern of the many.

Point 2. Despite the limitation a particular pattern will be approached, more and more accurately as more examples come in. That mathematical pattern is a bell-shaped curve. For a large total number of strikes, but a few strikes per square, the pattern used is called the Poisson distribution. For different numbers other curves appear, of the same general shape—the "normal distribution" is an important instance for physics.

Point 3. Statistical methods are not limited to rockets. Wherever events occur with random fluctuations about an average, the same mathematics, the same curves, appear. Thus *Gravity's Rainbow* is not exaggerating the universality of the Poisson distribution when it claims:

> But to the likes of employees such as Roger Mexico it is music, not without its majesty, this power series
>
> $$Ne^{-m} \left(1 + m + \frac{m^2}{2!} + \frac{m^3}{3!} + \ldots + \frac{m^{n-1}}{(n-1)!} \right)$$
>
> terms numbered according to rocketfalls per square, the Poisson dispensation ruling not only these annihilations no man can run from, but also cavalry accidents, blood counts, radioactive decay, number of wars per year.... (V140/B163)

The majesty is not so striking in the Newtonian clockwork view of the universe. The Poisson distribution tells us only of the results of small, random ignorances of the situation, and so it does not "rule." Individual events cannot be predicted by it. The exclamation points in the equation, by the way, do not express emotion—they are a conventional mathematical shorthand for "factorials": $3! = 3 \times 2 \times 1$.

Yet the curve is convenient, and statistics work. The curve is abstract, but allows predictions of real patterns. So too was the classical prediction of the ideal path of a rocket an invisible but useful concept. The shape of the simplest rocket path, due only to the unbalanced force of gravity, is a parabola, "that purified shape latent in the sky" (V209/B244). The mathematical shape of the Poisson distribution that gives us the chances of strikes in different places has roughly the same form in the center: a gentle, curving arc. Something like a rainbow.

The title *Gravity's Rainbow* is not an exact correspondence to either image from science, but does suggest both the typical path that Newton's universe predicts for a rocket under the influence of gravity, and the mathematical shape of the distribution of rocket strikes. Does the universe we live in conform to a ruling, absolute destiny that determines life and death, as the powerful double image at first suggests? That is a central question of the novel.

The first section of this essay showed that a gravity's rainbow, the life-or-death determining path of the rocket, could in principle be entirely determined. But in practice, as the second section has shown, only statistical judgments, good but never perfect, are available to us. At this point, then, the images from science have shown the possibility of control, but not its certain existence. We may still suspect that the terror of life and death, war and peace, are controlled, but we have not directly observed that control.

The Statistical Law

The statistical mechanics we have just discussed could be considered as a convenient solution when the facts, although knowable in principle, are difficult to obtain. The predictions made by such physics, like the distribution of rocket hits, will of necessity be only statistical themselves.

The second law of thermodynamics, by contrast, is a new law, covering a behavior of the universe not discussed by Newtonian physics. The first law of thermodynamics, by the way, turns out to be the conservation of energy—that energy can neither be created nor destroyed but only transformed from one state to another.

The second law places the barb on the arrow of time. Consider the following possible behavior on the part of a section of the universe. The remains of a V-2 rocket lie over several acres, in fragments. The vicinity is scattered with debris of smashed buildings and dirt thrown up from a crater. Suddenly the dirt around the crater flies up in the air, and falls back into the crater, smoothing out the ground. Simultaneously the fragments of the smashed bricks fly up, reassemble as bricks, and fly to the exact positions they each originally had in the walls of the building. The mortar and glass do likewise, so that the entire building complex reassembles itself in a few seconds, on top of the just-filled crater. There is still a hole in the top of the building, however, but suddenly, flying tail first out of that hole, appears the reassembled V-2 rocket. It seems to suck the roof of the building up with it, restoring it to its proper place and leaving a perfect roof as the rocket recedes up into the air.

Certainly we would recognize this scene as impossible. Perhaps it is a description of a film run backward. But we know it could not happen as described. Why? Surprisingly, nothing at all in Newtonian physics makes this scene impossible, or even unlikely. All the laws of Newtonian physics would be obeyed. The energy for the debris to fly up would come from the material and the ground giving up a little heat, and that heat turning to energy of motion. The reverse happens all the time: the debris came to a stop because its energy of motion was converted to heat energy by friction. Here, we are just running that phenomenon in reverse. Step by step, the strange scene is completely plausible in a Newtonian clockwork physics.

Yet we know such things do not happen. A rock flying at a window may result in smashed fragments of glass. Glass never spontaneously reassembles from the fragments into pane, ejecting a rock. That Newtonian physics fails to describe one behavior as impossible while predicting the other to be common indicates that Newtonian physics fails to give us a complete picture of our universe. We need another law.

Gravity's Rainbow gives us dozens of examples of these impossible phenomena, sometimes through reversed film images, sometimes through dreams or drugs.

> It is the dope that finds *you*, apparently. Part of a reverse world whose agents run around with guns which are like vacuum cleaners operating in the direction of life—pull the trigger and bullets are sucked back out of the recently dead into the barrel, and the Great Irreversible is actually reversed as the corpse comes to life to the accompaniment of a backwards gunshot (you can imagine what drug-ravaged and mindless idea of fun the daily sound editing on this turns out to be). (V745/B870)

Guns that destroy are much easier to find than those that heal. Destruction is simpler than construction. Do all these examples prove that God and nature are basically destroyers, or that at best "every true god must be both organizer and destroyer" (V99/B115)?

Thermodynamics is a powerful metaphor for raising the question and linking it to the fundamental problem of the nature of time. For one way to look at all the apparently irreversible phenomena we have considered is that they deal with the direction of the flow of time. Needed was a law to predict what processes are forward in time and what must be impossible or backward in time. That law is the second law of thermodynamics. We shall define it and discuss how it functions in Pynchon's metaphors. The law has a curious history, having been invented independently by several people over nearly a century, and in such different forms that it was not until the end of the nineteenth century that the various forms were recognized as being equivalent to each other and to the statistical laws discussed in the preceding section.

A modern statement of the second law would be that for the universe as a whole, or an isolated part of it, processes forward in time tend to increase disorder. There are of course mathematical formulations of the law, and *disorder* is carefully defined as *entropy*. But even without mathematics, this law already seems to describe what features all the previously mentioned examples have that makes it so easy for us to distinguish the forward and backward instances of time. A rocket explosion *disorders*: it is not expected that an explosion ends with smashed buildings reordered.

The identification of the common feature of all forward time processes, disordering, is a clever achievement. The surprising and disturbing word in the second law is *tend*. The law does not demand that the universe always behave this way, only that it tend to. This implies that violations are possible. Shake a box of coins, and every once in a while they will all appear heads up. You might continue to shake boxes of coins, and have a dozen in a row become all neatly ordered heads up. That is unlikely, but not impossible. Since the law says *tend*, no violation of the second law has happened.

The second law for complex systems like all the bricks in a house, or a falling V-2, is very reliable indeed. When other phenomena were being uncovered that consistently violated known laws at the end of the nineteenth century, physicists were more willing to give up on Newton's laws than the second law of thermodynamics. But the second law is not absolutely reliable—it is strictly a statistical truth, a truth about the universe that is only generally true.

Unlikely happenings occur. That does not violate the second law, as we have indicated. The association of unlikely happenings with time reversal is an accurate exposition of the fundamental concept of the second law. *Gravity's Rainbow* uses that association to reinforce the novel's film motif, but also to point out how often the "impossible" is only the unlikely.

Some of the time reversals are not even truly unlikely. A supersonic rocket can be seen before it is heard. "Imagine a missile one hears approaching only *after* it explodes. The reversal! A piece of time neatly snipped out...a few feet of film run backwards...the blast of the rocket, fallen faster than sound—then growing *out of it* the roar of its own fall, catching up to what's already death and burning...a ghost in the sky...." (V48/B55). Once again the V-2 is the concrete example, obeying the second law's demand for entropy while presenting us with a reversal, in perception if not in physics, of the normal time sequence. Time-reversal images in *Gravity's Rainbow* do not prove that entropy can be overcome. For many characters in the novel, however, any perceived challenges to disorder and death offer hope. The hope of these false time reversals does in fact lead to a much more subtle challenge to entropy.

A spectacular new use of the second law in science and in *Gravity's Rainbow* is the application of that law to life itself.[7] The life process at first seems to be a violation. Humans start as conjunctions of two very simple biological units, a sperm and an egg. Somehow that combination begins ordering the medium around it, assembling trillions of atoms in self-replicating units, more and more complexly ordered, to produce a human being. Does biology violate the second law? A broader view of the universe permits a simple no. The human (or insect or plant) is not isolated. If it were entirely isolated, it would quickly wither and die, becoming properly disordered. For life to survive, it must consume energy, creating disorder elsewhere. Consider the debris of disassembled foods each of us leaves behind in a lifetime.

Further, life has no equilibrium state, and is continually changing —it is not possible to observe simple before-and-after states (like the box of coins before and after shaking). The rules of "nonequilibrium" thermodynamics are more complex than the simple version of the second law given above, and biophysicists are still trying to determine how life fits into the scheme of a universe that is generally quite good on obeying the tendencies to disorder described by the second law.

Gravity's Rainbow is filled with images of biological order springing from disorder.

> . . . Corydon Throsp . . . liked to cultivate pharmaceutical plants up on the roof . . . , most returning, as fragments of peculiar alkaloids, to rooftop earth, along with manure from a trio of prize Wessex Saddleback sows quartered there by Throsp's successor, and dead leaves off many decorative trees transplanted to the roof by later tenants, and the

odd unstomachable meal thrown or vomited there by this or that sensitive epicurean—all got scumbled together, eventually, by the knives of the seasons, to an impasto, feet thick, of unbelievable black topsoil in which anything could grow, not the least being bananas. (V5/B5–6)

The compost-garden image is the most straightforward example of life cycling from disorder to order in temporary, local contradiction to the second law. The litter on Slothrop's desk (song and music, pieces of jigsaw puzzles, perhaps a picture of an explosion, a sexy pinup, intelligence summaries, a shoe polish can and *News of the World* [V18/B20–21]) takes a full page to describe, and the life that will arise from the debris is *Gravity's Rainbow*, the novel itself. Industrial processes, such as the production of steel using coal from long-dead forms of life (V166/B194), is another example, and one that later links the production of the V-2 to the life process. "Beyond simple steel erection, the Rocket was an entire system *won*, away from the feminine darkness, held against the entropies of lovable but scatterbrained Mother Nature . . . " (V324/B377). The rocket has been assembled by living beings from raw materials scattered by nature all over the earth.

Other compost heaps lie scattered about *Gravity's Rainbow*, not yet having spawned life. Slothrop's last appearance in the novel arises from a "compost-heap" of memories, including one of clearing literal heaps. Slothrop is waiting, "not a thing in his head, just feeling natural" (V626/B729), for nature to begin the cycle again.

Biological life remains an incompletely resolved challenge to the second law, and there was yet another challenge developed in the last half of the nineteenth century by physicist James Clerk Maxwell. He proposed a thought experiment that demonstrated a hypothetical way to violate the second law of thermodynamics. Although there was no practical means of performing the experiment, it could be thought, and it violated no other laws of physics.

Maxwell's Demon was the personification of this purely theoretical challenge to the second law of thermodynamics. The idea was that a tiny, intelligent being (a miniature demon) could operate on an atomic level: opening and closing atom-size doors, for example, to sort fragments. Because the demon acts on an atomic scale, he is negligibly bothered by friction, which wastes energy and creates disorder. The demon might patiently sort the random vibrations of atoms, allowing only those random motions that create order and blocking the motions that would create disorder or make no change. Thus the demon could reverse weathering and mechanical decay. Indeed, if he operated long enough, he could reassemble the smashed buildings and people blown apart by the V-2.

The demon would not even require any energy to create order by sorting. He would simply select from the natural, but orderless, random energies of vibration of atoms. He could even provide more useful energy. In the most common imaginary example of the imaginary demon, he sorts the atoms in a box so that the faster moving ones wind up on one side (producing heat there) while the slower ones are left on the other side (cooling it). From the temperature difference produced, one could run a steam engine. The sorting demon would be a permanent solution to the energy crisis.

Nobody knew then (or knows now) how to create any device to function as the demon would. That in no way diminished the seriousness of the challenge Maxwell's Demon presented to science. Since a device was conceptually possible that would always violate the second law, the law was not even statistically reliable, and so not much of a law. The demon violated no known law, except the second law of thermodynamics. So either the second law had to go, or there was another as yet uninvented fundamental law that prevented the demon from existing. The reliability of the second law was unquestioned. Physicists would have rather given up Newton's laws, or Maxwell's laws of electricity and magnetism, than admit a failure of the second law. We shall see in a few paragraphs that a new fundamental law to slay the demon was indeed found.

Thermodynamics is not without a remaining hint of the demon even today. Physicists no longer take seriously any mechanical device challenging the ultimate march toward chaos promised by the law, but life still represents an incompletely understood process that does sort, build, and order. In the Pynchon literary canon, Maxwell's Demon is the occasional unexpected act that changes the direction of the narrative, and so orders the novel in a new way. In "Entropy," *The Crying of Lot 49*, and *Gravity's Rainbow*, surprise, often in the form of a small character figuratively identified with the demon, often interrupts and reorders the narrative. The demon is named in *Gravity's Rainbow* (V239/B278) and then more fully described (V411/B479–80). His other appearances cannot be certified, but his presence may be suspected whenever a small, demon-like character disrupts the action and starts things off on a new track. When Slothrop's pants are stolen, for example, we catch one glimpse of the thief: "From way down the hall, a tiny head appears around a corner, a tiny hand comes out and gives Slothrop the tiny finger. Unpleasant laughter reaches him a split second later . . . " (V199/B231).

The demon is supposed to function because he need only sort and direct. He does not have to move things himself, which would require energy and create entropy. In most physics texts the demon is seen opening and closing doors, screening out the slow atoms from the fast on one side of a divided box. That image might explain the two screen-door salesmen briefly mentioned in *Gravity's Rainbow* (V447/B521 and V665/B774). The image is certainly responsible for Mister Information's description of the pointsman, who "hardly has to work at all" and sorts people between Happyville and Pain City (V644/B751). The demon does require information, to tell the fast atoms from the slow, the Elect from the Preterite. That essential need for information led to the demise of the demon in twentieth-century physics. Information, which nineteenth-century physics had thought could be obtained with no energy expenditure, was discovered to require a minimum, a quantum, of energy for each bit of data acquired. A demon who would sort trillions of atoms would require trillions of quanta, and in fact would require more energy to operate than he could produce. His entropy production would thus exceed the order he created. The relation between information, energy, and entropy was a major theme for "Entropy" and *The Crying of Lot 49*, and as the Mr. Information passages of *Gravity's Rainbow* indicate, the pattern continues as one of the science themes of this novel.[8]

Slothrop himself, like Oedipa Mass, functions in a sorting-demon manner. He tries to sort and order the events of his world and his history. He does stumble upon hints of order, and conceives numerous possible hidden orders, although he never achieves full understanding or completes an ordered pattern. Yet he survives, and escapes the undesirable orders some want for him and the complete disorder others would impose.

The statistical truths of the Poisson distribution and of thermodynamics represent the middle ground between the complete understanding promised by the Newtonian paradigm and the permanent incompleteness that was to come.

God the Higher Mathematician

The third and final great theme from science that structures *Gravity's Rainbow* is "modern" twentieth-century physics. Whereas thermodynamics and statistical mechanics offered extensions and new modes of viewing the clockworks, the new physics represents an entirely new model for the universe, a model that cannot exist in mechanical terms, as the miniature clockwork solar systems could in the Newtonian universe.

The language of modern physics speaks of multidimensional spaces, probability matrices, and wave states. New mathematical forms are fully manipulatable, and produce predictions for the behavior of the physical world, yet they do not provide the concrete images that comprised the earlier world views and so graphically served as image and metaphor in the rocket and the compost garden. Modern physics does provide new arguments about world view, however, and images of this physics in *Gravity's Rainbow* serve as the extreme alternative to the paranoia of the Newtonian determinists.

Albert Einstein began striking off at one new angle in 1905 with the special theory of relativity, and completed this new structure in 1916 with the general theory. Relativity does not play a major role in the imagery of *Gravity's Rainbow*, however. Relativity does not say that everything is relative—rather, it sets up new relationships between previously unrelated fundamentals: time, space, mass, and gravity. The universe is as deterministic in these new relations as it was in the old. But now time and space are not the independent, universal, absolute concepts they once were. In relativity they may change, dilate and contract, depending on the nature of the observation made on them. Mass and gravity and time and space interact. Gravity's influence is more than just one of the forces exerted on a rocket. Now we see gravity, created by the presence of mass, as changing (in a well-equationed manner) the time and space around any mass.

The universe as a whole responds to the dominant force of gravity in the currently accepted model. The universe began in a great explosion about fifteen billion years ago. The space between the galaxies of stars, planets, and dust has been expanding since then. But the mutual gravitational attraction of all mass has been slowing the expansion of the universe. Depending on the latest estimate of the total mass, and hence the strength of the gravitational forces, the attraction may be enough to eventually halt the expansion and bring the universe back together, to *decrease entropy* in a great reversal of the initial bang. This theory of an oscillating universe is paired with the possibility that there is not enough mass, and the universe will continue to expand, to the dispersal of matter and energy and the final domination of entropy.

Casual references to cosmological terms (i.e., the red shift of the color spectra of the spiral nebulae was proof of the expanding of the universe [V754/B880]) appear in *Gravity's Rainbow*, but the cosmological picture is merged with the earlier classical images of life and the rocket rising and falling again. A brilliant passage near the end of *Gravity's Rainbow* begins by referring to the classical ideal rocket path, the mathematically infinite parabola:

> It Begins Infinitely Below The Earth And Goes On Infinitely Back Into The Earth it's only the *peak* that we are allowed to see, the break up through the surface, out of the other silent world, violently (a jet airplane crashing into faster-than-sound, some years later a spaceship crashing into faster-than-light) Remember The Password In The Zone This Week Is FASTER—THAN, THE-SPEEDOFLIGHT Speeding Up Your Voice Exponentially— . . . at each "end," understand, a very large transfer of energy: breaking upward into this world, a controlled burning—breaking downward again, an uncontrolled explosion...this lack of symmetry leads to speculating that a presence, analogous to the Aether, flows through time, as the Aether flows through space. The assumption of a Vacuum in time tended to cut us off one from another. But an Aether sea to bear us world-to-world might bring us back a continuity, show us a kinder universe, more easygoing....
>
> So, yes yes this is a scholasticism here, Rocket state-cosmology... (V726/B847)

The oscillations of the universe and of life, as symbolized by the rise and fall of the rocket, challenge the ultimate disorder of entropy. They suggest a broad pattern of cyclic birth, death, and rebirth in a new order and imply a grand, if impersonal, ordering.

Relativity elegantly enlarges the classical picture, and in *Gravity's Rainbow* it provides an extension of the clockwork universe—at once more flexible and surprising, but just as subject to the suspicion of control.

The Universe Itself Is Uncertain

In the 1920s, physics developed a new model that is a real alternative to the clockwork universe image that provides *Gravity's Rainbow*'s determinists with a physical environment to complement their political and personal maneuvers. That alternative was the *quantum physics* of Neils Bohr, Edwin Schrödinger, Werner Heisenberg, and Max Born. A great controversy about the interpretation of this new physics arose at the time, and is not yet laid to rest. Einstein himself, who helped create the quantum physics with his demonstration of the quantum nature of light in 1905, never accepted the establishment view that the quantum theory tells us of essential, unavoidable uncertainties in the universe. Not merely uncertainties in measurements due to neglected Newtonian forces, or statistical conveniences, these are uncertainties in the nature of knowledge itself.

The "Copenhagen Interpretation" of quantum physics describes a universe that appears to obey rigid rules, like Newtonian mechanics or Einsteinian relativity, only when we look at large masses of matter. The essential uncertainties in quantum theory are inversely proportional to the mass of the entity observed. For large masses (a speck of dust and up), the infinitesimally small uncertainties are beyond detection. When we look at masses the size of atoms and bits of atoms, however, the uncertainties are as large as the measurements, and classical predictions of behavior are wrong. The predictions of quantum physics often tell us not of a single expected result but of two (or more) completely different possible behaviors for an experiment, and the odds of observing each. But that is all. The individual experimental observation may go either way, and we can only know the odds. Even the most fundamental laws may lack certainty—a particle trapped in an atom by forces from which it cannot obtain the energy to escape may suddenly appear outside the trap. The greater the holding forces, the less likely the escape, but the odds are not zero unless the forces are infinite.

If you have listened to the clicking of a Geiger counter detecting the radioactive disintegrations from the radium dial of a watch face, you have heard the sounds of essential uncertainty. Classically, the particles in the nucleus of a radium atom are trapped. They do not have enough energy to escape the nuclear forces. Yet every so often the classically unchangeable nucleus disintegrates and in its place is a lighter nucleus, and a previously trapped fragment appears outside the nucleus flying away to interact with the counter and cause a click. There is no way to predict when a particle will make its totally unclassical and impossible escape. We can give superb statistics, however. On average, half of a collection of radium nuclei will remain stable for 1,620 years (radium has a "half-life" of 1,620 years). But that is an average, determined by measurements of billions of atoms. An individual atom may remain stable for billions of years—indeed, some radium atoms around today have been here since the creation of our solar system five billion years ago. Yet any atom may disintegrate a fraction of a second after its creation. The weaker the forces holding the nucleus together, the shorter the average time of stability and the more frequently a gram of the material will have atoms disintegrating. Thus we have both highly and slightly radioactive materials. The statistics are superb for the huge numbers of radioactive atoms in a grain of substance. Yet every click of that counter is individually unpredictable. The clicks are truly random.

One image from this physics is the branch point, a situation presenting a distinct number of possibilities. The atom of radium can remain whole or it can disintegrate. The "choice" between these branches is completely random. Neither history nor a deterministic god can alter the odds or close off a fork. In *Gravity's Rainbow*, these forks include capture or escape, Election or Preterition, or multiple choices of action.

The engineer Beláustegui, a "prophet of science" (V383/B446), is a clear contrast to the Newtonian engineer Pökler, since Beláustegui "knows his odds, the shapes of risk are intimate to him as loved bodies. Each moment has its value, its probable success against other moments in other hands, and the shuffle for him is always moment-to-moment. He can't afford to remember other permutations, might-have-beens—only what's present, dealt him by something he calls Chance and Graciela calls God" (V613/B714). In one surrealistic scene, Slothrop is involved with an inept crew:

> There's no real direction here, neither lines of power nor cooperation. Decisions are never really *made*—at best they manage to emerge, from a chaos of peeves, whims, hallucinations and all-round assholery. . . . Its survival seems, after all, only a mutter of blind fortune groping through the heavy marbling of skies one Titanic-Night at a time. Which is why Slothrop now observes his coalition with hopes for success and hopes for disaster about equally high. . . . It does annoy him that he can be so divided, so perfectly unable to come down on one side or another. (V676–77/B788)

Einstein refused to accept the Copenhagen interpretation of quantum theory, which held that the statistical rules of the theory are a true statement of limits on knowledge of the universe. The universe itself must not be fuzzy, said Einstein. He battled the Copenhagen interpretation, and the Heisenberg "uncertainty principle," by challenging its physics, but never succeeded in showing a fatal flaw or planning an experiment that disproved the quantum theory. He never gave up his philosophical objection, however, that (in his own summation) "God could not be so cruel as to play dice with the Universe."[9]

In *Gravity's Rainbow*, dodo exterminator Frans Van der Groov ponders his own version of the question of meaning behind the cycle of life and death. Might it all have no determined purpose like salvation? He too concludes "God could not be that cruel" (V111/B129).

In the previous section, we saw that in the Newtonian picture

God could completely determine a clockwork universe, but men had to be content with statistical information about the world. The possibility of control, by a god or a god-like power, was still present. What changes with the physics of quantum theory is that the universe itself becomes fuzzy, not merely man's limited knowledge of it. Even a god would lose control. This loss of even the possibility in principle of control is crucial to science, and to *Gravity's Rainbow*.

Many characters in *Gravity's Rainbow*, however, do accept that the universe is merely statistically determined. Roger Mexico works with the conveniences of classical statistical mechanics, devised to overcome ignorance of small perturbations and unmeasured forces. Yet he is aware of the more essential uncertainties undermining the very paradigm of mechanism:

> ". . . there's a feeling about that cause-and-effect may have been taken as far as it will go. That for science to carry on at all, it must look for a less narrow, a less...sterile set of assumptions. The next great breakthrough may come when we have the courage to junk cause-and-effect entirely, and strike off at some other angle." (V89/B102–3)

Drug salesman Wimpe uses the Heisenberg "uncertainty principle" explicitly:

> "We seem up against a dilemma built into Nature, much like the Heisenberg situation. There is nearly complete parallelism between analgesia and addiction. The more pain it takes away, the more we desire it. It appears we can't have one property without the other, any more than a particle physicist can specify position without suffering an uncertainty as to the particle's velocity—" (V348/B405)

Enzian gives a more hyperbolic description:

> "Well, I think we're here, but only in a statistical way. Something like that rock over there is just about 100% certain—it knows it's there, so does everybody else. But our own chances of being right here right now are only a little better than even—the slightest shift in the probabilities and we're gone—schnapp! like that." (V362/B421)

Enzian would disagree with Einstein. The message of history for the Herero is that "there was no difference between the behavior of a god and the operations of pure chance" (V323/B376).

The rocket, which has served in *Gravity's Rainbow* as symbol for both the clockwork mechanism, in flight, and the statistical conveniences, in impact distribution, once again is the image for a now essential uncertainty. As Enzian sees it,

> "One reason we grew so close to the Rocket, I think, was this sharp awareness of how contingent, like ourselves, the Aggregat 4 could be— how at the mercy of small things...dust that gets in a timer . . . corrosion, a short, a signal grounded out, Brennschluss too soon, and

what was alive is only an Aggregat again, an Aggregat of pieces of dead matter, no longer anything that can move, or that has a Destiny with a shape. . . ." (V362/B422)

A universe with no possibility of control, by God or mortal, would be a frightening thing indeed. Philosophers of physics might not go that far since playing the odds is entirely practical, and close to certainty for objects much bigger than atoms. Here *Gravity's Rainbow* is concerned only with science as principle, not the practicality.

Tchitcherine lives because he is successful in surviving plots against him by good luck. He is open to many possibilities and allows chance to "determine" his fate. Chemistry joins physics in *Gravity's Rainbow*'s description of Tchitcherine:

. . . He is a giant supermolecule with so many open bonds available at any given time, and in the drift of things . . . others latch on, and the pharmacology of the Tchitcherine thus modified, its onwardly revealed side-effects, can't necessarily be calculated ahead of time. (V346/B402–3)

Tchitcherine is literally as well as figuratively an example of chemical technology. Like another character from *V.*, his body is full of new alloy replacement parts.

Byron the Bulb is also a survivor like Tchitcherine, apparently thanks to chance. "Through his years of survival, all these various rescues of Byron happen as if by accident" (V653/B761). Byron's indefinitely long life is a normal statistical possibility (the Poisson distribution curve for bulb life never reaches zero percent even for very old bulbs).

In the new paradigm, these survivors cannot take comfort in assuming that fate, or God, has been looking after them. Neither man nor God could determine events, for good or for evil, if the metaphor of an essentially fuzzy universe is to be accepted.

This hopelessness, and inability either to grieve or to rejoice at turns of events, is the final deadly alternative to the brutal determinism that chose the metaphor of a clockwork universe, in which individuals had no control because more powerful forces ruled. The alternative to that paranoia is anti-paranoia: "where nothing is connected to anything, a condition not many of us can bear for long" (V434/B506). Anti-paranoia, through the metaphor of quantum physics, is the appropriate reversal of paranoia, with its metaphor of a classical clockwork physics.

Strategies for Success?

Three distinct images from science—the eighteenth-century clockwork universe, the nineteenth-century statistical rules, including thermodynamics, and the essential uncertainties of twentieth-century quantum theory—have served as metaphors for the strategies for success that characters in *Gravity's Rainbow* adopt. The V-2 rocket neatly encapsulates all three metaphors. The rocket is analyzed technically with each of these scientific tools. Characters must understand the rocket through both science and metaphor, since it is the life-and-death element of their environment.

> But the Rocket has to be many things, it must answer to a number of different shapes in the dreams of those who touch it—in combat, in tunnel, on paper—it must survive heresies shining, unconfoundable...and heretics there will be: Gnostics who have been taken in a rush of wind and fire to chambers of the Rocket-throne...Kabbalists who study the Rocket as Torah, letter by letter—rivets, burner cup and brass rose, its text is theirs to permute and combine into new revelations, always unfolding...Manichaeans who see two Rockets, good and evil, who speak together in the sacred idiolalia of the Primal Twins (some say their names are Enzian and Blicero) of a good Rocket to take us to the stars, an evil Rocket for the World's suicide, the two perpetually in struggle. (V727/B847–48)

Science provides both the focused image and the philosophical world views to attempt the survival task.

Have the three images from science aided their various adherents? Tyrone Slothrop wishes to escape control and understand the forces that want to control him. That requires his understanding the entire covert military-industrial complex. Although Slothrop does wander without others successfully working their will on him, his understanding of the hidden forces remains an incomplete collection of suspicions, coincidences, and alternative plots. Like Oedipa Maas in *The Crying of Lot 49*, he uncovers enough evidence to begin a hundred investigations, but reaches no ultimate conclusions. Along his search, he has been exposed to each of the alternative world views from paranoia to anti-paranoia, and yet we last see him with "not a thing in his head" (V626/B729). None of the metaphors from science has remained with Slothrop.

We leave other characters with clear evidence of survival and even success. Geli gets her man at last, but the only explicit tool she uses, besides persistence, is witchcraft. Here is a metaphor clearly external from the choices in science that *Gravity's Rainbow* has offered. The narrator affirms that category of alternative to the science metaphors after the final scene with Geli, Tchitcherine, and Enzian: "This is magic. Sure—but not necessarily fantasy" (V735/ B857).

Alternatives to the world views with science as metaphor are many, and are expressed by other characters. Thanatz is the "leading theoretician" of Sado-anarchism (V737/B860), and Blicero has a mystical belief in the Rocket as a promise of transcendence. No predominant pattern of earthly success follows any of the theoretical approaches, and neither salvation nor success is identified with any one theoretical system in *Gravity's Rainbow*.

Science as Style

So far we have considered science as metaphor. But the images from science also serve as symbol and motif in *Gravity's Rainbow*. Another novel might use images of animals, colors, or habits as symbols to be placed in the fictional landscape to provide continuity or effect. *Gravity's Rainbow* uses words and shapes from science for these special effects, quite separate from their metaphoric meaning.

One key motif is the repetition of an image, widely separated by events and pages of *Gravity's Rainbow*. This effect provides an almost subliminal continuity, and one that achieves a sense of déjà vu for the reader. One of these images is an elongated "s" shape. It is literally the integral sign from calculus, a shorthand for a mathematical operation of adding up the values of a function over a range of possibilities. The s-shape is often a double "s" in mathematics, adding up values over two ranges. We have already described the basic process in an earlier section. An actual integral sign appears in the novel as a mathematical pun (V450/B524), but images of s-shapes appear sporadically in the novel even in places where the mathematical meaning is irrelevant. Spokes on a pulley are "shaped like Ss" (V4/B4); Katje lies "S'd against the S" of Slothrop (V198/B231); the layout of the Mittelwerke plant is like "the letters SS each stretched lengthwise" (V299/B348). The literal correspondence of these shapes to calculations of integral calculus to get the rocket's path is called to the reader's attention partway through the novel (V300–301/B349–50).

Images of crystals also recur dozens of times throughout the novel from dirt, "crystallizations of all the city had denied" (V4/B4) to lava, "a city in a myth, under the threat of some special destruction—engulfment by a crystal lake . . . " (V718/B837). In science, crystals are an interdisciplinary subject of study that bring together physicists who study the structural order, chemists who look at the bonding order, and mathematicians who examine the order dictated by crystal symmetries. For scientists, crystals are *regular*, highly ordered structures. In *Gravity's Rainbow*, crystals serve as contrast to the irregularity in human affairs. Crystals do not provide the basis for a rival theory to the second law of thermodynamics because they result from the release of energy to the larger environment (a cooling of material is the common way to form atoms into crystals). And a highly crystalline structure is never living. So crystals in *Gravity's Rainbow*, of snow, cocaine, or terror, are images of order at the price of death. That alternative to order by plot, paranoid or otherwise, is a constant presence throughout all the different approaches to life represented in *Gravity's Rainbow*. These images of crystals may be contrasted with the compost-garden image (discussed earlier) that represents the possibility of fecundity in chaos. The chances for life amid the death-dealing of *Gravity's Rainbow* are small, but finite. Thus compost gardens are not as frequent as crystals.

The repeated images we have discussed so far also function in one of the most remarkable of *Gravity's Rainbow*'s stylistic effects. The patterns are not clearly evident on first reading. Later recognition of them confirms a barely perceived regularity and produces a certain surprise in the reader, who now sees order where before there was confusion. This effect reaches its full strength with the final stylistic trick to be considered here, the role of fantastic facts.

At first glance, the fantastic in *Gravity's Rainbow* stands out. Character's names are obvious symbolic devices (Pointsman, Enzian and Blicero, Roger Mexico, Jessica Swanlake). Byron the Bulb is a typical invention, an extreme and yet slightly familiar fantasy, like the folklore alligators under the city of New York in *V*.

And equally fantastic at first reading are such items as:

a rocket engineer standing at the target, ground zero, to watch a V-2 descent;

a chemist devising the structure of benzene from a dream of a snake;

and several more we have already mentioned:

a single mathematical function that describes cavalry accidents, blood counts, radioactive decay, number of wars per year, and rocket strikes;

a scientific theory that allows the impossible to happen often on an atomic scale;

scientists seriously discussing a demon.

These last two groups of fantastic-sounding items are in fact literal truths. Many of the most fictional-sounding events, particularly ideas from science, are not fiction but are sufficiently unknown to the public so that most readers assume them to be invented.

At some time, perhaps well after reading the novel, one is likely to come across a reference to these memorable "inventions" in a nonfiction source. The effect is most upsetting. There is a tinge of shock, and wonder if somehow the nonfiction has been influenced by *Gravity's Rainbow*. That is just the hint of paranoia-like suspicion that occupies most of the characters in the novel. This stylistic device, of selecting little-known but fantastic-appearing facts, is one of *Gravity's Rainbow*'s most innovative uses of science.

Many of these references to science are minor. A spy is named Sammy Hilbert-Spaess (V217/B253), but few readers will have come across a reference to the mathematical formalism called Hilbert space. The *Rücksichtslos* lists at a permanent angle of 23° 27' (V448/B522), and that is a little more likely to be noticed, since students in introductory astronomy courses everywhere learn that the earth itself lists at that angle with respect to our orbit around the sun.

Other fantastic facts are more important. They are repeated images in *Gravity's Rainbow*, and are major themes in science itself. The Poission distribution is used just as described in *Gravity's Rainbow*. A Poisson distribution analysis of "flying bomb" strikes appeared in a technical journal after the war, with a suggestion that this analysis might be a good teaching exercise.[10] Quantum theory does permit classically impossible disappearances of atomic fragments (although not in practice as dramatic as a person or a rock disappearing). Perhaps even stranger, Enzian's description of rock consciousness echoes a serious discussion in modern quantum mechanics about the role of consciousness as a "hidden variable" in the theory.[11] Maxwell's Demon was a serious topic, only dismissed in the twentieth century when quantum theory proved an energy source would be required to obtain information to operate any sorting device, even atomic in scale.

The repeated image of the German chemist Friedrich August Kekulé von Stradonitz, dreaming of a snake swallowing its own tail, is an important autobiographical description for the study of creativity. It is discussed at length in works like Arthur Koestler's *The Act of Creation*.[12] Kekulé's dream led to one of the major concepts of modern chemistry, and was crucial in the development of the German chemical industry.

By the mid-nineteenth century, chemists, including Kekulé, were trying to describe all organic matter as consisting of repetitions of basic building blocks, molecules. There had to be thousands of types of molecules, but each type was a specific mixture of several atoms, like carbon, hydrogen, and oxygen. Chemists suspected that the physical arrangement of the atoms in each type of molecule might be an important factor in determining the behavior of the chemical, but there was no way to observe molecular structure directly. One central puzzle was the structure of benzene, a molecule of six carbon atoms and six hydrogen atoms. This molecule represented an enormous class of important chemicals, but the structures proposed, such as a linked double chain of carbons and hydrogens, were not consistent with the known properties of the atoms or the molecule.

Kekulé's solution for the structure of benzene came to him in a dream. Chains of atoms writhed like snakes in his dream, when suddenly one of the snakes began swallowing its own tail. Kekulé awoke realizing that benzene could consist of a ring of atoms. This single concept clarified all the work previously done on the structure of organic chemicals, and initiated the modern science of organic chemistry.

Kekulé's story functions not only as a "fantastic fact" in *Gravity's Rainbow* but also serves to represent the underlying nonrational components of science and technology. Although lay people, scientists, and engineers in the novel (and too-often outside fiction) tend to treat science as only a great catalog of facts and laws, many aspects of the process by which science develops remain as mysterious as the process of conceiving a poem or a novel. The social, historic, and personal influences on the activity of science are an emerging field of study.[13]

The adventures of the German rocket engineer, Franz Pökler (V424–26/B494–97), have a literal counterpart. The engineer who commanded the Peenemünde site, Walter Dornberger, described standing at ground zero to watch a V-2 come down.[14] The real engineer's enthusiasm for technological challenge, and his dispassionate view of the ultimate results of his work, makes a model every bit as frightening as any of the bizarre models in *Gravity's Rainbow*. Many of the details of the actual work on the rocket are very close to *Gravity's Rainbow*'s descriptions (V239/B278, V452–53/B527–28, V517–18/B602–4). One other minor point from literal V-2 history: "Enzian" was the code name for a rival rocket project, but one that was never completed.[15]

Science in *Gravity's Rainbow* has two complementing roles. The metaphors from science, which we discussed first, reinforce the importance of the choices of world view made by the characters. It is harder to dismiss an unpopular choice when we see that it is parallel to a major theme in the development of science. On the other hand, literal facts from science are used for their *un*believability, to create an air of strangeness that will promote disequilibrium as the reader discovers the reality of what seemed invention.

Gravity's Rainbow demonstrates more clearly than any other work of modern fiction how science can be incorporated as a tool for metaphor and style. Science illustrates the struggle to understand life and death. Yet science in no way impresses itself on that struggle as the only useful tool.

The fundamental choices between belief in order and determinism versus a belief in disorder and lack of control are expressed in scientific images. Yet these two extremes are sterile for mankind. If determinism is absolute, no one, not even a Pointsman, can be sure that he is in control and not some higher force that wants him to think so. On the other hand, the chaos of anti-paranoia denies the possibility of self-control along with all forms of determinism.

The metaphors and images from physics in *Gravity's Rainbow* illuminate and inform our understanding of approaches to accepting the human condition. We must exist in a universe filled with coexisting extremes: order and chaos, predictability and uncertainty, life and death. How do we feel about this coexistence of opposites? In this essay, we have seen how science has changed the way it regarded these coexisting extremes several times. Those great choices in world view, the changing paradigms of science, have counterparts in the paradigms with which nonscientists view the human universe. In *Gravity's Rainbow*, the parallels have been made explicit and fascinating. Science in *Gravity's Rainbow* is not an escape from human problems but rather a valuable tool with which the novelist reflects those problems. *Gravity's Rainbow* presents the unifying view that all our pursuits are common responses to the same problem—how to regard a universe that demands coexistence between extremes.

The metaphor is of significant value in clarifying our choices. The unity of human problems spans the "dimple of a ditch"[16] between artificial barriers separating science and the humanities. If *Gravity's Rainbow* helps answer in the affirmative the question of whether science has relevance to fundamental human problems, then efforts to understand the science in this difficult novel will have been worthwhile.

1. Because science and technology play such major roles in *Gravity's Rainbow*, they are discussed to some extent in nearly every critical essay on the novel. Most treatments are limited to one or two topics of science, such as entropy or statistics. Joseph W. Slade, *Thomas Pynchon* (New York: Warner Paperback Library, 1974), identifies many aspects of science and technology in Pynchon's work. Two recent publications deal, as does the present essay, with the use of historic paradigm changes in science as a whole: Robert L. Nadeau, "Readings from the New Book of Nature: Physics and Pynchon's *Gravity's Rainbow*," *Studies in the Novel* 11: (1979): 454–71; and John Stark, *Pynchon's Fictions* (Athens, Ohio: Ohio University Press, 1980).

2. See Mathew Winston, "The Quest for Pynchon," in *Mindful Pleasures*, ed. George Levine and David Leverenz (Boston: Little, Brown & Co., 1976), pp. 251–64.

3. For an overview of the development of science, including the Newtonian universe, see Jacob Bronowski, *The Ascent of Man* (Boston: Little, Brown & Co., 1973); chapter 7, "The Majestic Clockwork," is a good introduction to these ideas. For a more detailed and academic introduction to Newtonian mechanics, including projectile (i.e., V-2) motion, see Robert H. March, *Physics for Poets* (New York: McGraw-Hill, 1970).

4. Calculus images are also treated in articles by Lance W. Ozier, "Antipointsman/ Antimexico: Some Mathematical Imagery in *Gravity's Rainbow*," *Critique 16*, no. 2 (1974), pp. 73–90; "The Calculus of Transformation: More Mathematical Imagery in *Gravity's Rainbow*," *Twentieth Century Literature* 21 (May 1975): 193–210.

5. For an excellent review of the development of ideas about randomness in science,see Stephen G. Brush, "Irreversibility and Indeterminism: Fourier to Heisenberg," *Journal for the History of Ideas* 37 (1976): 603–30.

6. Thomas Pynchon, *The Crying of Lot 49* (New York: Bantam, 1967), p. 23.

7. The discussion of this theme is based in part on Alan J. Friedman and Manfred Puetz, "Science as Metaphor: Thomas Pynchon and *Gravity's Rainbow*," *Contemporary Literature* 15 (Summer 1974): 346–59. A nonmathematical review of the underlying science, so close to Pynchon's treatment that it might be suspected as a source, is L. Brillouin's "Life, Thermodynamics, and Cybernetics," *American Scientist* 37 (October 1949): 554–68. A technical review of the status of the issue is Illya Prigogine, Gregoire Nicolis, and Agnes Babloyantz, "Thermodynamics of Evolution," *Physics Today*, November 1972, pp. 23–28, and December 1972, pp. 38–44. A recent discussion of these topics in Pynchon's work is Daniel Simberloff, "Entropy, Information, and Life: Biophysics in the Novels of Thomas Pynchon," *Perspectives in Biology and Medicine* 21 (1978): 617–25.

8. See also Alan J. Friedman, "The Novelist and Modern Physics: New Metaphors for Traditional Themes," *Journal of College Science Teaching* 4 (May 1975): 310–12; Speer Morgan, "*Gravity's Rainbow*: What's the Big Idea?," *Modern Fiction Studies* 23 (1977): 199–216; and Lois Parkinson Zamora, "The Entropic End: Science and Eschatology in the Works of Thomas Pynchon," *Science, Technology, and the Humanities* 3 (Winter 1980): 35–43. A useful introduction to this topic is the earlier exposition by Anne Mangel, "Maxwell's Demon, Entropy, Information: *The Crying of Lot 49*," *Tri-Quarterly* 20 (1971): 194–208.

9. An excellent overview of these great themes in modern physics is Adolph Baker, *Modern Physics and Antiphysics* (Reading, Mass.: Addison-Wesley, 1970).

10. R. D. Clarke, "An Application of the Poisson Distribution," *Journal of the Institute of Actuaries* 72 (1946): 481. I am indebted to Charles Clerc for pointing out this reference to me. See also Khachig Tölöyan, "The Fishy Poisson: Allusions to Statistics in *Gravity's Rainbow*," *Notes on Modern American Literature* 4 (1979): unpaged.

11. The relations between consciousness and quantum theory are still not quite an accepted field of physics, but some fascinating speculation has occurred: see Jeffrey Mishlove, *The Roots of Consciousness* (New York: Random House; Berkeley, Calif.: Bookworks, 1975), pp. 279–93.

Alan J. Friedman

12. Arthur Koestler, *The Act of Creation* (New York: MacMillian, 1964; New York: Dell Publishing, 1967), pp. 118, 169–71.

13. See, for example, Jacob Bronowski, *A Sense of the Future* (Cambridge, Mass.: MIT Press, 1977); Gerald Holton, *Thematic Origins of Scientific Thought: Kepler to Einstein* (Cambridge, Mass.: Harvard University Press, 1973); and Thomas Kuhn, *The Structure of Scientific Revolutions*, 2d ed. (Chicago: University of Chicago Press, 1970).

14. Walter Dornberger, *V-2* (New York: Viking, 1954).

15. *History of German Guided Missiles Development*, ed. Th. Benecke and A. W. Quick (Brunswick, Germany: Verlag E. Appelhans &Co., 1957), p. 6, "Enzian."

16. "An Interview with Nabokov," *Wisconsin Studies in Contemporary Literature* 8 (Spring 1967): 140–41.

Film in *Gravity's Rainbow*

By Charles Clerc

> The rhythmic clapping resonates inside these walls, which are hard
> and glossy as coal: Come-*on*! *Start*-the-*show*! Come-*on*! *Start*-the-*show*! The
> screen is a dim page spread before us, white and silent. The film has
> broken, or a projector bulb has burned out. It was difficult even for us,
> old fans who've always been at the movies (haven't we?) to tell which
> before the darkness swept in. (V760/B887)

In the final scene of *Gravity's Rainbow*, headed "Descent," the
audience ("us"—the readers, and, by implication, everybody) is
gathered into a darkened theater whose walls are black, attention
riveted upon a blank screen. We do not know for certain why it has
become "white and silent." We are left rather like Archibald
MacLeish's circus audience in the sonnet "The End of the World":*

> And there, there overhead, there, there hung over
> Those thousands of white faces, those dazed eyes,
> There in the starless dark the poise, the hover,
> There with vast wings across the cancelled skies,
> There in the sudden blackness, the black pall
> Of nothing, nothing, nothing—nothing at all.

Although audience reaction in the poem and the novel is similar,
the situations are of course very different. In one we are at a circus;
in the other we are waiting for a movie to start up again. Both convey a sense of impending doom: MacLeish by the final lines of the
preceding octave, "Quite unexpectedly the top blew off"; Pynchon
by the later references to "the Rocket falling nearly a mile per
second, absolutely and forever without sound . . . above the roof
of this old theatre. . . . " But whereas MacLeish's circus audience

---

*From *New and Collected Poems 1917–1976*, by Archibald MacLeish. Copyright ©
1976 by Archibald MacLeish. Reprinted by permission of Houghton Mifflin
Company.

sees only a nihilistic void, Pynchon's movie audience retains an image, "a film we have not learned to see...it is now a closeup of the face, a face we all know—" Perhaps it is the face of the "human figure, dreaming of an early evening in each great capital luminous enough to tell him he will never die, coming outside to wish on the first star"—thus, each of us, Everyman. It may be the face of Gottfried encased in his Imipolex shroud in the Rocket. It may be a transmogrification into the face of "a bright angel of death." Maybe it is the face of God or Satan. We find the answer within ourselves, or not at all, compelled as we are for comfort to take the hand of the person nearest us, follow the bouncing ball, and sing a hymn (V760/B887).

The main purpose of comparing the MacLeish poem and Pynchon's final scene is to reveal their basic metaphorical difference. The circus was a widely popular form of entertainment early in this century, and, to convey his effects, MacLeish relied upon a traditional symbol: the circus as life. Appropriately, the MacLeish poem appeared at the advent of talking movies: 1926. Pynchon's novel, published nearly fifty years later, brings to bear the imprint of cinema upon modern life. It demonstrates the pervasive influence of movies in all facets of our culture, down to indelible effects upon individual sensibilities. The parenthetical question "Old fans who've always been at the movies (haven't we?)" contains an underlying assumption of our familiarity with movies: they entertain us, take up our time, occupy our thoughts and conversations, affect some of our actions, and maybe even give form to our lives.

In verifying this widespread appeal, Pynchon shows a sound knowledge of movies and the film industry. He ranges from embryonic beginnings through the heyday of Hollywood up to the early 1940s, with major emphasis in between upon the pre-Hitler Golden Age of German expressionism. Except for the ending, time "present" in the novel establishes a chronological limit beyond which Pynchon cannot go: immediate post-World War II. So all the references to cinema, with the exception of an anachronistic minor western, predate 1946 and help keep the novel a very faithful period piece.

Pynchon works film into the novel in a variety of ways. He introduces fresh, if occasionally contradictory, perceptions about the relationships of film and life, especially as they reveal multisided realities. He incorporates cinematic techniques into the texture itself so that the novel is like a movie. He relies upon cinema as a source for metaphors, images, symbols, and associations. His supplemental usage of film also helps him reveal characters, mostly their psychological states. The novel dramatizes the literal power the film industry and movies exert in influencing people and shaping situations. Uses of cinema also enforce his other thematic concerns: the conflict between illusion and reality; modern man's need for entertainment, particularly humor; the robbing of true sensory responses by vicarious experience; and the good and bad effects of the all-too-human bent for fantasizing. Finally Pynchon conveys a nostalgic mood for silent films and early movies.

Like a rainbow, *Gravity's Rainbow* spans the entire arc of cinema: from technical processes of invention to the writer's script to motion picture-making to final appreciation by an audience. Selected examples of each should suffice to illustrate this range. (A) *Invention*. Aside from his other functions as scientific genius, the mysterious Laszlo Jamf also figures in the filmic process. Like an Edison in America or the Lumière brothers in France, he makes a contribution to the technical advancement of film by the invention of Emulsion J, which renders "the human skin transparent to a depth of half a millimeter, revealing the face just beneath the surface. This emulsion was used extensively in von Göll's immortal *Alpdrücken*, and may even come to figure in *Martín Fierro*" (V387/B451). (B) *Film script*. Parts of the Pynchon novel itself illustrate uses of the film script. Felipe's treatment of *Martín Fierro* and a mini-scenario narrated by Osbie Feel also illustrate the creative process that serves as inception of most movies. (C) *Movie-making*. Numerous details are given of how von Göll made his films, including specific techniques of camera angles and distance, movement, imagery, and cutting. Pynchon also weaves in information about real directors: "The countdown as we know it, 10-9-8-u.s.w., was invented by Fritz Lang in 1929 for the Ufa film *Die Frau im Mond*. He put it into the launch scene to heighten the suspense" (V753/B878). Acting is included in this category, and it too exists at both fictional and factual levels. We learn about the careers and performances of a star actress like Greta Erdmann or a leading man like Max Schlepzig, in addition to real movie celebrities like Brigette Helm and Rudolf Klein-Rogge, who starred in such films as *Metropolis* (1927) and *Dr. Mabuse, der Spieler* (1922). Some slight attention is also paid to minor cast members and extras, to cameramen and technicians, and extends even to post-scenario conduct, like the orgy that occurred on the *Alpdrücken* set when Greta's child Bianca was conceived. Besides professionally made motion pictures, film is also utilized to relay messages "in code" and for purposes of propaganda, behavioral conditioning, and spying. (D) *Appreciation by an audience.* Franz Pökler and Tyrone Slothrop represent two major types of fans who retain and react to countless images from the movies. Reception by the public extends in various other ways, both fictional and factual: for example, to Blodgett Waxwing's addiction to westerns, to Mitchell Prettyplace's humorously elaborate criticism of *King Kong,* to [Paul Joseph] "Goebbels's private collection" of erotic films.

II

An important advance made by Pynchon in treatment of film concerns our understanding of reality. He broadens our perspectives by showing that reality may exist in layers beyond our ordinary three-dimensional perception. Moreover, we are being asked implicitly not to rely on a single interpretation of reality—there are many. It would help if we responded to film in the ways of people from nonliterate, nonvisual, non-Western cultures (Marshall McLuhan described them in *Understanding Media*), as if we were entering other worlds. We must dispense with reliance on specific cause and effect—we have to look to hidden forms that produce magical results: realities for them. Thus Pynchon compels us to readjust our positioning with regard to the conventional opposites of reality: imitation and illusion. What seems imitative takes on life of its own, and in the process reveals its reality. What has seemed to be illusory proves real.

A few examples can quickly illustrate the principles of crossovers between life and "imitations" of life through film. The countdown in Lang's *The Woman in the Moon* became the countdown used by NASA in rocket-firing. The reality of the filmic experience, even as a silent, is as valid as the so-called real one. The former brought about the latter—art precedes life, as it were. Von Göll makes a telling remark when he learns that the Schwarzkommando do exist after he has made an intentionally spurious piece of film about them. Convinced that his film has brought them into being, he says, "It is my mission . . . to sow in the Zone seeds of reality. . . . My images, somehow, have been chosen for incarnation" (V388/B451). Although admittedly "megalomaniacal" and comic too, his way of seeing represents prescient transmogrification, in which realities exist before and behind the illusion of reality. When members of an audience later enact roles from cinema, particularly in psychological projection, they are responding as if the filmic situations have been real. Consider ramifications of von Göll's *Alpdrücken,* when husbands in the audience were so sexually aroused by the film that they went home and impregnated their wives. (Masturbation and nonconjugal coupling resulted as well.) Earlier, at the time of the shooting of the film, the cast and crew were so aroused that a gang-rape occurred that was not part of the film. The lead actress was impregnated, and, moreover, the director let the camera run on to record the orgy. Surely one experience was no less "real" than the other. Many years later Greta asks her newest lover Slothrop (at the time bearing her former lover's name) to beat her in ways similar to the punishment inflicted upon her in the past—the act even takes place on the same dusty torture rack in the same film studio. These experiences exist apart spatially and temporally, but they are interconnected realities. Time and space are inseparable, of course, but priorities exist in the two respective art forms. Fiction can handle differences of time; film has only one time: the present. On the other hand, the one principle most organic to film is space. From yet another point of view, the realities of *Alpdrücken* and *Gravity's Rainbow* reveal varied forms of creativity. Children are created from a film that was itself created: all creations of a created novel.

But if we are drawn by Pynchon into new possibilities for seeing ontologically, the way is not straight and true—it is fraught with contradiction and paradox because Pynchon also shows that filmic illusion is quite distinct from reality and suffers from limitations and shortcomings.

One limitation of film emerges when Katje is being spied upon by a camera at the Chelsea maisonette (V92–94/B107–9). She is described entirely in objective cinematographical terms. After a tracking close-up, Pynchon steps away from the position of camera-man, behind the surface of the frame, to begin subjectively exploring what cannot be seen: "inside herself, enclosed in the *soignée* surface of dear fabric and dead cells, she is corruption and ashes." The passage devoted to what the "camera records" helps identify character and vivify mood, but we also learn the distinction between inner and exterior modes. The camera cannot penetrate into the inner being. Fiction thus has the advantage of exploring psychological states, of rendering attributes of thought. However, the reality of the camera's picture is certainly as real as the subject itself.

In terms of technique, multiple strategies of interpretation and perception are afforded Pynchon when he can conjoin insights as writer and compositional effects as cinematographer. We see Katje through the camera: "widest lens-opening . . . extra tungsten light laid on . . . frame stopped and prolonged." Subtly the camera eye of the author takes over to observe the cameraman as voyeur, Katje as subject, Osbie Feel as chef; then to rove outward to the long rain's "freezing descent" and the "city, in all its bomb-pierced miles: this inexhaustibly knotted victim." Sound effects of "gutters singing" and past "rocket blasts near and far" accompany this panning. Once again "in a frame's passage," the camera defines Katje for a "celluloid instant poised." Then by swift associational stimuli, the kitchen oven becomes the fearful ovens that threatened Katje in the past (the Witch's, Blicero's and Nazis'). Furthermore, dimensions of meaning for the future are added because this segment of film will be used to condition an octopus and set in motion the series of events leading to Slothrop's flight.

On occasion in the novel, ordinary reality is taken as filmic substance. For example, Slothrop regards bombed-out Berlin as he would the preparation and expense of a movie scene: "dark-clothed extras waiting in queues for some hypothetical tram . . . this burned tenement so amazingly detailed—They sure must have the budget, all right" (V374/B435–36). The passage reveals the extent to which Pynchon plays with inversion of "illusion" and reality. Ordinarily a movie scene attempts to duplicate the reality of an actual scene, but here his character is looking at real life as if it were a movie set: starving people are "extras," the tenement is "amazingly detailed." Hence, the humorous and ironic conclusion that "They sure must have the budget."

In various other situations of *Gravity's Rainbow*, characters and people make little or no distinction between film and traditional reality—they are virtually equalized. Farfetched as it may seem, a linkage is established between Slothrop and the American gangster John Dillinger. Both men are influenced by movies that they imitate, both are "framed," both are sequentially shown as victims of craven authority, both become, one by death, the other by perplexing disappearance, the stuff of which myths are made:

> John Dillinger, at the end, found a few seconds' strange mercy in the movie images that hadn't quite yet faded from his eyeballs—Clark Gable going off unregenerate to fry in the chair, voices gentle out of the death-row steel *so long, Blackie*…turning down a reprieve from his longtime friend now Governor of New York William Powell, skinny chinless condescending jerk, Gable just wanting to get it over with, "Die like ya live—all of a sudden, don't drag it out—" even as bitchy little Melvin Purvis, staked outside the Biograph Theatre, lit up the fatal cigar and felt already between his lips the penis of official commendation—and federal cowards at the signal took Dillinger with their faggots' precision… there was still for the doomed man some shift of personality in effect— the way you've felt for a little while afterward in the real muscles of your

face and voice, that you *were* Gable, the ironic eyebrows, the proud, shining, snakelike head—to help Dillinger through the bushwhacking, and a little easier into death. (V516/B601)

It is an extraordinary passage. Need we be reminded, the ambush of Dillinger occurred on the night of July 22, 1934, outside the Biograph Cinema in East Chicago. A force of about fifteen FBI agents, led by the head of the Chicago office, Melvin Purvis, had set a trap for the bank robber and notorious escape artist who had become, only the month before, Public Enemy Number One. Dillinger emerged from the theater at about 10:30, in the company of two women, his girl friend Polly Hamilton and her friend Anna Sage, the FBI's informant, subsequently dubbed The Lady in Red. When Dillinger attempted to escape toward an alley, he was shot dead.

The movie Dillinger had seen, the title of which is left unspecified in the passage, was *Manhattan Melodrama* (produced by MGM in 1934, directed by W. W. Van Dyke II, and starring Clark Gable as Blackie Gallagher, William Powell as Jim Wade, Myrna Loy as Eleanor). The plot line was a Hollywood staple: two boyhood buddies growing up on opposite sides of the law. The devil-may-care gambler-racketeer-turned-murderer becomes in his own way more heroic than the law enforcer-politician, especially as he goes off jauntily to the electric chair. The inversion of the Dillinger–G-Man story is as consistent as the inversion within the movie story. Dillinger is more hero than criminal; the supposedly good forces of law and order are made infamous: Melvin Purvis is "bitchy" and "little"; the other G-Men are "faggots" and "cowards"; and Purvis's reward for success is "the penis of official commendation between his lips." Obviously, the bureau's position was just the reverse; in fact, Chief J. Edgar Hoover used the case to promote the glory and infallibility of the FBI. Pynchon's view, however extreme it may appear, is not without support. To this day, a vocal minority persists in its condemnation of the killing and the FBI ballyhoo surrounding the case.

Other ramifications of the mise-en-scène are worth examining. The Dillinger inset is placed next to the scene in which Närrisch, as protective cover for von Göll's escape, awaits his death: "down to the last tommygun of his career, foreign and overheated." Naturally von Göll, whose values are based upon movies, argues that nothing serious will happen to Närrisch. Slothrop thinks he knows better: "this ain't the fuckin' *movies* now" (V527/B614). Närrisch has no movie images, "no sources of mercy" to comfort him (it turns out he did not need them anyway), as Dillinger did in Pynchon's imaginative re-creation. The Dillinger passage thus creates the illusion that illusion is preferable to reality, as if the artificiality of emulating a screen star is beneficial in an otherwise-all-too-real and cruel world. For Dillinger, empathy-fakery—"the shift of personality"—is merciful, brings him courage, and eases him into death. Or another way to regard the changeover is to see realities existing side by side—one merely moves from one to the next.

Furthermore, Dillinger has become mythicized by a cult following. He is an object of veneration at the dopers' hangout in Berlin, aptly named the Club Chicago: "Oversize photos of John Dillinger, alone or posed with his mother, his pals, his tommygun, decorate the walls" (V368–69/B429). His blood, soaked up in clothing, checks, newspapers, bits of cloth by the crowd at the ambush site, becomes memento, fetish, sacrament of sorts. Significantly, Seaman Bodine, who was in Chicago at the time, takes the last opportunity when he sees Slothrop to give to him the fragment of an undershirt stained by Dillinger's blood, surely an action indicative of the passing on of the mantle into myth (V741/B864–65).

Effects of the passage double back upon themselves. Clark Gable was for Dillinger what Dillinger and Slothrop become for their admirers: something else beyond person, larger than life, legendary. Unreal as Blackie Gallagher was, he became real for John Dillinger in Pynchon's view, so real that the "shift of personality" could occur. It is an act of transcendent simulation, a process of which Pynchon is keenly aware. If it can so invade lives, then logically the division between fact and fiction, between illusion and reality, between history and dreaming, grows even more narrow.

But, back again on the other side, the separation may be such that it cannot be breached, for Pynchon also suggests that any imitation of life—the illusion given by film—is untrustworthy. It distorts and falsifies, it cheapens and removes: "[Analytic legacy] brought the technicians at Peenemünde to peer at the Askania films of Rocket flights, frame by frame, Δx by Δy, flightless themselves...film and calculus, both pornographies of flight." The films are pornographies of flight because they are vicarious, artificial; they are reduced to stills. The actual experience has been missed—the excitement of flight is substituted for. Spontaneity is lost with the imposition of scientific analysis and control. For these reasons, Pynchon refers to the films as "reminders of impotence and abstraction" (V567/B661). So imitation in this sense is bad, negative, and divisive because it abstracts real life, it vitiates potency, it subdivides the unity of a singular experience.

Among its myriad thematic subjects, *Gravity's Rainbow* plays up the importance of entertainment in human life. Without making value judgments, Pynchon works mostly with filmic associations that are banal, clichéd, romanticized, to show the all-pervasive reach of pop culture. Much of such entertainment is helter-skelter and purposeless—a means of wiling away the precious commodity of time. Life on the screen becomes a substitution for life as it is, hence the highly ironic tone of the lyrical Christmas passage in which "the lads in Hollywood [are] telling us how grand it all is over here, how much fun" (V135/B157). Obviously war is neither grand nor fun—any illusions about it merely reflect self-deception. A similar acknowledgment of falseness comes in the description of Paddy McGonigle's Irishness. On the screen, the Irish are stereotyped, oversimplified, conventionalized, distorted "through every wretched Hollywood lie" (V641/B747). And yet a curious paradox emerges: perhaps illusion is necessary at times in the face of life's too frequent awfulness. Maybe the Pynchon persona, like Blanche in *A Streetcar Named Desire* or Dr. Relling in *The Wild Duck*, would say, if he or she had the opportunity, that we need our illusions, we need magic—we cannot survive without them because our own pitiable beings are too inadequate to be self-supportive. Beyond the necessity for escape and entertainment, we seek fulfillment, even the identity of other lives, in film.

Pynchon seeks a double effect: the real world is the reel world, and vice versa. One is reminded of the pun tucked away in the poem about King Kong (to be discussed in a later section). The director Carl Denham makes "the unreal reel / By shooting at it, one way or the other." A camera does indeed make the unreal into a film reel. In turn the film reel makes the unreal seem real and become real (as the terror of Kong becomes real for the heroine). Denham shoots at the unreal with a camera and also with a gun to make it reel, i.e., stagger. All become different manifestations of reality.

Although Pynchon employs numerous movie references that are concrete and specific, his imagination also tends to manifest itself in general filmic analogues. He can achieve parody and at the same time implant symbolical and historical associations. A case in point is Pirate Prentice's surreal vision of *"a giant Adenoid,"* which "once blocked the distinguished pharynx of Lord Blatherard Osmo" (V14/B16). As the Adenoid grows and grows in its unstoppable rampage in London, we recollect its screen cousins: The Thing, The Blob, The Devouring Slime, The Mutant Amoeba—all those rampant creatures or organisms that glutted their way through all those science fiction horror fantasies. Here Pynchon achieves comedy because the engorged victims wind up laughing and enjoying themselves. However, he rarely settles for mere parodic analogue. When the Adenoid is pacified by cocaine—the appropriateness of the organ to the narcotic hardly escapes notice—we are in turn prodded into varied associations, whether Freud's addiction, opiated war veterans, the drug culture of the 1960s, or the widespread use of cocaine in the 1970s and 1980s.

In ways as multiplotted, crowded, and frenetic as Griffith's *Intolerance* or Altman's *Nashville*, Pynchon's novel has filled the screen. Techniques aside, it is thus quite possible to take the novel itself as film, an episodic World War II movie showing definite leanings toward the genre of musical comedy. A number of factors contribute to this impression. One results from a felicitous circumstance of typography. The original publisher, Viking Press, divided the chapters by a sequence of seven squares, representing in the manner of a logogram both frames and the sprocket holes of a film projector. (The Bantam edition reduces to one square for chapter demarcation.) The word *catch* repeated again and again in the next-to-last page may suggest a film catching in the projector. Then the conclusion of the novel provides further support to the film metaphor by suggesting that the readers have been viewers. So "audience" has extended outward from characters like Pökler and Slothrop and Waxwing to those of us "who've always been at the movies." There we are, jammed into a theater, presumably the Orpheus in Los Angeles but generally the theater of life, where we have been witness to cluttered sequences of events, to mind-boggling bombardments of images. The final bombardment is to take place, literally and metaphorically, when the film breaks off. The blank page of the book after "Now everybody—" is as blank as the screen. We are left in equipoise, doomed by the past, bound in hand-joined brotherhood in the present, awaiting an unknown but of course clearly reckoned future. The terrible import of descending rocket and looming blankness warn of the plight of modern civilization. Yet, for all its bleakness, the novel also posits affirmative possibilities by elevating consciousness, by acknowledging our bond of humanity, and by predicating a chance in the world to reverse the progress of the rocket.

III

Most of the American movies cited in the novel are of the popular and commercial variety, which is to say that one does not turn to

Gravity's Rainbow for aesthetic recommendations of the world's great art films. These movies are designed to satisfy the needs of a mass culture for sheer entertainment, escapism, titillation of the senses, humor. They also happen to reveal a certain yearning for the nostalgia of adolescent movie-going. Although Pynchon decidedly leans toward fantasies and thrillers for thematic development, his use of American film titles is quite eclectic, as the following categorized list shows: HORROR: *King Kong* (1933), *Frankenstein* (1931), two spin-offs, *The Bride of Frankenstein* (1935) and *The Son of Frankenstein* (1939), *Dracula* (1931), *White Zombie* (1933), *Dr. Jekyll and Mr. Hyde* (three major productions in 1920, 1922, 1941); ODDITY: *Freaks* (1932); COMEDY: *My Little Chickadee* (1940), *A Day at the Races* (1937); MUSICAL: *Flying Down to Rio* (1933), *Meet Me in St. Louis* (1944); FAMILY SAGA: *A Tree Grows in Brooklyn* (1945); RELIGIO-MUSICAL: *Going My Way* (1945); CHILDREN'S FANTASY: *The Wizard of Oz* (1939); WESTERN: *The Return of Jack Slade* (1955 [the lone anachronistic entry]). Pynchon also refers to animal fantasies like *Dumbo*, Donald Duck and Porky Pig cartoons, and to mysteries and adventures about Fu Manchu, Tarzan, Zorro, the Green Hornet, Superman, and the Lone Ranger. Other American pictures alluded to, but not specified by title, include *Stanley and Livingstone, Gunga Din,* the previously noted *Manhattan Melodrama*, the Rin-Tin-Tin and Andy Hardy series, in addition to similar series-type pictures with Nelson Eddy and Shirley Temple. Other genres, such as gangster, pirate, and spy films, are made evident in the emulative action of characters; thus on occasion the novel takes on aspects of genre films.

Significantly, too, the German movies are mostly expressionistic fantasies. There are ten in all: five are imaginative, and five are actual silent films made by Fritz Lang during the 1920s. The ficti-tious von Göll movies are *Alpdrücken* (*Nightmare*), the unreleased *Das Wütend Reich* (*The Mad Kingdom* or *The Fanatical Reich*), and *Good Society*. Other movies in which Greta Erdmann appeared include *Weisse Sandwüste von Neumexiko* (*White Desert of New Mexico*) and *Jugend Herauf!* (*Upward Youth!*—a pun on "Juden Heraus!" or "Out with Jews!"). The Fritz Lang silents are *Der Müde Tod* (*The Weary Death* or *Destiny*) (1921); *Dr. Mabuse, der Spieler* (*Dr. Mabuse, the Gambler*), in two parts (1922); *Die Niebelungen* (in two parts, *Siegfried* and *Kriemhild's Revenge*) (1924); *Metropolis* (1927); and *Die Frau im Mond* (*The Woman in the Moon*) (1929). (The only other film mentioned from another country is *October*, directed by Sergei Eisenstein, and first shown in Russia in 1928.)

Emphasis upon expressionistic fantasies by Pynchon is perfectly suited to his narrative methods and to his thematic intentions. These films by and large reject imitation of external reality or deliberately distort it. They stress inner feelings and qualities by either transforming exterior facts into interior elements or by externalizing psychic states. The desired effects of atmosphere, texture, and tone are achieved by subjective camera techniques (including pioneer use of a moving camera as a narrative tool), distortive lighting, bizarre sets, and so on. Affinities with *Gravity's Rainbow* are readily apparent. Surface reality is deliberately distorted to express what Pynchon and his characters believe to be inherent reality. Solipsism is a vital ingredient, whether it dictates the perceptions of an author like Pynchon or an expressionist director like Lang or the fictitious von Göll. Accentuation of the self, individualistic vision of the world, warping of reality are among factors that come to have historical significance from the standpoint of some cultural historians who have detected a connection between these films and the emergence of Nazism. The degree of influence may be debated, but it is certainly safe to say that these films were somewhat instrumental in shaping German culture in the period between the two wars.

The uses made of *Dr. Mabuse* typify the multilevel artistry of which Pynchon is so capable. Cinema and fiction mutually support one another, and in their relationship to fact, they also create a continuity of analogous meanings that eventuate in allegory. First, *Dr. Mabuse* parallels situations of manipulation and control in *Gravity's Rainbow*. (The original is not to be confused with its many sequels, especially the major one by Lang, *Das Testament des Dr. Mabuse* [*The Last Will of Dr. Mabuse*], 1932. It was an anti-Nazi picture confiscated by officials of the Third Reich; directly afterward Lang fled to America.) Dr. Mabuse, who uses a variety of disguises to conceal his identity, relies on hypnosis to control his victims and to overcome his opponents. As mastermind of a gang of criminals, he gains by chicanery his fortune and power. When eventually he is hunted down and cornered, he goes mad. The movie, on the one hand a thriller, is also a study of an amoral tyrant whose position of eminence has been fostered by a depraved, chaotic world. Pökler yearns to be a Mabuse, "vital and proud," a man of "charismatic flash" who gives way to whatever avaricious and violent impulses come over him—of course Pökler is more victim than "the savage throwback." Through Pökler, Pynchon sets up *Dr. Mabuse* as *cinéma à clef*: "You were meant to think of Hugo Stinnes, the tireless operator behind the scenes of apparent Inflation, apparent history: gambler, financial wizard, archgangster" (V579/B674). If such is the case, Stinnes was still alive at the time of the movie's release (he was born at Mülheim an der Ruhr on February 12, 1870, and died in Berlin on April 10, 1924). As an industrialist of enormous wealth and power, "the Wunderkind of European finance" (V284/B331), he controlled holdings in coal mining, ocean and river transportation, iron and steel production, newspapers, power plants, estates, and hotels. He was also influential within the military-industrial complex, heading the mobilization of German war industry in World War I, and in politics in postwar Germany. At his death his far-flung industrial empire was liquidated.

A third parallel beyond a real-life financial wizard and a cinematic one may be found in a characterization within the novel itself. The Dr. Mabuse figure is Blicero/Weissmann. He is obsessed, depraved, cunning, anarchical, antisocial. The enslavement of Katje and Gottfried for his own sexual perversions and the hypnotic manipulation of a select staff for the building of the Rocket are a microcosmic form of Dr. Mabuse's machinations. The strongest parallel is in their fates, for quite like Dr. Mabuse, Weissmann becomes at war's end "a screaming maniac. . . . Things were falling apart, and he reverted to some ancestral version of himself, screamed at the sky, sat hours in a rigid trance, with his eyes rolled clear up into his head" (V465/B542). As the movie implicitly criticizes society for engendering a Dr. Mabuse, so the novel implicitly recognizes the national fanaticism from which the power of a Weissmann springs. Of course, this very kind of society allowed and indeed encouraged the emergence of a Hitler. With history thus providing yet another parallel, the use of the Dr. Mabuse film becomes both prophetic and profound.

Der Müde Tod plays like a distant melancholy air in the novel as a reminder of the omnipresence of death and figures in the persistent thematic commingling of love and death. *Die Frau im Mond* and *Metropolis*, as science fantasy films, would naturally hold more appeal to a character like Pökler. Toward *Die Frau im Mond*, he was "amused, condescending. He picked at technical points" (V159/B186); but *Metropolis* is in his eyes a "great movie" (unlike the director himself, who is on record as never having liked it). Pökler is taken by it because of its prophetic vision of a future society, "a Corporate City-state where technology was the source of power, the engineer worked closely with the administrator, the masses labored unseen far underground, and ultimate power lay with a single leader at the top, fatherly and benevolent and just" (V578/B673).

In connection with prophecy, von Göll sees a time when film will be a dominant force in life: "Someday, when the film is fast enough, the equipment pocket-size and burdenless and selling at people's prices, the lights and booms no longer necessary, *then...then...*" (V527/B614–15). Although he does not complete the prediction, its meaning is multishaded: film will be so ubiquitous everybody will be using it; people will be leading staged lives; the control of directors will be expanded; life will have become like the movies.

Parallels to *Die Niebelungen*, especially by way of the novel's epical and mock-heroic qualities, are also evident, but limitations of space prevent a comparison because it requires extensive delineation of plot and character. One other film, *The Wizard of Oz*, can be mentioned briefly for its contribution to theme. The epigraph to part three (V279/B325) cites Dorothy's remark to her dog upon their arrival in Oz: "Toto, I have a feeling we're not in Kansas any more...." Slothrop's escapades and encounters in the Zone are roughly akin to Dorothy's in her fantasy land. The Oz motif is depicted comically during one chase scene when a navy corpsman helps Slothrop escape: " 'Follow the yellow-brick road,' hums Albert Krypton, on pitch, 'follow the yellow-brick road' . . . " (V596–97/B695). (The name Krypton connects to another well-known fantasy.) However, the Zone is as different from Oz as the objects of Dorothy's and Slothrop's quests. If the Secret Rocket (or Blicero) is the Wizard, then the Wizard has been inverted for diabolic purposes. Another use of the Oz motif occurs in the brief history of Amy Sprue, one of Slothrop's "crazy kinfolks" in early America. Although she "was not, like young skipping Dorothy's antagonist, a mean witch. . . . They busted her for witchery and she got death" (V329–30/B383). Although the novel's mean witch, Pointsman, goes unscathed, at least Slothrop's most persistent antagonist, Major Marvy, gets his just deserts. As everybody knows, Dorothy never left Kansas—it was all an entertaining dream. But Slothrop did leave America, and, though the "poor ass-hole . . . can't let her go." (V623/B726), he discovers, to his dismay, that you can't go home again.

IV

Although a great majority of film references in *Gravity's Rainbow* are to the professional American and German movie industry, other kinds of film-making play a part too. Newsreels showing current events were once a staple companion of feature films. They were particularly useful in World War II as a means of dispensing information about the war, often for propagandistic purposes, by both the Allies and Axis powers. In the novel, viewing or working with newsreels is mentioned in connection with Slothrop, Ensign Morituri, Pirate Prentice, and Ronald Cherrycoke. For instance, Morituri edited "newsreels to make the Axis look good and the other side look bad" (V473–74/B552). One newsreel, FROM CLOAK-AND-DAGGER TO CROAK-AND-STAGGER, achieves a comic effect by virtue of its parody of the newsreel technique used to show the rise to power of Citizen Kane—it employs reverse procedure to show fall and dissolution. This British-made "government newsreel" is both surreal and satiric as commentary on the fate of former employees of the Firm too maladjusted to endure civilian status. (See V542–43/B631–32 for a description of demobbed Lucifer Amp.)

Virtually all serious aspects of technical filming are relegated to the German side of the story, like "the Askania films of rocket flights" and engineers sitting around "looking at movies of dials." Uses made of film by the British and Americans are either surreptitious or silly. For instance, the hidden camera spying on Katje at the Chelsea maisonette records her movements for the specific purpose of conditioning the octopus Grigori for his attack upon her. Katje discovers the film when the war is over.

Spliced on at the end of this footage is "what seems to be a screen test of Osbie Feel," a scenario for a movie he has written entitled *Doper's Greed*. It is an absurd western featuring "two trail-weary cowboys, Basil Rathbone and S. Z. ('Cuddles') Sakall" and the town sheriff, "the Midget who played the lead in *Freaks*." (His name was Harry Earles.) It "goes on for an hour and a half," complete with Jewish-accented dialogue and whacky action. Katje concludes that the film has been deliberately planted and contains "a message, in code." She breaks the code, sees it as "a prophecy. A kindness," packs her belongings, leaves the White Visitation (V533–35/ B621–24), and later tags on to the Counterforce. Although the coded movie does indeed bring a revelation, it is a farcically complicated way of relaying a message and makes yet another comic comment on the absurdity of bureaucratic military schemes.

Film is also used for propagandistic deceit: like the phony Schwarzkommando footage shot in England by von Göll, using mostly members of PISCES made up "in plausible blackface, recruited for the day, the whole crew on a lark." The film, "only three minutes and 25 seconds of which will be viewable," is to be transported to Holland "to become part of the 'remains' of a counterfeit rocket-firing site in the Rijkswijksche Bosch" (V113/B131). Again, The Firm has gone to extreme measures in the execution of complex schemes that produce little or no meaningful result, except for affecting the movie director.

The workings of the film industry as a business figure less prominently in the novel than diversified cartels like IG Farben. Nevertheless, one German film conglomerate known as Ufa (for Universum-Film-Aktiengesellschaft) is important. Ufa was initially subsidized and promoted by the German High Command in 1917, primarily as a means of spreading war propaganda and uplifting morale through film. The government later detached itself from Ufa. Although small independent film-makers continued to operate in Germany, most leading film companies were to come under the umbrella of this huge combine. Ufa was instrumental in major ways in the creation of Germany's Golden Era of cinema in the 1920s. It took pride in its artistic accomplishments and its image worldwide. All of Germany's great directors—Lang, Pabst, Lubitsch, Murnau, Wiene (and the fictional von Göll)—made films for Ufa, and most of Germany's leading actors and actresses (including the fictional Greta Erdmann and Max Schlepzig) appeared in its many productions. In the mid-1920s, Ufa produced the greatest number of films in Europe (for example, 228 feature films in 1925 alone), although it did need help from American companies to solve its financial problems. Furthermore, Ufa exerted international power in the film industry, as is shown by von Göll's connections in South America for film stock through IG (V387/B451) and by connections to Lyle Bland, powerful American businessman and Slothrop's uncle. In addition to its sizable movie-studio facilities, including a large, up-to-date complex at Neubabelsberg near Potsdam, Ufa owned many movie houses. One of them on the Friedrichstrasse in Berlin (topped by "two tall phallic electric columns") was familiar to both Pökler and Weissmann. In 1933, as both a repressive and exploitative measure, Ufa was taken over by the Nazi regime. In this state of control, its function was to please and promote the Nazi government, especially by inculcation of party doctrine. (By then many German film-makers and actors from Ufa had emigrated to America, specifically to join the movie industry in Hollywood.) So in some fifteen years Ufa had come full circle—and its ruination in war was inevitable.

As is often the case in *Gravity's Rainbow*, when Pynchon shows a grasp of large conceptual workings of war or science, technology or industry, he can also reduce to small telling details. For example, the massive film industry is utterly dependent for its existence upon a single instrument: the camera. In turn it cannot function without smaller components. As if to emphasize the significance of technological minutiae, Pynchon pays homage to lenses as he writes about the Erdmanns: "strained through glass, warped in and out the violet-bleeding interfaces of Double and Triple Protars, Schneider Angulons, Voigtländer Collinears, Steinheil Orthostigmats, the Gundlach Turner-Reichs of 1895" (V484/B564). These and other lenses helped cinema grow by meeting demands for speed and a high standard of definition.

If Pynchon can work down the scale seriously, as he does from industry to lenses, by the same token he can work down it comically for international politics. What he does to the enormously significant Potsdam conference in Germany in 1945 serves as a delightful example. World leaders met to divide Europe, primarily Eastern Europe, then under the control of the Russians. Besides territorial adjustments, the agenda was taken up by the problems of war reparations, issues of election and freedom of the press, disposition of confiscated goods and industrial capital, and declaration of a position to be followed on Franco's Spain, which had been sympathetic with Germany. Here, then, were weighty issues that would affect every future generation around the globe—but Pynchon is having none of them. He plays down the conference and makes mock of it in various ways. First, he converts it into a boffo showbiz farce. Second, he severely limits our perspective of the conference by choosing to present it from Slothrop's viewpoint. Third, he sends Slothrop on a mission to Potsdam under circumstances that provide a sharp contrast to the gravity of the political event. In his outlandish Rocketman helmet and cape, Slothrop must sneak onto villa grounds, past guards and wire, and find a cache of hashish previously hidden there by Seaman Bodine. As he digs up the hashish, there are sounds from the balcony and he ducks for cover:

> Footsteps approach, and over the railing leans—well, this may sound odd, but it's Mickey Rooney. Slothrop recognizes him on sight, Judge Hardy's freckled madcap son, three-dimensional, flesh, in a tux and am-I-losing-my-mind face. Mickey Rooney stares at Rocketman holding a bag of hashish, a wet apparition in helmet and cape. Nose level with Mickey Rooney's shiny black shoes, Slothrop looks up into the lit room behind—sees somebody looks a bit like Churchill, lotta dames in evening gowns cut so low that even from this angle you can see more tits than they got at Minsky's...and maybe, maybe he even gets a glimpse of that President Truman. He *knows* he is seeing Mickey Rooney, though Mickey Rooney, wherever he may go, will repress the fact that he ever saw Slothrop. It is an extraordinary moment. Slothrop feels he ought to say something, but his speech centers have failed him in a drastic way. Somehow, "Hey, you're Mickey Rooney," seems inadequate. So they

stay absolutely still, victory's night blowing by around them, and the great in the yellow electric room scheming on oblivious.

Slothrop breaks it first: puts a finger to his mouth and scuttles away, back around the villa and down to the shore, leaving Mickey Rooney with his elbows on that railing, still watching. (V382/B444–45)

Our total experience with "the great conference" comes down to Mickey Rooney on a balcony. The ploy by Pynchon is a skillful absurdity. As a surreal contemporary form of the mock epic, it is outrageous in its boldness, funny in its implications, and of course downright silly. Yet, if we are going to meet with a reversal of expectations, than this bizarre zeugma does not disappoint. Earth-shaking actions are ignored, the most powerful political leaders in the world become mere background players, and the foreground is occupied by the quintessence of harmless juvenility: "Judge Hardy's freckled madcap son" with his "am-I-losing-my-mind face." It is indeed "an extraordinary moment," less for Slothrop and Mickey Rooney than for the reader of contemporary fiction who must adjust to the wrenching together of high art and low comedy with no holds barred. It is a humorous filmic device *sui generis*.

V

Significantly, the three major fictionalized filmic stories involving Gerhardt von Göll, Greta Erdmann, and Franz Pökler exist at three basic levels: director, actor, spectator. The film *Alpdrücken* confirms these roles: von Göll, a man of sweeping imagination with a bent for the fine details of organization, made the movie. He directed Greta, whose sensual beauty prompted lechery in the males of the audience: "How many shadow-children would be fathered on Erdmann that night?" (V397/B463). A specific case of erotic stimulation: Franz Pökler, whose child Ilse was conceived directly after he saw *Alpdrücken*. So the major structural triad of shaper-interpreter-receptor is clearly drawn by that single movie. Moreover, their lives and personalities, their very beings are directly related to film and constitute three distinct parts of a Germanic entity. All of them underwent dramatic changes through the rise and fall of the Third Reich.

For most Germans at war's end, life has become a yawning abyss; but for director von Göll, it has become a vastly rewarding, free-wheeling big business. "Der Springer"—his nickname means jumper, leaper, or, specifically, knight in chess—is a magnate among black marketeers.

In some ways, von Göll is a study in contradictions. As a director, he was passionately devoted to his craft: framing techniques, wipes, symbolic lighting, dissolves, and so on. Yet he was not above meretricious commercial enterprise, if we are to judge by the "dozens of vaguely pornographic horror movies" (V393/B458) he directed. He showed integrity and independence when he attempted to make the movie *Das Wütend Reich* about the deranged king of Bavaria, Ludwig II. Yet to pacify the Nazis, he "compensated" with the acceptable *Good Society*. He combines other contradictory qualities of elegance and coarseness, empathy and indifference, refinement and arrogance.

In another way his character is quite clear-cut. He is selfish, ruthless, and expedient. Both as a black marketeer and as a director, he is in a position of power. He sees himself as a ubiquitous god figure, one of the Elite who can comprehend the cosmic design of darkness and light *in toto* (V495/B577). He gains monomaniacal control over people and things. His directorial power was such that he gave people identity by naming them (Greta and Schlepzig were two); in black-marketeering, "his corporate octopus [is] wrapping every last negotiable item in the Zone" (V611/B712); he uses people as he wishes (Slothrop, Närrisch, the Argentines among them).

For all his personal flaws, a basic artistic motive drives von Göll. "Once an intimate and still the equal of Lang, Pabst, Lubitsch" (V112/B131), he still seeks independent control: "This film director turned marketeer had decided to finance all his future movies out of his own exorbitant profits. 'Only way to be sure of having final cuts' " (V386/B449). If in the old days he was considered "a genius," it is made clear that "commerce has not taken away [his] Touch: these days it has grown more sensitive than ever" (V112/B131).

Having been inflated by the results of the Schwarzkommando footage, he looks forward to the time when he can shoot the Argentine epic *Martín Fierro*. He is aware, as is the novelist himself, of the necessity for audience appeal: "Keep the customer happy" (V386/B449). For this reason, von Göll wonders which part of the film to do first: Part I depicting Martín's life of rebellion, or Part II dramatizing his life of assimilation with "a very moral ending," in other words, the part in which Fierro sells himself out. The Argentines are justifiably skeptical of von Göll's trustworthiness as they wait for him toward novel's end. Sets are already prepared: real buildings—"nothing will be struck" (yet another example of fantasy taking on a reality of its own). It seems doubtful that von Göll will ever appear to make the movie. The impression left is that his artistic drive as director has been perverted by trafficking in drugs or use of them. His final project "which will never be completed" is "a really offensive and tasteless film" called *New Dope*, perhaps merely fantasy, since the movie is "going on, under the rug" and is about "a brand new kind of dope that nobody's ever heard of"—all the images of the movie run in reverse. In this episode, von Göll is seen sitting on "an unusually large infant's training toilet" as he "blithers" nonsense (V745–46/B869–70). Yet our last image of him recaptures, by way of a mystical moment, the past when he was in a directorial capacity: "on his camera dolly, whooping with joy, barrel-assing down the long corridors at Nymphenburg. (Let us leave him here, in his transport, in his innocence...)" (V750/ B875).

In sum, von Göll is a chameleonic, opportunistic entrepreneur, a talented director obsessed by the art of movie-making and the multirealities of film, a charismatic and not entirely unlikable figure. As he has mastered film, he has mastered survival in war. And it is a keen novelistic stroke to make him a successful, if unsavory, businessman, for, after all, movie-making, which may aspire to art, is uppermost a profit-making business.

Unlike him, Greta (also Margherita and Gretel) Erdmann has been debauched by film and ruined by war. Once an ethereal "doll," her beauty has become "fattening, wrecked" (V365/B425). She is a fear-riddled, pitiful, cruel woman driven by murderous, sadomasochistic impulses.

Manufactured stardom contributed to her downfall, as it has many a cinematic sex object. She was a star in Germany in the twenties and thirties, a director's "creature" promoted into an "Anti-Dietrich." She played many roles that left her "more identities than she knew what to do with" (V482/B562). She was always told what to do by men, "who to be," and how, whether "languid, exhausted . . . chased . . . submissive . . . ravished . . . dismembered." Once on her own against best advice she tried to make it in Hollywood but failed, and at her return to Germany, after a year she exhibited suicidal tendencies and descended deeper into neurasthenic breakdown.

Like so many other characters, she makes no distinction between so-called outer reality and filmic reality. For example, during the time when she is with Slothrop she hears shots in the streets and takes "the explosions as cue calls for the titanic sets of her dreams to be smoothly clogged with a thousand extras: meek, herded by rifle shots, ascending and descending, arranged into patterns that will suit the Director's ideas of the picturesque" (V446/B520–21). Her masochistic behavior during the period with Slothrop is, again, an extension of her brutalized past, including the *Alpdrücken* experience. Typically too, she has had man trouble, whether from lovers or husbands. She romanticizes her love for her former leading man Max Schlepzig (one of the false identities coincidentally assumed by Slothrop)—they were "the Reich's Sweethearts" (V395/B460). Schlepzig subsequently disappeared during the Nazi purge of Jews in 1938. Whether he was indeed putative father of her child Bianca is doubtful because the *Alpdrücken* sex orgy also involved a host of "jackal men" wearing black hoods or animal masks. As Stefania says, "Margherita's problem was that she always enjoyed it too much, chained up in those torture rooms. She couldn't enjoy it any other way" (V461/B538). Marriage to a valise-bearing sadomasochist like Miklos Thanatz has hardly improved her lot. Their sadomasochistic appetites were further whetted by their experiences while entertaining German troops at concentration camps, "the barbed-wire circuit," and later at the Holland rocket sites, where Greta encountered the diabolical Captain Blicero and the erotic enticement of Imipolex G.

In her corruption, Greta became more perpetrator than victim. Affected by deep-seated anti-Semitism, arising out of her own fear that she may be Jewish, she murdered Jewish boys in the black mud pools of the resort town of Bad Karma (V475/B554). The last murder attempt, prevented by Ensign Morituri, occurred the day before war broke out, September 1, 1939. The crimes went unsolved, and she went unpunished. At war's end, she degrades others, as she is herself degraded. In her need to receive and to administer pain, her treatment of her daughter reveals a deeply tormented state. Almost as a parody of an extreme "stage mother," she loves and hates and corrupts her own daughter. Hints are dropped that she may even have killed her aboard the *Anubis*, but there is also conflicting evidence that Bianca may have accidentally drowned. Again, as with other ambiguous situations, we do not know exactly what happened.

The fresh flower that Greta wears daily belies the deadness of her soul. The woman in black seen and feared by Greta at the spa is a mirror of herself. On every hand, the paranoiac Greta feels the presence of "them" and of death. Fearful of the dead boys rising from the rivers, she is terrified at the sight of Slothrop coming out of the water after he had fallen boarding the *Anubis*. She quakes at the fear of evil in herself: "when I was a child, they said not to look in the mirror too often or I'd see the Devil behind the glass" (V444/

B518). The reflection now in the postwar "summer of '45" is inescapable. Trapped by her decadence, haunted by the ghosts of the past, half mad, she drifts across the landscape like some precursor of Munchian angst, emitting with every cry and moan a silent, primal scream of alienation, for having been "left nothing but God's indifferent sunlight in all its bleaching and terror" (V364/B424).

As an object of adoration and lust, she symbolizes woman victimized and manipulated by a male-oriented, sexist-militaristic society. Its perversions convert her into depravity, its furies pursue her into paranoia. But other symbolical resonances are equally significant. She is perverted Earth Mother (Erdmann = earth man); she is a perverted form of Mother Germany. It is almost too ironic that her constant ally is a Japanese whose name is Morituri ("Those about to die"). The fate of war-torn Germany itself is tied into these archetypes: beauty turned into ugliness, ambition into despair, power into passivity, illusion into the reality of depravity and suffering, destruction and death. The surrogate earth mother gives birth to mutants; the real one inflicts punishment on her own; the seductress turns into tortured torturer, so in love with sex and violence and death that she thrives on the blood of her whipped thighs and the embrace of a corpse in the frozen streets. The latest sight of her is a fitting close: a spectral apparition in a black chemise, hysterical, adrift on the *Anubis*, the ship of fools intended for the Elect, the damned being brought to judgment. Thus embodied in her story are the consequences of the triumphant yet desperately troubled rise and the shattering fall of the Third Reich.

If Greta's story scrapes the nerves, the story of Franz Pökler touches the heart. Its strategic position, an entire uninterrupted middle section (V397–433/B462–505), suggests its importance. Other brief episodes treating Pökler's life appear elsewhere (V154–64 and V575–80/B180–91 and B670–76), but the central narrative remains the most cohesive and comprehensible story in the novel.

Pökler is the classic dupe, the deluded follower who lives a secondhand life, the victim of manipulative leaders, the victim of his own weaknesses, his misplaced idealism, his divided loyalties. He is torn by his love for his daughter and devotion to his work as a rocket engineer. Our compassion for him results from this divisiveness.

It is of considerable significance that he is a "fanatical movie hound" (V577/B672), positive proof, as Slothrop observes, that "German movies have warped . . . outlooks" (V474/B552).

Pökler's experiences with movies reflect a dreamlike, surreal state. Although he "loved films," he watched them "nodding in and out of sleep." His wife Leni wonders how he can "connect together the fragments" (V159/B186). Once when he distributed handbills advertising a "film fantasy," he discovered that the theater scheduled to show it was being torn down. Fantasy indeed compounds fantasy and leads to a surreal condition; he is as deceived as the people who will come to see the fantasy and find nothing there— only the reality of fantasy. Films are at least partially responsible for the change in Pökler's professional pursuits, as he dreams, making his own "dramatic connections," about the roles played by his favorite actor Rudolf Klein-Rogge, "the lion" (in opposition to "too tame, too gentle" roles played by matinee idol Bernhardt Goetzke):

> Metropolitan inventor Rothwang, King Attila, Mabuse der Spieler, Prof.-Dr. Laszlo Jamf, all their yearnings aimed the same way, toward a form of death that could be demonstrated to hold joy and defiance, nothing of bourgeois Goetzkian death, of self-deluding, mature acceptance, relatives in the parlor, knowing faces the children can always read.... (V579–80/B675)

Ironically, the truth of his life is far removed from these fantasies of recklessness. He is no "lion," in Jamf's words; he exists exactly as Leni thought of him: "swimming his seas of fantasy, deathwish, rocket-mysticism—Franz is just the type they want" (V154/B180). Theirs was a doomed marriage of opposites: Leni was intuitional, active, perceptive; he, logical, acquiescent, deludable; she, lively and emotional; he, straight and boring. He had been shaped (in a sense, like Slothrop) by his teacher Jamf and then became incapacitated by the desertion of his wife and loss of his child, so much so that "he couldn't even go to the movies" (V402/B468). The only human meaning attached to his life, aside from the companionship of his trusted friend Mondaugen, springs from his daughter, "fathered" by erotic projection "on Greta Erdmann's silver and passive image" (V576/B672). *"That's how it happened. A film. How else? Isn't that what they made of my child, a film?"* (V398/B463). It is not difficult to see why he is known as "the cause-and-effect man" (V159/B186).

As a result of his own inertia, Pökler falls increasingly under the control of Major Weissmann (Blicero) during years of rocketry research and development, all pointing toward culmination in work on the 00000. Weissmann arranges that for two weeks each year, first at Peenemünde and then at Nordhausen, Pökler will be visited by his daughter, who had earlier disappeared into a "re-education camp." However, he is never sure that the alterably different girl who makes her annual appearance and vacations with him at the children's resort Zwölfkinder is his own Ilse. He remains unable, even unwilling, to ascertain consanguinity. For him, a daughter of some kind is better than none at all. A resentful, angry martyr, limited by his pedestrian rationality, frustrated by his loneliness, ineptness, and malleability, he accepts his plight and continues to tolerate monastic overwork. The only way he can retaliate is by committing (or fantasizing) "incest" with each "daughter," acts surely meant to convey his moral outrage.

Pynchon brilliantly works from mathematics to rocketry to human lives (and later to timeless geological processes) to relate this compelling story. Two crucial passages illustrate the intricate linkage:

> Meantime Heinkels were also dropping iron models of the Rocket from 20,000 feet. The fall was photographed by Askania cinetheodolite rigs on the ground. In the daily rushes you would watch the frames at around 3000 feet, where the model broke through the speed of sound. There has been this strange connection between the German mind and the rapid flashing of successive stills to counterfeit movement, for at least two centuries—since Leibniz, in the process of inventing calculus, used the same approach to break up the trajectories of cannonballs through the air. And now Pökler was about to be given proof that these techniques had been extended past images on film, to human lives. (V407/B474)

> So it has gone for the six years since. A daughter a year, each one about a year older, each time taking up nearly from scratch. The only continuity has been her name, and Zwölfkinder, and Pökler's love— love something like the persistence of vision, for They have used it to create for him the moving image of a daughter, flashing him only these summertime frames of her, leaving it to him to build the illusion of a single child...what would the time scale matter, a 24th of a second or a year . . . ? (V422/B492)

The physical principles, resources, and shortcomings of motion pictures are made to function here in multiple ways. Pökler, visited by a "daughter" for only a brief period each year, first sees her in stilled frames. Time is stopped for him, frozen; but to gain life, it has to move for him. The movement of film is obtained from a succession of related still images. Even as his mind moves them, Pökler is well aware that the frames of a film only give the illusion of continuous motion. As an engineer, he has been witness again and again to "the rapid flashing of successive stills" that merely "counterfeit movement" (first passage). Furthermore, Pynchon plays on the phrase "persistence of vision" (second passage), which relates to film's illusion of continuity. Its speed is twenty-four frames per second, obviously too fast for any single frame to be detected by the eye. Technically, the quirk in human perception is thinking that one still sees something for a fraction of a second after it has disappeared. The idea behind persistence of vision works so well in this episode because Pökler persists in retaining the effect of an image after the cause is removed—in this case Ilse. He also knows that the individual frames are no substitute for organic reality. Paradoxically, even if we partake of direct experience our senses may distort what we have taken to be reality.

Pökler is victimized by this complex quandary. He observes only isolated fragments, he invalidates their reality, he questions his participation in real experience, he recognizes that distinctly different stillnesses and moments have been falsified into an illusion of movement and continuity (thus, contradictorily, creating its own reality). Nonetheless, out of his own human need, he speeds up those frames so that they become for him a unified developing child. "Love" causes that "persistence of vision" to occur. Pökler's mental set demands this unity. The "continuity" of an Ilse provides order and meaning to his otherwise barren, fragmented existence. To understand Pökler, we might remember what Graciela Imago Portales tells herself in another context (V388/B452): "There are worse foundations than a film."

The trajectory of a rocket is traceable in the same way from innumerable frames: blast-off, ascension, peak of flight, fall, and crash. So a human life: birth, growth, maturity (including peak of experience), decline, death. So, were it filmable, the history of earth in a rock—it too can be considered a movie:

> Rock's time scale is a lot more stretched out. "We're talking frames per century," Felipe like everybody else here lately has been using a bit of movie language, "per millennium!" Colossal. But Felipe has come to see, as those who are not Sentient Rocksters seldom do, that history as it's been laid on the world is only a fraction, an outward-and-visible fraction. That we must also look to the untold, to the silence around us, to the passage of the next rock we notice—to its aeons of history under the long and female persistence of water and air (who'll be there, once or twice per century, to trip the shutter?), down to the lowland where your paths, human and mineral, are most likely to cross.... (V612–13/ B713–14)

We need a closer eye for the earth's mysteries. We need to look underneath the "outward and visible" to the inward and invisible. By a certain stretch of the imagination, it is the principle of *camera obscura* extended—inverting an image of what is outside to form on the inside. Were we only able to get "inside" the camera, then the projector, the rock, ourselves—. Interestingly here, persistence of vision becomes "persistence of water and air"—aeons of history. Pynchon is saying in brief that truth can be found, especially in nature, if we had the time and perception to search it out.

Because lines between reality and deception are ill-defined and because Pökler cannot cope with the fuzziness of their demarcations, he cooperates perforce in perceiving a synthetic whole. It is for this reason that framing in the novel takes on the added meaning of being trapped or fixed by a fraudulent scheme, as in "to frame" or "frame up." In the generalized section "Listening to the Toilet," Pynchon does not mention Pökler, but one statement summarily applies to him: "you are trapped inside Their frame with your wastes piling up, ass hanging out all over Their Movieola viewer, waiting for Their editorial blade" (V694/B809). Editors, directors, authorities, the powers—"They" are always in control.

Like so many other events in the novel, we cannot be sure of the outcome of the Pökler story. As instructed by Weissmann at the end of the war, Pökler awaits the return of his daughter to the rusting, abandoned Zwölfkinder (twelve children). In spite of the torment undergone by Pökler, as well as by his former wife (who has become the whore Solange in Berlin), a note is struck that would indicate an affirmative ending, if not specifically a reunion. Some few at least— Slothrop, Roger Mexico, Bianca in death—manage to escape the frame; we can conjecture that perhaps Ilse is another:

> [Solange (Leni) is dreaming of] Ilse, riding lost through the Zone on a long freight train that never seems to come to rest. She isn't unhappy, nor is she searching, exactly, for her father. But Leni's early dream for her is coming true. She will not be used. There is change, and departure: but there is also help when least looked for from the strangers of the day, and hiding, out among the accidents of this drifting Humility, never quite to be extinguished, a few small chances for mercy.... (V610/B710–11)

So, Ilse, "the movie child," returns from the nightmare into which she was born, the nightmare out of which she was conceived. (How appropriate that *Alpdrücken* means *nightmare*.) Ilse relates to the other children as intricately as Pökler relates to von Göll and Greta Erdmann. They need not know each other—Ilse does not ever meet her substitutes or Bianca; von Göll and Greta never lay eyes on Pökler. Yet a net of complicity binds them all. The girls provided as surrogate daughters were bait; out of them from the known Ilse, Pökler devised his image of a single child. As von Göll manipulates and Greta hallucinates, he extrapolates. His child, the other girls, and Bianca are all movie children. They are all the "same" child, as is every child "fathered" on the movie image of Greta, Temptress, Earth Mother, Terrible Mother, at the erotic inspiration of von Göll's artistic child *Alpdrücken*. In time they become orphans of the Nazi juggernaut, unwitting victims of a mother country that perpetrated a war beyond their control.

Pökler remains its most touching adult victim on the home front. In a broad sense, he becomes symbolic of the typical German noncombatant in World War II. Despite his own skepticism and hardship, he fulfilled his duties. The entire Pökler section exudes a kind of sympathy for the nonpolitical citizen, the starry-eyed scientist, the patriotic but uninformed worker, the little man and "his poor harassed German soul" (V426/B497). It sees him as exploited and deceived and abused by feckless authority. But at the same time, it also makes clear the dangers of a vicarious, immobilized existence, a failure to act, deliberate withdrawal—a passive lie of life in which illusion must become the reality. Thus Pökler is not only the victim of others, he is the victim of himself and his own incapacities and fantasies.

VI

Tyrone Slothrop is the single character who seems most deeply immersed in the images and patois of cinema, but his responses, by and large, are emulatory. Thus he is being treated separately from von Göll, Erdmann, and Pökler. His life is more an external byproduct of film than theirs.

For the sake of comparison, we can begin by putting two Tyrones in the same pod. The first is that dashing adventurer of such costume epics of the 1940s as *The Black Swan, Captain from Castille, The Prince of Foxes,* and *The Mark of Zorro.* Then there is the second in a Wagnerian opera costume (pointed helmet sans horns, a full cape of green velvet, a pair of buckskin trousers), spurred by the motto "No job is too tough for Rocketman" (V371/B432). It is one thrilling escapade after another for the two Tyrones: in and out of the clutches of heinous villains, in and out of the arms of pliant females. From there the similarities diminish. That other Tyrone was strikingly handsome, neat and trim, rarely paranoid, lithely powerful, and always got what he was after. This Tyrone is ordinary looking, sloppy and a bit pudgy, always paranoid, virtually powerless, and never does find what he is after. Although the other Tyrone also appeared in some serious films, he could almost never play roles that were either comic or absurdist. So while Tyrone Slothrop is supposed to conjure up both identification with, and inversion of, that namesake of his, he also leaves the old-fashioned Tyrone Power in the dust.

Comedy, absurdity, and fragmented complexity need to be added. In his perigrinations over Europe, Slothrop outdoes to burlesque extreme the escapades of a hero-buffoon like Adrien (Jean-Paul Belmondo) in *That Man from Rio* (French, 1964). Substitute Brazil for Europe, substitute a search for a lost Indian treasure for Imipolex G or the Schwarzgerät, substitute the villains for Major Marvy and henchmen of PISCES, match the outrageous pursuits and escapes, and you begin to get the mix. Throw in a generous dash of the zany antics of the Keystone Cops and *It's a Mad Mad Mad Mad World*, spice it with the satiric military, bureaucratic, and technological absurdities of a *Dr. Strangelove* or *Catch-22*, and you arrive at some semblance of the formula for this madcap but fundamentally serious comedy. It is serious because Slothrop's paranoia is founded upon fact. Mad, destructive forces are at work about him. To escape them, he assumes multiple forms, which may be measured by the number of his aliases (besides Rocketman, Ian Scuffling, Max Schlepzig, Plechazunga, the Pig-Hero) or his guises of clothing: pig suit, white zoot suit, Russian army uniform, and tuxedo. But the chameleonic nature of the Slothropian persona has been mostly established by cinema. He is a thinking, walking, sleeping conglomeration of many movie beings.

Because he is a vehicle as well as a character, Slothrop becomes the perfect instrument by which Pynchon can show impressionability and convey the enormous influence of cinema upon the human psyche. Slothrop has been brainwashed by all the movies he has ever seen. Conversing with Squalidozzi, he can quote at length "Saturday-afternoon western movies dedicated to Property" (V264/B307). He combs "his hair into the usual sporty Bing Crosby pompadour" (V184/B214). Having once sent away for "a whole Mustache Kit, 20 different shapes from Fu Manchu to Groucho Marx," he is prepared for becoming an "Errol Flynn [who] frisks his mustache" (V248/B289). At the Potsdam conference, "some [American newspapermen] think he is Don Ameche, others Oliver Hardy. Celebrity? what is this? 'Come on,' sez Slothrop, 'you just don't know me in this getup. I'm that Errol Flynn' " (V381/B443). He warns Katje during a fight: "I'm the Cagney of the French Riviera, so look out" (V222/B258). To deny his sex appeal, he draws a comparison of himself with "some kind of a Van Johnson or something" (V182/B212). He assumes different voices, depending upon his situation: he can sound "like Cary Grant" or he can interject "in a Groucho Marx voice." When compelled to dissemble with Major Marvy he tries "for a Russian accent, which comes out like Bela Lugosi" (V557/B649). In dreamy sleep, " 'Oh my goo'ness,' Slothrop keeps saying, his voice exactly like Shirley Temple's, out of his control" (V493/B574). His comically classic warning "Don't fuck with the Rocketman!" is delivered to the gangsters "so they'll remember, kind of a hiyo Silver here" (V435/B507). By himself in a meadow or in the mountains, he hums "exactly the breathless, chin-up way Fred Astaire did" (V561/B654) and he masters on bagpipes "that dreamy tune Dick Powell sang in the movies, 'In the Shadows Let Me Come and Sing to You' " (V622/B725).

His sensory responses, sometimes filtered through the omniscient narrator, are equally steeped in film. He associates the look and conduct of others with filmic types ranging from child stars like Shirley Temple and Margaret O'Brien to adult stars like Rudolph Valentino and Carmen Miranda to creatures like the Frankenstein monster and King Kong. MPs in pursuit of an escapee named Hopper are "as demoralizing as a close-up of John Wayne (the angle emphasizing how slanted his eyes are, funny you never noticed before) screaming 'BANZAI!' " (V256/B298). Once when Slothrop himself contemplates escape to Africa, he decides against it because there's "nothing *there* but natives, elephants, 'n' that Spencer Tracy" (V266/B309).

Slothrop has done more than merely absorb sight and sound from the screen. He has become so accustomed to theater surroundings that he knows when he is being followed by the noise he does not hear: "Even in movies there's always someone behind him being careful not to talk, rattle paper, laugh too loud: Slothrop's been to enough movies that he can pick up an anomoly like that right away" (V114/B133). In France he is reminded of an erotically droll date to see *Meet Me in St. Louis* back at the Empire Cinema in London, when he "recalls doing the penis-in-the-popcorn-box routine there with one Madelyn" (V252/B293).

Hollywood is Slothrop's dream factory, and on occasion he gives way to wishful thinking about it. In a tight predicament outside the Potsdam conference, he fantasizes that he could "end up getting a contract for the rest of his life with a radio network, o-or even a movie studio!" (V381/B444). Given to evening-star wish fulfillment, he categorizes his hopes, one of which is "Let me go to Hollywood when this is over so that Rita Hayworth can see me and fall in love with me" (V553/B644). And when Slothrop dreams, he dreams about movies and about actresses.

These examples go beyond merely illustrating the extent to which Slothrop has been saturated by cinema: they show Pynchon's triple-edged technique. A character is given some grounding in reality by use of specific references to the pop culture out of which he comes. Furthermore, the references show how the character is to be seen and judged, whether by enacting specific mimicry or a general role, such as "Slothrop is the character juvenile tonight" (V437/B509–10). Most importantly, these references heighten parts of the character that are intentionally superficial, that show a weakness for fantasizing, and that reveal a lack of individual identity. It could also be argued that Slothrop is actually given more life because he has so many identities. Certainly all the merely celluloid impressions make more fitting and credible the eventual disappearance of Slothrop when he is *"stripped. Scattered all over the Zone. It's doubtful if he can ever be 'found' again, in the conventional sense of 'positively identified and detained' "* (V712/B830). Had he sufficient personal identity from the start, there might be cause for dissatisfaction in a readership used to more decisive treatment of a main character. However, in this case, a lack of resolution works surpassingly well, especially in its implicit ironies. Insofar as the protagonist is concerned, well over 300,000 words have led us to naught: his flight and quest dissipate into inconclusiveness, and we never know what happens to him. The identity that he so desperately seeks is denied him, from the outside by The Firm, from the inside by his certain non-selfhood. Cinema has contributed immeasurably to his loss of being. Existing as he does at times surrealistically, composed as he is of many identities, none of which represents a wholly integrated person, we are more easily persuaded of his evaporation. Yet it is also important to see him along the way reduced to a primitive state, man at one with nature: "He's kept alone. . . . He's letting hair and beard grow. . . . He likes to spend whole days naked, ants crawling up his legs, butterflies lighting on his shoulders, watching the life on the mountain, getting to know shrikes and capercaillie, badgers and marmots" (V623/B725). It is then fitting that afterward he be "scattered."

Paradoxically mythic dimensions are added because he becomes larger than life, by having less life than he might. This kind of magnification occurs in both cinema and fiction. We have seen it in screen heroes from Sam Spade to Shane, in screen antiheroes from Hardy's Laurel to Bonnie's Clyde—all nonpersons. Similarly in fiction, mythic qualities accrue to a laconic romantic like Gatsby, a monomaniacal sea captain like Ahab, an enigmatic killer like Joe Christmas. They too are, relatively speaking, nonpersons who remain memorable for reasons other than intensive depth of characterization. The outlandish Slothrop belongs in this gallery. It is indeed an achievement by Pynchon to create a mythically evolving character in the face of deliberate fictional handicaps, such as placing emphasis upon humor of the absurd and making little concession to criteria of mimesis.

VII

The preoccupation with cinema so evident in Slothrop, Pökler, Erdmann, and von Göll is counterbalanced by an apparent lack of interest by five other major characters: Weissmann, Tchitcherine, Katje, Enzian, and Geli Tripping. Movies seem to figure hardly at all in their lives, mainly because their reality is of a quite different order. A demonic Kurtz figure like Weissmann would naturally find little or no attraction in popular forms of entertainment. He enacts, rather than living vicariously. The same may be said of Geli Tripping, who, for all her dedication to supernatural forces as a novice witch, is natural, realistic, and practical. When Slothrop meets her, we are told specifically that "the movies had not prepared him for this Teutonic version here" (V330/B383). Disinterest in movies does not mean that these characters are kept immune from cinematic treatment, but what few references there are, especially in connection with Tchitcherine and Enzian, might just as well have been avoided. Although Katje is appropriately unsuitable as cinematic subject, she does figure in on three occasions: she is the object of the hidden camera at her arrival in London, she engages in a brief exchange with Slothrop on *My Little Chickadee*, and she views the "code" film *Doper's Greed* made by Osbie Feel.

Pynchon chooses to have the disinterest of this preceding group understood, without specifying it, unlike the direct tactic employed on a minor character such as Närrisch who "hasn't been to a movie since *Der Müde Tod*. That's so long ago he's forgotten its ending, the last Rilke-elegiac shot of weary Death leading the two lovers away hand in hand through the forget-me-nots" (V516/B601–2). Also, as if to clarify a situation, Pynchon's technique sometimes is to work by a negative metaphor. For instance, he has Pirate Prentice complain during his "Kipling Period" in India in 1935 that there was "no Cary Grant larking in and out slipping elephant medicine in the punchbowls out here" (V13/B15).

For other principal and minor characters, Pynchon employs a variety of cinematic approaches, ranging from multireferences to a single association that functions somewhat like a Dickensian tag.

For instance, Jessica Swanlake is likened solely to Fay Wray, who played the heroine of the original *King Kong;* and Džabejev, Tchitcherine's driver, is a consistent poseur as Frank Sinatra. Among numerous other examples, Leni Pökler has a "long Asta Nielsen upper lip" (V415/B484); Shirley in the Red Cross Clubmobile is "a pretty girl with a Deanna Durbin hairdo" (V599/B698); Dr. Muffage enunciates certain words "remarkably like James Mason" (V592/B690). Prentice is seen in various cinematic contexts, from his Irish grin like "your Dennis Morgan chap" to the knob of his walking stick, which resembles W. C. Fields. An assortment of references about Roger Mexico ranges from Dracula to Douglas Fairbanks. He and Jessica are the novel's only "normal" lovers, yet their romance takes on cinematic qualities that heighten its illusoriness. When they first met, he was driving by in a car as she was on the roadside struggling with a bicycle, her skirt hitched up—"It was what Hollywood likes to call a 'cute meet' "; that same day they go to see "that awful *Going My Way* (V38/B43–44). Afterward, most of their time together is spent in love-making trysts during which they engage in "flip film-dialogue, scenarios they make up to play alone for themselves." Also, Roger is jealous because Jessica is bound to another man (Jeremy/Beaver). Trying not to think about them together, Roger tells himself, "you're better off up at the Tivoli watching Maria Montez and Jon Hall" (V121/B141). The movie is very likely one of a half-dozen third-rate exotic romance-adventures made by this handsome Hollywood team between 1942 and 1945. The thought by Mexico is thematically revealing. Unable to cope with the reality of a frustrating love affair, he can think about finding comfort, solace, and escape in celluloid romance. Vicarious and unsatisfying as it may be, it would at least be less hurtful.

For sheer versatility in cinematic associations, no one can match Seaman Bodine, the "spirited salt" who "specializes in supporting roles." He can do "a William Bendix imitation" with "a sincere little break in his voice. . . . He can do a perfect Arthur Kennedy-as-Cagney's-*kid-brother*, how about that? O-or Cary Grant's faithful Indian water-bearer, Sam Jaffe. He is a white-hat in the navy of life, and that extends to vocal impressions of the fake film-lives of strangers" (V684/B798). Pynchon also reverses the process to extend cinematic associations to real personages; for example, Pökler on D-Day thought when he heard General Eisenhower announcing the invasion of Normandy that "it was really Clark Gable . . . the voices are *identical*" (V577/B672); or, as another, Albert Speer, Nazi minister for armament and war production, looks "remarkably like American cowboy actor Henry Fonda" (V448/B523).

The advantage of these similes is that they establish quick identification, albeit less with voices. The faces of a Groucho Marx or a Henry Fonda come readily to mind, although the reader must keep a mental clock set to avoid anachronisms of age. The faces recalled are of actors in their prime, anywhere from thirty to forty to fifty years ago. Furthermore, the simile takes for granted that the reader is able to make the comparison. In other words, as a fan who has "always been at the movies," the reader is expected to know each face or manner of voice. If the reader does not, the comparison is perhaps pointless. When Pynchon cites popular, enduring movie stars, he is on safe ground, but when actors are less well known— say, Deanna Durbin or Dennis Morgan, George Formby or Brigette Helm—the connection may be lost upon his audience. The problem is compounded for the reader unfamiliar with mediocre movies of the thirties and forties.

Filmic references extending beyond the main chronology of the novel into the fifties do not get any easier. A case in point: the "Bengt Ekerot/Maria Casarès Film Festival" in the Zhlubb episode ORPHEUS PUTS DOWN HARP. Pynchon was very likely amused by the concept as he developed it. Aside from the fun being poked at Richard M. Nixon, he clearly intends the title as a parody of the most extreme of arty film festivals. But the joke is also quite recondite. Ekerot played black-hooded, black-caped Death in Ingmar Bergman's *The Seventh Seal* (*Det Sjunde Inseglet*) (1956), and, similarly, Maria Casarès played Death in Jean Cocteau's *Orpheus* (*Orphée*) (1950). The symbolic associations with deadly authority, with a repressive, paranoiac Nixon administration, with the Rocket to be poised over the theater are all artistically valid, but questions remain: Is the initial joke too private? Is it appreciated only by film scholars and trivia buffs? The writer faces a two-sided problem when using movie allusions, metaphors, associations: they may be either too obvious or too obscure. The obscure references may be missed by the audience; the obvious comparisons may be regarded as inferior because they are crude, unimaginative, and easily made. In either case, the chief disadvantage of this sort of metaphorical writing is the ephemeral nature of topical references. If there is a defense of Pynchon, it might be found in a rephrasing of Francois Truffaut's remark: "I don't want to make films for people who don't read," that is, "I don't want to write novels for people who don't know film."

Pynchon does not consistently rely upon specific comparisons to movie stars. Other references to minor and incidental characters are general for either appearance or behavior: Gwenhidwy bends "like a screen lover" (V171/B200); Private Paddy ("Electro") McGonigle is "one of those million virtuous and adjusted city poor you know from the movies" (V641/B747); Otto chases seagulls "hands out in front of him silent-movie style looking to strangle" (V495/B577); at the spa Bad Karma, there are men with "faces shaven very smooth, film star polished" (V477/B556); on the *Anubis*, Karel is "posing as a film producer" (V461/B537); even a weapon, the "8 mm French Hotchkiss when fired goes haw-haw-haw-haw, just as nasal and debonair as a movie star" (V697/B813).

In view of the intense appreciation of film shown by many of the characters, it is inevitable that certain addictions and cults would become evident. One example of the fan who particularizes by favoritism is the rocket assistant Drohne, who has "seen every one of [Greta's] films" (V487/B567). The ultimate devotee of the American western is Blodgett Waxwing. This "well-known [stockade] escapee" is so addicted to cowboy movies that he openly risks "a death rap" in order to see them at U.S. Army bases:

> . . . He loves those shit-kickers, the sound of hoofbeats through a metal speaker across a hundred yards of oildrums and deuce 'n' a half ruts in the foreign earth makes his heart stir as if a breeze blew there, he's got some of his many contacts to run him off a master schedule of every movie playing in every occupation town in the Theatre, and he's been known to hot-wire a general's jeep just to travel up to that Poitiers for the evening to see a good old Bob Steele or Johnny Mack Brown. . . . He has seen *The Return of Jack Slade* twenty-seven times. (V246–47/ B287)

The final example points up ridiculous excess of both film scholarship and cultism. The film critic Mitchell Prettyplace has devoted himself to "a definitive 18-volume study of *King Kong*." Besides "every shot including out-takes raked through for every last bit of symbolism, exhaustive biographies of everyone connected with the film, extras, grips, lab people," it includes "interviews with King Kong Kultists, who to be eligible for membership must have seen the movie at least 100 times and be prepared to pass an 8-hour entrance exam" (V275/B320).

VIII

A consideration of cinematic metaphor in *Gravity's Rainbow* has to start with large operative concepts; then it can focus down upon specific application. The word *theater* provides a starting place. Its denotations and connotations extend beyond a structural building, beyond performance or literature, beyond facade or pretense to war, a theater of war, in this case the geographical area of Western Europe. The phrase is easily transposed into war as theater, as we see in the opening description of the Evacuation as "all theatre" and by repetitive use of the same phrase or others like "become theatre" or "elaborate theatre" in a half-dozen other contexts of war. A variation is to be found in Enzian's thought: "It means this War was never political at all, the politics was all theatre, all just to keep the people distracted" (V521/B607), apparently from underlying power struggles. From war as theater, we can link up to the already discussed artistic concept of novel as film. Next we turn to audience to deal with the vicarious experience of World War II. Since by now that war period is a generation or two away, the experience of it for many people has come from film. Those three concepts—theater-of-war, novel-as-film, war-as-film—establish a broad metaphorical framework for the novel.

Specific metaphors from film are utilized in various ways: to show settings, to depict actions, to establish character groupings, to describe clothing, to convey moods and feelings. The tropes are more than casually cinematic; they originate, specifically or generally, with movies, and often they make direct references to movies.

Metaphors of setting range all the way from rooms to buildings to towns. A room is "a De Mille set"; to Slothrop, the Reichstag building in Berlin looks like King Kong squatting down in the street; at the Potsdam conference, "the whole joint is lit up like a Hollywood premier" (V380/B443); when Tchitcherine was stationed in a remote Russian village in Seven Rivers Country, he discovered that "because of the earthquakes, nobody built higher than one story and so the town looked like a Wild West movie: a brown dirt street, lined with grandiose two- and three-story false fronts" (V338/B393).

Fittingly, some action takes place in and outside movie theaters and inside film studios. Among examples, Greta once met "V-Mann Wimpe in the street, in Berlin, under a theatre marquee whose sentient bulbs may have looked on, a picturesque array of extras, witnesses to grave and historic encounters" (V464/B541). At one point, Slothrop is kidnapped by Tchitcherine and taken to his headquarters in an abandoned film studio in Neubabelsberg, the former German movie capital. The Russians drug Slothrop with sodium amytal, interrogate him, then leave him. When he revives, he takes note of the surroundings, where he will shortly meet Greta and re-create the past. The passage is cited in its entirety to point up Pynchon's evocative power and his eye for detail:

> Aha! Canvas flats. It's a movie set. . . . a dilapidated old studio, dark except where yellow sunlight comes through small holes in the over-head. Rusted catwalks, creaking under his weight, black burned-out klieg lights, the fine netting of spider webs struck to graphwork by the thin beams of sun.... Dust has drifted into corners, and over the re-mains of other sets: phony-gemütlich love nests, slant-walled and palm-crowded night clubs, papier-mâché Wagnerian battlements, tenement courtyards in stark Expressionist white/black, built to no human scale, all tapered away in perspective for the rigid lenses that stared here once. Highlights are painted on to the sets, which is disturbing to Slothrop, who keeps finding these feeble yellow streaks, looking up sharply, then all around, for sources of light that were never there, getting more agitated as he prowls the old shell, the girders 50 feet overhead almost lost in shadows, tripping over his own echoes, sneezing from the dust he stirs. (V393/B457)

Descriptions of clothing are tailored for ready identification with the trademark apparel of specific actors and actresses of the period from the mid-twenties into the early forties. These include "Garbo fedoras," a Bing Crosby baseball cap, "George Raft suits," "a flopping Sydney Greenstreet panama hat," and extend to the size of Norma Shearer's wardrobe. As part of the development of the Polish undertaker scene, Pynchon describes a fantasy world in which appear dwarves riding bareback on large birds and wearing "*Carmen Miranda* hats, for example, bananas, papayas, bunches of grapes, pears, pineapples, mangoes, jeepers even *watermelons*" (V664/B774). Surrealistic passages of this kind show that in terms of both comic and tragic vision Pynchon's kindred spirit in the arts is Hieronymus Bosch. As might be expected, cowboy-movie getups appear. For instance, at a party attended by Slothrop, Raoul roams "around in a ten-gallon hat, Tom Mix shirt and brace of sixguns with a Percheron horse by the bridle" (V245–46/B285). Aspects of the western motif also function in ironic ways: the German Gustav, a former Storm Trooper, "thinks Post Toasties is the name of some American Führer, looking vaguely like Tom Mix or some other such longlip bridlejaw cowboy" (V717/B836). The juxtaposition of "Führer" and "cowboy" illustrates Pynchon's flair for oxymoronic pairings. This one combines incongruity with an ironic reversal of expectation that has a ring of truth. Tom Mix did have the steely-eyed look of a tyrant, as John Wayne had a slant-eyed oriental look.

Even "code-names" during wartime spring from film, as Horst Achtfaden says of the Elektromechanische Werke. Workers were named after "characters from a movie. . . . The other aerodynamics people were 'Spörri' and 'Hawasch.' I was called 'Wenk' " (V455/B531). The unspecified movie is Lang's *Dr. Mabuse, der Spieler.* (Other character surnames were: Told, Carozza, Hull, Pesch, Fine, Karsten, Schramm.)

Specific moods are conveyed by direct reference to movie stars: discontent and nicotine nervousness in the women's battery in London, when Maggie Dunkirk says to Jessica that she "thought it looked somewhat like a bloody Garbo film around here" (V127/B148); stillness and comic grotesquerie in Säure's story to Slothrop of the permanganate shortage: "There crept over Berlin a gigantic Laurel and Hardy film, silent, silent" (V375/B437); unshakable melancholy and worry in Alfonso Tracy: "Even Laurel & Hardy doesn't work for me anymore!" (V583/B679).

Various kinds of personal feelings are revealed by cinematic tropes: pain, when Slothrop is "lost, alone with that sovereign Nazi movie-villain fist clamping in his bowels" (V360/B419); ominousness and fear, at the first sight of Waxwing, who is "the meanest customer Slothrop has seen outside of a Frankenstein movie" (V246/B286); sorrow and poignant isolation, experienced by Bianca, who "dreams often of the same journey: a passage by train, between two well-known cities, lit by that same nacreous wrinkling the films use to suggest rain out a window" (V471/B549); surprise and terror, registered in a rocket bomb victim "the snowy roofslates fallen across half your bed, the cinema kiss never completed" (V49/B57).

Character grouping, too, is done by generalized cinematic metaphor. The comparison is easily made because such grouping is a staple of compositional images in the movies, whether a collection of young radicals, newborn babies, or show biz types. The first example also includes a reference to a Russian film. "Rudi, Vanya, Rebecca, here we are a slice of Berlin life, another Ufa masterpiece, token La Bohème Student, token Slav, token Jewess, look at us: the Revolution. Of course there is no Revolution, not even in the Kinos, no German *October*, not under this 'Republic' " (V155/B181). From an attenuated portion of the Roseland Ballroom toilet scene, corpses are described as "stiffs humped under the snow in the Ardennes [that] take on the sunny Disneyfied look of numbered babies under white wool blankets, waiting to be sent to blessed parents . . . " (V70/B81). Slothrop has no trouble getting past the

Potsdam conference guards in his Rocketman attire because they are used to "a strange collection of those showbiz types" (V380/B443).

The use of groups of children in movies has not escaped Pynchon's attention. He satirizes it through the profitable exploitation that Clayton "Bloody" Chiclitz envisions of the thirty children employed in his black-market fur operations:

> "My dream," [Chiclitz] admits, "is to bring all these kids back to America, out to Hollywood. I think there's a future for them in pictures. You heard of Cecil B. De Mille, the producer? My brother-in-law's pretty close to him. I think I can teach them to sing or something, a children's chorus, negotiate a package deal with De Mille. He can use them for the real big numbers, religious scenes, orgy scenes—" (V559/B651)

In turn, Major Marvy insists that "they ain't goam be *singin'* "— De Mille would use "them little 'suckers for *galley slaves*! *Yaah*-ha-ha—yeah they'll be chained to th' oars, just haulin' ass, rowin' old Henry Wilcoxon away into th' sunset to fight them Greeks or Persians or somebody." The alert reader might well wonder how someone as dumb as Marvy would know Henry Wilcoxon's name. Be that as it may, Chiclitz roars, "Never, by God," and delivers his pun on "forty million Frenchmen can't be wrong." The exchange is comic, the pun is clever, the disagreement is of negligible import, yet the undercurrent of seriousness cannot be ignored. Whether the basis is fantasy or reality, exploitation nevertheless exists. The business of war has become the business of peace, and even children have become a commercial commodity. They join the many other characters of the novel who have been trapped by circumstances, or, more aptly, framed.

IX

It would appear that virtually all cinematic references to this point have been handled by Pynchon in traditionally fictional ways, but he goes well beyond conventional trappings of the novel when the form of the movie subject matter takes over. His introduction to the Komical Kamikazes: "Something *right outa Hollywood*. . . . Yes, it *is* a movie! Another World War II situation comedy" (V691–92/B806) or his acknowledgment of "a bad cinema spring" (V628/B732) give hint of a partial progression, but both of these passages serve to illustrate that he is still maintaining a novelistic stance. It is when he abandons this position for direct involvement as screenwriter or film-maker that the most notable transformation is evident. On these occasions, he converts the novel into film script form or his writing at strategic moments takes on the peculiar professional idiom of a scenario or he sees in the manner of a film-maker. For instance, to set a scene, he writes: "Lovely morning, World War Two" (V125/B145). Although the scene direction is simple, it is also grandoise in scope. Other examples are less exaggerative. He provides scenario direction for time at the head of an episode: "Just before dawn" (V329/B382). As the lead into another section, he dictates time and weather condition: "A windy night" (V591/B689).

These are relatively simple examples of scenarist writing, but they give some sign at least of a change of novelistic position. Similarly there are sequential differences in use of dialogue and dramatic action. When the novelist is briefly reviewing Närrisch's life as henchman, there is an apparent distance between him and subject matter: " 'Cocaine—or cards?' (an old movie line the gunsels loved to use that summer)" (V517/B602—it is from Lang's *Dr. Mabuse, der Spieler*). Pynchon does not just reuse the movie line, he comments upon it. The distance narrows at a sadomasochistic reconciliation between Slothrop and Greta: "Not exactly the scenario she wanted but close enough, sweetheart" (V446/B520). He is still commenting, but film language has become more entrenched. Finally, the distance is bridged and authorial position transformed at a direct instruction, like the one at the preparation for the Rocket firing in The Clearing: "There ought to be big dramatic pauses here" (V757/B884). In short, the screenwriter has taken over.

Editing methods and optical effects are used on occasion in precise ways: for "a shy fade-in" by Greta; in "cutaways" from Katje to the octopus Grigori on film at "The White Visitation"; in a "dissolve" as Pirate Prentice and Katje dance; by "camouflage in German Expressionist ripples"; in "Gnostic symbolism in the lighting scheme of the two shadows, Cain's and Abel's" in *Alpdrücken*. Technical use of camera, like crane and zoom shots, is evident in two other passages, the first of which again illustrates Pynchon's familiarity with expressionistic German techniques: "From overhead, from a German camera-angle, it occurs to Webley Silvernail, this lab here is also a maze" (V229/B267), in the second, from the point of view of Enzian, the eye becomes a telephoto lens tilting rapidly across the landscape: "*Zoom* uphill slantwise toward a rampart of wasted, knotted, fused, and scorched girderwork" (V520/B606).

When Pynchon specifies a functional camera distance and expressionistic lighting in film script language, he hits full stride, as in the scene when Pointsman fantasizes winning the Nobel Prize: "Here's a medium shot, himself backlit, alone at the high window in the Grand Hotel, whisky glass tipped at the bright subarctic sky" (V142/B165). This is an outstanding instance of novelist writing as scenarist and novelist seeing as film-maker. Fictional rendition has been given over to locationing of camera lens, to placement of lighting, to directorial positioning of an actor playing a role, for which, to heighten the ironic illusion, he has no chance whatever of achievement. An even more cinematically sophisticated scene occurs in the paraphrased script that Felipe is writing for von Göll for the projected *Martín Fierro* film:

> A shadowed plain at sundown. An enormous flatness. Camera angle is kept low. People coming in, slowly, singly or in small groups, working their way across the plain, in to a settlement at the edge of a little river. Horses, cattle, fires against the growing darkness. Far away, at the horizon, a solitary figure on horseback appears, and rides in, all the way in, as the credits come on. At some point we see the guitar slung on his back: he is a payador, a wandering singer. At last he dismounts and goes to sit with the people at the fire. After the meal and a round of caña he reaches for his guitar and begins to strum his three lowest strings, the bordona, and sing: (V386/B449–50)

The Spanish lyrics follow. Most film scripts do not carry instructions for musical scoring, let alone lyrics, since, after all, the musical background for a movie is a composer's business. Ordinarily music is provided after a film is shot. Pynchon, however, shows he can work in the Hitchcock mode by "visualizing" the music during the formative script stage. Thus he can be screenwriter, director, and composer all at the same time. Certainly in several of the filmic scenes, Pynchon displays an innate sense of musical effectiveness. In another brief passage of parodic narrative, he combines instruction for camera distance with notation for musical accompaniment: "*Our captain, Frau Gnahb, heads into the Greifswalder Bodden, to comb the long firths for her quarry. After an hour* (comical bassoon solos over close-ups of the old recreant . . . " (V527–28/B615). Like the choice of the guitar for the opening of the Argentine film, the choice of bassoon in solo seems just right in capturing the humorous mood of this situation: a salty old woman guzzling a mind-blowing drink as she pilots her boat. On yet another occasion, Pynchon not only thinks out possible orchestration for his scene, he also visualizes deployment of the musicians in a way that provides lyrical and seriocomic commentary on his character Pökler, who is awaiting Ilse at Zwölfkinder: "If there is music for this it's windy strings and reed sections standing in bright shirt fronts and black ties all along the beach, a robed organist by the breakwater . . . " (V398/B464).

Two instruments, the harmonica and the small toylike kazoo, dominate others, especially because they are so clearly linked to Slothrop as comic Pied Piper. He eventually plays both professionally, if we are to accept as reliable the clue that "there's supposed to be a last photograph of him on the only record album ever put out by The Fool, an English rock group—seven musicians posed. . . . There is no way to tell which of the faces is Slothrop's: the only printed credit that might apply to him is 'Harmonica, Kazoo—a friend' " (V742/B866). A major musical motif is established by repetitive appearance and sound of harmonica and kazoo, notably culminated by the "harbodica" craze sweeping Los Angeles in the key Richard M. Zhlubb scene. Both instruments are associated with good, with pleasure, with "brotherhood." The kazoo sound is most effectively incongruous and intrusive in Slothrop's dream, the opening of the fourth part, which occurs in the form of a film clip featuring Bette Davis and her companion Margaret Dumont. The latter was a veteran character actress noted for her roles as a regal and wealthy widow whose patience remains imperturbable through the zany antics of the Marx Brothers in such films as *Duck Soup, A Day at the Races,* and *A Night at the Opera:*

> Bette Davis and Margaret Dumont are in the curly-Cuvilliés drawing-room of somebody's palatial home. From outside the window, at some point, comes the sound of a kazoo, playing a tune of astounding tastelessness, probably "Who Dat Man?" from *A Day at the Races* (in more ways than one). It is one of Groucho Marx's vulgar friends. The sound is low, buzzing, and guttural. Bette Davis freezes, tosses her head, flicks her cigarette. "What," she inquires, "is *that*?" Margaret Dumont smiles, throws out her chest, looks down her nose. "Well it *sounds*," she replies, "like a ka*zoo*." (V619/B721)

If there is a dominant kind of dramatic action binding the novel, it is the chase. Pynchon acknowledges appreciation of this staple tradition of suspense, adventure, and comedy by a film-oriented audience when a chase is about to get under way following Roger Mexico's revenge against the postwar Firm at Twelfth House: "aficionados of the chase scene, those who cannot look at the Taj Mahal, the Uffizi, the Statue of Liberty without thinking chase scene, chase scene" (V637/B742). Escapes and chases are also vital to the thematic thrust of the Raketen-Stadt section, in which the Floundering Four, including Tyrone as a typical American teenager, engage in "many, many go-rounds" with "Pernicious Pop" (beginning V674/B785). The various sequences, including a dog chase by Mexico and Pointsman, a wild chase in the tunnels of Nordhausen, and the duel between pie-throwers Slothrop and Schnorp in a balloon gondola and Major Marvy and his beer-sodden cohorts in a rusty old reconaissance plane, all smack of modernized Keystone Cops routines. Ironically, the pursued, Slothrop chief among them, are most susceptible to capture when they are motionless and least expecting it.

To culminate the motif of the chase, Pynchon devotes a brief section, "Chase Music," to heroes associated with this traditional form of action. These include literary and movie heroes and comic book characters: Philip Marlowe, the Lone Ranger, Superman, Sub-mariner, and Plasticman. The section is ironic, preceding as it does "The Countdown" to the firing of the 00000 Rocket. In all cases the chase heroes, who are used to appearing in the nick of time, arrive "too late" in their rescue missions.

X

Both serious and comic elements of narrative chase and thematic disjunctiveness conjoin in repeated references to a particular movie: *King Kong* (not to be confused with the flashier but inferior second version). They place emphasis upon a misunderstood preternatural creature loose in a technological society and add solidity to the underpinning of other thematic subjects like alienation, exploita-tion, and deception. The society that has exploited the ape must suffer for a time, as the creature lashes out against it, but eventually the creature has to be destroyed. Pynchon works ambivalent sides of the fence in imparting terror of the monster within society while at the same time conveying sympathy for it as pariah. As perhaps the most enduring monster movie ever made, *King Kong* is funda-mental as archetype for primitive rather than man-made nemesis.

Apart from its droll, ironic humor, the epigraph to part two on King Kong (V179/B209) reveals a basic deceptiveness, not unlike the connivance used on Ann Darrow (Fay Wray) by entrepreneur-producer-director Carl Denham (Robert Armstrong). As a penni-less, hungry waif, Ann is ripe for a promise of stardom, after having been caught stealing an apple from a fruit-vendor in a depression-ridden early scene. In the novel, Slothrop is dispatched to the French beach resort for reasons other than what he thinks. Both Slothrop and Katje become victims of an elaborate hoax, although Slothrop is the less-knowing of the two. His Beauty is no wide-eyed innocent Fay Wray—it is the jaded, enigmatic Dutch spy Katje Borgesius on assignment. Her Rescuer is no strapping First Mate Jack Driscoll (Bruce Cabot)—it is the plump, callow Slothrop, led into an affair for purposes of observation and the gaining of information. Their Beast is no gigantic ape—it is the pampered, well-conditioned Grigori, "the biggest fucking octopus Slothrop has ever seen outside of the movies" (V186/B217). Pynchon has a good deal of fun with the leitmotif of "Beauty and the Beast," in contrast to the movie itself, with its solemn opening pronouncement from an old Arabian proverb and its mournful concluding summary by the impresario that "it was Beauty killed the Beast."

However, comic aspects hardly constitute an accurate measure of the Beast motif in the novel. Its repercussions are serious elsewhere. For Jessica, in her "Fay Wray number," the Beast is evoked in varous ways: fears of the unknown, "The War . . . the paranoia, the danger . . . busy Death" (V628/B732), and, importantly, the pull of love that she feels for Roger. Their erotic abandonment has helped free her from repression, and yet she is afraid of it. This "kind of protective paralysis" leads her to reject Roger for the security of a life with stodgy "old Beaver" at war's end. Her fears are "for the Fist of the Ape, for the lights of electric New York white-waying into the room you thought was safe, could never be penetrated...for the coarse black hair, the tendons of need, of tragic love" (V275/B320).

A "much more likely candidate" for "the Fist of the Ape" is Katje because she has known real terrors. Unfortunately, they have deadened her and left her at the abyss of an existential void. To Pökler the ape is merely in inferior infancy, for German films like *Metropolis* are far more advanced over American movies: "Klein-Rogge was carrying nubile actresses off to rooftops when King Kong was still on the tit with no motor skills to speak of" (V578/B673). For Freudian Edwin Treacle of PISCES, feelings about blackness are related "to feelings about shit, and feelings about shit to feelings about putrefaction and death" (V276/B321). In the "Shit 'n' Shinola" section, the Pynchon narrative voice surfaces to lambast again that triad of white society's fears: blackness-shit-death.

The most intricately developed thematic idea is the connection between King Kong and blacks, especially the Schwarzkommando, the black rocket troops who are considered mutants in an Aryan Nazi society. Furthermore, the mutant ape is likened to mutant rocketry, and both ape and rocket are linked by phallic imagery: the ape atop the Empire State building and the potent 00001 rocket spawned out of A-4 research and development:

> So, when laws of heredity are laid down, mutants will be born. Even as determinist a piece of hardware as the A4 rocket will begin spontan-

eously generating items like the "S-Gerät" Slothrop thinks he's chasing like a grail. And so, too, the legend of the black scapeape we cast down like Lucifer from the tallest erection in the world has come, in the fullness of time, to generate its own children, running around inside Germany even now—the Schwarzkommando. . . . (V275/B320)

These sexual and racial motifs are linked by deft artistry. The Schwarzkommando are descendants of the Hereros, a tribe virtually exterminated by German troops in Southwest Africa in 1904. They, too, were "scapeapes," victims of fear and prejudice. Yet some survived and were transported to Germany, where they were still to be regarded as black "devils," children of the first "scapeape." Their leader Enzian in his "Illumination" had "coupled with a slender white rocket." The past thus recurs in this symbolic recent action by relating to Enzian's boyhood homosexual liaison with Weissmann in Africa in the 1920s.

In turn, this consistent thread of homosexuality ties to Slothrop. It contributes to his fear of blacks and increases his paranoia. In two surrealistic scenes (the Roseland Ballroom Toilet and the Transvestites' Toilet), ape and black merge to produce his mental images of sodomy, in the former scene to fear of assault while defenseless, in the latter to latent attraction, when, by appearing in drag in a Fay Wray gown, he reveals his "repressed desire to be sodomized, unimaginably, by a gigantic black ape" (V688/B803).

The identification with Fay Wray ties in to the touching poem about King Kong that follows, particularly as it reflects and distorts the movie's romantic psychodrama. *King Kong* is indeed a sentimental, exotic romance banked upon the fires of "impossible love"—as the critic Prettyplace says, "You know, he *did* love her, folks." Adapting to a lyrical tone as narrator is Ann Darrow/Fay Wray; the "you" is the ape. The setting is Skull Island, where the ape is to be captured by the enterprising showman Denham. Unexpectedly, Ann is kidnapped by the natives and offered up as a sacrifice to placate the beast. She waits in terror of "the night's one Shape": blackness, the ape. Smitten by her blonde, puny charms, he protects her while fighting off attacks of hideous prehistoric creatures: a dinosaur, a giant snake, a pterodactyl. She undergoes several "Falls," including a visual one from the claws of the pterodactyl that has swooped down upon her, another far into the water in the arms of her rescuer Driscoll while King Kong is busy disposing of the great flying reptile. In America, the beast of course will take the longest Fall of all:

> At that first moment, long before our flight:
> Ravine, tyrannosaurus (flying-mares

And jaws cracked out of joint), the buzzing serpent
That jumped you in your own stone living space,
The pterodactyl or the Fall, no—just...
While I first hung there, forest and night at one,
Hung waiting with the torches on the wall.
And waiting for the night's one Shape to come,
I prayed then, not for Jack, still mooning sappy
Along the weather-decks—no. I was thinking
Of Denham—only him, with gun and camera
Wisecracking in his best bum actor's way
Through Darkest Earth, making the unreal reel
By shooting at it, one way or the other—
Carl Denham, my director, my undying,
Carl...
Ah, show me the key light, whisper me a line....
                                                            (V689/B803)

The Carl-Ann relationship is not unlike the director-actress ties
between von Göll and Greta that accentuate control and subordi-
nation. Also, while the "Jack" in the poem refers to first mate
Driscoll, it might also be taken as double entendre for Jack Kennedy,
on the basis of the prose postscript about "dames" employed "to
cringe from the Terror," who when home from work "fall asleep
just like us and dream of assassinations, of plots against good and
decent men." In its style and thematic content, the poem is among
the best of the songs, limericks, and miscellany inserted into the
narrative.

Compared with *King Kong*, references to other horror films like
Frankenstein and *Dracula* are minimal, but they too are highly
supportive of theme. For example, on several occasions Slothrop
and Roger are likened to Dracula and to Bela Lugosi. These metaphors and images gain import as Jessica rationalizes riddance of her
lover: "Already she's beginning to think of their time as a chain of
explosions, craziness ganged to the rhythms of the War. Now he
wants to go rescue Slothrop, another rocket-creature, a vampire
whose sex life actually *fed* on the terror of that Rocket Blitz—ugh,
creepy, creepy" (V629/B733). From another point of view, it is
really the Rocket that has been the vampire. Slothrop and Mexico,
like Pökler and his fellow German engineers, are "all equally at the
Rocket's mercy." So whether regarded as a blood-sucking, life-
draining creature or as a Frankenstein monster out of the control of
its creator, the Rocket is a possessive, demoniac force. It becomes a
symbol of rampant but fascinating evil. The monster stalks from
our fears of the excessiveness of scientific research and technological assemblage, the vampire arises from our deep-seated fears of

sex, the devil, night, pain, and death. Hope of afterlife may also be a
factor, that is, the obverse may be present in the love of death. Thus
it is possible for the Rocket to achieve dimensions that are hallu-
cinatory, supernatural, malevolent, but, contradictorily, compelling. (We reason: the more potent our rocketry, the "safer," the
more "peaceful" we are.) As configurations of debased humanity,
monster and vampire reflect ourselves, the dark places of the
psyche: deep, unknown, terrifying, yet in the race to death, paradoxically, comforting. As is characteristic of him, Pynchon relies
upon the movie transmogrifications, rather than upon the original
literary sources, Mary Shelley's *Frankenstein* (1818), and Bram
Stoker's *Dracula* (1897). Once again, this emphasis reinforces the
value of extraliterary matters. Films reflect us and affect us—look
to the media for the message.

XI

Foremost among Pynchon's achievements is the opening up of
the novel to new potentialities: more diverse form, freer content,
innovative techniques. As he boldly erases boundaries between real
and unreal, between unreal and surreal, so he blurs demarcations
between novel and film. This is not to say that film and fiction can
be equated. Their essential differences will always prevail unless at
some future time language is changed into explicit yet highly
sophisticated picture-symbols, capable of imparting the most subtle
nuances. For now, the frame or sequence of film is not the page of a
book; printed words are not camera images. Nevertheless, like the
sister arts of poetry and painting, affinities do exist between fiction
and film. The crucial issue remains one of judgment of the distance
that separates them. For Sergei Eisenstein, they were very close; for
Ingmar Bergman, they are poles apart.

In his attempt to narrow the distance between them, Pynchon
reverses the traditional transposition from novel into film. He is by
no means the first writer to employ cinematic techniques in the
novel, but he is clearly in the forefront in expoiting new blends.
Believing as he does that movies are one of our strongest cultural
influences, he concomitantly demonstrates that the form and
content of cinema can become integral to fiction. Thus it is quite
possible to create a novel that can function as a movie and emulate
its methods. Quick cuts, dominant contrast, flashbacks and flashforwards, montages, dissolves, texturing, medium-long-close
shots, freezing, and a host of other cinematic devices, associations,
and tropes heighten the affinites of the two art forms. The ties

within this sibling relationship are further strengthened because Pynchon is an enthusiastic movie buff and because he has a facility for precise movie language.

A proviso is needed to forewarn that some of Pynchon's techniques are potentially hazardous if placed in unskilled hands. One kind of risk worth examining briefly is the possible application of similar techniques to television. Filmic references and allusions represent a shorthand method of writing, whether of image, metaphor, association, or symbol. No lengthy exposition is needed: a phrase like "she wore a Garbo hat" is direct and succinct. The danger lies in its topicality—its roots are at best loosely planted in a transitory milieu. Pynchon came out of a movie generation; the next appeal may well be to the television generation: he was as fat as Cannon, his head gleamed like Kojak's, he wore a Columbo coat. How enduring are these metaphors? We know they are ephemeral as a few seasons. The next step is to draw images from advertising, as the young are prone to do. The shorthand method of pop-top culture robs the imagination: it makes for laziness, for shoddiness, for superficiality of response, for shallowness of perception. We become the gulls of meretricious hucksterism and commercial entertainment. There is no doubt about Pynchon's artistic mastery, especially the splendid reels-within-reels effects gained by scaling his novel to a 1940s movie that also utilizes two preceding decades of movies. When techniques like his are intentionally used to establish cultural historicity, to show how interchangeable film and reality may be, to illumine mental sets of characters, to reveal the perniciousness of movie lies, to heighten ludicrousness, they can be powerful artistic tools. Badly used, they can debilitate a work of literature by their superficiality and inconsequence. The use that the fiction writer makes of television in the future thus may become the crucial issue.

Pynchon's treatment of audience also bears mention. The presence of an audience should convey feelings of conviviality, sharing, union, yet for Pynchon the mere fact of an assemblage can never provide solace for loneliness. In one of the key passages of the novel, a touching commentary on life, he underscores the inevitability of human isolation: *"we will never know each other*. Beaming, strangers, la-la-la, off to listen to the end of a man we both loved and we're strangers at the films, condemned to separate rows, aisles, exits, homegoings" (V663/B772). The ostensible subject is the brief alliance of Enzian and Katje to learn the fate of Blicero, whom they "both loved." Below the surface lies recognition of pervasive strangeness in a strange land. By design, chances of reciprocal love or lasting allegiances are abrogated. "Rows, aisles, exits" establish physical separation of course, but it is the word *condemned* that carries the greatest weight. We enter as strangers, we leave as strangers; those separate "homegoings" to which we are condemned reinforce our essential aloneness. In an earlier lyrical passage devoted to bereavement of Bianca, the narrator addresses the "you" who is "slouched alone in your own seat, never threatened along any rookwise row or diagonal all night." Since "you'll never get to see her . . . somebody has to tell you" (V472/B551). For all its attempts to communicate, to bridge distance, to penetrate barriers of protectiveness and incomprehension, we sense in the voice the futility of breaking through the predetermined order of human isolation.

Gravity's Rainbow is a book that illustrates perhaps for the first time the workings of an "auteur" theory of fiction. For purposes of filmic analogy, it takes only a slight stretch of the imagination to regard Pynchon as much "director" of this work as its writer. He has cast his novel like a movie, with leads, with strong supporting players, with bit parts, with numerous extras. His characters rarely take over to pursue lives of their own; they are firmly in a directorial grip that guides them in directions he wishes for us to follow. He has created a big picture, an epic picture, consisting of a dozen significant and complex story lines. Yet, though he has an interesting and powerful narrative to tell, emphasis is placed upon how he says what he has to say. In short, technique is vital. Similarly, Pynchon has liberated the novel in ways that resemble the liberation of film by auteur directors. He has done so by his own verve, by pyrotechnic skill, by forthright obscenity, by a high-spirited panache, by funny comedy, by a brooding air of mystery and anxiety, loss and pain. The novel is stamped by a force of personality and vision that is unique, and surely as identifiable as a film or series of films by a Bergman, a Fellini, an Antonioni, a Hitchcock.

Although comparisons with film directors may be invidious, they may help in establishing the tenor and thrust of Pynchon's fiction. His work reminds one of Jean-Luc Godard on film. Their ideological dispositions are markedly different. By and large, Godard falls short of Pynchon's intellectual magnitude, and, maybe most importantly, he lacks Pynchon's sense of humor. Nevertheless, there remain between them similarities in technical virtuosity and thematic density. Both are highly sensitive and vulnerable to their times, indeed, even haunted by their times. Both evoke the consequences of mechanical and brutalizing civilization through characters who are often vehicles. Both artists show a bent for excess and self-indulgence—on occasion they do not know when to stop. Their compulsiveness, diffusiveness, and extravagance may amount to excess baggage, but it is a small enough price to pay for genius.

By its uses of film, not to mention other advances, *Gravity's Rainbow* has done more than break new ground: the novel as genre will never be the same. Were film able to record the visionary upshot of William Blake or James Joyce, it would clarify the nature of Pynchon's vision alongside theirs. It would reveal his relevance, his contemporaneity, his accessibility, his warning. Films of rocket paths would do it. If Blake's vision were a rocket, it would proceed, manned but of course dearmed, ever heavenward—it would alight in God's lap. For the Joyce of *Finnegans Wake*, the rocket would circle forever, breaking the sound barrier of vocabulary, endlessly repeating cycles of myth. Pynchon's rocket comes down. Down and down. As apocalyptic writing, *Gravity's Rainbow* is unmatched in its creation of an aura of impending cataclysm. Teeming with life, his novel at its penultimate image leaves us at that blank screen, leaves us as destruction threatens from above at that "dim page spread before us, white and silent." It is a seared vision that seeing nothing sees everything.

Religion, Psychology, Sex, and Love
in *Gravity's Rainbow*

By Joseph W. Slade

Behind Thomas Pynchon's almost Emersonian faith in the unity of
Creation lies an extraordinary ability to synthesize diverse areas of
learning and discrete chunks of knowledge into a credible literary
cosmos. Pynchon's texts are worlds. Complete as they are, however, these worlds are rarely comprehensible to his characters. To
the men and women of *Gravity's Rainbow*, Pynchon's idiopathic
masterpiece, "texts" are bewildering, and the confusion adds
human dimension to events. Even the narrator of that book,
although hopeful that the universe he depicts is coherent, suffers
from a doubt that can escalate to agonized theological proportions.
When that happens, the religious implications of the novel's
emphasis on language and texts—the Word—become apparent.
Much of the force of the narrative derives from its evocation of the
sacred and from the narrator's obsession with Calvinist and Puritan
doctrine.

Marcus Smith has pointed out that the "apocalyptic and millenial
visions" of *Gravity's Rainbow* are reminiscent of the old Puritan
jeremiads, which prophesied the end of history for a people offensive to a righteous God.[1] Pynchon's jeremiad warns against the
excesses of a post-industrial society whose destructiveness is
symbolized by lethal weaponry. More significantly, it indicts the
Protestant tradition from which the destructiveness derives.
Pynchon's version of Protestant history condemns the Calvinist
compulsion to reduce the teeming fullness of the world to the two-
dimensional plane of economics. In building his markets, the
Protestant—the dominant political figure of modern Western
culture—has manipulated, exploited, and laid waste an organic
nature. Worse, he has impoverished himself spiritually, perhaps

beyond his ability to make amends. His greatest error has been to secularize his world: for that reason he can no longer read the primary text of Creation.

Viewed superficially, Pynchon's theological argument seems commonplace, a mere recapitulation of ancient disputes between champions of materialism and spirituality. If that alone were the weight of Pynchon's jeremiad, *Gravity's Rainbow* would earn its author no honor in this country or any other; conventional prophecies on the doom inherent in rampant technology and corrupt institutions have already become tedious. Fortunately, Pynchon does not root the sins of the present in historical materialism per se. Instead he charges that an impulse originally religious has led to the desacralization of nature, then compounds the irony by suggesting that remystifying human experience is possible because of the failure of Western institutions, by means of the technology he might be expected to discredit.

Nature for Pynchon is not pastoral but paradoxical, and the first assumption of the gospel according to this Thomas is doubt where most humans would prefer certainty. Nature's mystery, which should leaven man's ambition, derives from her capacity to surprise, to behave unexpectedly. Uncertainty is an index of the sacred—an assertion Pynchon amply illustrated in his second novel, *The Crying of Lot 49*—and human understanding of the sacred turns on a willingness to recognize chance. Nature may or may not play dice with the world; we can not know for certain, and that is the world's saving grace. Uncertainty is the beginning of mystery, and mystery is the beginning of reverence. By denying uncertainty, our Western culture has lost its capacity for reverence.

In explaining the loss, Pynchon adapts the sociological scheme of Max Weber in order to demonstrate a linkage between economic and political systems on the one hand and thermodynamics and religious sensibilities on the other. The device provides a framework for the sprawl of Pynchon's narrative. According to Weber, man counters alienation through a combination of "objectivity" and "rationalization." With objectivity he strips away illusions about the meaning of life; with rationalization he creates values and new meaning. Having no illusions, he is free to design his world. In fact, human freedom lies precisely in the ability to see life for what it is, to create meaning, and to act with purpose. But the discipline and asceticism that make possible rationalization can also lead to oppressive systems that control men. Weber identified the discipline and asceticism in our era as essentially Calvinistic, and found its most exemplary stage in America, although he observed its progress in Germany and the Low Countries as well. Put perhaps too simply and in somewhat more Pynchonian language than Weberian, the Calvinist, faced with the blankness and chaos of nature, transforms nature after his own design by bureaucratizing it and turning it to profit. The capitalist system he thus creates becomes oppressive; the bureaucracies reify and come to control their individual members. For Weber there was something tragic about this process of rationalization, of imposing design and pattern on nature, if only because he believed the process irreversible and inevitable in its homogenizing effect on humans. Although he spoke in sociological constructs, Weber was postulating a theory of systems analogous to theories of thermodynamics: closed systems decline into entropy. If nothing can halt the process, however, it can be slowed by what Weber called charisma. Systems can be altered, perhaps even rejuvenated, by the appearance of "irrational," charismatic figures and the *spiritual* movements they can engender. Pynchon will build his novel on this hope for spiritual change.

According to the quasi-Weberian scheme of *Gravity's Rainbow*, the Western Protestant has traditionally recoiled from the chaotic fertility of Creation, which he regards at best as "the entropies of lovable but scatterbrained Mother Nature" (V324/B377) or at worst as a blank, incomprehensible void, a zero, an impenetrable barrier. Toward the end of the novel, as the narrator lurches toward madness, as he prepares to reveal the identity of the Schwarzgerät, occurs a description of a steaming tropical jungle: "This is the World just before men. Too violently pitched alive in constant flow ever to be seen by men directly. . . . An overpeaking of life so clangorous and mad, such a green corona about Earth's body that some spoiler *had* to be brought in before it blew the Creation apart. So we, the crippled keepers, were sent out to multiply, to have dominion. God's spoilers. Us." (V720/B839–40). Like the images of miasmic marshes in *Death in Venice* or the alluvial savannahs in *Heart of Darkness* that so frighten Aschenbach and Kurtz, primeval scenes terrify Pynchon's Protestants, whose reflex is violence.

As an example of this reaction, Pynchon sketches the short history of an ultra-Calvinist Dutchman, Franz Van der Groov (an ancestor of Katje Borgesius). One of God's spoilers, Van der Groov virtually exterminates the dodo birds of seventeenth-century Mauritius because they seem too ugly and useless to be part of God's design, using a matchlock rifle of already obsolete manufacture. This latter point Pynchon insists upon by way of exonerating technology from the narrator's arraignment of human destructiveness. The dodo birds did not fit into any orderly pattern of creation that the Calvinists could discover, did not possess the power of speech, and thus could not be "saved" by God's "Word." After the slaughter, Van der Groov has a vision of the sanctification of the dodoes, "all brothers now, they and the humans who used to hunt them, brothers in Christ" (V111/B129). The mistake here, of course, is that the Word is false, for it is a human, not a divine, invention. The penalty for not conforming to this artificial plan is death: the Protestant will attempt to annihilate what he loathes and fears—he will kill in order to order. Then he will justify his insanity by allowing destruction to masquerade as salvation.

The Word is the product of a literate Western culture. Over and over the narrator alludes to the power of language: "There may be no gods, but there is a pattern: names by themselves may have no magic, but the *act* of naming, the physical utterance, obeys the pattern" (V322/B374). And again, "Names by themselves may be empty, but the *act of naming...*" (V366/B426). Language, by designating, divides the named from the rest of Creation, fixes it. That explains the survival of "the primitive fear of having a soul captured by a likeness of image or by a name" (V302/B352). Language confers control over nature; it is the most primal of man's technologies. In *The Presence of the Word* (1967), Walter Ong astutely remarks that the "desacralization of culture" began with the development of the alphabet.[2] Certainly Pynchon appears to follow Ong in his account of the Kirghiz tribesmen, whose sacred world is profaned by the imposition of the New Turkic Alphabet.

This subplot of the novel involves colonial oppression through linguistics. Once humans begin writing, Pynchon believes, that technology becomes as dangerous as Van der Groov's musket. The Soviets who overrun the Kirghiz are not Protestant, but they share with the West a fear of nature and a propensity toward deadly order, parallels Pynchon manipulates cavalierly, as if bureaucratic discipline were by definition a Protestant monopoly. At any rate, Tchitcherine the Russian has misgivings about his role as imperialist: "He had come to give the tribesmen out here, this far out, an alphabet: it was purely speech, gesture, touch among them, not even an Arabic script to replace" (V338/B393–94). As he listens to two of the Kirghiz singing duels, or ajtys, Tchitcherine "understands, abruptly, that soon someone will come out and begin to write some of these down in the New Turkic Alphabet he helped frame...and this is how they will be lost" (V357/B415). The songs will be lost because they are spontaneous expressions of a dialectic that transcends duality. To write them down will be to arrest what can only flourish as ephemeral yet dynamic oral culture. Yet even on this oral level, language facilitates analysis, the tool of rationalization, the process by which Western man subdues nature and creates his own systems of organization.

Language, mathematics, and science are forms of "name-giving, dividing the Creation finer and finer, analyzing, setting namer more hopelessly apart from named, even to bringing in the mathematics of combination, tacking together established nouns to get new ones, the insanely, endlessly diddling play of a chemist whose molecules are words..." (V391/B455). The more man analyzes, the more he sets himself apart from nature and the more he insulates himself from chance manifestations of the sacred. Of necessity the process demands the establishment of dualities: order as opposed to disorder, the rational as opposed to the instinctive, fragmentation as opposed to unity, and, among a host of others, death as opposed to life. Within the context of the narrator's mysticism, unbalanced as it is, the most pernicious of these is the distinction between life and death, the culmination of the relentless secularization that sprang from the original shrinking from chaos, for, as the narrator will attempt to demonstrate, order marches inevitably toward death.

The God of the Calvinists was order; disorder was an Other, sinister and intolerable. This duality the Calvinists capped with another. God, said the zealots, had his own system of order, fully determined. He had preordained the Elect and the Preterite. At first the theologians maintained that Election was mysterious, a matter of grace: no one knew whether he was a member of the Elect or the Damned until his death. This mystery, so long as it lasted, had at least the virtue of preserving some uncertainty and doubt, a pale reflection of nature's own randomness. The thrust of Protestant history, however, has been to eliminate mystery. Gradually, the Calvinist mind, hungry for assurance and control, decided that the signs of Election were worldly success and wealth, the trappings of capitalist status. If one was rich and privileged within the human system now emerging, he was a member of the Elect; if he was poor and powerless, he was relegated to Preterition. God's Word had ordained it so. The Elect, using this version of divine right, took over the system they had evolved by exploiting the Preterite, their power guaranteed by the Preterite belief in predestination.

This belief had been given substance by the Protestant co-option of Newtonian physics, whose "natural laws" advanced rationalization and secularization by giving authority to cause and effect and thus legitimizing determinism. Newtonian physics purports to render the universe intelligible and usable by humans. Merely to believe that such order and control is possible is to actualize it, as man's technology has so often proved.

As their power grew, the Elect—or rather, the Protestant economic polities of the West, at first called national states—extended their domain through colonization and imperialistic oppression, and cemented their control by political and psychological suasion. The terms *Election* and *Preterition* have fallen into desuetude, so thoroughly has the religious aspect of aggression been forgotten, but the categories have become engrained in Western consciousness. National economic institutions have changed their character, transformed into multinational corporations, but their power remains secure: the Preterite believe to some degree in the inevitable hegemony of the Elect if only because the latter have made their institutions perpetual. The multinational companies like Siemens, Shell, and GE—the "They" of *Gravity's Rainbow*—divide up the world with formal alliances such as the secret agreement between Standard Oil and I.G. Farben in 1936 to share markets and exchange some 2,000 patents. Being corporations, the multinationals have achieved the immortality that Daniel Boorstin attributes to modern business ventures,[3] a recognition dimly grasped by Pynchon's characters. "It is possible that They will not die," says Father Rapier," that it is now within the state of Their art to go on forever—though we, of course, will keep dying as we always have" (V539/B628).

The "other side" of the interface between life and death disturbs the narrator, who believes that the Elect are attempting to penetrate the last barrier. This outrageous notion may originate with Pynchon's reading of Weber's reflections on "the bureaucratization of spirit" and "the ghosts of dead religions" that haunt rationalized cultures; spirits and ghosts prowl the landscape and peer down from the skies in the novel. Concepts of death are central to the religious themes of *Gravity's Rainbow*. Construed in literate, linear terms, death is the negation of life, one pole of a duality, frightening, erotic, unknowable. Apprehended as one half of a dialectic, death is a phase of genesis and decay, a recurrent cycle of nature. Understood either way, death and dying are mysterious. Because any mystery loosens the grip of rationalization, "They" wish to bureaucratize the ranks of the dead by extending "control" through seances and spiritualist experiments at places like "The White Visitation," home of "PISCES—Psychological Intelligence Schemes for Expediting Surrender. Whose surrender is not made clear" (V34/B39). "There are sociologies," says Edwin Treacle, in an effort to widen Weber's insights, "that we haven't even begun to look into. . . . It makes no sense unless we also consider those who've passed over to the other side. We do transact with them, don't we? Through specialists like Eventyr and their controls over there. But all together we form a single subculture, a psychical community, if you will" (V153/B178–79). As the narrator grows more suspicious of any duality, as he vibrates to sensitivities he uncovers, as he ultimately begins to lose "control" of his narrative, he will insist that death is the deepest longing of Western humans.

Be that as it may, the narrator is on safer intellectual ground when he claims that rationalized systems, religious or political, "promote" death as a form of salvation, as a necessary sacrifice to ensure progress, as a means to an end. Wimpe the drug salesman explains this concept to Tchitcherine:

> "Religion was always about death. It was used not as an opiate so much as a technique—it got people to die for one particular set of beliefs about death. . . . But ever since it became impossible to die for death, we have had a secular version [dialectical materialism]—yours. Die to help History grow to its predestined shape. Die knowing your act will bring a good end a bit closer." (V701/B818)

The narrator's emphasis on death in this respect indicates the dimensions of control as he believes them to exist. What Protestant history has produced is a massive structure of discipline, the equivalent of a gigantic closed thermodynamic system, a world, in fact, that overlays the world of nature. "Another world laid down on the previous one and to all appearances no different. Ha-*ha!*" (V664/B774), the narrator laughs. Although in some respects this sphere of artifice is not real, it is the world in which men must live. It has a kind of unity, but because it is founded on analysis and differentiation it is an environment of synthesis, not paradox—dualities, not dialectics. Without a vision of natural wholeness, prevented by the fragmentation of Creation, modern man is alienated from nature and from his fellows. Rationalization has swept aside earlier cultures and religions. Gone are ritual, dogma, and tradition. Bureaucracy has destroyed intimate human relationships. Gone are the organic ties of family, friends, and folk. In their place are contractual bonds, formulas of impersonal trade, that render government, industry, education, religion, the military—every aspect of society—abstract and anonymous. The end excludes all but the necessary means.

To use the terms of Ferdinand Toennies, whose influence on Max Weber was large, *Gesellschaft*, or the complex of impersonal alliances characteristic of capitalism and nationalism, has displaced *Gemeinschaft*, or the more organic relationships characteristic of village, kinship, and religion. Westerners, says one of Pynchon's mouthpieces, have become "Christianized," "enfeebled by Gesellschaft and our obligation to its celebrated 'Contract' " (V465/B542). Contracts do not provide a sufficient ground for community, for spirituality, for a morality freed from hard institutional crusts. Like T. S. Eliot and Ludwig Wittgenstein, two early intellectual guides, Pynchon doubts that humanism can flourish in a secular world.

As reminder of the past and rebuke to the present, Pynchon weaves into his narrative once again the story of the Hereros of German Southwest Africa. In a 1968 letter to Thomas F. Hirsch, then working on a dissertation on the Hereros at Boston University, Pynchon confessed to a fascination with the Bondelswaarts that had begun when he incorporated a government report on the Herero uprising of 1904 and their subsequent near-annihilation by Lothar von Trotha into chapter nine of *V*. He had continued reading on the subject (he was obsessed with it, he told Hirsch), and was planning to use what he had learned in a new book to appear before long.[4] The experience of the Hereros anchors the Weberian framework of *Gravity's Rainbow*. The religion of the pre-colonial Hereros shaped their society, Pynchon wrote to Hirsch, discussing at some length the patterns and polarities of a Herero village. Western missionaries, especially the Germans, destroyed the healthy dichotomies and replaced them with categories. What had happened to the Hereros, Pynchon said to Hirsch, was what was then afflicting the buddhists in Vietnam: the grafting of a culture that prized classification and division onto one that exalted the holistic. The connection helps explain the hints that the narrator of *Gravity's Rainbow* is a Vietnam veteran strung out on mysticism and dope.[5]

The Hereros surface in *Gravity's Rainbow* as the Schwarzkommandos, troops forcibly expatriated to Germany. Their travail exceeds that of the Kirghiz tribesmen, since they are not only dragged from an oral-aural to a script-print stage of culture but are introduced as well to Europe's more lethal forms of rationalization. Although by Western standards they seem passive, the Hereros exhibit considerable strength. Pynchon had for some time wondered, he confided to Hirsch, why the Hereros had not overwhelmed von Trotha's soldiers with their superior numbers. He had read a pamphlet by W. P. Steenkamp entitled *Is the South-West African Herero Committing Race Suicide?* (Capetown: Unie-Volkspers Bpk, [1935?])[6] and dismissed its speculations on vitamin E deficiency, concluding instead that the Hereros' death wish stemmed from their religious orientation, which led them to feel that each human was part of all creation, a vision experienced as mysticism, rather like being high on drugs. Collective suicide, envisioned as a return to unity, seemed plausible considering their understanding of a holistic universe. Although that vision is common to most of the great religions, Christianity does not encourage it, Pynchon remarked to Hirsch. German Christianity in particular embodied the worst characteristics of Western rationalization.

Even in their captivity, the Schwarzkommandos of *Gravity's Rainbow* remain partly underacinated, having managed despite their training as rocket experts to cling to vestiges of tribal life. Survivors of von Trotha's campaign, the Schwarzkommandos trust in a mantra that means "I am passed over." The belief links them with the Preterite of the West but also enables them "to stand outside our history and watch it, without feeling too much" (V362/B422) as occupants of moments of stillness amid the West's linear rush toward rationalization. The posture is ambiguous, however, because it resembles a Western yearning for stasis.

The distinction that Pynchon attempts teeters on subtlety, for he wishes to draw a line between the Herero desire to commit tribal suicide as a form of return and the erotic love of death the narrator believes has infected Western culture. The distinction is further complicated by the Europeanization of the Schwarzkommandos, whose leader, Enzian, is—with a somewhat overcontrived appropriateness—a half-breed son of a Russian father, a half-brother to Tchitcherine, half-seduced by Blicero, and half-Westernized as a result. Such circumstances endow Enzian with a moral perspective while they at the same time doom the Schwarzkommandos as a group.

Enzian derives substance as a character and a leader from a mythic faith in divinity and in the doctrine of eternal recurrence. For him there is "no difference between the behavior of a god and the operations of pure chance" (V323/B376); his openness to chance lends him authenticity as a priest of Pynchon's theology. Enzian knows that mystery still supports the world despite the fascination with "masculine technologies, with contracts, with winning and losing" (V324/B377) in which he has been tutored by Blicero. In contrast to the Western conviction that humans are here "once, only once" (V539/B628), Enzian clings to patterns of "return" (V327/B380) and exalts the dialectics of recurrence, a metaphysical repetition that acknowledges chance while affirming continuity.[7] In recurrence time and the world stand renewed, and he who perceives the recurrence finds refreshment and regeneration. Enzian's faith in this ancient doctrine is not impervious to the encroachment of events; he understands that recurrence is to an extent a conceit, a metaphor for the relationship between life and death.

Yet it does help explain the actions of those who would hasten cycles of return and regeneration by adopting racial suicide:

> It was a simple choice for the Hereros, between two kinds of death: tribal death, or Christian death. Tribal death made sense. Christian death made none at all. . . . But to the Europeans, conned by their own Baby Jesus Con Game, what they were witnessing among these Hereros was a mystery potent as that of the elephant graveyard, or the lemmings rushing into the sea. (V318/B369)

Of the various kinds of animal totems in the novel—dodoes, pigs, aardvarks, lemmings—the last are most programmed for death, as if, Pynchon will imply, the lemmings had been built to Christian specifications. On the other hand, in their precolonial past the Hereros had chosen the aardvark as symbol of "fertility and life," but in Europe "its real status is not so clear" (V316/B367). Its diminished symbolic vigor notwithstanding, the aardvark still serves as totem for the Erdschweinhöhlers, the faction within the Schwarzkommandos whose members affirm life—and, if necessary, death—against the blandishments of their rivals, the Empty Ones. The Empty Ones have succumbed to Western linear time. "Europeanized in language and thought, split off from the old tribal unity . . . they calculate no cycles, no returns[;] they are in love with the glamour of a whole people's suicide" (V318/B369–70), and turn to masturbation, abortion, sterilization, and sexual aberrations that prevent fertilization, all of them subsumed under the "deviation" of suicide. By endorsing sterility and nonreproduction, the Empty Ones enter linear time and violate cycles of return.

As a corollary to their axiom of termination, the Empty Ones—in company with numerous other characters in the novel—wish for reversal of time. They dream of proto-continents, of edenic gardens, of open landscapes without labyrinths or fences of rationalization, of ways back to the past in contravention of linear time. Even the narrator on occasion admits to this longing:

> At least one moment of passage, one it will hurt to lose, ought to be found for every street now indifferently gray with commerce, with war,

with repression...finding it, learning to cherish what was lost, mightn't we find some way back? (V693/B808)

By contrast, Enzian is comfortable in cyclical time. His moral centrality stems from his knowledge that the Empty Ones are deluded. Listening to Ombindi, Enzian decides that the man is "at times self-conned as any Christian" when he "praises and prophesies that era of innocence he just missed living in, one of the last pockets of Pre-Christian Oneness left on the planet" (V321/B373). There is no way back in linear time to the Herero village or any other state of innocence, and no way to escape the consequences of living in a rationalized society. Eclipsed, hidden, distant, nature—or rather the romanticized image that each person carries with him— recedes before human consciousness as surely as the grids of Rilke's City of Pain overlay the mandalas of the ancient village.[8] To yearn for lost innocence is human, perhaps, but to act on the basis of such a tropism can be disastrous. That motivation drives Blicero, whose romanticism flowers into a megalomania with the same root as the despair of the Empty Ones.

For all its sketchiness, mandated by the shadowy presence of Weissmann in the novel, Pynchon's portrait of Captain Blicero reveals the essence of fascism. The welter of postwar events has obscured the outlines of Hitler's fanaticism, which rose out of a contradiction perverse enough to mock the paradoxes of nature. Pynchon grants Hitler's appeal by asserting that charisma can be revitalizing as well as dangerous (V81/B93) and reminds his readers that a swastika is also a mandala (V100/B117). Hitler idealized the past, romanticized the ancient heroic culture of the Teutonic peoples, strove to re-create tribes of Aryan barbarians hurling spears in the Black Forest, wanted to reestablish the "organic" ties of family and folk. In his 1937 essay "The Affirmative Character of Culture," Herbert Marcuse, one of Pynchon's influences, speaks of the "false collectivities" of race, folk, blood, and soil advanced by the Nazis as a kind of code signaling "renunciation and subjection to the status quo."[9] These contrivances underline Hitler's determination to use sophisticated technology and modern corporate structures to accomplish his goals: he wished to *engineer* an artificial return. That is why the architectural monstrosities of Albert Speer look to Pynchon like mileposts on a linear road to the past. Spurred by desires similar to Hitler's, Blicero attempts to break out of "this cycle of infection and death" (V724/B844), his term for the systems of rationalization he has correctly apprehended, in favor of a romantic love/death, a penetration of "the radiance of what we would become" (V724/B844). On the Heath, Blicero has "reverted to some ancestral version of himself. . . . . He had left 1945, wired his nerves back into the pre-Christian earth we fled across, into the Urstoff of the primitive German, God's poorest and most panicked creature" (V465/B542). Like so many others in *Gravity's Rainbow*, Blicero has been caught in the cleft between order and disorder. Repelled by disorder but aware of the deadliness of rigidity, he lusts after a pregnant stasis whose perfect embodiment is the moment just after rocket *Brennschluss* and just before the rocket's plunge, a moment frozen with potential, the interface between worlds—or so it seems. That moment, a vector poised above a zero, Blicero reserves for Gottfried, as appropriate to the "peace" of his name; it is a gift, of sorts, that Blicero has carefully prepared.

The moment is a rift in time, a singularity, a delta-t, and *perhaps* a convergence and simultaneous disjuncture of secular and sacred worlds. Repeatedly characters experience singularities, sometimes spontaneously, more often by contrivance. From a host of examples of the latter category, two will suffice. The first involves the Polish undertaker who courts lightning in the hope of catching the cusp of a revelation,

> a discontinuity in the curve of life—do you know what the time rate of change *is* at a cusp? *Infinity*, that's what! A-and right across the point, it's *minus* infinity! How's *that* for sudden change, eh? Infinite miles per hour changing to the same speed *in reverse*, all in the gnat's-ass or red cunt hair of the Δt across the point. That's getting hit by lightning, folks. (V664/B773)

Inside that moment, "it will *look* like the world you left, but it'll be different. . . . Another world laid down on the previous one and to all appearances no different. Ha-*ha*! But the lightning-struck know, all right!" (V664/B774). At such moments it is no wonder that a "way back" seems possible—but the moment is psychic and nonlinear.

The second example, less comic but equally dangerous in its implications, involves Leni Pökler, who participates in prewar Berlin street demonstrations to enjoy the thrill of potential annihilation by the police. As the mob surges toward the weapons of the authorities, fear itself evaporates as the moment of death becomes imminent:

> She even tried, from what little calculus she'd picked up, to explain it to Franz as Δt approaching zero, eternally approaching, the slices of time growing thinner and thinner, a succession of rooms each with walls more silver, transparent, as the pure light of the zero comes nearer.... (V159/B185)

Leni is an inarticulate cartographer of "parallel" worlds, a mystic persuaded by "metaphor" and "signs and symbols," willing to reach for manifestations of hierophany.

As usual with Pynchon's characters, however, perception and sensation are untrustworthy. Those who experience singularities cannot tell whether they are secular or sacred, whether the suspension of time holds the immanence of transcendence or merely the imminence of death. Although the ambiguity can be forgotten in the caress of the zero, the consequences—serenity or extinction— are very different. Gottfried's descent, for example, offers no promise of peace, not even for Blicero, a "master" of "illumination" (V758/B885).

In his madness, Blicero chooses an ancient fairy tale from the storehouse of German culture and casts himself as the wicked witch to Gottfried's Hansel and Katje's Gretel, a deliberate putting on of roles that Pynchon rounds out by describing Gottfried in the rocket as a "fawn."[10] Pynchon uses the Hansel and Gretel motif over and over, most amusingly in the scene with Mrs. Quoad ("I've had to become all but an outright witch" [V115/B134]) feeding candies to Tyrone Slothrop and Darlene, to make clear a major theme: that children are saved from menace only in fairy tales. The irony, of course, is that the novel's only real witch, Geli Tripping, will employ her powers in defense of love. By playing out the story—"the strayed children, the woodwife in the edible house, the captivity, the fattening, the Oven"—Blicero, Katje, and Gottfried establish a "preserving routine, their shelter, against what outside none of them can bear—the War, the absolute rule of chance . . ." (V96/B111). The house in the woods is a "Little State, whose base is the same Oven which must destroy it...." (V99/B115). But Blicero knows that "every true god must be both organizer and destroyer" (V99/B115).

Blicero manipulates such dualities. Obsessed by "bookish symmetries" (V101/B118), he must align opposites into a mandala-like pattern in order to "transcend." As witch, he represents mother and father, roles complementary to his bisexuality. As creator of the rocket 00000's *Schwarzgerät*, a black womb for a white human, he turns destroyer when he actually encases Gottfried in the weapon. Blicero then completes the charade apparently by stepping into the oven-like flames of the final lift-off. In a way, the game, the ritual, is more significant than its conclusion, which signifies the exhaustion of Blicero's perverse energy. He has persevered. When Katje "quits the game," Blicero plays it without her, at one point substituting Greta Erdmann for her in his need to construct a scenario of meaning in the midst of chaos.

Blicero's is a self-reflexive evil informed by awareness, even in his madness, of what he is doing. He suggests Calvinism curved back upon itself. The first of the famous Five Points advanced by John Calvin in his *Institutes of the Christian Religion* is the doctrine of total depravity, or man's "natural" inability to exercise free will as the result of corruption inherited from Adam's Fall. References to Calvin's First Point, from Nadine Slothrop's "I'm a wicked old babe, you know that. No hope for the likes of me...." (V683/B796) to Katje's condemnation of herself as "corruption and ashes" (V94/B109), abound in *Gravity's Rainbow*, reaching an apotheosis with Blicero: "The man's thirst for guilt was insatiable" (V323/B376), Enzian remembers. Blicero wishes to restore "the primacy of the 'conscious' self and its memories" (V153/B179) by freighting the psyche with guilt, then obliterating it in expiation. His self-loathing, so readily converted to fascism, is surpassed only by the narrator's. Blicero's hope that his perversity can exfoliate into Götterdämmerung pales beside the narrator's vision in his worst moments of man as the despoiler of the *whole planet*, a sin punishable by unspeakable apocalypse.[11]

Like Blicero, his former lover, Enzian needs meaning too. Sensitive to chance and impelled by duty to his tribe, he quests for "glimpses into *another order of being*" (V239/B279) associated with the Rocket. Blicero's Rocket is for Enzian not just the emblem of the West but also a symbol of wider importance, an annunciation that human control is not secure. Even though society's leaders claim that order and discipline protect all men from violence, chaos, and disaster, nothing can defend against the Rocket, as Enzian tells his companions:

> "It comes as the Revealer. Showing that no society can protect, never could—they are as foolish as shields of paper...." . . . "Before the Rocket we went on believing, because we wanted to. But the Rocket can penetrate, from the sky, at any given point. Nowhere is safe." (V728/B849)

In other words, the Rocket restores uncertainty, undermines order, and—in a sense—resacralizes the world. Even Imipolex G, the mysterious plastic so integral to Blicero's last act, has religious characteristics: it shimmers with stars like "points in the body of God," it possesses a "Region of Uncertainty," and—as screen for projectors of images "analogous to a motion picture," movies being imitations of life—it pulses with "indeterminacy" (V699–700/B815–16). Ambiguity rises to a remarkable pitch here as Pynchon appears on the one hand to shake his head at the human propensity to worship technology and on the other to insist that the things humans invent do have a spiritual presence. Nearly everything in *Gravity's Rainbow* has a dual aspect, in keeping with the novel's inquiry into the limits of contradiction. If fortuitous contradiction is a mark of the sacred, then paradox is the only paradigm for understanding. Rockets can be good or bad, nature soothing or horrifying, Rilke's poetry comforting to Slothrop or tormenting to Blicero, dialectics valid for Enzian or false for Tchitcherine. Western man may have reduced his world to dualities, to binomial codes, but, as Pynchon demonstrated in *The Crying of Lot 49*, resonant distances stretch between one and zero. That a rocket can be both profane and holy is no more startling than the contradictions inherent in language, whose power can freeze and fragment yet also exalt and protect—as Seaman Bodine and Roger Mexico learn when they employ word play to escape the Utgarthaloki menace (V714–17/B832–36). Language embodies paradox, as in the phrase "ass backwards" (V683/B796); and "Shit and Shinola" can impossibly "coexist" (V687/B801). Even the Kirghiz discover the power of the word: "this alphabet is really something!" (V355–56/B414). Language and mathematics, suspect as tools of rationalization, can produce mantras and music, spells of great potency and songs that are "magic capes." A kazoo, after all, can imitate the "Brennschluss of the Sun" (V711/B830); and Pynchon's style, in which allusions and connections are made idiom, spins puns, paradoxes, and metaphors into revelations of the sacred.

The Rocket, then, becomes iconic. Believers in signs of nature's dialectic, the Hereros adapt their village mandala to the A-4 itself, thereby bestowing on the weapon a holiness at once spurious and real. For them the Rocket is not so much an instrument of their vengeance or redemption as it is a dynamic symbol of creation and destruction. Enzian feels a kinship with the Rocket, he tells Slothrop, because the V-2 shares with humans a vulnerability to chance; the Rocket is "at the mercy of small things," accidents that can rob it of "life" (V362/B422). Like Rocketman, Slothrop himself, the Rocket cannot be totally programmed: ostensibly under the launcher's direction, the Rocket actually falls within an Ellipse of Uncertainty. Moreover, the Rocket's real launching pad rests on human dream, the hope of transcendence, of flight over human limitations, far above rationalized grids. Dreams are the source of all technological achievements, like Kekulé's wonderful discovery of the benzine ring, subject of a lament by the narrator:

> Kekulé dreams the Great Serpent holding its own tail in its mouth, the dreaming Serpent which surrounds the World. But the meanness, the cynicism with which this dream is to be used. The Serpent that an-

nounces, "The World is a closed thing, cyclical, resonant, eternally-returning," is to be delivered into a system whose only aim is to *violate* the Cycle. Taking and not giving back, demanding that "productivity" and "earnings" keep on increasing with time, the System removing from the rest of the World these vast quantities of energy to keep its own tiny desperate fraction showing a profit. . . . (V412/B480)

In this respect, Pynchon seems to have grafted Thorstein Veblen onto Max Weber. Veblen worshipped technology as the fountain-head of progress but despised the businessman as the perverter of the promise. "Captains of industry" bought and sold the bounty of creative inventors by exploiting markets, rigging shortages, and eliminating competition—the very practices of "Them" in *Gravity's Rainbow*. This affinity notwithstanding, Veblen would have balked at the spirituality with which Pynchon endows man's inventions. Secular though it is, the world that man has created intersects with whatever sacred worlds coexist with it through the medium of technology. Pynchon does not deny man's right to nature's bounty, nor his right to alter, only the "right" to use his control to oppress. Indeed, Pynchon can himself seem puritanical when he excoriates the entrepreneur for having broken a covenant based on the dream of progress, for betraying the promise of human ingenuity, for mis-using artifice consecrated by work and sacrifice.

Enzian is trying to forestall the inevitable. Although he too be-lieves in a Text that "will bring us back, restore us to our Earth and to our freedom" (V525/B612), near the end of his quest he finds what he fears is the real Text, the bombing patterns around Jamf Olfabriken Werke AG, which indicate the seamless transition from prewar cartels to postwar multicorporate systems. In pursuing his goal, Enzian has had to travel in *"their* time, *their* space" toward "out-comes the white continuum grew past hoping for centuries ago" (V326/B380). About time, however, Enzian is astute, for he re-spects the present, which he makes as tenseless as possible. Since linear history is irreversible, he must step out of sequential time, through a door in the present, into the Holy Center of the world. The route to this sacred place of renewal lies in myth, which pre-scribes fearsome quest, careful replication of ritual, and fidelity to divine tradition. At the head of the tribe, Enzian tracks Blicero's legendary white rocket, an instrument of death that carried life, to its point of firing, to the holy center of the new totem of his people, in order to assemble a copy, the black rocket 00001:

What Enzian wants to create will have no history. It will never need a design change. Time, as time is known to the other nations, will wither away inside this new one. The Erdschweinhöhle will not be bound, like the Rocket, to time. The people will find the Center again, the Center without time, the journey without hysteresis, where every departure is a return to the same place, the only place.... (V318–19/B370)

The duplication—ideally—will counter the unique destructiveness of the first launch, restore the covenant, and rejuvenate the wasteland, for Enzian will fire his missile at the very wellhead of the secular world, which must metaphorically intersect at that point with whatever other worlds there be. Enzian may be able to launch his rocket, but he cannot abrogate time without the assistance of the immortal Slothrop, the mediator between worlds, whose miraculous powers alone can effect the transformations that can make time "wither away." Only with Slothrop can rocket 00001 become a spiritual second chance for a rationalized culture. The Empty Ones wish only to destroy the oppressive systems: they will be satisfied if the black rocket's parabola spawns the rainbow bridge over which the disinherited Nibelungs of the earth can storm the citadel of the gods in suicidal Götterdämmerung. The rainbow Enzian hopes for is the sign of a new covenant; he would be a Noah left serene after the war's destruction has cleansed the planet. Whether Slothrop is to ride in this ark as the *Schwarzgerät* of rocket 00001, whether he is to find and decipher the true Text, or whether he is merely to provide the understanding necessary to redirect the technology of a lethal culture is never made clear, but it is clear that he holds promise. (In terms of the colonialism that makes up a significant theme of the novel, the implication is that America has an obligation to defend the freedom of the as yet incompletely rationalized Third World through technology.) For all of Blicero's ingenuity, Gottfried dies, the victim of a sexual love of death, of a longing for sterile release from control. This perversion of both sexuality and technology is the affliction of the wasteland, which suffers, in Eliot's words, from "death-in-life"--or, in the words of Walter Rathenau in the novel, from a movement "not from death to any rebirth . . . [but] from death to death-transfigured" (V166/B194). Slothrop, on the other hand, holds the potential for "life-in-death"; he is the redeemer of the wasteland. But Slothrop will not function as the link between secular and spiritual worlds, will not suspend time, will not achieve understanding, will not rejuvenate his culture.

Besides, when Enzian finds the Holy Center, if he finds it, the narrator knows that the West will erect on the spot a Rocket-City, as unlike the metaphorically renewed Herero village as Augustine's City of God was unlike the City of Man. Religious impulses are always rationalized: that is the revenge of linear time. The new "community," once rationalized, will not harbor those "heretics" who cling to whatever dualities can still evoke meaning, not even the simplest dichotomy of "the Primal Twins (some say their names are Enzian and Blicero) of a good Rocket to take us to the stars, an evil Rocket for the World's suicide, the two perpetually in struggle" (V727/B848).

On a personal level, however, Enzian must be content with a religious instant. So strategic a tranquility could easily degenerate into a view of rationality as profane as against a vision of intuition as sacred were it not for Pynchon's introduction of another variable in his theology. Its herald is Kurt Mondaugen, whose mysticism has been compounded from a fascination with technology and a period spent with the Erdschweinhöhle in Southwest Africa. From this blend Mondaugen draws "moments of great serenity" that contain "the pure, the informationless state of signal zero," a form of "electro-mysticism" (V404/B470). The allusions to electricity throughout *Gravity's Rainbow* are almost surely playful bows to Marshall McLuhan, whose works, Pynchon indicated to Hirsch, he had been reading.[12] McLuhan has much to say about the impairment of human faculties as the result of linear inroads of Western consciousness. Perhaps the most amusing of Pynchon's McLuhanesque devices is Byron the Bulb, whose career parallels that of Tyrone Slothrop.[13] In *Understanding Media*, McLuhan asserts that "the electric light is pure information. It is a medium without a message. . . ."[14] Byron functions as an immortal icon of the Preterite, a counterpart to other lights and illuminations, all symbols of information, haptic or not. Behind McLuhan, however, is something else.

The "informationless state of signal zero" is a measure of stasis and revelation in Pynchon's universe, and is connected with the zeros that replicate in the novel. Mondaugen's commentary polishes another plane in Pynchon's polygonal adaptation of Weber's theories. The characters' preoccupation with order and disorder, with life and death, and with information or its absence recalls one of their creator's earliest themes, borrowed from Henry Adams and refined from novel to novel: human history as thermodynamic process. Here the theme furnishes a locus for intersecting analogies. Weber wrote that rationalization, once begun, was irreversible. Linear, historical, one-dimensional, its course could be deflected only by the manifestation of "charismatic" figures around whom spiritual movements or followings would coalesce. In this way, a rigid system might be altered for good or ill—the novel mentions a range of charismatic candidates: Tyrone Slothrop, the

V-2, Malcolm X, Adolf Hitler, John F. Kennedy—until the press of rationalization rigidified or "routinized" in its turn the charismatic diversion. Pynchon can be flippant about the notion, as in the case of an interrogator asking Enzian if his own experience can "be described, in Max Weber's phrase, almost as a 'routinization of charisma' " (V325/B378), to which Enzian replies, "Outase [shit]," an answer that merely affirms the construct. Aside from its function in *Gravity's Rainbow* as a vehicle for social and political comment, then, the Weberian scheme articulates neatly with slightly reductive manipulations of thermodynamic laws and their corollaries in information theory, and beyond them, with reflections on life and death. By dealing with this matrix of metaphors, Pynchon again evokes a paradox of a religious cast.

That paradox has been formulated by Lancelot L. Whyte, who asks, "What is the relation of the two cosmic tendencies: towards mechanical disorder (entropy principle) and towards geometric order (in crystals, molecules, organisms, etc.)?"[15] Some mysterious dynamic governs the relationship, for order can persist in the midst of disorder, and, consequently, life in the midst of death. Indeed, life *is* order, whereas death is a form of disorder. Taken far enough, the paradox can open up metaphysical rifts of large span, since humans cannot know, with certainty, whether disorder—chance—is actually possible. For that reason, Pynchon has recourse to Heisenberg's principle of uncertainty, which legitimizes chance, and the principle of complementarity, which validates paradox. As Lewis Feuer has noted, these principles, fashionable in the twenties as buttresses for claims of free will, have worn thin today.[16] Although they do serve to counter the Newtonian determinism associated with Calvinism, Pynchon rests his theology more precisely on the laws of thermodynamics.

In *The Crying of Lot 49*, Pynchon toyed with Maxwell's Demon, a theoretical machine contravening the second law of thermodynamics, which holds that the entropy within a system tends to increase. A measure at once of the disorder and the homogeneity of a system, thermodynamic entropy has a mirror-image relationship to entropy within communications systems. In *Gravity's Rainbow*, Pynchon plays with this relationship. The greater the entropy of a message, the greater its unpredictability, the more information the message or signal carries. Moreover, according to the third law of thermodynamics, entropy tends toward zero as systems verge toward zero temperature. At absolute zero, motion ceases. Without motion there can be no information: the signal is zero. Ordinarily the cessation of energy means death, yet it can also metaphorically suggest mystic certainty, as it apparently does for Enzian, who is "closest to the zero" among Mondaugen's associates. Enzian enjoys metaphors, and can hope for rest and revelation from a "zero" state of induced serenity, while he himself stays in motion. For Blicero, on the other hand, metaphor merges into madness when he fires his rocket toward the frozen "zero" of the North Pole, an action that can only terminate in stasis.

For all his "serenity," Enzian is devoted to hard work, to the gathering of information. He is mindful of the history of his ancestors, who have always suffered from "lost messages. It began in mythical times, when the sly hare who nests in the Moon brought death among men, instead of the Moon's true message. The true message has never come" (V322/B374–75). Enzian wants to train the Empty Ones to live and to collect information (V525/B612). Gathering information is a negentropic process, a wresting of form from disorder. Life itself can flourish only when the order and disorder of a system are in viable balance. Human understanding of life and death can develop only when information—made possible by disorder—is available. "There's a real conversion factor," the narrator of *Gravity's Rainbow* maintains, "between information and lives" (V105/B122). The preservation of life and of human value calls for religious sensibility. As William Irwin Thompson has put it in *At The Edge of History*, a work influenced by Pynchon's *The Crying of Lot 49*, "Inverse entropy, the *conservation* of value in a world of chaos, comes from a religious transformation in which a disadvantage on one level of order becomes an advantage on a higher level of order. Every creation is preceded by the right kind of chaos needed for a universe."[17]

The "right kind of chaos" is, of course, World War II, a conflict so cataclysmic that it should have wiped humanity's slate clean. That is the hope, at least, of Squalidozzi and his fellow anarchists, "a community of grace" (V265/B308), who hope for a return to "unscribbled serenity." "In ordinary times," Squalidozzi explains to Slothrop, "the center always wins. Its power grows with time, and that can't be reversed, not by ordinary means. Decentralizing, back toward anarchism, needs extraordinary times...this War—this incredible War . . . " (V264–65/B308–09). The Weberian nature of linear time dooms Squalidozzi's hopes; like the Empty Ones, his U-Boat crew succumbs to "nostalgia" for a mythical past, and "only the hope of dying from it [nostalgia] is keeping them alive" (V384/B446). Eventually, Squalidozzi and his friends get sidetracked by Gerhardt von Göll, who promises to shoot a movie for them on Laszlo Jamf's "Emulsion J" filmstock, a film that will lead the anarchists "back to the Garden" (V388/B451) they dream of returning to. The Argentinians participate in this screwball project as a way of compensating for their incompetence as traders of information; when Squalidozzi entrusts a message for his underground to Slothrop, he never asks the name of his messenger. The ironies, though hilarious, are relevant to the religious theme of the novel. Graciela shares with Enzian a belief that God is chance (V613/B714), and the rest of the anarchists presumably believe in disorder, yet none of them can understand what they most desire. Worse, the film they want to make is about Martín Fierro (Pynchon is apparently having fun with the real film of that title), an anarchist "saint" who ends by embracing Gesellschaft. Still worse is the absurdity of people who love the open nature of the pampas choosing synthetic forms and images.

The situation of the Argentinians is less significant in itself than in the way it connects with the quest of Tyrone Slothrop, the "sudden angel, thermodynamic surprise" (V143/B167). In a sense, Slothrop is a human Maxwell's Demon, and, like his predecessor in *The Crying of Lot 49*, he is supposed to mediate between the world of thermodynamic reality and the human world of information. He is also something more, although just what is not clear despite, or because of, Pynchon's many clues. Laszlo Jamf code-named the young Tyrone "Schwarzknabe," a term that suggests Schwarzchild, the famous scientist of the early part of this century, whose name has been memorialized in (1) the Schwarzchild radius, a limit demarcating the gravitational contraction of stars that results in a "black hole" in space; (2) the Schwarzchild solution, a construct that provides a resolution of the Einsteinian field equations; and (3) the Schwarzchild singularity, a point where space is so curved by matter that its radius is zero and its density is infinite. Or, Slothrop may be a "black body," the study of whose emissions in terms of wavelength led Planck to the quantum theory, either because Slothrop is naturally an ideal body that absorbs all the heat or light radiation that falls upon it or because he has been so conditioned by Jamf's Imipolex G (or possibly, Emulsion J), perhaps in an experiment involving movies run backward (black body radiation can be approached in a laboratory). At any rate, Slothrop can apparently convert disorder—in the instance of rocket explosions—into order—in the instance of sexual potency. When he first appears in the novel, he is unconsciously comfortable with randomness, a condition symbolized by the amazing disorder of his office desk, and clearly on the side of life through his sexual, i.e., fertilizing, responses to death.

Like other names in *Gravity's Rainbow*, Slothrop's is suggestive. Blicero calls his lover Enzian, for example, after a passage in Rilke's poetry; but Enzian is also the name of a twelve-foot-long, 600 mph surface-to-air missile "passed over" in favor of the V-2 shortly after Wernher von Braun moved his rocket technicians to Peenemünde.[18] Jamf is an acronym for an American street term, "Jive-Ass Mother Fucker," denoting "the system." Slothrop's name, as Daniel Simberloff has noted, contains an acronym (S-l-o-th) for the second law of thermodynamics.[19] But the name also indicates the reason for Slothrop's failure as a messiah, as the "pig that wouldn't die" (V555/B647): he is too slow. At first Slothrop searches for information, about the V-2, about the *Schwarzgerät*, in an attempt to define himself and his miraculous powers, but he cannot process the information and eventually forgets why he is seeking it.

Other characters are far more adept as information gatherers and sorters: Pirate Prentice translates dreams and fantasies, Eddie Pensiero reads shivers, Säure Bummer reads reefers, and Miklos Thanatz reads whip scars. Mister Information dispenses data, and Byron the Bulb radiates pure information. But Slothrop radiates nothing. As he loses momentum in his quest, Slothrop's energy wanes. "Keep it bouncing," Pierce Inverarity advised Oedipa in *The Crying of Lot 49*, "keep [information] cycling." Slothrop cannot. Great as they are, his powers are not sufficient to explicate the paradoxical relationship of order and disorder in the world.

Scientists can resolve the paradox statistically, and the strongest characters in *Gravity's Rainbow* are skilled at statistics.[20] Mathematical odds are part of Enzian's faith. During one of their encounters, Enzian explains to Slothrop that human existence itself can be construed in terms of probabilities:

> ". . . I think we're here, but only in a statistical way. Something like that rock over there is just about 100% certain—it knows it's there, so does everybody else. But our own chances of being right here right now are only a little better than even—the slightest shift in the probabilities and we're gone—schnapp! like that." (V362/B421)

Enzian is the lesser of the novel's two statisticians; Roger Mexico is the more capable of mathematical notations of the universe and its transformations. Mexico comes closest to understanding that Slothrop is chance raised to near-divine order, a being fueled by the chaos manifested in the random rocket strikes that may or may not erect his penis. Mexico knows that indeterminacy can preserve humans from total programming.

Mexico resembles Slothrop: "they're two of a kind, aren't they" (V629/B733), Jessica Swanlake decides. Were Pynchon not so steadfastly anti-Christian, Roger might be a John the Baptist to Slothrop's Messiah. Mexico's "mother" is the War (V629/B733), for he too responds to disorder, and is in fact dependent on it: "The day the rockets stopped falling, it began to end for Roger and Jessica" (V628/B732). Mexico, the statistician willing to "junk cause-and-effect entirely, and strike off at some other angle" (V89/B103), maps rocket strikes and Slothrop's erections in Poisson distributions of probability, as if from an "angel's-eye view" of London. "Why is your equation only for angels, Roger?", asks Jessica: "Why can't *we* do something, down here? Couldn't there be an equation for us too, something to help us find a safer place?" (V54/B62).

To Roger is given a vision of the original Christ-child—with Whom it is easy to associate Slothrop—before His career succumbed to rationalization:

> But on the way home tonight, you wish you'd picked him up, held him a bit. Just held him, very close to your heart, his cheek by the hollow of your shoulder, full of sleep. As if it were you who could, somehow, save him. (V135–36/B158)

The passage occurs in perhaps the most beautiful scene Pynchon has ever written, the Evensong visit to a church "growing out of the earth" (V127/B148) by Roger and Jessica at Advent. In the scene, various themes come together as Pynchon underscores their importance by inserting an apparently offhand remark about a schizophrenic with powers similar to Slothrop's, a man who believes that "*he* is World War II." New offensives give him energy, like a "season of birth, of fresh beginnings." "Whenever the rockets fall—those which are audible—he smiles, turns out to pace the ward, tears about to splash from the corners of his merry eyes, caught up in a ruddy high tonicity that can't help cheering his fellow patients" (V131/B152–53). (Slothrop's powers are greater, of course, for he does not have to *hear* the rocket explosions.)

Inside the church, song—especially the lyrics of an exiled Jamaican, perhaps a kinsman of the Hereros—holds back the night outside, sets the War at a distance, though it is still close enough to intrude on the spontaneous community of worshipers. The War is in fact a mockery of community, of Gemeinschaft: "The War needs to divide this way, and to subdivide, though its propaganda will always stress unity, alliance, pulling together. The War does not appear to want a folk-consciousness, not even of the sort the Germans have engineered, ein Volk ein Führer—it wants a machine of many separate parts, not oneness, but a complexity...." (V130–31/B152). The narrator's sense of loss at this point is palpable:

> There must have been evensong here long before the news of Christ. Surely for as long as there have been nights bad as this one—something to raise the possibility of another night that could actually, with love and cockcrows, light the path home, banish the Adversary, destroy the boundaries between our lands, our bodies, our stories, all false, about who we are. . . . (V135/B157–58)

Slothrop is supposed to light the path. For much of the novel, he oscillates between the thermodynamic world of nature and the informational world of man, receiving messages from both but unable to interpret the signals from either. His penis erects in the midst of explosions when he takes in energy *and* also after his "study sessions" with German rocket manuals (V211/B245), when he takes in information of a more conventional sort. Slothrop, as a "natural" man in an artificial world, is unsuited for his environment, out of phase with both worlds, doomed always to miss *"his time's assembly"* (V738/B861). He is unequipped to function in the world of men for two reasons. The first is that he is lazy. Searching for information is like "LOOK-IN' FAWR A NEEDLE IN A HAAAAY-STACK" (V561/B654), hard, frustrating, often fruitless work. Toward the end of the novel, he comes across a message addressed to him on the wall of a public toilet: "Willst Du V-2, dann arbeite. If you want the V-2, then work" (V624/B726). The words recall the notorious German slogan of the concentration camps, "Arbeit macht Frei," or "Work makes you Free." The irony is that work does lead to freedom. Enzian tells Slothrop that he is free; later, he tells Katje the same thing, that she has *"been set free"* (V661/B770) as a "reward" for her services to "the Firm." *"Reward,"* she retorts; "It's a life-sentence" (V662/B772). Sartre could not put it more succinctly: the price of freedom is unceasing effort to collect and interpret information. Information is life.

The second reason for Slothrop's incompetence as a messiah is his fear of "buying and selling," the "real business of the War" (V105/B122) and of the modern human world. In this world, information is "the only real medium of exchange" (V258/B300), and Slothrop recoils; "no other Slothrop ever felt such fear in the presence of Commerce" (V569/B663). Eventually, because he is a "natural" phenomenon, a "singularity," he will return to nature, where, because man has overlaid the natural landscape with artifice, Slothrop will become invisible to his fellows. (Or, like a black hole in space-time, theoretically capable of bridging the world of universal relativity and the world of quantum mechanics, he collapses inward of his own gravity and becomes invisible because light cannot escape. "I don't know any more who Slothrop really was," says Katje; "There's a failure in the *light*" [V659/B768]. Or, as another possibility, Slothrop as a "black body" ceases to give off visible radiation because his "temporal bandwidth" narrows [V509/B593].) When Tyrone recovers his harmonica beside the mountain stream, his notes on the instrument work a kind of magic: "Slothrop, just suckin' on his harp, is closer to being a spiritual medium than he's been yet, and he doesn't even know it" (V622/B725). By becoming sound, he leaves the temporal boundaries of a script-print culture for the rich, imaginative enchantment of an oral stage; he regresses, from adult to child, and from the world of cities to the world of rural serenity. Slothrop is neither idiot savant nor romantic hero, however, although he seems so by contrast with Katje, who feels inwardly thwarted by a malaise that is urban-bred, "something not pastoral at all, but of the city, a set of ways in which the natural forces are turned aside . . . a city-darkness that is her own, a textured darkness in which flows go in all directions, and nothing begins, and nothing ends" (V661/B770–71). Like the counterculture children in America during the sixties, Slothrop returns to nature without understanding. Such a transformation is sterile. As Douglas Hofstadter would put it, Slothrop fragments because he can not achieve an "isomorphism," a transformation that preserves information.[21]

Slothrop *is* America: innocent yet ignorant, miraculous yet mundane, generous yet uncommitted. America was the land of promise, of second chances; she has failed her mission, as Slothrop fails his, not because of corruption but because of indifference. Slothrop cannot understand his dream that he and Jamf are one (V287/B334–35), which means that he is part of the system and that he cannot escape his responsibilities despite his desire to cast himself as a victim. He cannot comprehend his erection when he learns—*information* that reveals how he became part of the system—that Lyle Bland, the Slothrop Paper Company, Jamf, Harvard, and his own parents had conspired to use him (V285–86/B332–33); and the narrator, paranoid that he is, suggests the wrong conclusion: "His erection hums from a certain distance, like an instrument installed, wired by Them into his body as a colonial outpost here in our raw and clamorous world, another office representing Their white Metropolis far away...." (V285/B332). Slothrop comes to doubt that his "penis [is] his own" (V216/B252). But it *is* his own.

Slothrop lacks the courage to doubt his convictions. As a result, Slothrop functions as a diffident and inarticulate bearer of a blessing, a character-type that has become Pynchon's trademark. On one level, he fails as a redeemer of the modern wasteland because he loses his fertility as he loses his ability to convert information into understanding. Despite the many guises and names under which he appears in the novel, he cannot earn his real title, the one indicated in the incomplete word "G E N E R A T O R" (V734/B856) preserved in the graffitti that in Pynchon's fiction are the etchings of human longing.

On a more significant level, Slothrop fails as a mediator between worlds, or, more precisely, as an "angel" come to resacralize the human world. He is a form of grace, a reminder that chance still rules. Nature—earth, the World, the substratum and support of the rationalized human world—persists, and, because it does, so do the prospects for freedom and spiritual triumph. To rationalize the world is not to control it utterly, for "natural" surprise, described as chance, fortune, Murphy's Law, Gödel's Theorem, or just plain accident—the words that make up the vocabulary of Thomas Pynchon's liturgy—will always disrupt contrived order. Moreover, human systems ordered too rigidly will go entropic of themselves. The War Zone represents civilization's decay into a chaos (although some of the characters, even the narrator, suspect that the War is another form of control by Them) in which chance events, as reflections of nature's own aleatory behavior, are common. The uncertainty of the Zone offers hope that is soon defeated: an old world may or may not be dying, but a new one clearly is powerless to be born.

For all its artificiality, however, the rationalized world is real, not ersatz: humans must live in it and accept its limitations. As Miklos Thanatz learns, being a Preterite in the world means "he won't escape any of the consequences he sets up for himself now, not unless it's by accident" (V668–69/B779). The key word, of course, is *accident*, a form of grace that can temper iron determinism. Living in the rationalized world also means affirming rather than renouncing it, in the same spirit with which Rilke insists that humans must affirm death as well as life. Slothrop, whose coming has been foretold (he is "the pig that will not die"), is testament to the power of chance: his actions are not determined. Because randomness is the condition of his life, he could restore faith in a secularized society.

As is usually the case with messiahs, however, no one can comprehend his mysteries, least of all himself. He cannot remystify the world, and cannot affirm it, although he cannot die either.

In contrast to his ancestors, who collected "data behind which always, nearer or farther, was the numinous certainty of God" (V242/B281); and despite his "peculiar sensitivity to what is revealed in the sky" (V26/B30), Slothrop has difficulty dealing with revelations. It is hard to fault him for this failing, for what Pynchon has done in creating his slothful protagonist is no less than to anticipate the 1977 Nobel Prize for Chemistry, awarded for speculations on entropy that coincide remarkably with Pynchon's religious predilections.[22] Man has tried to make of his world a closed system that will not stay closed, thanks to singularities that actually quicken its energies, just as the universe itself has loci where entropy can be reversed.

Although his sexuality and his character are predicated on his ability to function randomly, Slothrop has been educated in the Protestant ethic. Manifestations of chance are foreign to his need for certainty, and he can cope with them only with a paranoia, "a Puritan reflex" (V188/B219) to signs of the sacred, and a mind-set he shares with the narrator and other characters.

Pynchon has thus gone beyond T. S. Eliot, that other critic of a secularized twentieth century, in suggesting that atrophied religious sensibility dictates the psychological aberrations of modern man. " . . . There is something comforting—religious, if you want—about paranoia . . . " (V434/B506), says the narrator. Paranoia is a legacy of rationalization, religious only in the sense that it arises out of the Protestant passion for certainty that touched off the rush to rationalization in the first place. The paranoid denies chance by insisting that nothing that happens is accidental, and thus closes himself off from actual manifestations of the sacred. Because it imposes a false gestalt on the information the individual receives, paranoia is thus at best inferior to true religious experience: " . . . It is nothing less than the onset, the leading edge, of the discovery that *everything is connected*, everything in the Creation, a secondary illumination—not yet blindingly One, but at least connected, and perhaps a route In for those like Tchitcherine who are held at the edge.... (V703/B820).

Slothrop fails as a redeemer when he cannot comprehend the nature of chance; he succumbs to "anti-paranoia, where nothing is connected to anything, a condition not many of us can bear for long" (V434/B506). Humans cannot function without a view of the world as stable and coherent, cannot cope with life without a belief in cause and effect, cannot survive in an environment without a degree of rationalization. But if paranoia reinforces the individual's faith in continuity and unity, it also impoverishes him spiritually.

To refuse to grant that chance is possible, to encourage paranoia, is to invite isolation, alienation, and anomie. By convincing himself that everything that happens is directed against him, the paranoid takes a solipsistic position that cuts him off from participation in the human community. By attributing menace to forces beyond his control, the paranoid sees himself as a victim and claims a refuge against taking responsibility for his actions. By assuming that *every* event is determined, the paranoid robs himself of surprise and the wonder of authentic revelation.

Outside Pynchon's variations on paranoia, *Gravity's Rainbow* draws for the most part on fairly conventional schools of psychology, some of which become the butts of humor, and most of which seem suspiciously involved with authoritative Protestant power structures. As Dr. Geza Rózsavölgyi of PISCES bashes his way through an explanation of the Minnesota Multiphasic Personality Inventory and the Rorschach tests with which he hopes to establish "control" over Slothrop, for example, the chaplain plaintively asks if there are scales for calibrating "*Human* values? Trust, honesty, love? Is there—forgive me the special pleading—a religious scale, by any chance?" (V81/B93).

Most of the psychologists in the novel, from Pavlov to Pointsman, are behaviorists interested in conditioning, which rests on determinations of cause and effect and implies a Newtonian model of the human mental universe. The System achieves its dominance by programming through culture and upbringing. Although most parents do not sell their children directly to "The Firm" as Slothrop's did, fathers and mothers do betray their offspring by molding them to the demands of a rationalized society. Aware of parental complicity, Leni Pökler does not wish to be a "mother" to her daughter: "How can I be *human* for her? Not her *mother*. 'Mother,' that's a civil-service category, Mothers work for *Them*! They're the policemen of the soul..."(V219/B256). Hansels and Gretels never know what they are getting when they reach for the gingerbread. Toward the end of his novel, Pynchon reminds his readers one last time of the duplicity of mothers: "Remember the story about the kid who hates kreplach?" The psychiatrist who advises the mother colludes in this instructive tale, which ends with the boy's discovery

of deception: " 'GAAHHHH!' screams the kid, in absolute terror—
'*kreplach!*' " (V737/B860).

Of the two, mothers are more insidious than fathers. If mothers
train their children for bureaucracies, fathers become impotent,
rendered ineffectual by officially sanctioned romantic dreams. Leni
Pökler

> knows about the German male at puberty. On their backs in the
> meadows and mountains, watching the sky, masturbating, yearning.
> Destiny waits, a darkness latent in the texture of the summer wind.
> Destiny will betray you, crush your ideals, deliver you into the same
> detestable Bürgerlichkeit as your father, sucking at his pipe on Sunday
> strolls after church past the row houses by the river—dress you in the
> gray uniform of another family man, and without a whimper you will
> serve out your time, fly from pain to duty, from joy to work, from com-
> mitment to neutrality. (V162/B189–90)

That males sell out quickly is obvious to their children, whose
hatred for their fathers curdles into contempt and indifference,
especially if the families are American. Lyle Bland's household is
typical. Bland is perhaps the most powerful man in America; on the
night he dies, his son goes to see *The Bride of Frankenstein*. Broderick
Slothrop is part of the "Father-conspiracy" (V679/B792) almost by
courtesy; he seems too foolish to be able to kill his son, as Tyrone
imagines him trying to do.

Although parent-child conflicts suggest Freudian topologies and
standard catalogs of repression, Pynchon stakes out a position at
some distance from Freud. For Pynchon the Oedipal complex is
more a symptom of an authoritarian social order than a source of
infection, or so the narrator indicates when he decides that the
Zone is a microcosm of the modern world:

> The Oedipal situation in the Zone these days is terrible. There is no
> dignity. The mothers have been masculinized to old worn moneybags of
> no sexual interest to anyone, and yet here are their sons, still trapped
> inside inertias of lust that are 40 years out of date. The fathers have no
> power today and never did, but because 40 years ago we could not kill
> them, we are condemned now to the same passivity, the same masochis-
> tic fantasies *they* cherished in secret, and worse, we are condemned in our
> weakness to impersonate men of power our own infant children must
> hate, and wish to usurp the place of, and fail.... So generation after
> generation of men in love with pain and passivity serve out their time in
> the Zone, silent, redolent of faded sperm, terrified of dying, desperately
> addicted to the comforts others sell them, however useless, ugly or
> shallow, willing to have life defined for them by men whose only talent
> is for death. (V747/B871–72)

Still, their helplessness makes parents agents of rationalization if only because they cannot resist the doctrines of commerce, payment, and exchange, "the damned Calvinist insanity" (V57/B66). The Counterforce, despite good intention, cannot surmount these temptations:

> They are as schizoid, as double-minded in the massive presence of money, as any of the rest of us, and that's the hard fact. The Man [Jive-Ass Mother Fucker?] has a branch office in each of our brains, his corporate emblem is a white albatross, each local rep has a cover known as the Ego, and their mission in this world is Bad Shit. We do know what's going on, and we let it go on. As long as we can see them, stare at them, those massively moneyed, once in a while. (V712–13/B831)

Ostensibly Freudian, the passage actually shifts the onus to Weber's repressive culture by asserting that economic constraints have entirely supplanted the ethical social norms that Freud found too rigid. The forms of guilt are different. Freud had great hopes for culture. He believed in the need "to strengthen the ego, to make it more independent of the super-ego, to widen its field of perception and enlarge its organization, so that it can appropriate fresh portions of the id. Where id was, there ego shall be. It is a work of culture."[23] Following Weber, Pynchon concludes that culture cannot liberate. Pynchon's civilization harbors different discontents.

Although Pynchon can hardly sidestep Freud's ideas, those he does borrow reinforce the novel's religious framework. Pynchon's affinities lie with T. S. Eliot rather than with mainstream psychoanalytic tradition, and his desire to hold a secular century accountable for its loss of faith makes him an indifferent psychologist. Besides, Freud's tripartite division of the self too much resembles the "false" dualities and boundaries rejected in the novel's historical survey of the West. Pynchon is far more comfortable with the lexicon of the behaviorists.

From its beachhead in childhood consciousness, the rationalized System can easily consolidate its power: the Preterite come to believe in the permanence of their disinheritance. By associating the Elect with the kind of deception practiced by mothers, Pynchon intimates that parental conditioning is just another category of artificial bureaucratization. By associating conditioning with Newtonian cause and effect, as spelled out by Pavlov ("His faith ultimately lay in a pure physiological basis for the life of the psyche. No effect without cause, and a clear train of linkages" [V89/B102]), Pynchon can exalt chance and paradox as sacred counters to the secular determinism.

Although "Their" power rests to an extent on behaviorist principles, it is also in Their interest to foster the concept of the romantic self, a tradition Pynchon believes is inherently dangerous (as manifest in Blicero) and near bankruptcy because it makes a fetish of the individual's search for an identity apart from his fellows and apart from the flow of life. They preach "your own individual life in time" (V697/B812), claims the narrator. Mondaugen the mystic has an answer, or at least a metaphor:

> Think of the ego, the self that suffers a personal history bound to time, as the grid. The deeper and true Self is the flow between cathode and plate. The constant, pure flow. Signals—sense-data, feelings, memories relocating—are put onto the grid, and modulate the flow. We live lives that are waveforms constantly changing with time, now positive, now negative. (V404/B470)

Other characters are more anguished. One of Pointsman's colleagues, Kevin Spectro, asks the Pavlovian, "When you've looked at how it really is, . . . how can we, any of us, be separate?" (V142/B165).

Dreams of destiny lead to sterile masturbation just as paranoia leads to solipsism, but the real threat arises from the isolation of the self, which permits Them to divide and conquer other humans. The concept of the romantic self stipulates a separateness made worse by epistemological confusion. Do human senses convey the world as it really is, with the consciousness largely passive, a theory sometimes known as the doctrine of immaculate perception, or do humans somehow project reality themselves, using stimuli shaped in personal configurations?[24]

Franz Pökler, for instance, must deal with this confusion when he cannot decide whether his daughter Ilse is really his own child. Pökler does accept the child as his own, and then, in a supreme act of courage, like Katje he "quit[s] the game" (V430/B502). His courage derives from his sojourn at Ground Zero, the V-2's test target, called the "Ellipse of Uncertainty," a safe place because the V-2 virtually never hits its target predictably. After this encounter with quasi-divine randomness and a night spent absorbing the information from a light bulb (V524–27/B610–15), Pökler emerges as the most moving character in Pynchon's book.

Although such episodes take the narrative some distance from conventional psychology, allusions to famous texts crop up frequently. From the many references to blackness and anality in *Gravity's Rainbow*, it is clear that Pynchon is invoking the works of Norman O. Brown, but not to the extent that one of the novel's critics claims.[25] The themes of Brown's *Life against Death* furnish Pynchon with a litmus test of conditioning. When Margherita

Erdmann taunts Slothrop with her fantasies of anal intercourse with black men, "hoping to trigger some race/sex reaction" (V446/B520), he does not respond. Although Slothrop dredges up culturally induced associations between blackness and excrement under sodium amytal, the linkages reflect adolescent anxieties exorcised by his surrealistic trip down the Roseland toilet: they have not crippled his consciousness.

Moreover, Brown's theories are a restatement of ideas drawn from Freud and Weber. Of the two, Weber takes pride of place among the influences behind *Gravity's Rainbow*. What remains of Freud in the novel is filtered through Weber, as in Pynchon's adaptation of paranoia to the imperatives of rationalization, and through Herbert Marcuse.[26] Marcuse, for example, sees promise in what he calls the "desublimation" of a rationalized culture, a goal that is to be accomplished through the "release of sensuality" and by the refusal of the individual to make sacrifices in the name of society. But he also stresses the power of rationalized structures and warns that established culture will probably co-opt rebellion, a notion that helps explain the failure of the Counterforce in *Gravity's Rainbow*.[27]

Ultimately, Pynchon could hardly be sympathetic to Freud's assertions that signs and symbols (especially of wit and humor, dreams, religion, and folklore) are the language of repression. Untrustworthy as they sometimes are, symbols, signs, and metaphors, particularly comic ones, are for Pynchon the crucifixes humans hold before vampires; they ward off evil—repression. Symbols are lightning rods for spiritual energy, drawing it to ground, sometimes literally, it would seem, as in the case of the Iron Toad (V603–4/B703–4) and other examples of electric revelation. *The Crying of Lot 49* described "the act of metaphor" as "a thrust at truth and a lie, depending where you were: inside, safe, or outside, lost." For all its ambiguity, the ability to metaphorize and symbolize is the most powerful weapon in the human psychological arsenal, and Pynchon's faith in its efficacy brings him down firmly on the side not of Freud but of his rival, Carl Jung.

Jung discounted many of Freud's theories, turning instead to a conviction that unsatisfied spiritual needs lead to personality disorders, a theme that Pynchon phrases and rephrases in *Gravity's Rainbow*. In opposition to Freud, Jung held that the libido is not an exclusively sexual force; for the Swiss it is the primal drive behind the will to live. A similar close association of libido with life clarifies Slothrop's negentropic function: his erections symbolize life itself. Allusions to Jung are frequent in the novel. Mondaugen's mystic vision (cited above), minus the electric terminology, might have been lifted from Jung's writings. Slothrop's ruminations on "four-fold expressions" (V624/B727) and the adventures of "the Floun-dering Four" (V674–81/B785–93), a sequence apparently spun out of childhood memory, recall Jung's fourfold division of the psyche.[28]

Rather more importantly for Pynchon's purposes, Jung recog-nized chance events as possible signs of the sacred and as indications of other worlds. With Wolfgang Pauli, Jung formulated a theory called "synchronicity," defined as "the simultaneous occurrence of two meaningful but not causally related events"[29] manifested apparently at random. Synchronicity represented Jung's attempt to use Heisenberg's principles to illuminate psychic states by wedding psychology and physics. In contrast to the Viennese school, which based its psychoanalytic methods on cause-and-effect relation-ships, Jung decided that causality was "a merely statistical truth and not absolute." Causality, he said,

> is a sort of working hypothesis of how events evolve out of one another, whereas synchronicity takes the coincidence of events in space and time as meaning something more than mere chance; namely, a peculiar inter-dependence of objective events among themselves as well as with the subjective (psychic) states of the observer or observers.[30]

As a theory, synchronicity articulates neatly with Jung's better-known theory of archetypes. About the latter the narrator of *Gravity's Rainbow* is typically paranoid, for he is afraid that rationalization can reach even into human dreams:

> It was nice of Jung to give us the idea of an ancestral pool in which every-body shares the same dream material. But how is it we are each visited as individuals, each by exactly and only what he needs? Doesn't that imply a switching-path of some kind? a bureaucracy? (V410/B478–79)

But Jung is postulating structures and linkages that subsist side by side with causal (or rationalized) order. At the deepest psychic level, humans do share a community of symbols, a true collectivity of which the corporate organization is only a parody. Moreover, Jung wishes to suggest that the two kinds of order can be bridged. In *Jung, Synchronicity, and Human Destiny*, Ira Progoff explicates Jung's think-ing in this fashion:

> The effective point of linkage is at the archetypal level. The specific archetypes that are active at the depth of an individual's existence are the means by which the general orderedness of the larger patterns of the macrocosm can come to specific expression at any moment of time. The archetypes are the vehicles by which the encompassing patterns of life are individualized in experience, and Synchronicity is the explana-

tory principle by which the chance and meaning of the intersection of these experiences in time may be recognized and comprehended.[31]

Jung believed that synchronicity was a key to religious experience. When archetypes surface in human experience, they reveal themselves in "auras" or "numinosity" of psychic intensity.[32] Unlike most psychologists, Jung thought that revelation could be authentic, and sympathized with those who put their trust in magic and dreams as avenues of religious expression. More than a few of the characters in *Gravity's Rainbow* clutch at omens, talismans, Tarot cards, astrology, sexual excesses, Kirghiz Lights, electric shocks, cabalistic practices, and drug rushes. Some of these, like the electric shocks, the drugs, and the sexual aberrations, do not produce authentic moments because they are contrived, deliberate, and self-conscious—incomprehensible, the narrator remarks, to "some angel stationed very high, watching us at our many perversities, crawling across black satin, gagging on whip-handles, licking the blood from a lover's vein-hit, all of it, every lost giggle or sigh, being carried on under a sentence of death whose deep beauty the angel has never been close to...." (V746/B871). Thwarted and frustrated by rationalization psychically internalized and culturally externalized, fearful of, but fascinated by, their own mortality, such characters push themselves to boundaries whose barriers remain impervious.

On the other hand, some characters do experience authentic revelation. Jung insisted that "spontaneity, even to the degree of absolute surprise,"[33] was essential to valid synchronistic events. If we assume that such events are spontaneous and authentic, the problem remains of knowing how to interpret them. Here training is desirable. Geli Tripping, in touch with chtonic powers, is an "apprentice-witch"; she must work in order to understand. When worlds collide, when "random" signals impact on consciousness, humans are usually too rationalized, too secularized, to achieve enlightment. Geli has learned to hold herself ready for synchronistic events; her magic merely opens doors between the psychic world of numinous archetypes and the physical world of statistical structures. Meaningful coincidence thus allows for the processing of information about both realms.

Despite many opportunities, Slothrop cannot muster enough effort to process his revelations. At times he seems to represent the abdication of the Protestant work ethic. "It'll get easier," says Semyavin when Slothrop complains about gathering data; "someday it'll all be done by machine. Information machines. You are the wave of the future" (V258/B300). Theoretically a "natural" information machine, Slothrop is twitted by the "Loonies on Leave" on the subject of "Entropy Management." One of the "nuts" hints that Slothrop's sources of information con him regularly, like three-card monte sidewalk dealers (V259–60/B301–2). The narrator embeds a Jungian explanation for Slothrop's growing inefficacy in the tale of Lyle Bland, the corporate czar. To get "a paranoid structure worthy of the name" out of Bland's many connections with industry would be difficult:

> Alas, the state of the art by 1945 was nowhere near adequate to that kind of data retrieval. . . . Those like Slothrop, with the greatest interest in discovering the truth, were thrown back on dreams, psychic flashes, omens, cryptographies, drug-epistemologies, all dancing on a ground of terror, contradiction, absurdity. (V582/B678)

Ironically, given his sins, Bland fares better than Slothrop as a medium of revelation. Bland's encounter with the sacred is refracted through Pynchon's comic genius. As a favor to a friend, Bland hires Bert Fibel to fix a shipment of pinball machines, all of which malfunction, either through "a randomness deliberately simulated" or "real random." Real or not, randomness usually signals the presence of another world, and the "surprise" here is that the other world is really there: the pinball machines house the inhabitants of "the planetoid Katspiel" (V584/B680) disguised as pinballs. As his reward, Bland is invited to join the Masons, to whom the pinball machines were consigned. Bland, made sensitive by his accidental encounter with the sacred, becomes a convert to magic and mystery:

> The magic in these Masonic rituals is very, very old. And way back in those days, it *worked*. As time went on, and it started being used for spectacle, to consolidate what were only secular appearances of power, it began to lose its zip. But the words, moves, and machinery have been more or less faithfully carried down over the millennia, through the grim rationalizing of the World, and so the magic is still there, though latent, needing only to touch the right sensitive head to reassert itself. (V588/B685)

The magic does work for Bland, who discovers in visions that the Earth is a unified "living critter." Bland steps out of time. Evidently his psychic journey is authentic, in contrast to those of other characters, who smoke, snort, or ingest narcotics, the principal drug being Oneirine.[34] Oneirine, another of Jamf's synthetics, produces dull hallucinations less important than the drug's property of "modulating" time. Gerhardt von Göll achieves a similar effect by running his final film, *New Dope*, backward to create the illusion of escape from temporal boundaries (V745/B869–70). Reversing time is far less urgent than real understanding. Bland may acquire it.

Slothrop does not. He "passes tests." He sleeps on Jamf's grave, and does not dream: "The absence of Jamf surrounds him like an odor, one he knows but can't quite name, an aura that threatens to go epileptic [Jung's term is *numinous*] any second" (V269/B313). (Byron the Bulb gives off information that can trigger epileptic fits in humans [V648/B756].) From this experience, he should realize that the mystery stimulus is irrelevant, that he is free, but he does not.

Because he does not, he never really understands that his sexuality is of the Earth itself, although he picks up clues before he floats off into the void of failed opportunities. Sexuality can be programmed to some extent by childhood experience and cultural reflex. Pirate Prentice can discharge semen to render a cryptographic message visible (a comic juxtaposition of sexuality and information-gathering) because he has been "conditioned to get a hardon in the presence of certain fetishes, and then conditioned to feel shame about his new reflexes" (V72/B82). With the message, The Firm has thoughtfully included a picture of a woman clad in "exactly the corselette of Belgian lace, the dark stockings and shoes he'd day-dreamed about . . . " (V71/B82). Margherita also wears a corset, which leads the narrator to reflect:

> How the penises of Western men have leapt, for a century, to the sight of this singular point at the top of a lady's stocking, this transition from silk to bare skin and suspender! It's easy for non-fetishists to sneer about Pavlovian conditioning and let it go at that, but any underwear enthusiast worth his unwholesome giggle can tell you there is much more here—there is a cosmology: of nodes and cusps and points of osculation, mathematical kisses...*singularities!* (V396/B461)

In this scene, Margherita has just met Slothrop, disguised as Max Schlepzig, "a random alias" (V395/B460), he tells her. "Random," she replies, out of her knowledge of the real Schlepzig, her costar in *Alpdrücken*; "another fairy-tale word." Hearing this new bit of information, Slothrop comes erect. Margherita asks Slothrop to whip her, to feed her "nostalgia" by providing "the pain of a return home" (V396/B461). At first reluctant, Slothrop is not sure how to proceed, "but somebody has already educated him." Almost in the same moment, however, he discovers that he cannot blame "his own cruelty" on conditioning. And when Slothrop recognizes his responsibility for his enjoying the beating he gives her, Margherita addresses him as the deity he almost is: "*God how you hurt me* . . ." (V397/B462).

Sadomasochistic acts are common in *Gravity's Rainbow* as attempts by characters to break through the boundaries of the individual self and to reestablish the sense of community that an impoverished spirituality has forestalled. Together the sadist and the masochist create a community of pain and shared fantasies within an erotic world of coherent proportions. No longer "strangers at the films," they are part of the film, the same film. Sexual perversions are reactions against the belief that life is determined, subject to social control. Implicit in the acts is a recognition of the limitations of the romantic self: the intent is to transcend that self by breaking free of its borders, perhaps by annihilating the self altogether in order to escape into void. In a rationalized culture, only sex and death remain mysterious. Aberrant behavior links the two under the banner of rebellion.

To participate in perverse acts is to join others in a theatrical uprising against an oppressive culture—or so the participants hope. The transgression of social taboos encourages mutual complicity, which in turn is designed to liberate. The release of sensuality counters social control. At least that is the argument, one version of which is advanced by Margherita's husband, Miklos Thanatz, a name that plays on Freud's concept of Thanatos. According to Thanatz, humans learn submission from their mothers, and as a result acquire the lust for dominance that is but the other side of the coin. He wishes to undercut the guilt-controls imposed by a rationalized society by fostering sadomasochism on a personal level. Playacting of this sort will rob the System of its power, as if by sympathetic magic:

> But why are we taught to feel reflexive shame whenever the subject comes up? Why will the Structure allow every other kind of sexual behavior but *that* one? Because submission and dominance are resources it needs for its very survival. They cannot be wasted in private sex. In *any* kind of sex. It needs our submission so that it may remain in power. It needs our lusts after dominance so that it can co-opt us into its own power game. There is no joy in it, only power. I tell you, if S and M could be established universally, at the family level, the State would wither away. (V737/B859–60)

The passage is a parody of theories advanced during the sixties. One of the gurus of that decade, Herbert Marcuse, did think that jettisoning guilt was a way of weakening a rationalized system:

> When in the context of an existence marked by knowledge it becomes

> possible to have real enjoyment without any rationalization and without
> the least puritanical guilt feeling, when sensuality, in other words, is
> entirely released by the soul, then the first glimmer of a new culture
> emerges.[35]

The "release of sensuality" would be accomplished, said Marcuse,
through what he called *desublimation*, an inversion of Freud's concept of sublimation, or the deferment of gratification for social
purposes.

On the other hand, Marcuse was quick to point out that the release of sensuality in a culture in which rationalization still held
"dominion" would result in desublimation with no real substance,
let alone true freedom for the individual. To the degree that
Western culture cements its hold over individuals by suppressing
the forms of sexuality and convincing humans to sacrifice themselves—or sublimate their impulses—for what Nalline Slothrop
(Tyrone's mother) calls "a Plan with a shape bigger than I can see"
(V682/B795), then giving free rein to sexuality would seem to be a
properly subversive response. But the chaos of the Zone—the
modern plateau of Western civilization—has merely loosened
certain sexual constraints, not abolished control; rationalization
still bestrides the culture and operates to channel impulses more
subtly. In such a society, Marcuse says in *Eros and Civilization*, the
apparently free libido

> continues to bear the mark of suppression and manifests itself in the
> hideous forms so well known in the history of civilization; in the sadistic
> and masochistic orgies of desperate masses, of "society elites," of starved
> bands of mercenaries, of prison and concentration-camp guards. Such
> release of sexuality provides a periodically necessary outlet for unbear-
> able frustration, it strengthens rather than weakens the roots of in-
> stinctual constraint; consequently, it has been used time and again as a
> prop for suppressive regimes.[36]

Deliberately, one suspects, Pynchon illustrates each of Marcuse's
examples in *Gravity's Rainbow*.[37] The sexuality released within the
context of a rationalized culture strengthens not Eros but Thanatos, for what Thanatz considers acts of liberation are merely
fantasies endorsed by the corporate state. "Look at the forms of
capitalist expression," Vanya tells Leni Pökler: "pornographies of
love, erotic love, Christian love, boy-and-his-dog, pornographies of
sunsets, pornographies of killing, and pornographies of deduc-
tion—*ahh*, that sigh when we guess the murderer—all these novels,
these films and songs they lull us with, they're approaches, more
comfortable and less so, to that Absolute Comfort. . . . The self-
induced orgasm. . . . Most of it's solitary. You know that" (V155/

B181). The more a culture promotes sexual release, through pornography and commercialization or exploitation of sensuality, the
more sexuality loses its erotic power to subvert control.

Thus, in searching for community, in trying to overcome isolation, the S and M enthusiast retreats to groupings of anonymity
that do not overcome the anguish of separation from his fellows. By
fitting their selves into stereotyped roles of master and slave, or
victimizer and victim, characters like Margherita and Thanatz enter
the anonymity of those types: their willingness masochistically to
accept pain or to inflict it sadistically attests to their interchange-
ability with one another. They aim at a fraudulent community, or
worse, at a fraudulent transcendence, a romantic rapture that is
death-oriented. When the burden of whatever autonomy is given to
the psyche becomes insupportable, they seek not to dismantle the
self's domestic bureaucracies but to obliterate them entirely.
Ironically, Blicero reproaches Katje for her desire to live, despite her
participation in his deadly fantasies:

> Her masochism . . . is reassurance for her. That she can still be hurt,
> that she is human and can cry at pain. . . . She raises her ass not in sur-
> render, but in despair. . . . But of true submission, of letting go the self
> and passing into the All, there is nothing, not with Katje.
> (V662/B771–72)

Pynchon's sources are grist for his comedy. Marcuse's reflections
crop up in many places in *Gravity's Rainbow*, but those concerning the
corporate co-option of the libido surface most amusingly in the brief
tale of James Jello. A rebellious crowd of workers sees "bareass
Crown Prince Porfirio with a giant halo of aluminum-shaving curls
on his head, his mouth made up with black grease, his soft buttocks
squirming against the cold refuse picking up steel splinters that
sting deliciously," whereupon "the march pauses in some confusion
as these most inept revolutionaries fall to arguing whether the apparition is a diversionary nuisance planted here by the Management, or whether he's real Decadent Aristocracy . . . " (V698/
B814). Marcuse extends the concept of co-opted desublimation into
the realm of human cultural types, and Pynchon follows him here as
well. Although certain figures of popular culture seem to oppose
the dominant social order, Marcuse thinks that what appears to be
aberrant, off-beat, or outlawed simply reinforces rationalization:

> the vamp, the national hero, the neurotic housewife, the gangster, the
> star, the charismatic tycoon . . . are no longer images of another way
> of life but rather freaks or types of the same life, serving as an affirma-
> tion rather than negation of the established order.[38]

That is why John Dillinger's bloody talismanic T-shirt cannot rescue Slothrop from dissolution, and why the Counterforce—freakish members all—cannot prevail. Even the drug subculture simply replicates the market economy of rationalized capitalism. Marcuse's warnings notwithstanding, Pynchon peoples his novel with freaks who do manage small insights even as they imitate more authoritarian power structures. When Seaman Bodine mounts the First International Runcible Spoon Fight, for instance, he invents a model of the War, a little corporate State whose legitimacy turns on the willingness of the combatants to fight for a cause. Since the enterprise is so clearly commercial, visible in a way that the economics of the War are not, St. John Bladdery and Avery Purfle, the contestants, refuse to fight to the death although they hear "Death in all its potency humming them romantic tunes, chiding them for moderate little men...*So far and no farther, is that it? You call that living?*" (V598/B697). If humans could "desublimate" the culture of which this prize ring is just a mockery, there would be no obscene War, no masturbatory Destiny, no corporate Thanatos. Numerous other popular types in the novel find minor illuminations, limited victories, small mercies; few effectively challenge cultural superstructures.

What saves these characters from what would otherwise be the weight of cynicism is the author's humanity, usually conveyed through comedy but just as often through a compassion that is Pynchon's ultimate claim to superlative artistry. Pynchon is nowhere more compassionate than in his depictions of authentic pain and shame. Measured against the debasement of spirit that Pynchon sees as the principal affliction of the twentieth-century wasteland, sexual aberrations, though frequently distasteful, are more human than alien. In an extended discussion of the most notorious scene in the novel, Paul Fussell, in *The Great War and Modern Memory*, decides that Brigadier Pudding's theatrical ritual of coprophagia furnishes modern literature with a perfect paradigm of the wasteland. The guilt, the humiliation, the excrement, the sterility combine in "the style of classic English pornographic fiction of the grossly masochistic type, the only style, Pynchon implies, adequate to memories of the Great War." The fantasies are condoned by the powers that be, but they are all that the Brigadier has. "It is a fantastic scene," says Fussell, "disgusting, ennobling, and touching, all at once."[39] In death Pudding joins the Counterforce, for all the good that it can do.

Not every character suffers from inner ordinances stiffened by external conditioning. Slothrop feels no shame at his sexual readiness, nor is he in love with his own or "his race's" death,[40] as his detractors claim (V738/B861). His fertility is divine, or, by way of saying the same thing, intensely human. "Fuck you" is "the only spell he knows, and a pretty good all-purpose one at that" (V203/B236). He encounters many females, but his intercourse with Geli Tripping best illustrates his potential. One fresh morning the two enjoy intercourse on top of the Brocken while the rising sun—itself a symbol of fertility—casts their copulating shadows on the World itself. Their images are godlike: "Geli grabs for Slothrop's cock. Slothrop leans to bite Geli's tit. They are enormous, dancing the floor of the whole visible sky" (V330/B384). The moment is delightful, merry, healthily erotic—one of Slothrop's finest. But it is flawed by Slothrop's inability to commit himself. He cannot love, and sex without love does not render wastelands fruitful.

During the course of an argument of the relative merits of Rossini and Beethoven, Säure claims that "with Rossini, the whole point is that lovers always get together, isolation is overcome, and like it or not that is the one great centripetal movement of the World. Through the machineries of greed, pettiness, and the abuse of power, *love occurs*. All the shit is transmuted to gold. The walls are breached, the balconies are scaled—listen!" (V440/B513). Earlier the narrator has observed that Rossini's *La Gazza Ladra* promises "love without payment of any kind...." (V274/B318); i.e., love free from the taint of contracts and rationalized exchange.

To say that such love is rare in *Gravity's Rainbow* is to understate. Love is a fragile shield in the armed camp of rationalization; the narrative twice repeats the slogan "An Army of Lovers Can Be Beaten" (V155, 158/B181, 185). That it can persist and defend at all is a matter of grace, but grace, as Edison said of genius, is mostly hard work in Pynchon's fiction. Even so, accident has a lot to do with love's occurrence. For example, Tyrone and Katje "are not, after all, to be lovers in parachutes of sunlit voile, lapsing gently, hand in hand, down to anything meadowed or calm. Surprised?" (V222/B259), asks the narrator.

Out of Slothrop's dreams emerges a mandala pattern of childhood, "The Floundering Four," one of whose aspects is "miraculous Myrtle," a girl with clear resemblance to Katje. For all her talents, of use to Slothrop in his pursuit of the "Radiant Hour," Myrtle, like Katje, lacks the ability to love; it is a "miracle" denied her (V675/B787). In the same passage, the narrator observes that homosexuals suffer from the same deficiency. That he is not referring to sterility per se is obvious from the narrator's earlier paean to homosexual love in the past, just at the onset of the waste-land, when faces could still be touched by signs of the sacred:

> In the trenches of the First World War, English men came to love one another decently, without shame or make-believe, under the easy like-lihoods of their sudden deaths, and to find in the faces of other young men evidence of otherworldly visits, some poor hope that may have helped redeem even mud, shit, the decaying pieces of human meat.... (V616/B718)

Now, the narrator complains, "In this latest War, death was no enemy, but a collaborator. Homosexuality in high places is just a carnal afterthought now, and the real and only fucking is done on paper...." (V616/B718). Or, he might add—on film, on plastic, on Imipolex G, on whatever surfaces will support an eroticism warped out of alignment with affection.

Actually, Pynchon implies in other places, the drawback to homo-sexuality is its narcissism, a fairly standard critique of homoeroti-cism. When Blicero torments Gottfried, for example, he torments himself. Love is supposed to proffer a window on the soul, not a mirror. The narcissistic aspect of his character diminishes Enzian, who can hardly bear the thought of Blicero's death because with-out his former lover "there is no heart, anywhere now, no human heart left in which I exist" (V660/B769). Redeemed to an extent by his willingness to open himself to risk, to "deepest possibilities for shame, for sense of loss renewed, for humiliation and mockery" (V659/B767), Enzian ultimately escapes gross polarities and binary deadlock by abstracting himself to a zero state of solitude. Duty, courage, and wisdom do not always grant what humans most desire.

The extremes of love in the novel are represented by Blicero and Roger Mexico. Blicero's ideal is passion enflamed: "not to love because it was no longer possible to act...but to be helplessly in a condition of love...." (V97/B112). He yearns to be cindered by radiance. Mexico, on the other hand, gravitates toward the some-what naïve faith that love will guide him "to life and to joy" (V126/B147). Having lost Jessica, he feels that "he's losing a full range of life, of being for the first time at ease in the Creation" (V629/B733).

But love is rarely so majestic, Pynchon seems to warn. Love is *real* enough—it radiates outward from the Advent church. That it per-sists is evident in the eagerness with which characters pursue it and in the poignancy with which they regard its loss. It survives in the many acts of kindness that illuminate the most trivial of encounters in the novel. Looking at Mexico and Jessica at a party, Pirate Prentice feels himself "suddenly, dodderer and ass, taken by an ache in his skin, a simple love for them both that asks nothing but their safety, and that he'll always manage to describe as something else— 'concern,' you know, 'fondness....' " (V35/B40). And, to cite only one other example, Nora Dodson-Truck pulls Carroll Eventyr inside her pentacle, "her way with anyone she loved. . . . One couldn't be too safe, there was always evil...." (V145/B169).

The need for safety can yield to the hunger for security, of course, and security is often at odds with personal freedom. Roger loses Jessica to Jeremy because the latter offers her middle-class stability and material comfort. Leni Pökler tries to love freely, without jealousy, without possessiveness, and without dependence on others. Her flight leads to a concentration camp, from which she emerges as the prostitute Solange, one "among the accidents of this drifting Humility, never quite to be extinguished, a few small chances for mercy...." (V610/B711). Brave as it has been, Leni's love has sustained massive defeats. That Pynchon endorses her efforts, however, is certain; he preserves her by "accident." What grace there is in Pynchon's world descends upon those who dare.

Against larger cabals, individuals oppose small conspiracies of compassion. Generous women—and one wonderful pig—provide Slothrop with companionship or sanctuary. Despite their preoccupation with dealing for profit, tough-guy black marketeers like Gerhardt von Göll and Blodgett Waxwing allow that friendship counts for something, and Pynchon even undercuts the sentimental cliché of the lone soldier covering the retreat of his fellows by convincing us that Klaus Närrisch sacrifices himself because he really cares. The death of Tantivy Mucker-Maffick leaves his loyalty to Slothrop untarnished, and Seaman Bodine tries to hold on to Slothrop when the latter fades into the cleft between worlds. Bonds of concern and affection unite the members of the Counterforce, at least for a time.

Yet individuals also betray their affections. It is easy to love in childhood, much harder in maturity, as perhaps only Leni Pökler fully understands. "We can get away," Bianca says to Slothrop; "I'm a child, I know how to hide. I can hide you too."

> He knows she can. He knows. Right here, right now, under the makeup and the fancy underwear, she *exists*, love, invisibility.... For Slothrop this is some discovery. (V470/B548)

The life expectancy of innocence is even shorter than that of love.

Doting girls become devious parents, members of the "Mother Conspiracy," and youthful swains become impotent fathers. The heroes of the Counterforce succumb to their own fears, become co-opted by the systems they have fought. Love grows fitfully in the interstices of continuously rationalized grids, like flowers along roads shortly to be interdicted. Sooner or later love becomes institutionalized, and institutions, by definition, belong to "Them."

But while it lasts, love shines. Spurred by love for his lemming, who is apparently racing toward suicide in the Baltic, confident that "love can stop it from happening" (V556/B648), Ludwig does rescue Ursula. Ludwig is a child, not yet corrupted by rationalization, although by the time he finds his pet he is well on his way to becoming a sexual entrepreneur. "So not all lemmings go over the cliff," says the narrator, "and not all children are preserved against snuggling into the sin of profit. To expect any more, or less, of the Zone is to disagree with the terms of the Creation" (V729/B851), which apparently does make a small place for love. Similarly, because as a witch she stands outside society, Geli Tripping can love Tchitcherine. She tracks him with painstaking devotion. Her magic and her labor secure the Russian's love. It is a triumph, but a rare one.

Rossini to the contrary, love does not serve as the axis of Pynchon's world. Yet it endures in the wasteland, against all odds, as Franz Pökler's story proves. When Pökler finally stumbles out of his cloister, he faces the ruins of his own and his race's humanity. In the concentration camp, among the stacked corpses, he overcomes his impotence with a gesture small but lit with love, and Pynchon sets his seal upon it. Pökler bestows his wedding ring on one of the few occupants still living in the charnel house, a woman chosen at *random*. The gesture gives meaning to Geli Tripping's song:

> Love never goes away,
> Never completely dies,
> Always some souvenir
> Takes us by sad surprise.
>
> (V289/B337)

---

1. Marcus Smith, "*Gravity's Rainbow*: A Jeremiad for Now," paper presented at the MLA convention, special session on Pynchon, Chicago, Illinois, December 1977.

2. Walter J. Ong, *The Presence of the Word: Some Prolegomena to Cultural and Religious History* (New York: Simon & Schuster, 1967), p. 162.

3. Daniel Boorstin, *The Americans: The Democratic Experience* (New York: Random House, 1973), p. 415.

4. Thomas Pynchon to Thomas F. Hirsch, January 8, 1968. I am indebted to Mr. Hirsch for bringing this letter to my attention.

5. See, for example, the "two station-marks . . . 1966 and 1971" (V739/ B862).

6. Pynchon also mentions several other volumes he consulted during the writing of *V.*, and Hirsch wrote back, suggesting books that Pynchon might want to look at. Thomas F. Hirsch to Joseph W. Slade, September 8, 1975.

7. The doctrine of eternal recurrence raises sticky questions, for recurrence implies a closed system, more or less determined, in which chance is not possible. Thomas Mann, who dealt with the same concept, and who may have influenced Pynchon, handled the contradiction in a particularly shrewd fashion: see Joseph W. Slade, "The Function of Eternal Recurrence in Thomas Mann's *Joseph and His Brothers*," *Symposium* 25 (Summer, 1971): 180–97.

8. Pynchon refers to Lewis Mumford's *The City in History* in his letter to Hirsch.

9. Herbert Marcuse, "The Affirmative Character of Culture," in *Negations*, trans. Jeremy J. Shapiro (Boston: Beacon Press, 1968), p. 125.

10. In the fairy tale, Gretel saves Hansel by pushing the witch into the oven. After various adventures, Hansel is changed into a fawn, but is retransformed to a man and marries Gretel.

11. Lawrence Wolfley, in "Repression's Rainbow: The Presence of Norman O. Brown in Pynchon's Big Novel," *PMLA* 92 (October, 1977): 873–89, suggests that Blicero speaks for the author, thus putting Pynchon in the odd position of appearing to defend a fascist mind-set he has written 760 pages to attack.

12. Pynchon to Hirsch, January 8, 1968.

13. Except that Byron at the novel's end is still giving off light, whereas Slothrop has disappeared.

14. Marshall McLuhan, *Understanding Media: The Extensions of Man* (New York: Signet, 1964), p. 23.

15. Lancelot L. Whyte, "Atomism, Structure, and Form," in *Structure in Art and Science*, ed. Gyorgy Kepes (New York: Braziller, 1965), p. 27.

16. Lewis S. Feuer, *Einstein and the Generations of Science* (New York: Basic Books, 1974), p, 174.

17. William Irwin Thompson, *At the Edge of History* (New York: Harper Colophon, 1971), p. 121.

18. Wernher von Braun and Frederick I. Ordway, III, *History of Rocketry and Space Travel* (New York: Crowell, 1966), pp. 110–11.

19. Daniel Simberloff, "Entropy, Information, and Life: Biophysics in the Novels of Thomas Pynchon," *Perspectives in Biology and Medicine* 21 (Summer, 1978): 617.

20. See Simberloff, pp. 619–20, for amplification.

21. Douglas R. Hofstadter, *Gödel, Escher, Bach: An Eternal Golden Braid* (New York: Basic Books, 1979), p. 9.

22. Dr. Ilya Prigogine, a Belgian chemist, won the prize for his study of chemical reactions in which substances interact with their surroundings toward greater order. Prigogine decided that the second law of thermodynamics operates only in closed systems. Life, however, is not a closed system.

23. Sigmund Freud, "New Introductory Lectures," in Standard Edition of *Complete Psychological Works*, ed. James Strachey (London: Hogarth and the Institute of Psycho-Analysis, 1964), 22:80.

24. For a fuller discussion of these analogies, see Joseph W. Slade, *Thomas Pynchon* (New York: Warner Paperback Library, 1974), chapter six.

25. See Wolfley, n. 11, above.

26. Marcuse's *Eros and Civilization* (New York: Vintage, 1955), seems to have been especially influential on Pynchon, particularly with the novel *V.*

27. Marcuse, *Eros and Civilization*, pp. 184–85. See also his "The Obsolescence of the Freudian Concept of Man," in *Five Lectures*, ed. Jeremy J. Shapiro and Shierry M. Weber (Boston: Little, Brown, 1970).

28. Jung's fondness for the Yang/Yin principle as an expression of the relationship between dualities is echoed in the novel as well.

29. Carl Jung, quoted in Arthur Koestler, *The Roots of Coincidence* (New York: Vintage, 1973), p. 94.

30. Carl C. Jung, "Foreword" to *I Ching: or Book of Changes*, trans. Cary F. Baynes from the German translation of Richard Wilhelm, 3d ed. (Princeton: Princeton University Press, 1950), p. xxiv.

31. Ira Progoff, *Jung, Synchronicity, and Human Destiny* (New York: Delta Books, 1975), p. 144.

32. Ibid., p. 108.

33. Ibid., p. 120.

34. Pynchon may have read Kenneth Anger's prospectus for *Kustom Kar Kommandos* or seen the single segment of this still uncompleted film. Described as an "oneiric vision," the film contains rainbows and rites not dissimilar to those in *Gravity's Rainbow*. See P. Adams Sitney, *Visionary Film: The American Avant-Garde* (New York: Oxford University Press, 1974), pp. 124–28.

35. Marcuse, "The Affirmative Character of Culture," pp. 116–17. W. T. Lhamon believes that Pynchon pays a kind of homage to Marcuse in setting *V.* in 1955, the year of publication of *Eros and Civilization* (W. T. Lhamon to Joseph W. Slade, November 20, 1979). I am indebted to James Seaton's "Critical Theory and Popular Culture: The Example of Marcuse," *Markham Review* 9 (Spring, 1980): 56-59, for much of the discussion here.

36. Marcuse, *Eros and Civilization*, pp. 184–85.

37. See the orgy on board the *Anubis* (V466–68/B543–46), the Mecklenburg dog village (V614/B715–16), and the homosexual 175-Stadt (V665–67/B775–77).

38. Herbert Marcuse, *One-Dimensional Man* (Boston: Beacon Press, 1954), p. 59.

39. Paul Fussell, *The Great War and Modern Memory* (New York: Oxford University Press, 1977), pp. 330, 333.

40. Slothrop responds sexually to chaos, and perhaps to things artificial or "dead," but such responses do not indicate that he is in love *with* death.

The New Consciousness
and the Old System

By Raymond M. Olderman

Gravity's Rainbow records the crisis of a new world view trying to emerge from the ruins of World War II. It records a change in Western consciousness—the decay of an old way of describing reality and the struggle to articulate a new way. It is a controversial book because for many readers its narrator reveals a new consciousness. The very idea that a new consciousness and a new description of reality has emerged in the latter half of the twentieth century polarizes people, particularly in the religious and intellectual communities. In Pynchon's history of Western consciousness, the old world view—with its rationalism and institutional religions, its Newtonian science and great chain of being—has entropied. It has reached a doddering old age and become a romantic totalitarianism of the soul; it has become the launching pad for the Nazi mind.

The new world view, on the other hand, has been trying to get off the ground for some time. It has emerged slowly from evolutionary theory and from a post-Einsteinian conception of physical reality. It broke into mass political life in the sixties. Since then the polarization between those who find hope in the possibility of a new consciousness and those who believe in the continued truthfulness of the old world view has intensified. I think *Gravity's Rainbow* speaks profoundly to those who believe in a new consciousness. It comes closer than anything before it to synthesizing a new world view and embodying that view in the behavior of humans. It is an apocalyptic book in the sense that it speaks in code to a community of outsiders who share belief in a new consciousness but find themselves losing hope.

In the late sixties and early seventies (a period Pynchon

specifically refers to), such people called themselves "freaks." *Gravity's Rainbow* records the interplay between freaks and defenders of the old world view, and it offers a sympathetic critique of the freak's version of the new consciousness. Most important, it demonstrates how the new world view and the new consciousness coexist in each of us with the old consciousness and its dying world view. Defenders of the old world view are "straights." But we all have both straight and freak aspects of consciousness that coexist like the left and right hemispheres of the brain. By embodying these two interacting aspects of our personal and communal consciousness in individual characters, Pynchon is able to literally set two conflicting world views in motion. And he is able to imply through his narrator a more incisive world view than either straight or freak.

The old world view is equated with the Father, with Patriarchy, with the "White Metropolis," with the Man, with Them—and it primarily has hold on the men of *Gravity's Rainbow*. It has created a "branch office in their brains" and a "colonial outpost" in their bodies. Men like Slothrop, Tchitcherine, Enzian, Pökler, Mexico, Pirate Prentice, Fat Ludwig, Lyle Bland, and Igor Blobadjian have to go through a spiritual/political journey in order to escape their own patriarchal behavior. As I shall try to show, the journey forces them to abandon their absolute straightness, their solipsistic machismo, and become freaky. They have to escape the Major Marvy part of their consciousness, find someone like Geli Tripping, and be transformed—whisked away to the invisible realm of the "Titans' subcreation." But, they cannot simply transcend—as Bland and Blobadjian do—they must be transformed, returned to earthly life from the realm of the freak, returned as a new creature embodying a new interplay of straight and freak consciousness.

Freaks are a new kind of cultural and literary outsider. They are inside-outsiders—people who perceive themselves as trapped in the System, and who want Out. Their journeys begin with some revelation of the System's injustice. As they travel outward, they keep uncovering new dimensions of the insider's world, moving from discovery to discovery, recognizing the System to be a series of interlocking institutions. Ideally, they also uncover the metaphoric systems of interpretation that interlock to give power to institutions. Ultimately, the journey turns toward pursuit of a new consciousness that can exist outside the reigning institutional and metaphoric System, outside the realm of the old consciousness. It becomes the pursuit of mystery rather than solution, not an escape from reality but a return to reality in its multiple fullness.

The key element of the journey is the encounter between freak and straight. Such encounters happen often, and their function is to reveal the world views of both freak and straight, and to mark the freak's particular stage of progress toward getting Out of the System. In *Gravity's Rainbow*, the encounter between freak and straight is played within a perceptual framework of such breadth and profundity that it is transformed from a simple cultural phenomenon into a genuine feature of a complex emerging world view. As I hope to demonstrate, this encounter embodies a genuinely mythic struggle between two aspects of an evolving communal consciousness; between a new world view and an old world view; between yin and yang; change and stability; multiplex, stoned thinking and single-dimension, linear thinking; between nonordinary and ordinary experiences; between new gods and old; between life and death.

The terms *freak* and *straight* are problematic because of their cultural usage, but they are necessary to reveal how Pynchon transmutes the terms of a living cultural phenomenon into a complex philosophical perspective. Further, since he is affirming something that is more than a philosophical perspective—he is affirming a living possibility—it is important to use terms that link his profundity to observable culture. Clearly, Pynchon demonstrates that each of us is both freak and straight, and the rich interplay such a concept provides is the dynamic underlying his synthesis and critique of the freak world view. It is the dynamic underlying his full-fledged alternate description of the physical, spiritual, and moral cosmos.

There are, however, less complex uses of this encounter, and before examining Pynchon's profound creation, it might be helpful—in understanding the extent of his accomplishment—to discuss some basic features of the encounter using examples from places where straight and freak are taken more literally. In a simple encounter between a straight and a freak, the straight always has the ultimate power—always. Invisibility is the freak's only protection. Unless freaks remain invisible, they cannot protect the flickering dimensions of their world view from either destruction or co-optation by the straight world. Invisibility is the currency of the freak world. With it the freak can keep moving, perhaps find the way Out, perhaps become statistically lost, a single particle responding to "the law of large numbers"—uncertainly located. It would be very difficult, if it were necessary, for a freak to actually hide from the straight world since that world is so densely layered, so nearly omniscient, so clearly omnipotent. But, fortunately, hiding is unnecessary because straights cannot see beyond incon-sequentially weird appearances to what is invaluably freaky. When they do, they are no longer straight. Freaks can remain invisible right out in the open if they accept their invisibility along with the useful but sad knowledge that straights will never comprehend them.

In any encounter with a freak, straights generally feel they are "winning" the meeting, coming out on top, virtuously using their power to dominate a weak type of person who needs, and probably even wants, domination. But because straights embrace the ordinary, freaks have the advantage that comes with a fuller awareness of what is happening—including an awareness of the straight's desire to dominate. It is this situation that tinges all en-counters between straight and freak, whether they are confronta-tions or simple exchanges, with the comic. The freak, or the inside-outsider, borrows from the tradition of the oppressed to create a new version of the mythical trickster. Even in the most complex versions of the inside-outsider, an element of the trickster always remains because the trickster is both humorous and invisible—two instruments of survival necessary in the freak world view. Here is a basic example of the trickster-freak in action, taken from Richard M. Dorson's collection of what he calls a genuine, hippie folk culture:

> One late afternoon, this hippie walked into a grocery store and said, "I'd like to buy some dog food."
> The storeowner looked at him and asked him, "You got a dog?" The hippie replied, "Yes." He said, "Well, prove it to me."
> So the hippie goes out the door, half an hour later comes back, shows the owner the dog, the owner sells him the dog food, and the hippie goes about his way.
> About half an hour later the same hippie came in, said, "I'd like some birdseed." The storeowner looked at him, said, "Do you have a bird?" The hippie replied, "Yes." Storeowner said, "Prove it to me."
> So he goes out, comes back about half an hour later, has this bird in a bird cage, says, "Here." So the storeowner sold him the birdseed and he walks on.
> About half an hour later he comes in with a shoebox under his arm, with a hole cut in the top. Storeowner looks at him and says, "What do you want?" He said, "Stick your hand in this box." Storeowner stuck his hand in the box, and was feeling around and said, "What's in here?" The hippie replied, "What does that feel like to you?"
> Said, "Feels like shit."
> Said, "That's right. I want a roll of toilet paper."[1]

This is an old joke remade. Freaks are eclectic; they value multiple perspectives and new connections. Their humor, like all freak enterprises, borrows from everyplace it can—from slapstick to verbal wit. In its new form, the joke revolves around a simple piece of stoned thinking. In response to the straight storeowner's literal-minded approach to reality, and his attempt to dominate, the hippie makes a connection about the general principle the storeowner is acting from and applies that to a specific gesture of rejection. The gesture itself provides extra connections for the stoned thinker. Freaks love to joke about the straight world's distaste for all things organic—and about shit in particular. They see the straight world as obsessed with hiding and saving shit in big toilet rooms as ardently as they hide and save money in big bank vaults. It is a standard connection in the freak world view. Both Ishmael Reed and Thomas Pynchon use it to make further suggestions about the straight's attitude toward the nonwhite races, toward the ego's relationship to the Other, and toward the whole nature of change and of death. Straights always want to hang on to things: "Shit, money, and the Word," Pynchon says, are "the three American truths" (V28/B31).

A somewhat more sophisticated development of the basic encounter between freak and straight appears in Gurney Norman's *Divine Right's Trip,* the novel from *The Whole Earth Catalog.* When Divine Right and Estelle visit the luxurious camper of the Lone Outdoorsman for steak and TV, their meeting is like an encounter between total aliens. One of the freaks—Divine Right—doesn't have it together, is stoned and loose-ended, and is potentially vulnerable to blowing his invisibility as a freak. Not having it together is the psychological counterpart to a failure in connection-making—a cosmic failure to a freak, since a successful trip outside the System is dependent on making connections. "The failure to make connections," says E. L. Doctorow in *The Book of Daniel,* "is complicity in the system." The danger involved in this failure is not that Divine Right might get caught by the straight, by the Lone Outdoorsman, but that he will end up acting like a straight and risk getting caught up in the straight world. But Estelle *does* have it together, and—like many other female freaks in current fiction—she handles the situation. The Lone Outdoorsman is, of course, Fatherly throughout the entire encounter—Fatherly is the major role for straights.

The incident of their encounter is much too long to quote, but in its course the straight evokes the logic of authority, Archie Bunker style, in order to construct a rationale for a narrow set of prejudices based on thoughtless devotion to form and order. The freaks pile up connections all around the straight, but he never notices. He is not left out; he is not humiliated for someone else's sport; he cannot lose. He has authority on his side—and besides, how could he ever possibly be left out? By definition, the freaks are outsiders, and the straight hardly ever forgets that fact. Contrary to the expected, this *increases* the freaks' fun. It affirms their invisibility, gives them a sense of distance from the System and therefore a sense of both spiritual progress and political virtue. And it leaves them safe to pursue a way Out—safe from the constant threat of violence, the rioting policeman that occupies the heart of the straight world's response to anything it cannot dominate. It is as if all their connections are happening in another dimension, unwinding all around the straight, who marches on with sturdy linear confidence that nothing is happening anywhere around him except a little noise. The reader waits for a collision, but it never comes. The freaks do not need to win—they do not need the straight's recognition of narrowness. They want to enjoy an event, not a victory.

The freak and the reader may be in on the joke, but the joke in the freak world view is not on people—it is on decayed forms of consciousness, thought, attitude, behavior, language, outlook, and belief. When people participate with earnest conviction and confidence in decayed forms of any kind, they become laughable—sad and dangerous, too, but laughable. In the encounter between straight and freak, the straight invariably is trapped by devotion to old forms because he or she does not make connections that stray beyond metaphors made by others. Such a position limits the imagination. It makes the straight dour and given to overkill—instead of new insights and connections, the straight must reassert the same connections, pushing harder, louder, longer. When freak humor gets very broad, as with Pointsman in *Gravity's Rainbow*, the straight can become an old-time villain whose power over the freak always fails because the villain gets tangled in the elaborate rules of his own machinations. When freak humor gets "heavy"—weighted with serious or cosmic connections—the straight's inability to change, to let go, puts him or her squarely in the kingdom of death. "You eat rays and for snacks you munch on sound," Ishmael Reed says of the straights, or Atonists, as he calls them:

> Loading up on data is slumber and recreation is disassembling. Transplanting is real big here. Sometimes you play switch brains and hide the heart. Lots of marching. Soon as these Like-Men disappear walking single file down the hall here comes another row of you. The Atonists got rid of their spirit 1000s of years ago with Him. The flesh is next. Plastic will soon prevail over flesh and bones. Death will take over. Why is it Death you like? Because then no 1 will keep you up all night with that racket dancing and singing. The next morning you can get up and

build, drill, progress putting up skyscrapers and . . . and . . . and . . . working and stuff. You know? Keeping busy.[2]

Freaks, on the other hand, are relatively free from devotion to form and particularly free from linear cause-and-effect logic, free to inhabit elaborate fantasies from a variety of perspectives, and to pursue connections for the sake of the process. They do not need to get anything done—except to preserve freakiness itself, to preserve a minority way of life largely invisible to the majority, to keep intact the possibility of alternate realities. Much of the freak world view is dependent on the connections made in that stoned dimension invisible to straights. Verbally, it can be an incredible weaving of dreams, visions, fantasies, movie clichés, and mind games. To the freak, all these intangibles are features of reality and are valid experiences just as much, or nearly as much, as any physical action in the tangible world. Like seventeenth-century metaphysical poets, freaks delight in bizarre connections, in following the process of stoned thinking in order to visualize the connections being made. The content of the connections is less important than the process of connecting. As Pynchon often indicates, one thing that connection-making can lead to is a sense of the mysterious connectedness of things; it can lead to a model of the mystic's experience with unity. Connection-making also buffers freaks from alienation and assures them that there are mysterious continuities in the universe; it aids them in pursuing a way Out of the layered fantasies of the System. By exploring the multiple possibilities of any given set of connections, the freak gains access to the unseen dimensions of reality. The opening pages of *Gravity's Rainbow* present what could be Pirate Prentice's dream, or an allegorical statement by the mysterious narrator, or a fantasy that Pirate has to manage for someone else— like the fantasy of the giant Adenoid he manages for Lord Blatherard Osmo. Before we can figure it out, we are thrown into new connections—Pirate's bananas, incoming rockets, song-and-dance routines, the machinations of the Firm, and so on. To make the reverberating connections demanded by these pages, a reader must have something like a freak's love of altered perceptions and a freak's tolerance for uncertainty.

The freak's world is not absurd; it may be surrounded by absurdity as it is surrounded by straights, but it has its covert continuities. The freak world view—in its more profound versions, as in *Gravity's Rainbow*—helps provide the balance of a potentially kinder universe, a universe of possibility *and* probability where all things are animated, overflowing with life, and waiting to "get it to-

gether." The freak world view celebrates the possibility of action—
even if the action is invisible. It celebrates the continuance of life
and the secret preservation of alternate realities. Without it, freaks
know themselves to be a scattered community—waiting in the
kingdom of death.

II

> You go from dream to dream inside me. You have passage to my last
> shabby corner, and there, among the debris, you've found life. I'm no
> longer sure which of all the words, images, dreams or ghosts are "yours"
> and which are "mine." It's past sorting out. We're both being someone
> new now, someone incredible.... (V177/B207)

In *Gravity's Rainbow*, freaks and straights are not only people, they
are aspects of a single individual's consciousness and aspects of a
communal consciousness. The conflict between them is transformed into a conflict with multiple reverberations, aimed finally at
demonstrating fundamentally different ways of dealing with the
underlying structures of reality. And yet, for Pynchon there is one
point of similarity between straights and freaks—the persistent
desire to get *Out*. For straights, getting Out means getting out of
life and its endless uncertainties, its potentials for chaos. For freaks,
it means getting out—sometimes at any cost—of the interlocking
layers of the single vision that dominates our world. For both,
getting Out leads to the "sterile grace" of transcendence, whereas
Gravity's Rainbow affirms both a realm of possibility outside the
visible and the multiple worlds of maya. It affirms "physical grace."
Its vision is essentially comic in the traditional sense, where life is
affirmed and gravity's embrace is returned, comic in the Dantean
sense. For a writer to gain credibility with a comic vision, he or she
must demonstrate that the vision is not naïve—that it takes account
of, and encompasses, what goes on in the world. *Gravity's Rainbow*
seems to take account of everything. It reveals a fully mature consciousness available to the human race if we can survive.

According to *Gravity's Rainbow*, all systems of science, art, religion,
politics, and economics—all systems of any kind—are simply
metaphoric descriptions that participate in reality but are not
reality in its entirety. Pynchon supplies enormous amounts of information from within each metaphoric system. The reader sees
the world as it is organized and explained by physics, history,
mythology, theology, popular culture, cybernetics, literature,
chemistry, mysticism, biology, politics, economics, psychology, and
so on. The reader must be able to alter his or her perception so as

not to be trapped in a single metaphoric description. The inability to alter perception is a measure of a person's straightness—whether the person is a character or a reader. If I were to discuss *Gravity's Rainbow* using all metaphors from physics, say, I would not be wrong; I would simply be confined to one dimension within a multidimensional world. Such a trap is itself a metaphor for how the straight mode of consciousness makes us live—confined to a single system of explanation, unconnected from everything outside that one system, and destined for rigidity.

Straights confuse a single interpretation of reality with reality. They say: you *are* your psychology, or the universe *is* certain physical laws. This mistake is known as literalization of metaphor, the mistake of thinking two terms of a metaphor are identical. It fosters devotion to authoritative systems of explanation, and is a central feature of the straight world's narrowness. For example, Pointsman—the anal-retentive villain—makes his first appearance with his foot literally in a toilet, and he literally introduces Slothrop to the multiple tentacles of the System by tricking him with an octopus. But perhaps the most blatant literalization belongs to the Undertaker, who dresses himself in a complicated metal suit to draw electricity, to get hit by lightning. His is the ultimate literalization of the search for enlightenment, and is emblematic of the cosmic foolishness inherent in all merely systematic approaches to truth. In fact, in super-straight sincerity the Undertaker undertakes *his* search because "he thinks it will help him *in his job*. Can you dig *that*, gates?" (V665/B775).

The freak's fascination with multiple perspectives becomes in *Gravity's Rainbow* a recognition that all perspectives are related to systems of metaphor, and metaphors are a "thrust at truth" only insofar as they recapitulate the underlying structures of reality— for example:

The parabola.

History as a metaphoric system describes the rise and fall of individuals, families, governments, and civilizations; the Rocket rises and falls betrayed by gravity; our celebrated sexual drives rise and fall; all biological life rehearses this same movement. It is as if all our systems were interpretations of a *shape* that exists between the points of a rise and fall. It is as if all our system-makers hung their interpretations on a curve they cannot see:

> But it is a curve each of them feels, unmistakably. It is the parabola. They must have guessed, once or twice—guessed and refused to believe—that everything, always, collectively, had been moving toward

that purified shape latent in the sky, that shape of no surprise, no second chances, no return. (V209/B244)

All our metaphoric systems attempt to explain this underlying latent shape of reality, the shape of the rainbow. But, no two people see the same rainbow; it is a shape constantly moving in time and space relative to the observer. That means rise and fall are also points relative to the observer. The rise of white America, for example, is the fall of Indian civilization. What we normally define as birth and death is a product of our own observation. The parabola that connects one person's birth and death, one civilization's rise and fall, can be altered by altering the angle of observation or intersection and the parabola becomes a part of a cycle—rise and fall become only two points in a process not of birth and death but of continual alteration, continual change. And change, like the parabola, turns out to be

> not, as we might imagine, bounded below by the line of the Earth it "rises from" and the Earth it "strikes" No But Then You Never Really Thought It Was Did You Of Course It Begins Infinitely Below The Earth And Goes On Infinitely Back Into The Earth it's only the *peak* that we are allowed to see. . . . (V726/B847)

Thus, in *Gravity's Rainbow*, all metaphors concerning the organic cycle, the benzene ring, mythology's great return, and Wagnerian operatic cycles are connected as attempts to explain a basic feature of reality—the way the parabola of visible life becomes an invisible cycle, the way altered perception alters form, the way continual change actually operates. The parabola is an underlying structure from which we extrapolate our comprehension of reality. In fact, the word *parabola* and the word *parable* have the same root and are the underlying structure for the changing perspectives that create *Gravity's Rainbow*.

The Rocket rides the parabola. It is a complex symbol of our individual perspectives—our sets of connections. It is a physical counterpart that makes visible a specific metaphoric system used in order to explain, embody, or literalize the basic shape of the parabola, one basic shape of reality. A rocket is like a world view. Everyone is trying to assemble a rocket. Literally, they want the weapon that will dominate the postwar world. Symbolically, they are assembling a set of metaphors to explain reality, and vying to complete the assembly first in order to dominate the consciousness of the postwar world. The rocket launched by Weissmann and the rocket built for launching by Enzian symbolize two poles in a single set of metaphors and connections that are still coming down on us, that *have* dominated the consciousness of the postwar world—and the religious, political, social, economic, and moral systems of the postwar world—until it is at the point of literal and symbolic explosion. Because we are ruled by a single metaphoric system of explanation—an explanation of the basic structures of reality—we are ruled, in effect, by the consciousness of the straight.

The freak's fascination with connections becomes, in *Gravity's Rainbow*, a demonstration of underlying connections between all our systems of order and explanation. There are horizontal connections and vertical connections. The horizontal connections provide a series of insights into relationships *within* a single metaphoric system. A reader, or character, can get lost tracing down all the connections that relate, say, within the psychological system of metaphors—the Freudian connections of sex, shit, and death; the Pavlovian connections concerning the operations of the opposite; the introduction of behavioristic connections, and so on. Pynchon warns against this trap repeatedly by continually making overt vertical connections *between* metaphoric systems—the connection of "shit, money, and the Word," is a shorthand example of how psychological, economic, and religious systems of metaphors have some deeper underlying structure.

In making vertical connections, the reader or a character brings together two or more whole systems of metaphor—two or more *sets* of horizontal connections. Connecting psychological systems to economic systems, for example, we connect, as Enzian does, everything related to the individual's domination by a father figure to everything related to proliferating cartels—the connection reveals the shape of the white man's fascination with a single authority, with absolute dominance and submission, with winning and losing, with sadomasochism, racism, shit, the penis, the Rocket's penetration, sexism, death, resistance to change, manly pursuits, masculine technologies, manipulation of the market, accumulation of power, political intrigue, and so on. Although Enzian makes these vertical connections, he is also somehow infected by their substance, as he is infected by Weissmann, as by implication we all are. If Enzian ever does launch anything, it might be something *opposite* to Weissmann's rocket, but not, I believe, essentially *different*. They exist within the same dying metaphoric system. It is, after all, Thanatz—death— who gives Enzian the last clue necessary for launching.

If we continue to make vertical connections, we can, for example, see the white man's psychology and the cartel as part of a historical system, as symptoms of the scientist's concept of entropy, as part of a political movement toward fascism, or as symptoms of cultural and human evolution heading toward a potential dead end. The more vertical connections we make, the less we are trapped in a metaphoric system, the more chance we have of being a medium of change, of doing something to alter the consciousness launched by World War II. The more vertical connections we make, the higher we move toward "the *peak* that we are allowed to see,""that purified shape latent in the sky."

Vertical connections are the chief source of difference in the encounter between freak and straight. The freak's invisible dimensions are invisible to the straight because they are arrived at through vertical connections, whereas the straight is confined to horizontal repetitions. The freak, the inside-outsider, moves outward and upward when he or she makes vertical connections, moving away from the core of the System. A new stage of the journey is completed each time he or she understands a metaphoric system well enough to stand back from it, grasp it as a metaphoric system, and connect it to other metaphoric systems he or she has understood. Each time a system is understood, the freak experiences a revelation that aids in peeling away another layer of the System's hold on his or her consciousness.

Freedom from the problem of confusing metaphoric systems with reality provides access to a second underlying structure in *Gravity's Rainbow*—the turning face or reversal. At the moment of some revelation in a character's life—or in the reader's comprehension—the narrator often describes the slow turning of some mysterious face. The character sees that face as belonging to something, being, or concept that is clearly beyond the realm of his or her normal experience. The word *interface* is often used to describe complex juncture points between two realms; but the image of the turning face is used as a symbol for the revelation of truth—it can be the truth associated with a single dimension of life or that truth revealed in the holiest and most liberating of "peak experiences."

I believe the basic human urge to experience some version of the nonordinary, of revelation, is offered by Pynchon as a major conscious or unconscious motivation for all his characters and, by implication, all of us. It moves them to get off the ground, to trace the path of the parabola's movements, to follow the shape of their own connections, to embrace some version of the Rocket and rise against gravity with undefined hopes. On the last page of the book—or in the last frame of the film that *Gravity's Rainbow* both becomes and denies, the film snaps, and we get the opportunity to participate with Gottfried in a peak experience, in a singular moment of revelation, for "in the darkening and awful expanse of screen something has kept on, a film we have not learned to see...it is now a closeup of the face, a face we all know—"

Everyone in Pynchon's world—whether aware or not of being motivated by revelation—is trying to get off: on dope, on sex, on power, on violence, on death, on spiritual promise itself. Everyone is, in a sense, also trying to find a reversal mechanism—to know in advance that some mechanism exists which follows rise and fall and allows people individually and/or collectively to fall and then rise again. The entire action of *Gravity's Rainbow* can be viewed as a series of searches for this mechanism—sometimes called the *Schwarzgerät* or "the next highest assembly." Everyone's search begins by using his or her own metaphoric system to ask: What mechanism will reverse the fall of the Slothrop family and by clear analogy the fall of America, Western civilization, and civilization as a whole? What mechanism will reverse the conditioned rise and fall of Slothrop's penis, conditioned to rise on the promise of death? What mechanism will reverse entropic movement of all physical, biological, and communications systems, the movement toward randomness and the loss of energy? What mechanism will reverse gravitational collapse and thrust us beyond the black holes of inner and outer space? What mechanism will reverse the lemmings' rush toward death?

Gravity's Rainbow is filled with metaphors of reversal—that is part of its overall comic vision. For example, the straight version of reversal lies in the fall of the Rocket itself, *a reversal of order*:

> Imagine a missile one hears approaching only *after* it explodes. The reversal! A piece of time neatly snipped out...a few feet of film run backwards...the blast of the rocket, fallen faster than sound—then growing *out of it* the roar of its own fall, catching up to what's already death and burning...a ghost in the sky.... (V48/B55)

This is Pointsman's approach to reversal. He is a representative straight, a slightly distorted mirror image of Weissmann. Pointsman's name means control-man; Weissmann is white-man; together they are a comic-book duo of bad guys; together they are the Man. Pointsman is the Man with his foot in the toilet, the Man as castrater, the Man as anti-black, the cause-and-effect Man. For him the Rocket, which both symbolizes and fulfills his own system of connections, always leads to death. That is what he and the consciousness he represents has made of the parabola—a weapon against life, the pathway of death.

Pointsman is trapped within a single metaphoric system, the Pavlovian system. He cannot make vertical connections—his revelation cannot be of truth; it can only be the revelation of his own system's ultimate stage. Thus he makes the pursuit of truth, and of the turning face, into a Pavlovian pursuit. That is, he literally stalks a very specific dog and believes that catching the dog will provide him with truth, with revelation. He fantasizes a scene where the turning face itself (described V142/B166) is the face of that dog. The dog's name in German means "victory over the nightmare of death." Here is the ultimate truth of Pointsman's system, and it is a key to the consciousness of the straight in *Gravity's Rainbow*. Nearly every character who expresses the straight mind experiences the desire to violate the cycle of life and achieve victory over death. None of them wants to willingly return gravity's embrace. Even that highest of human experiences, the peak experience, the revelation of truth, is shackled to a grim contest with death. The straight consciousness, or the straight part of everyone's consciousness, interprets the rise and fall of the parabola of visible life as nothing more than a movement toward death, and seeks the reversal of this movement *only* through victory over the cycles of change that underlie all life. It wants to prevent change and thereby achieve immortality. It is the consciousness of the lemming rushing to embrace the thing it fears.

But, in *Gravity's Rainbow*, one lemming—incredibly enough—is saved. The Rocket's reversal of order does not have to mean what Pointsman and the straight consciousness interpret it to mean. " . . . The Rocket has to be many things, it must answer to a number of different shapes in the dreams of those who touch it . . . " (V727/B847). The image of the Rocket's blast and light coming before the sound is also the perfect image of how revelation strikes individuals and perhaps societies: first the light and explosion and dislocation of direct experience, and then the sound, the creation of the Word. The reversal mechanism everyone in the book is after is revelation itself. Revelation is the underlying structure that ties together the multiple meanings of the parabola and the turning face—it is one of the most dominant metaphors in all of Pynchon's work. Only revelation can reverse the movement of all systems toward death. It is the mechanism that provides new energy to a decaying world; it is intuition; it is the stuff of Kekulé's dream; it is spiritual insight; and it is the *influx of something wholly new from outside* the physical, personal, social, political, and spiritual universe. It is the outside piece of information that shatters the closed order of any given system.

Revelation reverses by transforming—it reverses in the sense of altering a direction rather than unmaking that which has been made. As science would insist, it does not precisely reverse the direction of time, but transforms the direction of choice patterns, altering the direction of probabilities. Revelation is a spiritual metaphor, but it has its counterpart in other metaphorical systems. Psychology now calls it the peak experience. Evolution calls it mutation. Physics calls it a singularity ("Singularities are entry and exit points of that which is beyond space-time projecting itself into space-time").[3] On the political level, revelation is a metaphor for change coming *only* from outside a given system.

The freak pursuing vertical connections, hoping to get off far enough to be Outside the System, must become adept at experiencing revelation, and then be transformed into a mutant. In *Gravity's Rainbow*, Geli Tripping is the model of a successful mutant, but her function is to act on others as an agent of transformation rather than to be a pilgrim who reveals the process of becoming. The *journeying freak*, on the other hand, must locate the source of the System in order to get Out, must locate the genesis obscured by so many interlocking metaphoric systems. The System in *Gravity's Rainbow* has its source in that part of human consciousness which is *susceptible* to fascist-totalitarian explanations of experience. It is a part of everyone's consciousness, the part that commands us not to look outside the authoritative system of explanations because nothing lies out there but chaos; the part that confuses a failure of imagination with lack of order. In the name of order, the straight part of our consciousness traps us in a single metaphoric system—in the name of order, the straight part of our consciousness has trapped *itself* within that single metaphoric System which has dominated nearly all of earth's creation since at least World War II:

> Taking and not giving back, demanding that "productivity" and "earnings" keep on increasing with time, the System removing from the rest of the World these vast quantities of energy to keep its own tiny desperate fraction showing a profit: and not only most of humanity—most of the World, animal, vegetable and mineral, is laid waste in the process. The System may or may not understand that it's only buying time. And that time is an artificial resource to begin with, of no value to anyone or anything but the System, which sooner or later must crash to its death, when its addiction to energy has become more than the rest of the World can supply, dragging with it innocent souls all along the chain of life. Living inside the System is like riding across the country in a bus driven by a maniac bent on suicide. . . . (V412/B480–81)

For the freak to get off the bus, to get Out of the System, he or she must *get out of his or her own head*, or, more accurately, get out of the straight part of his or her consciousness. This is possible only in those peak experiences of revelation. There, the inside-outsider can see outside his or her straightness, and perhaps be transformed to a mutant, a bearer of a new consciousness better able to live in symbiotic balance with the universe and therefore better able to survive beyond the death throes of a dying world view.

Consciousness itself lies behind the mystery that permeates *Gravity's Rainbow*; in fact, it underlies everything in Pynchon's universe. It is an entirely animated universe—this is the basis for the book's optimism about the continuance of life. All things are living participants in consciousness; the balls in a pinball machine are not inert metal: they are "sentient all right, beings from the planetoid Katspiel" (V583–84/B680). Living nerve cells talk about their fearful trip to the "Outer Level." The earth itself is a "living critter" whose trees are the dendrites of its nervous system. The Rocket "lives an entire life" in the five minutes between rise and fall. The most informed and illuminated revolutionary in the book is a light bulb who makes speeches. Even Slothrop's roll of fat speaks to him and tells him to get off his ass. Everything is infused with conscious, sentient life; everything speaks. Consciousness provides the unity of all creation. But all sentient life also participates in the creation of consciousness. Unity is not preexistent; it does not exist in some separate platonic realm. It is created from multiplicity, from the changing contribution of all living things. Therefore, the physical dimensions of reality are no more or less illusory than the spiritual dimensions. Everything is always in the process of altering unified consciousness by the contribution of its individual consciousness. This is an important feature of Pynchon's vision in *Gravity's Rainbow*. It is one of the things that makes reading the book so difficult—the book modulates from consciousness to consciousness without warning as if it were moving from point to point within a single consciousness, as if the individual consciousness were only as separate as raindrops in a raincloud.

As a scientific metaphor, "consciousness [may be] the missing hidden variable in the structuring of matter."[4] As an evolutionary metaphor, consciousness is that which is intermingled through all creation, and all creation potentially moves toward greater unified complexity as consciousness moves toward understanding itself. As a religious metaphor, consciousness is a God or divinity revealed to be both a unity and a multiplicity in constant change as all things participate in its creation and all things are created through its workings. As a moral and political metaphor, consciousness is that which must be liberated from the influence of a fascist/totalitarian domination.

Because we all participate in the creation of consciousness, the narrative voice in *Gravity's Rainbow* scolds us often as "glozing neuters." Force and counterforce alike are guilty of fascist/totalitarian thinking and of unwillingness to acknowledge participation in the creation of fascist/totalitarian systems. We see ourselves as filmgoers, objective observers—passive viewers of a creation categorized and wholly separate from us:

> Well, if the Counterforce knew better what those categories concealed, they might be in a better position to disarm, de-penis and dismantle the Man. But they don't. Actually they do, but they don't admit it. Sad but true. They are as schizoid, as double-minded in the massive presence of money, as any of the rest of us, and that's the hard fact. The Man has a branch office in each of our brains, his corporate emblem is a white albatross, each local rep has a cover known as the Ego, and their mission in this world is Bad Shit. We do know what's going on, and we let it go on. (V712–13/B831)

Such chastisements distinguish the more balanced narrator from indecisive freaks like Slothrop, and remind us that the new consciousness has yet to embody itself in an effective counterview to the old.

To understand the balance between freak and straight that *Gravity's Rainbow* is reaching for, we must comprehend the spiritual and political significance of revelation—the change that comes from outside the known system. Revelation begins with a glimpse of what underlies metaphor itself, a glimpse of truth and at unity of consciousness, and it proceeds toward active *change*. A change that comes from outside the System must come from outside that part of universal consciousness which I have described as straight. As ubiquitous as the System is, finding outside information is not hopeless—Pynchon makes continual reference to Gödel's theorem and Murphy's law to assure us that no system can account for everything. Reversal is possible; its mechanism is revelation, and the key to revelation is the consciousness of the freak. The freak consciousness, or the freak part of our mutual consciousness, freed from bondage to a single perspective, a single metaphoric system, actively in pursuit of that surprise from out of the sky, is the true "singularity," the entry and exit point for revelation. Existing as it does within each consciousness as well as within mutual consciousness, the freak is that thing which is both inside and outside—once it is recognized. In cybernetics the freak is the much-hunted-for self-regulating mechanism that keeps a system alive.

There is in all this an ultimate, cosmic joke played on the inside-outsider, played on the individual freak who discovers that there is no such thing as inside and outside. The very success of his or her journey guarantees that some System will be constructed—and reveals that the journey toward a new consciousness must be continuous. Revelation must be continuous, for with each success some new literalization comes into being and some new version of the System is created. Dressed in a system, the freak is no longer invisible; he or she creates a new order of straights and is dependent on new freaks to begin peeling it all away again. Revelation is a metaphor for the underlying structure of discovery; without it the freak becomes straight. Without the freak in us, change is impossible. As Pynchon says, reversal is possible from "only the stray freak particle, by accident, drifting against the major flow" (V51/B59). The encounter between straight and freak, then, participates in the cosmic comedy of all change.

One way *Gravity's Rainbow* suggests for the freak to get outside the straight consciousness is to check his or her responses to paranoia. In the general sense that freaks use the word *paranoia*, any system of connections is ultimately paranoid. When the pattern of connections is mistaken for reality, you are trapped in your paranoia at the center of your own system. Unless everything is connected, something will be left out. If you are unable to accept the existence of valid patterns, valid explanations of life wholly outside your own, then any strange experience becomes a negative sign of the Other. Everything outside your pattern for explaining experience is connected to the pattern as *threat*. What threatens your explanation of life threatens you. The world, then, is fully explained. Freaks believe everyone is paranoid. They constantly remind themselves and others of their paranoia, checking to see if the threat is real, that is, checking to see if what they have interpreted as threat can be connected in some other way. Straights are paranoid, too, but they will not admit it because their brand of paranoia is part of the official reigning authoritative viewpoint. Straights are not used to examining their connections, so they are not used to spotting the point where they slip over into the bizarre. Freaks test their paranoia to preserve their invisibility; straights ignore their paranoia to preserve their Byzantine schemes.

Paranoia, of course, has its positive and negative dimensions; connections can lead both to a cosmic sense of the unity of things and to insane behavior of many kinds. Paranoia in *Gravity's Rainbow* recognizes the existence of other orders behind the visible. It is an anti-entropic force, a counterpart to gravity itself, pulling random events in to its own center of organization; it is the drive in all humans, straight and freak, to construct patterns that make meaning of life:

> . . . It is nothing less than the onset, the leading edge, of the discovery
> that *everything is connected*, everything in the Creation, a secondary illumi-
> nation—not yet blindingly One, but at least *connected*, and perhaps a route
> In for those like Tchitcherine who are held at the edge.... (V703/B820)

Tchitcherine is held at the edge of revelation, at the edge of the
Kirghiz Light, because the straight part of his consciousness makes
him always employ paranoia to look Inside for truth, as if it lies in
the inner circles of the Communist party or the narcissistic circles
of the self. Later, the wonderful witch Geli Tripping will teach him
the freak's use of paranoia to move Outward invisibly toward
revelation; she will magically turn him inside-out.

Paranoia is a metaphoric name for the drive that potentially leads
humans *toward* revelation, toward change and the reversal of any
given system's decay. It is also a metaphor for a conflict that provides the dynamic behind our drive to experience revelation.
Humans are driven to create patterns that explain experience and
provide a model of normalcy, and humans are also driven to experience nonordinary modes of reality. This creates a conflict
between the need to order life and the need to depart to another
kind of order. It is a conflict as important to a metaphoric explanation of daily living as the conflict between Eros and Thanatos—and I
suspect *Gravity's Rainbow* reveals both conflicts to be metaphors for
the same underlying structure. Humans make connections until
they have a satisfying explanation of experience. As life progresses,
the explanation becomes a clear but often unseen limitation, and
the individual responds to what Andrew Weil calls a natural cyclic
impulse to experience nonordinary states of reality.[5] Both the
straight and the freak, of course, share this paranoia-producing
conflict, but their response is crucially different.

The straight's devotion to a single set of metaphoric explanations
puts him or her in terrible bondage to external control. He or she
must continually capitulate to anything that promises to maintain
the appearance of validity—anything that promises to keep the
ordinary patterns intact with the minimum of oscillation.[6] This is
the key to Pökler's place in *Gravity's Rainbow*. He illustrates a way of
dealing with life that makes the straight consciousness susceptible
to fascism/totalitarianism. Further, in response to the need for
nonordinary modes of reality, the straight cannot rely on any
experience that would come from outside his or her single metaphoric system—he or she cannot rely on revelation, on real change.
Thus the straight's system must provide *escapes* from the ordinary
patterns of life without risking involvement in any new set of patterns—the escapes must be sanctioned by the very system the

straight wishes to escape; the illusion of courage and danger must be maintained within a context of hidden safety from change—titillation replaces revelation, pornography replaces passion.

According to Pynchon, the escapes sanctioned by our culture that entrap the straight consciousness in the illusion of escaping the ordinary are primarily: sex, death, spiritual detachment, movies, and dope. For example, the illusion of escape from the ordinary is raised to a scientific principle cozily compatible with fascism by Laszlo Jamf. Jamf, a key mystery figure in the background of almost all aspects of fascist development in *Gravity's Rainbow*, tells his students that the ionic bond would liberate them from the ordinariness of the covalent bond—instead of carrying the "lunch-bucket in to the works every morning with the faceless droves," they could transcend and, like the ionic bond, "move beyond life, toward the inorganic." (V580/B675–6)

The connection between the fascist mind and the straight consciousness is made most clear by Weissmann/Blicero. He uses and reuses with kinky variations every escape the System offers but always remains trapped within the System, dominated by his attachment to the technological interpretation of maleness and of meaning. And yet his words make it equally clear that all of us are susceptible to straight and fascist thinking; straight and freak alike respond to this plaintive death wish:

> "I want to break out—to leave this cycle of infection and death. I want to be taken in love; so taken that you and I, and death, and life, will be gathered, inseparable, into the radiance of what we would become...." (V724/B844)

The expression of this attitude puts Weissmann/Blicero at some center point between freak and straight—but not a balanced center point. He pursues the Outside, the nonordinary experience, as desperately as a freak does, but his straightness condemns him to repetition of the System's escapes rather than revelation—it condemns him to decadence. He is dangerous precisely because his motivating plea—to transcend rather than to transform—is so attractive in its many guises that it can fool both freak and straight. But for Pynchon transcendence is a "sterile grace," and actual death is one of its conditions.

On the other hand, the successful freak—responding to the need to experience nonordinary states of reality—pursues altered perception, discovers a new set of patterns, a wider cycle of paranoid connections, and is either moved further on a vertical progress through metaphorical systems toward revelation or is simply satisfied, at least temporarily, with a new outlook on life, with making changes. In *Gravity's Rainbow*, everyone participates in the possibilities of both the straight consciousness and the freak consciousness. Sometimes, for example, Slothrop is a freak getting out of the System, and sometimes he is a straight escaping life. It depends on how he alters his normal patterns—how he deals with his paranoia. Basically, when he makes vertical connections and moves to a new order of perception, he is a freak—as when he discovers the dimensions of the political plot against him and joins the world of the dopers. When he lives within a single set of perceptions, he is a straight, as in the beginning of the book. He is a more subtle mix of freak and straight toward the end of the book. He is freak enough to see outside the reigning system of metaphors and to connect to the earth as a living creature instead of as a dead rock, but he is too trapped by the doper's side effect—a narrow and detached sense of the moment—to move further toward revelation. The clues we are given near the end of the novel seem to indicate that Slothrop is in a delicate stage of his invisibility. He has been too straight, too literal about invisibility itself. Pig Bodine, one of Pynchon's mystery people, gives Slothrop a magic talisman to help him further on his journey, but the narrator reads Slothrop's tarot and says they are the cards of a "tanker and feeb." (V738/B861)

Slothrop the American needs a reversal, a new counter-entropic principle to help him hold things together again, to reverse his scattering. Scattering is like embracing the flow of entropy, like suffering a gravitational collapse, disappearing into a black hole. Slothrop will gain insight into mysteries that exist beyond man-made laws of nature, but unless he comes out some other side into a new universe, he will just simply be gone. I think the experience implied in scattering is another doper's side effect. It is when the doper has glimpsed infinity or mystery and does not want to come back to daily life.

Scattering is a difficult stage in the freak's journey because it also plays a positive role in throwing off the rigidities of the System—it plays the role of "deconstruction." It is the stage in which the mysteries of chaos are revealed, but it can be an addictive stage. If Slothrop stays scattered, he will be living entirely in the doper's world; he will become straight, dead to the world, by denying other dimensions of life; he will be trapped on the island of the lotus-eaters. Although scattering gives Slothrop a much-needed access to heaven and an identification with nature, he must, in the world of gravity's rainbow, come back to daily life, down to earth. It is a principle of Pynchon's vision: "eerie and messianic" as gravity may be, we must *return* its embrace. It may be necessary to fall into a black hole, or to become a doper, or a deconstructionalist—it may be necessary as a part of the journey Out of the System; but it is significant that Pynchon leaves Slothrop, the representative American, in a so delicate and unresolved stage. Either he will pass a crucial test, or his journey will be over. The delicacy of this stage with its fatal attractions is reflected in the scattered effect of the book's last sections. It is as if Pynchon were indicating the spiritual state of American freakdom—a little too strung out, so that its world view is scattering at a dangerous rate.

It is interesting that Geli Tripping, freak queen and agent of transformation, passes over Slothrop to choose the Russian, Tchitcherine, whose transformation and subsequent disappearance from the book is acted out in the physical world when he ends his vendetta against his black brother—a gesture of profound importance in Pynchon's world. Perhaps Tchitcherine is chosen because he *personally* deserves it. He is a "giant supermolecule" who keeps his bonds open for new links; who believes the State should "persist no longer than the individuals in it" (V338/B393); and who finds comfort in "the dialectical ballet of force, counterforce, collision, and new order" (V704/B821). Perhaps Geli chooses Tchitcherine simply because she loves him; or perhaps she loves him because he has been held for so long on the edges of illumination; he is so ripe for revelation that he is perhaps beyond the knowledge and temptations of scattering. But not so Slothrop.

Gravity's Rainbow sets up a continuum from the straight consciousness to the freak consciousness, roughly from Major Marvy to Geli Tripping, but everyone is a mixture of kinds of consciousness. The unity of consciousness in Pynchon's world is no simple union of opposites: the underlying structure of reality is a continuum, an interplay, a set of movements connected invisibly like ripples in a pond, like arcs of a gravitational field, or dancers connected by the pulse of the music. The continuity of reality is an "assertion through structure" like "living genetic chains"—it is a series of points in a field of consciousness connected by an unknown number of shapes, shifting according to the participation of each point. When we isolate a moment in time and examine a single character—Pökler or Mexico, who are a lot alike—he or she will in that moment be participating in some specific act that could be labeled freak or straight. But each character is a different point on the overall continuum, the overall unified consciousness of the book. Within each individual, the freak and the straight mix in varying degrees to dominate the actions of the individual at any given moment. If a proper balance exists, the straight aspect of consciousness should provide the basic patterns that explain experience and the freak aspect of consciousness should provide the kind of departure from the ordinary that allows the influx of energy and change. The balance is crucial. The freak can no more do without the straight than can the straight without the freak. Their interdependence is like the relationship between technology and magic, analysis and intuition, practicality and fancy, entropy and energy, death and "death transfigured," parent and child, the left and right hemispheres of the brain, male and female "principles." In *Gravity's Rainbow*, the encounter between straight and freak takes on the significance of all these relationships. Dynamic balance is the ideal that underlies Pynchon's comic vision; it is the highest good of the new consciousness, and it promises restoration of sanity to all systems: personal, social, political, economic, and metaphysical. But this balance never exists in the world of the novel except as a latent shape, a true *possibility*—we can glimpse it only when we share in the overall time scheme of *Gravity's Rainbow*. Understanding the time scheme helps the reader enter the invisible zone of the book; it gives access to the place from which the narrator sees and describes the cosmic comedy of changes.

"Personal density . . . is directly proportional to temporal bandwidth." This is the proposition, we are told, that will one day be called "Mondaugen's Law," and it explains the general time-scheme of *Gravity's Rainbow*: " 'Temporal bandwidth' is the width of your present, your *now*. It is the familiar ' Δt' considered as a dependent variable. The more you dwell in the past and in the future, the thicker your bandwidth, the more solid your persona" (V509/B593). If your sense of the *now* includes a wide range of past *and* future, then your personal density is high. Past and future are no longer "in" the past and "in" the future; they are both part of the present; they are "in" the *now*. You are very here. If, like Slothrop, your sense of the *now* involves only the single still frame of the moment, then your persona will have little density—you will be unable to hold things together; you will lose your gravity and scatter as Slothrop does. Such a concept explains how the rocket launched on the first page of the book and Weissmann's rocket and Enzian's rocket are all the same Rocket that is coming down on all of us on the last page of the book. The book is all happening within the *now* as it is related to the narrator's personal density. The narrator's temporal bandwidth, or *now*, is wide enough so that within the time range of the book—roughly 1937 to some unspecified future moment of the Rocket State (excluding some overtly "historical" excursions to the time of the Puritans or of Rome)—everything is happening *now*. This explains what might appear to be anachronisms; it explains how the freaks of the World War II period are related to the freaks altered by the events of the sixties—it is all part of the same moment.

This use of time also provides the freak reader with some sense of his or her history—current freaks are avatars of a kind of consciousness that has a tradition at least as old as the world from the outset of World War II and connecting to all kinds of freaks, outsiders, Preterite of other times. It also provides a new synthesis and perspective on an old freak problem: a freak can respond to those spiritual disciplines that advise embracing the moment and still be politically and socially aware simply by widening his or her temporal bandwidth. Thus the spiritual realm can be embraced as well as the multiple realms of the body. The expansion of individual consciousness necessary to do this is, I think, part of the book's importance. *Gravity's Rainbow* is not an anti-novel—in Pynchon's world there could be no such thing—it is a counter-novel, and like the Counterforce, it is part of an overall movement to preserve and expand alternate modes of reality, part of a larger continuity.

The precise range of the temporal bandwidth of *Gravity's Rainbow* is precisely chosen to cover a specific period where the palpable decay of an old world view dominates consciousness and makes straights of most of us. The *range* of temporal bandwidth is also a matter of balance. If the period of the *now* extended further back in time, the book would have even more density, but it would risk that kind of detachment which claims to see the "big picture" and is less concerned with any single feature of its landscape. (Von Göll, der Springer, claims this perspective, and he is a film director—film and calculus, the narrator tells us, are both "pornographies of flight.") The time range of the book is, however, broad enough from past to future for us to see in operation the hardening of the straight consciousness, the loss of energy and tolerance for change—the deadly trap of a single perspective:

> The Oedipal situation in the Zone these days is terrible. There is no dignity. The mothers have been masculinized to old worn moneybags of no sexual interest to anyone, and yet here are their sons, still trapped inside inertias of lust that are 40 years out of date. The fathers have no power today and never did, but because 40 years ago we could not kill them, we are condemned now to the same passivity, the same masochist fantasies *they* cherished in secret, and worse, we are condemned in our

weakness to impersonate men of power our own infant children must hate, and wish to usurp the place of, and fail.... So generation after generation of men in love with pain and passivity serve out their time in the Zone, silent, redolent of faded sperm, terrified of dying, desperately addicted to the comforts others sell them, however useless, ugly or shallow, willing to have life defined for them by men whose only talent is for death. (V747/B871–72)

Only from the lofty position of the narrative voice are we allowed to view fully the continuities between straight and freak that exist in each of us—only when we are tuned to the book's concept of time. Given the opportunity to see "outside" of time as it is normally lived, the reader is given the spiritual opportunity to glimpse the possibility of balance, and to glimpse the multiple possibilities of our common future—with balance and without. The reader can participate in the prophetic experience, and more easily embrace the comic sense of life's larger dimensions.

III

When we zoom in from the narrator's timeless perspective to the actual time-bound world of the characters' lives, to what scientists call the Zone of the Middle Dimensions, the continuities are off balance. If we read human possibilities from this perspective, from the eyes of the individual characters, then the straights dominate in the world, and the straight state of consciousness dominates the freak in almost any given individual. Down in the daily life of the Zone, there is "the persistence, then, of structures favoring death," (V167/B195) and the continuities are invisible. We see only the divided poles, the encounter between 1 and 0, between rigid straight and largely unsuccessful freak. The humor of this confrontation, the humor of the freak world view, is actually everywhere in *Gravity's Rainbow*. The book is, among other things, a terrific comic book for synthesis freaks, pitting the floundering freak against the evil forces of death. It is like pitting a silly, cosmic Captain Marvel against that scientist, Sivana, who wanted to rule the world—the one who says "heh, heh" all the time, as the narrator does, for example, when reading Slothrop's tarot cards.

In the freak world view, heroes are always vaguely comic, touched with the ineptitude of the outsider. They can never really win victories against straights. They can only win survival. And even that is usually by accident and because of the blind narrowness of the straight. Slothrop as freak does pretty well for a while, escaping from the evil scientist Pointsman, trying to stay invisible, running around in a Rocketman or a Pigman suit, arising grossly from garbage cans—and all the time trying to find out about "The Penis He Thought Was His Own." In his travels, Slothrop encounters the king of the straights, Major Marvy, military buddy of industrialist Bloody Chiclitz. Marvy is forever chasing Slothrop, and the book is filled with good old-time chase scenes like: Slothrop racing through the bowels of the Mittelwerke with Major Marvy hot on his heels singing Rocket Limericks:

> There once was a fellow named Moorehead,
> Who had an affair with a warhead.
> His wife moved away
> The very next day—
> She *was* always kind of a sorehead.
>
> (V307/B357)

And, as Marvy—the drawling juicer, the foul racist, pisser on electric toads of manhood, *reducto ad absurdum* of John Wayne's absurdity—as Marvy gets closer, his limericks get grosser:

> There once was a fellow named Slattery
> Who was fond of the course-gyro battery.
> With that 50-volt shock,
> What was left of his cock
> Was all slimy and sloppy and spattery.
>
> (V311/B361)

Of course, Slothrop gets away and lives to fight back in an aerial pie fight, but the chase goes on until in a magnificent comic reversal all this penis preoccupation comes to a jovial end—so to speak. Evil scientist Pointsman sends a couple of hack doctors to perform a castration on Slothrop, who at the time is trying to get some ID papers and is kicking around in his pig suit. Unbeknownst to Major Marvy, an accidental switch occurs and everyone ends up with his or her just deserts: Marvy gets a pig suit; Pointsman gets Marvy's balls; and merry Slothrop gets away with Pig Bodine, Albert Krypton, and Shirley the Red Cross Lady.

Later in the book, we get a still more blatant comic-book, fantasy version of the major conflict between an ineffectual counterforce and the male/penis/death-oriented world of the Father figure—it is the "Floundering Four" against the "Paternal Peril," against "Pernicious Pop": "Onward to rescue the Radiant Hour, which has been abstracted from the day's 24 by colleagues of the Father, for sinister reasons of their own" (V674/B786).

In all these encounters, the roles of straight and freak remain clear. The straight world would turn synthesis into synthetics—into plastic whose virtues are the virtues of the fascist/totalitarian cartel of the spirit: "Strength, Stability, and Whiteness." THEY are the War. The freaks are still able to love, to be innocent, to look for life without cynicism. In Roger Mexico's encounter with Britishman Beaver—that gentleman of old England who whisks away the woman Roger loves—we see a more sophisticated version of the freak's conception of the straight:

> Damned Beaver/Jeremy *is* the War, he is every assertion the fucking War ever made—that we are meant for work and government, for austerity: and these shall take priority over love, dreams, the spirit, the senses and the other second-class trivia that are found among the idle and mindless hours of the day.... Damn them, they are wrong. They are insane. (V177/B206)

Roger is the inside-outsider just alerted to the meaning of being Inside. He is a model of the freak trapped in a straight world and forced to confront his own straightness. He escapes Pökler's fate only by virtue of this somewhat accidental confrontation. He discovers Pointsman's fingers in his love-pie and turns against the straight world. For a while he rides high—pissing in grand fashion on one of Pointsman's top-level meetings and tormenting Beaver:

> . . . At a prearranged spot in a park, two unemployed Augustes leap out in whiteface and working-clothes and commence belting each other with gigantic (7 or 8 feet long) foam rubber penises, cunningly detailed, all in natural color. These phancy phalli have proven to be a good investment. (V708/B826)

Together with Pig Bodine, Roger has his ultimate confrontation with Jeremy when he tries to gross out everyone at a very posh dinner, shouting out a menu like: "snot soup" and "pus pudding" and "menstrual marmalade" and "clot casserole" and so on. He does gross people out, but he loses Jessica. He is a novice freak and must, after his initial freak-out, begin learning the lessons of invisibility. His loss of Jessica is a serious loss—Roger is Pynchon's *spokesman* for love. (He is not as successful at actually loving as Geli Tripping is—he needs a little magic in his freakery.) And love, believe it or not, is the most important counter-entropic force in the book, the heart's own force of gravity. Roger's desire to win against the straight is doomed. To win is to be straight. Roger understands the freak's dilemma in moral terms; after his attempt to win, he begins to understand the relationship of the counterforce to the force:

> Roger must have been dreaming for a minute here of the sweaty evenings of Thermidor: the failed Counterforce, the glamorous ex-rebels, half-suspected but still enjoying official immunity and sly love, camera-worthy wherever they carry on...doomed pet freaks. . . .
> . . . In the middle of all that he has to walk (*ow*, fuck) right into the interesting question, which is worse: living on as Their pet, or death? (V713/B831)

This is what the actual confrontation between freak and straight is about—a choice between living as an alien or embracing the death culture and death itself. Everything in *Gravity's Rainbow* participates in this struggle—even the music of Rossini and Beethoven. In the beginning of the book, Pirate Prentice may win his bizarre contest with the giant Adenoid; but in the end, the Adenoid turns out to be Richard M. Zhlubb, night manager of the Orpheus Theatre. The Man, who puts down the " 'irresponsible use of the harmonica' or, actually, 'harbodica,' " archly believes that "an unauthorized state of mind" can be the result of an attempt to "play a chord progression on the Department of Justice list." (We all know who this Richard M. Zhlubb is, heh, heh.) Although a few freaks successful at invisibility manage to win a little love and a little of the heart's ease—like Leni Pökler/Solange and Fat Ludwig with his lemming—losing is an old game to freaks. That is because freaks, when they know themselves and the inside function of their freakiness, are meant for balance, not for victory. But the straight part of every freak's consciousness registers each loss as one more shove toward a willing departure from the cycles of life.

In *Gravity's Rainbow*, consciousness of new connections provides the real counterforce to the kingdom of death. Balance is possible, and the likelihood of our achieving it is part of the book's subject. The ending offers a large range of probabilities concerning this likelihood and concerning the shape of the future. Contemplating the ending is, for me, as mixed an experience as any contemplation about life. I am filled with contradictory conclusions: we are about to die; we are about to submit to fascism/totalitarianism; we are seeking balance; we have always had this threat and promise hanging over us and we always will; a new consciousness is coming into being; and so on. The continued existence of the freak is hopeful, but the broad separation between the freak part and the straight part of our consciousness not only turns us into cartoons, it also can mean contradictory things. Either the freak has become visible in our daily world to remind us of the need for change, or the freak and straight have flown further apart, dividing consciousness, continuing entropic disintegration.

But although a new world view has failed to take hold, the *revelation* of a new consciousness has clearly arrived. In *Gravity's Rainbow*, it is the consciousness of the "Titan," and Pynchon's narrator seems to promise its survival. It is embodied most nearly by Geli Tripping, who, through her freaky witchery, saves Tchitcherine. It is Geli who is given the privilege of witnessing the mad vitality of the Creation:

> This is the World just before men. Too violently pitched alive in constant flow ever to be seen by men directly. They are meant only to look at it dead, in still strata, transputrified to oil or coal. Alive, it was a threat: it was Titans, was an overpeaking of life so clangorous and mad, such a green corona about Earth's body that some spoiler *had* to be brought in before it blew the Creation apart. So we, the crippled keepers, were sent out to multiply, to have dominion. God's spoilers. Us. Counter-revolutionaries. *It is our mission to promote death.* The way we kill, the way we die, being unique among the Creatures. It was something we had to work on, historically and personally. To build from scratch up to its present status as reaction, nearly as strong as life, holding down the green uprising. But only nearly as strong.
> Only nearly, because of the defection rate. A few going over to the Titans every day, in their striving subcreation. . . . (V720/B839–40)

Geli's magic spell transforms Tchitcherine. She is the spiritual daughter of Oedipa Maas—the product of Pynchon's immaculate conception and revelation in *The Crying of Lot 49*. She is the agent of revelation striking Tchitcherine as lightning struck that Undertaker in his metal suit. Tchitcherine is a military man and is literally "more metal than anything else." He is carried by Geli at least beyond the edge of the illumination he always sought, into the invisible world of the Titans' subcreation. It is Pynchon's best union of freak and straight, effective enough to deflect Tchitcherine from the vendetta against his black brother in order to create a consciousness so new that its invisibility for the rest of the book is complete. Despite the straight consciousness, "the crippled keepers," a freak can still play the role of what the physicists call a "singularity"—letting in the light from someplace outside our decaying systems. *Gravity's Rainbow* is more positive than either of Pynchon's earlier works. It is itself a "singularity," letting in the light of a magnificent consciousness, creating a kinder universe than the one implied by the separate pieces of information absorbed by that consciousness. The light of revelation has so clearly dawned on the narrator—we are told so on the second page—that it is as if Pynchon has developed a depth of soul only hinted at in his earlier works. The threat of death still hangs heavily as does the threat of fascism/totalitarianism, but clearly Geli Tripping is among us, the change of consciousness has been revealed, and we must wait to see its impact on life (V4/B4–5):

There is no way out. Lie and wait, lie still and be quiet. Screaming holds across the sky. When it comes, will it come in darkness, or will it bring its own light? Will the light come before or after?
But it is already light.

1. Richard M. Dorson, *America in Legend* (New York: Pantheon Books, 1973), pp. 299–300.

2. Ishmael Reed, *Mumbo-Jumbo* (New York: Bantam, 1972), p. 71. Like *Gravity's Rainbow*, *Mumbo-Jumbo* provides a more profound synthesis of freak mythology than is demonstrated in the stereotypic encounter we are all familiar with. Ironically, however, actual experience seems to provide many examples of the *simplest* encounter between stereotypic freaks and straights. One such actual encounter is recorded by Richard Fariña in an essay called "The Monterey Fair" in *Long Time Coming and a Long Time Gone* (New York: Random House, 1969), pp. 135–54. Fariña describes Joan Baez, himself, Thomas Pynchon, and some others in an encounter with some John Birchers. Pynchon is aptly mysterious.

3. Bob Toben, *Space-Time and Beyond* (New York: Dutton, 1975), p. 145.

4. Ibid., p. 11.

5. Andrew Weil, *The Natural Mind* (Boston: Houghton Mifflin, 1972), pp. 21–22.

6. Tim Tillotson and physicist Robert March, of the University of Wisconsin, Madison, have helped me with much of the science in *Gravity's Rainbow*. Professor March interprets the formula "which describes motion under the aspect of yaw control" as a metaphoric capitulation to the fear of oscillation, an explanation of the "deep conservatism" of the young engineers excited by cybernetics. See V239/B278.

Freedom and Knowledge in the Zone

By James W. Earl

Gravity's Rainbow is a philosophical novel. By this I mean that its major themes, the ideas from which its plots, characters, and symbols are generated, correspond to perennial problems of Western philosophy. Foremost among these is the problem of free will and determinism; and closely related to it is the problem of rational and intuitive knowledge. For Pynchon, as for many thinkers, these two issues are not easily separated: rational analysis and determinism appear to be natural allies, opposed to irrational intuition and freedom. Pynchon, of course, is an artist and not a systematic philosopher; his ideas are highly eclectic and do not belong to any definable movement, system, or school of thought. But his philosophy is clearly the product of a very broad familiarity with contemporary ideas, and we can show the harmony of his vision with several well-defined currents in modern thought.

The struggle between freedom and determinism is played out large in *Gravity's Rainbow* in Slothrop's Progress: whether or not and how Slothrop can free himself from the control of Jamf, the IG, Pointsman, and the Firm is the central issue of the book's main plot. By the time Slothrop enters the Zone, our impression (and his too) is that he is the totally conditioned man, programmed, manipulated, and monitored since infancy by conspiracies within conspiracies; he is a test case, the perfect "fox" for testing and perfecting Pavlov's and Pointsman's theories of behavioral determinism.

Slothrop's subjugation to these forces is symbolized by "The Penis He Thought Was His Own," which may seem at first a fanciful and comic symbol. But the penis is not a purely comic organ; it has been a symbol for serious matters for a long time. In the first full treatment of the problem of free will, Saint Augustine argued that man is free, except for his unruly penis, which disobeys the will as man disobeys God, and so is a paradoxical symbol of both man's freedom and the subsequent enslavement of his will to the senses.[1] The sexual response is a natural focus for any discussion of free will, since it is so clearly a *response* and not an act of will. For the same reason, it is a natural focus for the modern behaviorist studying his determined stimulus-response mechanisms. Jamf's grotesque study of Infant Tyrone's tiny penis is not so farfetched: several studies have actually been done of infantile erections.[2]

Slothrop's erections represent the many powerful automatic response mechanisms in our behavior. The general force of the symbol in regard to the theme of free will is elaborated for us in relation to Pirate Prentice: "Like every young man growing up in England, he was conditioned to get a hardon in the presence of certain fetishes, and then conditioned to feel shame about his new reflexes" (V71–72/B82). This simple model is later refined to a "cosmology" of anxiety-producing "singular points" (including rocket launchings as well as sadomasochistic paraphernalia) that serve as fetishes stimulating erections (V396/B461–62). The conditioned and uncontrollable sexual response and the guilt it generates are an important tool society uses to control the behavior of its members; Pointsman and the Firm use it to manipulate a number of characters in the book. This sociopolitical interpretation is spelled out (in only slightly exaggerated form) in Thanatz's theory of "sado-anarchism" (V737/B859–60).

The automatic penis is such an appalling symbol of man's un-freedom, of course, because sex would seem to be man's most intimate contact with nature, and the surest route to his freedom from social control. But this natural freedom has to be won back from society's various pornographies, imitations of nature. In spite of all the control over him, in spite of the penis "installed, wired by Them into his body" (V285/B332), early in the book Slothrop begins having periodic intimations of a freedom he cannot quite comprehend:

> There are times when Slothrop actually can find a clutch mechanism between him and Their iron-cased engine far away up a power train whose shape and design he has to guess at, a clutch he can disengage, feeling then all his inertia of motion, his real helplessness...it is not exactly unpleasant, either. Odd thing. (V207/B241)

In these spells, Slothrop begins to glimpse *"another order of being,"* "an identical-looking Other World," and is left afterward with a sense of "self-sufficiency nothing could get inside" (V239–40/ B279). So even as he is first beginning to detect Their control, he senses the possibility and pleasure of this limited freedom, a freedom from all but nature's controls, like the freedom of the rocket after *Brennschluss*—no more guidance, no more feedback, only the inertia of motion that is gravity's parabolic rainbow. When Slothrop finally enters the Zone, he is welcomed by Enzian, who boldly announces his freedom to him: "But you are free. We all are" (V288, 661/B336, 770). So Slothrop's odyssey into the Zone to discover the secret of his childhood that connects his erections to the rocket becomes also the gradual realization of his disengagement from the forces of control, and also his growing ability to love.

The many forces so sternly opposed to the idea of human freedom in the book are more or less abstract and invisible; the most visible is Pointsman the behaviorist, who epitomizes its most conscious and evil form. But behaviorism is only the theoretical and experimental arm of a larger determinism that claims to control all events according to a strict mechanistic causality that denies the existence of both will and chance—"No effect without cause, and a clear train of linkages" (V89/B102). Pointsman makes it clear that his behaviorism depends upon the universal validity of this causality and rational analysis, and as he searches for the connection between Slothrop and the rocket, he thinks, "When we find it, we'll have shown again the stone determinacy of everything, of every soul" (V86/B99–100). "The ideal, the end we struggle toward in science, is the true mechanical explanation" (V89/B102). This frightening attitude represents the main thrust of the European philosophy of science and culture from Spinoza to the positivists of the late nineteenth century. It is summed up by Otto Liebmann in his *Climax of Theory* (1884):

> In every possible instance, rational science, as distinguished from childish superstition, depends upon the universal assumption that a strict causal nexus underlies even our consideration of inaccessible reaches of overt events, and that such partial events exactly match the otherwise sporadic and fragmented pattern of our experience of this causal nexus. Still, the difficult problem—that of reconciling this fundamental scientific conviction with moral freedom of the will and with logical freedom of thought—is transcendent; but regardless of how the solution is sought, it absolutely must not be allowed to interfere with the epistomological questions. This would be an extraneous and disruptive intrusion and would only create confusion.[3]

In spite of the clarity of his convictions, Pointsman himself is a bundle of contradictions and ironies. He dreams of finding "an exit out of the orthodox-Pavlovian" (V141/B165), but he cannot free himself. In other ways, too, he wants to be different than he is, but he cannot control his own behavior. "He's creepy. He's even aware, usually, of the times when he's *being* creepy—it's a certain set to his face-muscles, a tendency to sweat...but he can't seem to *do* anything about it" (V141/B164). Although his *behavior* is strictly determined (by what?), his *thought* is not. He is not entirely determined, and Slothrop's case seems to provide him an opportunity to free himself from his own hopeless conditioning: "It has to be more than the simple conditioning of a child, once upon a time. How can he've been a doctor this long and not developed reflexes for certain conditions? He knows better: he knows it is more" (V143–44/B167–68). But Slothrop is only the means for him to free himself enough to reach the ultimate Reward of his Pavlovian's Progress, the Prize; and his deepest commitment regarding Slothrop is, after all, "*We must never lose control*" (V144/B169).

An even deeper irony is hidden in Pointsman's name. We are given an etymology of sorts late in the book:

> He is the pointsman. He is called that because he throws the lever that changes the points. And we go to Happyville, instead of to Pain City. . . . He hardly has to work at all. The lever is very smooth, and easy to push. Even you could push it, Skippy. If you knew where it was. But look what a lot of work he has done, with just one little push. He has sent us all the way to Happyville, instead of to Pain City. That is because he knows just where the points and the lever are. He is the only kind of man who puts in very little work and makes big things happen, all over the world. (V644–45/B751)

This image is not Pynchon's invention; the pointsman recurs in modern discussions of free will, as a metaphor, in fact, for the free will itself. James Clerk Maxwell first developed the metaphor of "singular points" in his essay "Science and Free Will": "At these points, influences whose physical magnitude is too small to be taken account of by a finite being, may produce results of the greatest importance."[4] Sir James Jeans, in his popular *Physics and Philosophy*, elaborates the metaphor:

> The course of a railway train is uniquely prescribed for it at most points of its journey by the rails on which it runs. Here and there, however, it comes to a junction at which alternate courses are open to it, and it may be turned on to one or the other by the quite negligible expenditure of energy in moving the points. Maxwell thought that the human body might come to similar junctions, at which it could be turned into one course or another by the action of the mind, without any expenditure of mechanical energy—the body is the train, the mind is the pointsman.[5]

The psychoanalyst Ferenczi also uses the image: "The will is not like the locomotive that dashes along on the rails: rather it resembles the pointsman."⁶ Pynchon's use of the name Pointsman, and his remark that "even you could push it, Skippy. If you knew where it was," are clues that we should see through Pointsman's rigid determinism, and see the irony in his inability to be his own pointsman, though he tries to be everyone else's.

Pointsman's philosophical position is made most explicit in his discussions with Roger Mexico. "If ever the Antipointsman existed, Roger Mexico is the man" (V55/B63). As a statistician interested in probabilities, Mexico shares none of Pointsman's assumptions about rational analysis and mechanistic causality. And Pointsman is horrified by the implications of Mexico's probability theory—his ability to predict the shape of future events in large numbers, and his absolute inability to apply his knowledge to particular events. Probability theory presents the determinist with a conundrum: Mexico's events are both random (free) and ordered (determined). Mexico calculates the strict and predictable order that underlies random events in large numbers (indeed, all events)—an order that can be described mathematically, but cannot be explained causally or even rationally. Why should random events obey any laws at all? What are (to use Arthur Koestler's term) "the roots of coincidence"? Statistics and probability theory uncover a deep flaw in the notion of mechanistic causality, which is the basis of classical scientific thought as well as our commonsense interpretation of experience. Pointsman thinks,

> How can Mexico play, so at his ease, with these symbols of randomness and fright? Innocent as a child, perhaps unaware—perhaps—that in his play he wrecks the elegant rooms of history, threatens the idea of cause and effect itself. What if Mexico's whole *generation* have turned out like this? Will Postwar be nothing but "events," newly created one moment to the next? No links? Is it the end of history? (V56/B64–65)

He is both right and wrong. He is right in suspecting that the whole generation has turned out like this. By the end of the book, Mexico's generation will have learned to recognize and reject the behaviorist's lockstep mechanism of cause and effect, the stimulus-and-response; they will come to reflect a new historical order, freed from mechanism, causality, determinism, conditioning, and even from rationality itself—a Counterforce, determined only to be free, in the belief that there is an underlying natural order even to its own randomness. Roger confronts Pointsman directly on the subject of analysis and causality:

> "I wonder if you people aren't a bit too—well, strong, on the virtues of analysis. I mean, once you've taken it all apart, fine, I'll be the first to

applaud your industry. But other than a lot of bits and pieces lying about, what have *you* said? . . . There's a feeling about that cause-and-effect may have been taken as far as it will go. That for science to carry on at all, it must look for a less narrow, a less...sterile set of assumptions." (V88–89/B102–3)

Roger is righter than he knows; in fact, he will be just about the last one to grasp the full significance of his position. Osbee Feel will have to explain it to him, when Roger cannot understand that the Counterforce must be a nonrational nonstructure: "*They're* the rational ones. We piss on Their rational arrangements" (V639/ B744). The twin themes of human freedom and irrationalism, their necessary relation to each other, and their relation to the philosophy of modern science, lie at the very center of *Gravity's Rainbow*.

The object of Pointsman's fear is hardly new. A century ago, Tolstoy ended *War and Peace* with an essay on free will and necessity in history, which could hardly be a more appropriate backdrop for our discussion. The notion of cause, Tolstoy argues, has always been essential to our understanding of history; but cause is just another word for necessity, and so the rational analysis of causes and effects is actually a denial of that freedom of will which we experience in ourselves. This is a paradox: "Reason gives expression to the laws of necessity. Consciousness gives expression to the reality of our free will."[7] But the discovery of general laws of history has added a new dimension to the problem:

Ever since the first person said and proved that the number of births or crimes is subject to mathematical laws . . . from that moment the foundations on which history was built were destroyed in their essence.[8]

Unlike Pointsman, however, Tolstoy does not fear the discovery of such laws; though they utterly devalue the notion of cause (which, he concludes, cannot be applied to history), they reveal a higher structure in which necessity and free will no longer appear mutually exclusive—in fact, they are no longer very meaningful terms. The essay concludes by referring us to this higher and invisible structure: "In the present case, it is essential to surmount a consciousness of an unreal freedom and to recognize a dependence not perceived by our senses."[9]

Pointsman can see only chaos in the abandonment of causality. He would rather recognize in human behavior a dependence upon stimuli than upon such invisible forces as Tolstoy and Mexico point to. His error is in not realizing that this new situation does represent a new *order*, even though it marks the end of the old familiar one we thought essential. For even if Mexico's statistical laws are not grounded in cause and effect and cannot predict a precisely determined Laplacian future, they are still, after all, derived from experience, and the shape of history is implicit in them. The world remains orderly, even if we come to see it as constituted of random events with no causal links—*too* orderly, in fact, for the true paranoid. Slothrop discovers the historical basis of these laws in the Spielsaal, where the games of chance reveal the same unfathomable laws as the regularity of Roger's rocket-strikes and Their control over him and Katje: "The odds They played here belonged to the past, the past only. Their odds were never probabilities, but frequencies *already observed*. It's the past that makes demands here" (V208/B243).

Although Pointsman's fear may seem more or less common-sensible to us, it is in fact out of step with the general development of modern science, which he thinks he serves. There really *is* a feeling about that cause and effect may have been taken as far as it can go. Acausality, randomness, probability, and uncertainty have become part of the scientist's stock-in-trade, and theoretical tools have been developed for dealing with them. It is Pointsman, not Mexico, who is out of step with science and the modern world.

In the new Wonderland of the physicist, the mysterious obedience of events in large numbers to laws like Mexico's Poisson equation leads us to principles of order and symmetry in the universe that are themselves beyond the reach of rational analysis. Man has always suspected the existence of such principles, and has given many names to his suspicions. Werner Heisenberg calls it "the central order," and declares, "In the beginning was symmetry."[10] All the supernatural elements in *Gravity's Rainbow* can be interpreted in terms of this dualism between the order we perceive in the world and "another order of being," the "identical-looking Other World," our intuition of greater, invisible, and incomprehensible forces, which gives us the sense of haunting and unaccountable structures in the world and in history.

Quantum and relativity theory have brought us to what seem to be the outer limits of rational thought, where mathematics, common sense, and imagination confront the dead end of paradox. Paradox itself has become such a fundamental part of physical theory that it has been elevated to the rank of a principle: Niels Bohr's principle of "complementarity" simply asserts that mutually exclusive interpretations of phenomena are a basic fact of life in the new physics. *Contraria sunt complementa*, Bohr inscribed on his crest.

Quantum theorists have learned to accommodate themselves to descriptions of reality that conform to neither logic nor language. The "picture" of reality that results does not include "things," but "events"—and not even events in the normal sense, but the probabilities of events, tendencies for events to happen. Reality is conceived of as not Being but Becoming, process rather than state. Heisenberg explains that the probability that governs atomic events in quantum theory "is a quantitative version of the old concept of 'potentia' in Aristotelian philosophy. It introduced something standing in the middle between the idea of an event and the actual event, a strange kind of physical reality just in the middle between possibility and reality." This reality can hardly be described:

> The language has already adjusted itself, at least to some extent, to this true situation. But it is not a precise language in which one could use the normal logical patterns; it is a language that produces pictures in the mind, but together with them the notion that the pictures have only a vague connection with reality, that they represent only a tendency toward reality.[11]

Mechanistic science from Galileo to Maxwell conformed reasonably well to our everyday notions: things moved in time through space according to causal laws. Perhaps we did not understand *how* the earth could hang unsupported in space, perhaps it did not seem commonsensible, but we could at least imagine it, we could form a picture of it in our minds. The nature and workings of the atom, however, or space-time, cannot be imagined at all. Now the physicist confesses with the poet that "the deep truth is imageless."

In the study of atomic particles and the quantum, and the new interpretation of space and time, when the scientist brought his old assumptions to reality in its most fundamental forms, philosophical issues began to intrude into the laboratory itself. The Michelson-Morley experiment in 1887 and the discovery of the quantum in 1900 provided the first irrefutable scientific evidence that not only is the world we are familiar with not at all what it seems, but also that our minds are not exactly suited to grasp the real nature of space, time, matter, or cause. The great physicists of the time, like Maxwell, Mach, and Planck, turned in the end to explore the philosophical implications of their scientific work, especially the problems of perception, causality, and free will. This new situation and its implications, and its continuing conflict with the old assumptions, provide the setting and themes of *Gravity's Rainbow*—the lingering survival of the mechanical world view after its time.

The scientist has finally come around to what has been obvious to philosophers for a long time, certainly since Kant—that our normal understanding of reality is affected by the structures of the mind and its perceptions. One would think, then, that this old-but-new problem would have given a new impetus to the study of the mind. And indeed, psychoanalysis in its many forms, language theory, anthropology, and a number of related disciplines, more unified than is often thought, have been concerned to establish a science of the mind that would complement and validate the advances made by the other sciences.

But there has been one peculiar holdout: in 1913 psychological behaviorism was established in a manifesto by J. B. Watson, as a science singularly devoted to the avoidance of the philosophical problems of knowledge, consciousness, and the mind, which had just taken on a new importance in other sciences; concomitantly, behaviorism devoted itself to the mechanical-causal model of stimulus-response, contrary to the most fundamental contemporary scientific and philosophical developments. Behaviorism's mechanistic assumptions defy the universal agreement among scientific theorists in other areas that a mechanistic philosophy of science is no longer tenable.

So, to return to our book: here is Pointsman, the representative of an intellectual order flourishing well beyond its time, hopelessly out of touch with modern science, terrified by Roger Mexico's innocent equations, dedicated to finding "the true mechanical explanation," the "stone determinacy of everything, of every soul," and exploiting his partial truths to the enormous detriment of the other characters and human values generally. Certainly people can be conditioned; Jamf, Pointsman, and the Firm—the whole structure of society—demonstrate this, as does our everyday experience. But does this mean that conditioning is the fundamental principle of human learning and behavior, and that we cannot (or should not) free ourselves from it?

Pynchon is saying that freedom is possible; we can at least free ourselves from all but the laws of nature—and even the laws of nature are no longer the hard mechanical laws of the old science. The universe we must live in, according to James Jeans's famous remark, is "more like a great thought than like a great machine."[12] The congruence of natural and mental laws, which allows the harmonious relations of our minds and our behavior and experience, gives rise to a new and slightly mystical form of philosophical idealism.

So far as the inanimate world is concerned, we may picture a substratum below space and time in which the springs of events are concealed. . . . But as we pass from the phenomenal world of space and time, we seem, in some way we do not understand, to be passing from materialism to mentalism [idealism], and so possibly also from matter to mind. It may be then that the springs of events in this substratum include our own mental activities, so that the future course of events may depend in part on these mental activities. . . . The classical physics seemed to bolt and bar the door leading to any sort of freedom of the will; the new physics hardly does this; it almost seems to suggest that the door may be unlocked—if only we could find the handle.[13]

For Jeans, then, our experience of free will is the seeming influence of our mental activities upon the world. The most important evidence of this free will is the way our intelligence works against the law of universal entropy. Our free intelligence, he concludes, is very similar to Maxwell's sorting Demon, guiding events at those "singular points" where there are choices to be made.[14]

In the Zone, where all barriers are down, where the "laws" of society and the "laws" of behavior have temporarily collapsed, poor Tyrone Slothrop wanders unsuspectingly into a demonstration of this new order (actually the oldest order of all) of free and random events guided by higher laws, conforming to higher and mysterious structures. He becomes "the figurehead for the latest passage" (V238/B277), flailing his arms and unknowingly blazing a trail for the Counterforce to follow. He *is* a test case—not the test of absolute determinism, however, but just the opposite: proof that *freedom* is at least *possible*. He stumbles accidentally upon what Enzian is struggling so hard to find: "Somewhere, among the wastes of the World, is the key that will bring us back, restore us to our Earth and to our freedom" (V525/B612). Like the Grail, or like grace, this freedom is most easily found when you are not looking for it. The Zone is one of those Maxwellian singular points at which one is free; Slothrop discovers this while meditating on his ancestor William Slothrop, who was another such point:

> Could he have been the fork in the road America never took, the singular point she jumped the wrong way from? . . . It seems to Tyrone Slothrop that there might be a route back—maybe that anarchist he met in Zürich was right, maybe for a little while all the fences are down, one road as good as another, the whole space of the Zone cleared, depolarized, and somewhere inside the waste of it a single set of coordinates from which to proceed. (V556/B647–48)

He understands "this network of all plots may yet carry him to freedom" (V603/B703). And later we find him meditating: ". . . In each of these streets, some vestige of humanity, of Earth, has to remain. . . . Finding it, learning to cherish what was lost, mightn't we find some way back?" (V693/B807–8). And he succeeds to an extent. He is restored to the earth and his freedom, though in a way he could not have anticipated, totally alone:

> He likes to spend whole days naked, ants crawling up his legs, butterflies lighting on his shoulders, watching the life of the mountain, getting to know shrikes and capercaillie, badgers and marmots. . . . Now, in the Zone, later in the day he became a crossroad, after a rain he doesn't recall, Slothrop sees a very thick rainbow here, a stout rainbow cock driven down out of pubic clouds into Earth, green wet valleyed Earth, and his chest fills and he stands crying, not a thing in his head, just feeling natural.... (V623–26/B725–29)

As Pynchon depicts the struggle between the old order and the new, there is no question of their moral values: the old order is that of mechanism, society, and death, and the new is of freedom, nature, and life. How the conflict between the mechanistic order and the natural order is developed in the novel is too large a topic for a short paper, but I can point to certain imagery, lines of development, and conclusions. These lead to a vision of the possibility of human freedom based on the dissolution of social structures founded on reason and analysis, and the restoration of a natural order, a recognition of "another order of being," Tolstoy's "dependence not perceived by the senses," the "springs of events" in Jeans's "substratum" of the universe.

If the theme of Return I have just sketched out seems too optimistic to really be Pynchon's, I hasten to add its apocalyptic corollary. For it is now too late in history for the world, or even society, to effect such a return. Only the individual can recover this freedom, and to do so he must step outside the social order to escape the mechanistic controls it exerts over him. So when Slothrop "returns," he becomes invisible to those around him; he becomes an exile from the army, from America, from his family, and even from his friends. Similarly, when Katje and Prentice enter the Counterforce, they do not find a society there, but only a collection of individuals dropping out each in his own direction; and they realize that their new situation alienates them forever from the People they have only lately learned to love:

> "But the People will never love you," she whispers, "or me. However bad and good are arranged for them, we will *always* be bad. Do you know where that puts us?" (V547–48/B638)

They share a vision of the coming apocalypse, and "dissolve now, into the race and swarm of this dancing Preterition" (V548/B639).

This negative aspect of Return applies to Enzian too. Even

though he is the chief theoretician of Return in the book, who can remember his African homeland, "one of the last pockets of Pre-Christian Oneness left on the planet" (V321/B373), he is also the chief theoretician of No Return. The linear and apocalyptic direction of modern history (the "one-way departure") was revealed to him in his childhood: when he returned alone to rejoin his tribe, it had been destroyed by the Europeans (V323/B375). For the Hereros, the only possible Return is tribal suicide, since "the Eternal Center can easily be seen as the Final Zero" (V319/B371), and Enzian's Return will be his death.

Why is the return to our earth and to our freedom possible only at such high cost? Partly because we must renounce society, for it is the modern world itself we must return *from*. To understand society and its silent tyrannical rule over us, we have to understand analysis, which for Pynchon is the trademark of the European Kingdom Of Death: "Europe's Original Sin—the latest name for that is Modern Analysis" (V722/B842). Analysis is the cause of Europe's irreversible fall from that natural state to which we must return by ourselves.

The relationships between rational analysis, free will, and determinism are old problems. Zeno spotted the paradoxes of analysis almost as soon as it was invented. Reason has never been able to deal directly with time, motion, and change, but instead divides, categorizes, and freezes them; by its nature it sees a line or trajectory as a series of points, and sees a process as a series of states. To do so, of course, it has to invent the notions of points and moments, without extension or duration; and explaining the relation of such notions to real space and time is not easy. Reason is at home with Being, and so sees it everywhere; but it finds Becoming a problem because it cannot be analyzed—because we cannot stop it to look at it and describe it. Unfortunately, the world is always becoming, and Being eludes us there—it is hard to find, but all too easy to think about.

The analytic approach to the world has had great practical success, of course, but at very high cost. Analysis leads us away from all those intuitional and irrational truths that non-European cultures prize so highly and the Western intellectual usually holds in contempt, and that impeded the development of genuinely scientific traditions outside Europe. Analysis actually leads us away from reality itself, as Pynchon says when he refers to "the German mania for name-giving, dividing the Creation finer and finer, analyzing, setting namer more hopelessly apart from named" (V391/B455). It is interesting to note that even in the construction of the Rocket, the problems of guidance have to be solved by a team of mystical engineers, with their Demian-metaphysics, rocket-Zen, and electro-mysticism (V403–4/B469–70). The thorough antirationalism of *Gravity's Rainbow* cannot be overstated.

European science and technology were able to progress so extraordinarily only by ignoring certain problems of philosophy created by our insistence that thought be rational and our devaluation of intuition as a form of knowledge. The scientific elaboration of a mechanistic world view depends upon the infinitesimal calculus, which ignores Zeno's paradoxes by simply assigning a term to the infinitesimal instant and point, delta-t. The delta-t does not solve the philosophical problem, of course; it simply names it and allows us to manipulate the name in order to solve all sorts of practical problems. It is virtually a symbol of this one aspect of reality we cannot understand, one of the borderlines of rational knowledge, the name we give to our inability to grasp reality clearly as it is, as an unbroken continuum in space and time. The delta-t is not just another mathematical tool, it is a compromise with reality and thus a reminder of the incomprehensibility of the world around us and the limitations of our reason. In *The Crying of Lot 49*, Pynchon described it as

> a vanishingly small instant in which change had to be confronted at last for what it was, where it could no longer disguise itself as something innocuous like an average rate; where velocity dwelled in the projectile though the projectile be frozen in midflight, where death dwelled in the cell though the cell be looked in on at its most quick. (Pp. 95–96)

In *Gravity's Rainbow*, the same theme is developed on a much grander scale in the pervasive imagery of film. The relations of time, analysis, calculus, behaviorism, freedom, and social order are all explored in this imagery. The illusion of movement in film symbolizes the falsification of time, motion, and change that is produced by reason's division of them into successive instants and points. "Film and calculus, both pornographies of flight. Reminders of impotence and abstraction" (V567/B661). We can see how broad the theme's implications can be in the story of Franz Pökler:

> There has been this strange connection between the German mind and the rapid flashing of successive stills to counterfeit movement, for at least two centuries—since Leibniz, in the process of inventing calculus, used the same approach to break up the trajectories of cannonballs through the air. And now Pökler was about to be given proof that these techniques had been extended past images on film, to human lives. (V407/B474)

Blicero, in whom Europe's love affair with the forces of death is symbolized, plays Pointsman with Pökler. Like Pointsman, he too is a behavioristic social engineer, and his cinematic methods for behavior modification are emblematic of the dangers to human values posed by the philosophical error that underlies the rationalistic and mechanistic interpretation of the world—all the more dangerous in an age that no longer believes in God or the soul, and so has mechanized everything, including historical and social forces, life itself, and human thought and behavior, "everything, every soul."

Pynchon is not the first to use the image of the cinema to explain the relations of reason and mechanism. Henri Bergson, in his enormously influential *Creative Evolution* (1907), wrote a history of Western philosophy as the progressive elaboration of the error he calls "the cinematographical illusion." He describes a "cinematograph" (for an audience that had not yet become thoroughly conditioned by the movies), and then proceeds:

> Such is the contrivance of the cinematograph. And such is that of our knowledge. Instead of attaching ourselves to the inner becoming of things, we place ourselves outside them in order to recompose their becoming artificially. . . . Perception, intellection, language so proceed in general. Whether we would think becoming, or express it, or even perceive it, we hardly do anything else than set going a kind of cinematograph inside us. We may therefore sum up what we have been saying in the conclusion that the *mechanism of our ordinary knowledge is of a cinematographical kind.*[15]

This kind of knowledge has evolved in us for a good purpose, which is the successful manipulation of reality in everyday practical affairs, like the making and using of tools. But whatever its practical virtues, this kind of knowledge is not suited for the discovery and description of the true nature of the world in science or philosophy, since it is such a profound falsification of reality. He goes on to say, however, that this error can be corrected. Bergson asks that we develop a second form of knowledge, one that can perceive the "duration" of reality directly, and thus perceive the creative life force, the *élan vital*, that infuses the material world. Readers of *Gravity's Rainbow* will recognize in this program the very heart of the book's moral vision:

> This second kind of knowledge would have set the cinematographical method aside. . . . [This] other knowledge, if it is possible, is practically useless, it will not extend our empire over nature, it will even go against certain natural aspirations of the intellect; but, if it succeeds, it is reality itself that it will hold in a firm and final embrace. . . . For, as soon as we are confronted with true duration, we see that it means creation, and that if that which is being unmade endures, it can only be because it is

inseparably bound to that which is making itself. Thus will appear the necessity of a continual growth of the universe, I should say of a *life* of the real. And thus will be seen in a new light the life which we find on the surface of our planet, a life directed the same way as that of the universe, and inverse of materiality. To intellect, in short, there will be added intuition.

The more we reflect on it, the more we shall find that this conception of metaphysics is that which modern science suggests.[16]

This intuitive key to Life is the key Enzian searches for among the wastes of the world, which can restore us to our earth and to our freedom. Compare to Bergson's vision those given to so many characters in *Gravity's Rainbow*, most clearly to Slothrop (V626/ B729), Lyle Bland (V590/B687–88), and Geli Tripping (V720/ B839–40).

Bergson's "Vitalism," the Philosophy of Life, plays an important role in the history of European thought; in many respects it is a revival of the Romantic philosophy of Schelling a century earlier, which had briefly interrupted the development of mechanism with a philosophy of organic nature. For Schelling the world of nature (including history and culture) could not be analyzed because "it is not simply a sum total of geometric arrangements and mechanical laws, but an organic whole of structures and powers."[17] For the Romantics, Nature remained a riddle, beyond our powers of scientific understanding, accessible only to intuition. Bergson's renewed attack on analysis, aided by modern scientific developments, inspired in turn a number of related philosophical movements, among which was Whitehead's attempt to synthesize recent developments in his own "Philosophy of Organism." Such philosophies share an almost Oriental insistence on the living wholeness of the world, as well as its hiddenness from thought. The act of apprehending this transcendental Nature is therefore an act of self-transcendence, of intuitive unification with the world. In his criticism of this philosophical attitude, Theodore Litt complains that it "allows the dissolution of personal existence, an irremovable feature of this doctrine, to become so obvious."[18]

With all this in mind, we can return to our earlier question concerning Slothrop's own personal dissolution: why is his freedom possible only at such high cost? We can begin to see it as a predictable result of his growing sense of the unity of the world (his paranoia, "the onset, the leading edge, of the discovery that *everything is connected*" [V703/B820]), and his own unity with it (finally "just feeling natural"). What Enzian says of Blicero can also be said of Slothrop: "Whatever happened at the end, he has transcended.

Even if he's only dead. He's gone beyond *his* pain, *his* sin—driven deep into Their province" (V660–61/B770).

We need to elaborate the meaning of this dissolution, which be-sets many of the book's characters besides Slothrop—notably Blicero, and Pirate and Katje, who "dissolve now, into the race and swarm of the dancing Preterition." But dissolution is a symbol with many meanings, which in large part constitute the philosophical context of the book. They can all deepen our understanding of the book's themes, and show how they are related to analogous or identical themes developed in philosophy.

This is the particular theme we have been developing in *Gravity's Rainbow*: first, that rational analysis, as the modern world's charac-teristic mode of life, has stolen man's freedom by seducing him intellectually into a "stone determinacy" at every level of his being; second, that we can return to our freedom, but only individually and alone—only at the cost of relinquishing society, because society cannot see its own enslavement to reason, does not understand its dangers, and so pushes it upon us aggressively, wrongly, and mortally, even if innocently; and third, that our solitary return into freedom is experienced both by society and ourselves as a dissolu-tion—a loss of the self that is, paradoxically, an act of identification with the world and all of those who constitute the very society we cannot belong to.

As elaborate as this theme appears, it is not Pynchon's alone. In fact, it was very much in the air as Pynchon was writing *Gravity's Rainbow*. We can find it in ideas as diverse as the popular psychoana-lytic vision of Norman O. Brown, the anthropology of Lévi-Strauss, the philosophy of Husserl and Heidegger, and elsewhere too. But these few will serve our purpose here. Each provides us with a partial commentary on Pynchon's theme.

The first is Norman O. Brown, whose plan for personal and social salvation is outlined in his book *Love's Body*. The penultimate chapter of the book is entitled "Freedom," and that this freedom implies some form of self-annihilation is clear from the title of the final chapter, "Nothing." Following Freud, Brown sees in the mind and in history the struggle of the two instincts Love and Death, and like Pynchon he sees Europe as essentially the Kingdom of Death—and Death is Analysis.

> Is there a way out; an end to analysis; a cure; is there such a thing as health? To heal is to make whole, as in wholesome; to make one again; to unify or reunify: this is Eros in action. Eros is the instinct that makes for union, or unification, and Thanatos, the death instinct, is the instinct that makes for separation, or division.[19]

Unification is accomplished by the acceptance of the symbolic consciousness: "Symbolism is mind making connections (correspondences) rather than distinctions (separations). . . . Freud says, symbolism is on the track of a former identity, a lost unity . . . the unity of the whole cosmos as one living creature."[20] This lost unity is not only psychic; it is not just the recovery of the unified self: "The integration of the psyche is the integration of the human race, and the integration of the world with which we are inseparably connected."[21] This integration is a return not just to another kind of thinking but to the roots of nature and the origin of symbols, a return to the body, the rediscovery of our full sexuality, Brown's notorious "polymorphous perversity." The descent into this psychosexual inferno in search of oneness is "a perpetual promenade right in the forbidden zone. . . . Go down and stay down, in the forbidden zone; a descent into hell."[22] The application of these ideas to *Gravity's Rainbow* is too transparent to require explanation; I rehearse them here to arrive at Brown's twin conclusions: freedom, and the subsequent dissolution of the ego in its union with the world.

> To become conscious of our participation in the creation of the phenomenal world is to pass from passive experience—perception as impressions on a passive mind—to conscious creation, and creative freedom. . . . Apocalypse is the dissolution of the group as numerical series, as in representative democracy, and its replacement by the group as fusion, as communion.[23]

The individual ego, according to Brown, is an illusion "which disintegrates at the moment of illumination."[24]

Second is Claude Lévi-Strauss, whose structuralism may seem an unlikely analogue of these ideas because of its highly analytic nature. But behind and prior to Lévi-Strauss' analyses, we find an active intuition, and we also find a motive, a concern for the crisis of modern European culture. He ends his autobiographical *Tristes Tropiques* with a moving explanation of why he fled France to live among the South American Indians. Of primitive life, he says:

> In that mythic age, man was no freer than he is today; but only his humanness made him a slave. Since his control over nature remained very limited, he was protected—and to some extent released from bondage—by a cushioning of dreams. As these dreams were gradually transformed into knowledge, man's power increased and became a great source of pride; but this power, which gears us, as it were, to the universe, whose great deterministic laws, instead of remaining remote and awe-inspiring, now use thought itself as an intermediary medium and are colonizing us on behalf of a silent world of which we have become the agents.[25]

It is Europe that has to bear this responsibility for destroying the natural human condition, now having finally Europeanized America. It is the theme of Blicero's last lament, the White Man wondering how to atone for his crime: "America was a gift from the invisible powers, a way of returning. But Europe refused it" (V722/B842). Lévi-Strauss says,

> For us European Earth-dwellers, the adventure played out in the heart of the New World signifies in the first place that it was not our world and that we bear responsibility for its destruction; and secondly, that there will never be another New World. . . . Our world missed the opportunity offered to it of choosing between its various missions.[26]

And in a passage that brings to mind Geli Tripping's vision of mankind as "God's spoilers" (V720/B840), Lévi-Strauss pins the blame for our present condition on the unnatural progress of civilization itself:

> [Man] himself appears as perhaps the most effective agent working towards the disintegration of the original order of things and hurrying on powerfully organized matter towards even greater inertia, an inertia which one day will be final. . . . What else has man done except blithely break down billions of structures and reduce them to a state in which they are no longer capable of integration?[27]

Our growing communications produce "an evenness of level" that he likens to the physicist's concept of entropy, a familiar theme to Pynchon's readers. "Civilization, taken as a whole, can be described as an extraordinarily complex mechanism, which we might be tempted to see as an opportunity of survival for the human world, if its function were not to produce what physicists call entropy, that is inertia." He suggests renaming anthropology "entropology"—"the study of the highest manifestations of this process of disintegration."[28]

But Lévi-Strauss does not leave us with no exit. Like Bergson and Brown, he believes relief is to be found in the return from reason to intuition, a return to freedom and love. He concludes with an eloquent call to freedom, intuition, and the Earth, a commentary on all the themes of *Gravity's Rainbow* I have been discussing that will repay a very close reading:

> When the spectrum or rainbow of human cultures has finally sunk into the void created by our frenzy, as long as we continue to exist and there is a world, that tenuous arch linking us to the inaccessible will still remain, to show us the opposite course to that leading to enslavement; man may be unable to follow it, but its contemplation affords him the only privilege of which he can make himself worthy; that of arresting the process, of controlling the impulse which forces him to block up the

cracks in the wall of necessity one by one and to complete his work at the same time as he shuts himself up within his prison; . . . the possibility, vital for life, of *unhitching*, which consists . . . in grasping, during the brief intervals in which our species can bring itself to interrupt its hive-like activity, the essence of what it was and continues to be, below the threshold of thought and over and above society: in the contemplation of a mineral more beautiful than all our creations; in the scent that can be smelt at the heart of a lily and is more imbued with learning than all our books; or in the brief glance, heavy with patience, serenity, and mutual forgiveness, that through some involuntary understanding, one can sometimes exchange with a cat.[29]

The third and most important critique of Pynchon's ideas is the philosophy of Edmund Husserl. Husserl was the founder of the phenomenological movement, which gave rise to the more widely understood existentialism. We have only to think of the classics of existential literature to see their contribution to our search: Slothrop's dissolution is really no more puzzling than the dissolution of the ego we see in Sartre's Roquentin in *Nausea* or Camus's Meursault in *The Stranger*, when they realize their unsought-for illumination and freedom. The *essential negativity of freedom* is the theme of Sartre's monumental *Being and Nothingness*. And of Heidegger, Husserl's greatest successor, I will only say here that he provides the profoundest commentary of all on the ideas of *Gravity's Rainbow*, and I recommend to the philosophically inclined reader, especially his discussion of "Them" in *Being and Time*, and his meditation on Rilke's poem "The Force of Gravity."[30]

Husserl's own work is not as well known to students of literature because it is so difficult to vulgarize. His only popularizer has been Colin Wilson, whose most popular work, *The Outsider*, is a study of the Slothrop-theme in twentieth-century literature—the inevitable social alienation of the man who comes to realize his human freedom.

> The Outsider and freedom are always associated together. The Outsider's problem *is* the problem of freedom. . . . A man becomes an Outsider when he begins to chafe under the recognition that he is not free. While he is the ordinary, once-born human being, like Camus' Meursault, *he is not free but does not realize it*.[31]

This is an apt description of Slothrop, who must discover his bondage before he can discover his freedom from it, and whose final liberation makes him so much an Outsider that he actually disappears from view.

Phenomenology, like existentialism, is first of all a philosophy of *freedom*. It is an unthinkable proposition that man is not free, that he is determined by the external world, since that world can only be known in consciousness, and is in fact constituted in consciousness, actively as well as passively, according to the intentions of the ego. Second, it is a philosophy of *intuition*. The world of our experience, which we experience as pre-given to us, resides within consciousness and may be inspected directly. This pre-analytic inspection, which is carried out with no assumptions about either the world or the mind, is the phenomenological "reduction," and is the foundation of all true knowledge. Third, it asserts the essential *unity* of experience. All knowledge is synthesized in consciousness in such a way that "the ego contains no individual isolated *cogito* [act of consciousness]," but "all of existence is one universal synthetic unity."[32] Because consciousness, and thus the world, is a synthetic unity, our analytic constructions of it must be seen as an unreliable aspect of our own subjectivity. Everyday normal thinking naïvely assumes that the world known to consciousness is objective, and even objectivizes its own analytic constructions. But in the process of the phenomenological reduction, this naïve objectivism gives way to a comprehensive "transcendental subjectivism"; and in the process, the whole structure of mathematicized physical theory is reduced to small account in the constitution of real knowledge. According to Husserl, European science since Galileo has assumed "that perceived qualities are purely 'subjective' illusions and that 'true reality' is of a mathematical order." This is a profound error that ultimately leads to circular reasoning. "Only a more radical reflection which relates all of physics to the foregoing presence, to the 'pregivenness' of the life-world, can escape from this circle." The errors of objectivism and the mathematical analysis of the synthetic unity develop into Husserl's greatest theme in his later work, "The Crisis of European Humanity." In Europe, "there is a crisis in the very project of knowing."[33]

Husserl's philosophical program for establishing true knowledge is in certain ways a more detailed and rigorous Bergsonian vitalism. What we gain by thinking phenomenologically is "pure living."[34] Husserl's late thought revolves around two great concepts. First is the "life-world," characterized by synthetic unity and duration, the basis of our experience and consciousness, manifest and irreducible and therefore the reference of all true knowledge. Second, this knowledge is manifested not to itself, not to the whole of consciousness, but to a "transcendental Ego," "the pure subject, the 'I' that stands behind all appearances as their observer and behind all free acts as their agent," the ultimate ground of being, knowledge, and freedom. An arduous examination of the transcendental Ego leads Husserl to posit that "the transcendental Ego conceived as the perennial observer of existence can quite properly be said to be external to the world, just as the reader is external to the book and the audience is external to the play."[35] This Ego actually transcends the world of consciousness, and finally allows us to establish "transcendental intersubjectivity," that is, to escape from our captivity within the self, an escape into full knowledge, communion with other minds, and freedom.

The passage into full self-consciousness of the transcendental Ego is the passage out of Plato's cave into the blinding light of the truth, and the realization that all previous knowledge has only been the naïve acceptance of illusion. Colin Wilson compares this passage to the very same discovery we are led to on the last page of *Gravity's Rainbow*, where the book-as-film breaks off unexpectedly, and we suddenly find ourselves sitting in a theater staring at a blank screen:

> [The Outsiders'] problem is the unreality of their lives. They become acutely conscious of it when it begins to pain them, but they are not sure of the source of the pain. The ordinary world loses its values, as it does for a man who has been ill for a long time. Life takes on the quality of a nightmare, or a cinema sheet when the screen goes blank. These men who had been projecting their hopes and desires into what was passing on the screen suddenly realize they are in a cinema. They ask: Who are we? What are we doing here? With the delusion of the screen identity gone, the causality of its events suddenly broken, they are confronted with a terrible freedom. In Sartre's phrase, they are "condemned to be free." Completely new bearings are demanded; a new analysis of this real world of the cinema has to be undertaken. In the shadow world on the screen, every problem had an answer; this may not be true of the world of the cinema. The fact that the screen world has proved to be a delusion arouses the disturbing possibility that the cinema may be unreal too.[36]

This formulation applies equally to Slothrop and the Counterforce, and to the reader of the book and the reader of this essay too. We are all shocked in this way into a higher consciousness that can finally lead us to a transcendental freedom.

1. *The City of God*, trans. Henry Bettenson (Baltimore, Md.: Penguin Books, 1972), 14. 17.

2. M. Blanton, "The Behavior of the Human Infant during the First Thirty Days of Life," *Psychological Review* 24 (1917); H. M. Halverson, "Infant Sucking and Tensional Behavior," *Journal of General Psychology* 53 (1938); see P. Greenacre, *Trauma, Growth, and Personality* (New York: W. W. Norton, 1952), pp. 35–41.

3. In Ernst Cassirer, *The Logic of the Humanities*, trans. C. S. Howe (New Haven, Conn.: Yale University Press, 1960), p. 10.

4. In Lewis Campbell, *Life of James Clerk Maxwell* (London: Macmillan, 1882), p. 443.

5. Sir James Jeans, *Physics and Philosophy* (Cambridge: Cambridge University Press, 1944), p. 211.

6. Sandor Ferenczi, *The Theory and Technique of Psychoanalysis* (New York: Basic Books, 1926), p. 405.

7. Leo Tolstoy, *War and Peace*, trans. Constance Garnett (London: Heinemann, 1971), p. 1311.

8. Ibid., p. 1313.

9. Ibid., p. 1315.

10. Werner Heisenberg, *Physics and Beyond*, trans. A. J. Pomerans (New York: Harper & Row, 1971), pp. 240–41.

11. Werner Heisenberg, *Physics and Philosophy* (New York: Harper & Row, 1958), pp. 41, 181.

12. Sir James Jeans, *The Mysterious Universe* (New York: Macmillan, 1931), p. 158.

13. Jeans, *Physics and Philosophy*, p. 214.

14. Ibid., pp. 215–16. See also his *The New Background of Science* (Cambridge: Cambridge University Press, 1953), pp. 276–81.

15. Henri Bergson, *Creative Evolution*, trans. Arthur Mitchell (New York: Henry Holt, 1911), p. 306.

16. Ibid., pp. 342–43.

17. Cassirer, *Logic of the Humanities*, p. 6.

18. Ibid., cited on p. 8.

19. Norman O. Brown, *Love's Body* (New York: Vintage, 1966), p. 80.

20. Ibid., pp. 81–82.

21. Ibid., p. 87.

22. Ibid., p. 241.

23. Ibid., p. 255.

24. Ibid., p. 105.

25. Claude Lévi-Strauss, *Tristes Tropiques*, trans. J. and D. Weightman (New York: Atheneum, 1974), p. 391.

26. Ibid., p. 393.

27. Ibid., p. 413.

28. Ibid., pp. 413–14.

29. Ibid., pp. 414–15.

30. Martin Heidegger, *Being and Time*, trans. J. Macquarrie and E. Robinson (New York: Harper & Row, 1962), pp. 163–68; and "What Are Poets For?," in *Poetry, Language, Thought*, trans. A. Hofstadter (New York: Harper & Row, 1971), pp. 91–142.

31. Colin Wilson, *The Outsider* (New York: Delta, 1956), p. 113.

32. Edmund Husserl, *The Paris Lectures*, trans. P. Kastenbaum (The Hague: Nijhoff, 1975), p. 18.

33. Paul Ricoeur, *Husserl: An Analysis of His Phenomenology*, trans. Ballard and Embree (Evanston, Ill.: Northwestern University Press, 1967), pp. 153, 163.

34. Edmund Husserl, *Cartesian Meditations*, trans. Dorian Cairns (The Hague: Nijhoff, 1973), p. 20.

35. Kastenbaum, introduction to *The Paris Lectures*, pp. xlvi, xlvii, liii.

36. *The Outsider*, pp. 67–68.

Pynchon's Language:
Signs, Systems, and Subversion

By Charles Russell

> No things, but an iridescence in the void. Meaning is a continuous creation, out of nothing and returning to nothingness. If it is not evanescent it is not alive. Everything is symbolic, is transitory; is unstable. The consolidation of meaning makes idols; established meanings have turned to stone.[1]

The world of human meanings that Pynchon depicts is also "but an iridescence in the void." It is acutely aware that it rises out of nothingness and is ever threatened by a collapse back into nothingness. It is kept alive—kept animate—only by the continuous process of self-creation, of desire and assertion, that temporarily establishes the countless individual systems of personal and collective meaning that appear to give validity and stability to the world we inhabit. But, Pynchon also informs us, all too frequently the fear of the void compels people to mistakenly believe that the world they have created *is* secure enough to shut out the vision, if not the inevitable reality, of their own destruction. Ironically, however, the more they make idols out of their systems of belief, the more those meanings turn to stone. Their firmly held beliefs seem at first to be barriers against the darkness, but are ultimately rigid and as inanimate and as threatening as the void they would defend against. Invariably, this irony informs the apparently ineluctable processes of the creation and collapse of meaning systems throughout Pynchon's works.

Pynchon's three novels describe a rage for order run amok, a struggle for survival that in its excess has become suicidal. Each of his books, but especially *Gravity's Rainbow*, focuses on the fateful dynamics of the assertion and petrification of meaning systems, whether they be linguistic, religious, political, economic, scientific, or sexual; indeed, any pattern of order that people assign to their lives seems to follow the same semiotic logic, the same patterns of the creation, intensification, and final failure of essential meaning. Yet through Pynchon's parody of this semiotic rage, his own self-consciously excessive system-building, his mammoth creation of the evanescent world that makes up *Gravity's Rainbow*, he offers us an insight into, as well as a critique of, the stone idols of our culture.

There are many critical approaches to *Gravity's Rainbow*, but one of particular importance is provided by a study of the nature and limits of language systems and, by extension, all semiotic systems in the book. Pynchon's ultimately self-reflexive focus on the linguistic basis of meaning systems provides the thematic and formal coherence of the book as well as determines the distinctive qualities of his style and linguistic richness, particularly his wonderful use of metaphor. At the same time, these concerns clearly link this author and book to the dominant literary strategies of much of contemporary fiction. Indeed, *Gravity's Rainbow* is but one manifestation of a widespread literary fascination with the nature and limits of aesthetic and social language during the past two decades. Whether it be the books of Burroughs, Gass, Coover, Barth, Barthelme, or Reed, the "new" and poststructuralist novels of Robbe-Grillet, Sollers, or Maurice Roche, the writings of Handke, or of a myriad of South American fabulists, the fiction of our era offers a radical critique of art as language, of language as social behavior, and, correspondingly, of social behavior as versions of semiotic systems. These writers' preoccupation with language, especially with the ceaseless dialectic of assertion and collapse of meaning—of creation and deconstruction—generates the self-reflexive linguistic play that has become the primary aesthetic style of our period, the period known as the postmodern.

As an aesthetic concept, postmodernism emerges from literary modernism, with which, as its name suggests, it shares many defining characteristics. In the work of writers as diverse as Yeats, Eliot, Proust, Rilke, Joyce, Valéry, Kafka, Lawrence, and Pound, modernism's determining obsession may be seen as the stark confrontation of language and consciousness with that which lies beyond them—a confrontation revealed either in the authors' search for a more valid or primal level of meaning that might redeem the apparent valuelessness of the social world from which the writer was alienated, or in the aesthetic consciousness' dramatic opposition to the seeming meaninglessness of existence ever threatening humanity's meager realm of order and meaning. The self-consciousness of great modernist literature displayed an existential faith in the heroic integrity of human action and posited meaning in an alien and nonhuman cosmos.

Postmodernism retains and restates this fascination with order and potential disorder, with the power and desire of human language and consciousness to create a world of adequate meaning. But significantly absent from contemporary writing is any faith in, or even appeal to, an existent and more valid realm of being beyond the quotidian social order. There is no saving myth, no sustaining sacred belief, no valorization of the subconscious that can be asserted as more than a temporary expedient. There is barely any hope of significant social change that might alter the beliefs or social conditions of culture: certainly there is no developed conception of historical progress. Rather, it is entirely within the framework of socialized behavior—humankind's self-projected semiotic systems —that postmodernism situates us. It is the manifestations of private and collective consciousness that this new literature explores. And consciousness, in this our structuralist era, is deemed to be determined solely by language. Only that which enters into language has meaning; only that which finds articulation can be known. Consequently, the study of humanity's effort to establish a meaningful world is conducted most frequently through the analysis of how language is used in personal and collective discourse.

Furthermore, rather than privileging literature as a unique form of language as did the modernists and the New Critics, postmodernist writers recognize that literature is itself totally encapsulated within, and is a direct expression of, the reigning cultural codes of meaning, even if particular writers may be antagonistic to the ideological extensions of those codes. Consequently, many postmodern novels challenge the reader to explore the relation of the particular literary work to the social structure, behavior, and ideology of its culture. It is evident, for example, that the French new novelists, as well as Burroughs, Coover, Barthelme, and others—Pynchon primary among them—believe that inherited languages, and the social world built upon them, are not to be trusted. If no semiotic system can offer essential meaning, none can claim privileged or authoritative status. But it is precisely such claims that all too frequently are made by the institutions of power, manipulation, and exploitation in society. Rather than analyzing or attacking the particular actions or values of these institutions as entities, the contemporary novelist tends to depict them as ideological systems to which an aggressive, deconstructive semiotic analysis can be addressed. The logic of assertion and control, the limits of meaning, the internal dynamics and contradictions of the system thus become the focuses of the literary text.

Insofar as the literary work is implicated in that same culture, it demands of itself and its readers a constant critical self-reflexiveness. In effect, the postmodern work urges the demystification of language by and within the literary artifice. Each statement and each text must turn back upon itself to reveal and judge itself—its assumptions or pretensions to meaning, as well as its limits and arbitrariness. The essential message of the postmodern novel is, as N. O. Brown suggests, that meaning must be evanescent. It is only alive in the precarious free play of constant creation rising out of the necessary—and self-conscious—deconstruction of previous meaning. Furthermore, the contemporary novelist suggests that these processes of literary assertion and disruption, or of analysis and criticism, may provide paradigms for the individual's social and political responses to the culturally encoded meaning systems, the values and conflicts within modern society.

These postmodern revisions, or subversions, of the modernist rage for order are nowhere so evident as in the works of Thomas Pynchon. In fact, the central struggle in *Gravity's Rainbow* between the Firm and the Counterforce may be read as one expression of the conflict between these two views of the nature and power of language. On the one hand, the Firm's demand that its language and control systems be coherent, stable, and manipulable suggests the sinister dimension of the rage for order, while at the same time the dark romanticism rife within the Firm, particularly with Blicero and his guiding spirit, Rilke, reveals the passionate undercurrent of modernist despair and longing for what transcends their language. On the other hand, the Counterforce's much more tentative, self-deconstructive, and perhaps self-defeating play with language indicates both the liberating aspects as well as the severe limits of postmodern aesthetics.

The nature of signs, systems, and their subversion is thus one of the primary themes of *Gravity's Rainbow*. The work constantly directs our attention toward the process of human signification: how we give meaning and order to our world, how we interpret experience, and how we find ourselves trapped within the meaning systems we create. All the characters and societies that Pynchon depicts are obsessed with these processes of defining, explaining, and controlling their world. Each individual, group, or culture seizes upon particular names, theories, or signifying systems to lend validity to the patterns of action that characterize their behavior. Furthermore, almost all human activities, individual or collective, appear to combine to form a web of interconnecting meaning systems that are often at war with each other but that ultimately betray the same inherent, insane logic of control. Both the social and physical environment seem pregnant with meaning. It is as if we were surrounded by barely disguised language systems needing—demanding—to be interpreted. Everything potentially bears a message, from the sacred rainbow and the secular rocket to molecular patterns and the lay of the Colonel from Kenosha's hair (V643/B749). *Gravity's Rainbow* offers us a vast superstructure of these interpenetrating systems of meaning and control, be they malevolent or benign. It is a parodic panorama of life in late-capitalist, post-industrial society, in which individuals live at the mercy of diffuse economic, political, corporate, and technological orders, and struggle within behavioral patterns shaped by psychological, parapsychological, and sexual determinants. But even more diabolic, Pynchon implies, is that even if antagonistic to each other, all these systems are analogous. All behavior, all knowledge, all *reality* seem to exhibit the same structure and logic. Indeed, they appear to suggest, as many of the characters in the novel believe, that they are ultimately all connected and controlled by an omnipresent and malevolent agency. If such an agency exists, however, it is not a social entity like the ubiquitous Firm, but rather the passion of human consciousness and language to rigidly discriminate, name, and attempt to dominate experience, of which the Firm is only a particular, if excessive, manifestation. Language, which determines the structure, hence the operation, of consciousness and culture, consequently provides the universal analogy of control and decay in Pynchon's world. But if it often appears to be the villain of the work, it is also the primary agent of healthy creation and potential liberation from the reign of oppressive systems.

II

Although the Rocket is the focal metaphor of the book, in Pynchon's universe all human activities manifest the same record of fear, desire, and defeat. Enzian and Slothrop realize, just as Herbert Stencil does in *V.*, that finally the particular frame of reference does not matter. One can read the same message in the Rocket, the War, the Firm, or the detritus of people's lives in the Zone (V524/B611, V626/B727). However, it is around the Rocket, and particularly the scientific, technological quest that gives it birth, that the analogous relationship of language, science, and behavior, as well as the dangers of their excesses, are most apparent. For Pynchon the basis of the analogy lies in the similar tendencies of language, rational thinking, and scientific methodology to fragment undifferentiated experience into separate entities in order to recombine the fragments into a new, humanly governed order.

The process of naming, discriminating, and restructuring that is the foundation of scientific procedure and linguistic action is the source of human power as well as the cause and sign of humanity's fear and misery. The similarities between science and language are revealed, for example, to Blobadjian when he is transferred from committee work on the New Turkic Alphabet to a committee on molecular structure.

> How alphabetic is the nature of molecules. . . . "See: how they are taken out from the coarse flow—shaped, cleaned, rectified, just as you once redeemed your letters from the lawless, the mortal streaming of human speech.... These are our letters, our words: they too can be modulated, broken, recoupled, redefined, co-polymerized one to the other in world-wide chains that will surface now and then over long molecular silences, like the seen parts of a tapestry." (V355/B413–14)

Tchitcherine observes a similar tendency in Slothrop's subconscious fixation with compound words based on the word *black*. But here, the process of recoupling indicates a mania, an uneasy desire to distance oneself from some obsessive fear. "Has he by way of the language caught the German mania for name-giving, dividing the Creation finer and finer, analyzing, setting namer more hopelessly apart from named, even to bringing in the mathematics of combination, tacking together established nouns to get new ones, the insanely, endlessly diddling play of a chemist whose molecules are words...." (V391/B455).

These tendencies of language affect, if not generate, most of the narrative situations in *Gravity's Rainbow*. They exhibit, Pynchon would have us believe, a process inherent in all human endeavor—in social formation, ideology, science, technology, economics, politics, language, even dream. They are also the source of the hope and the failure, the idealism and the paranoia, the mania and the victimization that texture the novel.

These passages indicate the two common processes at the heart of all systems of articulation, interpretation, and manipulation: (1)

the fragmentation of experience by consciousness during the act of naming—the definition and discrimination of specific identities isolates them from their context and, in the process, provides the namer with a critical distance from the named and the world that threatens so; (2) the attempted reformulation (*reformation*) of the now isolated terms into a coherent and manageable system of language, knowledge, and power. The goal of such processes is the establishment of a human-oriented and possibly controllable alternative to the natural world.

These processes are the basis of the creation of the human realm. They allow the emergence of self-consciousness and critical perception of the world. The power they give to humans to create themselves seems magical and awesome. Twice variations on the phrase "names by themselves may be empty, but the *act of naming*..." (V366/B426, V322/B374) suggest the sense of mystery and might that the characters—and the narrator—feel in their language. Though Blobadjian is describing the creation of a written alphabet from a preexistent spoken language, his description applies to the creation of language itself from unarticulated experience. The appearance of a pattern in the tapestry, of a meaningful sound from the silence or clangor around one, represents the "redemption" of meaning, speech, or the letter from the "mortal streaming" of human experience. Words represent a liberation of humanity from its unselfconscious domination by nature, and they will also become the means of liberation from later oppressive social languages, from restrictive and codified social domination.

But these basic processes also indicate their own limitations, and the quotations from Blobadjian and Tchitcherine contain within them ominous suggestions of those factors of human consciousness that lead to the destructive excesses that dominate social behavior in *Gravity's Rainbow*. There is an obsessive need to make the creative process absolute—to ensure that the human world be composed solely of elements "cleaned," "rectified," and "redeemed" from the "lawless" element of experience. And as Tchitcherine suggests, the fragmentation of "Creation" increasingly separates namer from named until the names themselves become the endless and insane playthings of the namer, who comes to find the self enclosed—trapped?—within a world of its own construction. The motivating force implicit in these two passages is fear. The dark origin of language and consciousness, Pynchon suggests, lies in humankind's defensive reaction to the plenitude and flux of brute existence. Humanity is haunted by a fear of all that exceeds comprehension, of all that is undefined, unordered, and uncontrolled: in short, the nonhuman world out of which we arise and to which we must ultimately submit. The dread of this world and the anguished refusal to submit to it are traced in all the Firm's actions and systems of "control." If, in *V.* and *The Crying of Lot 49*, the fear of the inanimate and the void obsesses the characters, in *Gravity's Rainbow* all too many of the figures cling to the rigid, inanimate world of their own construction as a protection against overbearing life. At one point, the narrator expresses both a nostalgia for the lost world of primal existence and a bitter self-judgment about humanity's weakness:

> Human consciousness, that poor cripple, that deformed and doomed thing, is about to be born. This is the World just before men. Too violently pitched alive in constant flow ever to be seen by men directly. They are meant only to look at it dead, in still strata, transputrefied to oil or coal. Alive, it was a threat: it was Titans, was an overpeaking of life so clangorous and mad, such a green corona about Earth's body that some spoiler *had* to be brought in before it blew the Creation apart. So we, the crippled keepers, were sent out to multiply, to have dominion. God's spoilers. Us. Counter-revolutionaries. *It is our mission to promote death.*" (V720/B839–40)

The narrator's bitterness here expresses one more version of the underlying theme of so much of Western religion, philosophy, and poetry: the Fall is into consciousness, into language. The desire to know, and ultimately to control, existence is the primal transgression of humanity against the natural order, although here God is a coconspirator in this transgression. Culture, the projected world of human dimensions, presents itself in dramatic opposition to the ever threatening world of nature. At the heart of culture, consciousness, and language lies the fear of uncontrolled life; and finally, the fear of such life is the fear of death. The inevitability of death signals to Pynchon's characters their essential vulnerability and the foreboding collapse of their world. All conscious life, no matter how absolute it may appear to itself, knows that it may be visited at any moment by death. Pynchon's figures unfailingly await the appearance of the hand reaching down out of the clouds announcing their death, their *"debt to nature due"* (V26/B30).

Against this future, consciousness seeks to erect closed systems of belief, systems of interpretation, that would deny or disguise the "debt." To the Puritan believer (including Tyrone Slothrop's ancestors), for example, the hand that reaches down is the hand of God. Yet for the religious, the death that climaxes one's life in this frightening world also offers the possibility of transcendence and immortality. The Christian interpretation of existence, the System that ruled Western culture for so long, defines this life as fallen while at the same time providing the divine means of escape. The church offers an all-encompassing system that humanity apparently could not by itself consciously devise. Nevertheless, this religious paradigm continues the primal transgression. It negates given existence in favor of an alternative vision whose constant focus is the moment of impending death.

The Christian system offers escape from this death—for some. The world, as we learn from Pynchon's work, is divided into two groups, the Elect and the Preterite: those who know how to *interpret* the latent text of the Christian God in nature, who see the world and their lives as fallen, hence hate them and desire to escape; and those who do not perceive the text or who "misread" it, as does William Slothrop, who argues for the necessary role of the Preterite in creation. The division of humanity into these two groups is ultimately a question of the viability of a particular system of interpretation and of the power to enforce it. The Lord's division subjects some people to the righteous power of the Elect, who, in effect, need the Preterite to prove their own salvation. The Preterite are ever threatened by the possibility that they might be perceived as the dodoes of existence, ripe for victimization, if not extermination. But there does remain, in William Slothrop's and Pynchon's revisionist theology, the possibility that the Preterite might be the true innocents, and hence the only ones saved.

This religious extension of the question of meaning systems is important to the discussion precisely because the basic structure of Puritan Christianity is preserved within the ruling patterns of modern secular society (and similarly, William Slothrop's compassion resurfaces in Pynchon's sympathetic figuration of the modern Preterite). Both cultures manifest the same patterns of transgression against nature and the subsequent construction of regimented and oppressive societies obsessed by fears of their inadequacy. The Christian paradigm of the hatred of a fallen life governed by death, and transcendence found only through death, is reflected in the rocket-builders' obsession with death and the prophesy of Escape that the rocket offers.

But the shift from an absolute, externally defined system (God) to a human-oriented and established secular world makes humanity entirely dependent upon its own powers of control and transcendence. It is a faith that is not justified, as Roland Feldspath suggests. "Putting the control inside was ratifying what de facto had happened—that you had dispensed with God. But you had taken on a greater, and more harmful, illusion. The illusion of control. That A could do B. But that was false. Completely. No one can *do*. Things only happen, A and B are unreal, are names for parts that ought to be inseparable" (V30/B34). The modern world that Pynchon describes is one in which people strive desperately to substitute a rationalist, linguistically based system of meaning and interpretation for a presumed divine order. But having no recourse to divine sanction, the human order must of necessity be more complete, self-enclosed, and self-sufficient than its lot under the Christian dispensation. To be secure and self-sustaining, human understanding must tend toward totalization—toward an internally consistent and all-encompassing structure by which all social institutions and patterns of human behavior are mutually regulated.

This totalization of the human order is dependent on the construction of internally coherent and self-justifying systems of meaning—languages of absolute efficacy. Normally, any semiotic system is only as valuable as its operational ability to order and describe the "external" world. In Pynchon's universe, however, it is in the final interests of the ruling orders primarily that their language systems be unambiguous, invulnerable. The Firm, therefore, emphasizes three factors of semiotic systems: causality, exclusion, stasis. (1) The primary value of any such system— linguistic, behavioral, chemical—is its ability to provide explanations for, and predictions based upon, causality. Experience is analyzed and named in order to discern the principles of behavior that can be directly manipulated, hence the belief that "A can do B" or Pavlovian science's search for ultimate cause and effect. (2) Given this stress on causality, only that which supports the meaning system by verifying the principles of cause and effect can be admitted into consideration, thus Pointsman's inability to accept Mexico's Poisson equation, which can describe future events without providing either explanation or accurate prediction. (3) Ultimately, any system valorizing cause and effect tends toward absolute regimentation. It denies the possibility of change or the introduction of uncodified or resistant data. It seeks total precision and stability, as shown, for example, in Jamf's hatred of the covalent bond and his preference for the ionic "mineral" bond.

For Pynchon the Firm's movement from an interest in describing phenomena to its single-minded exclusion of any information that would threaten the description is a general law of human systemization. As has been frequently observed, all efforts at systemization in Pynchon's works invariably end by emulating the things they struggle against. Meaning systems may be anti-entropic, but the more they desire absolute invulnerability, the faster their own entropy increases. In *Gravity's Rainbow*, the scientific, psychological, and linguistic systems that seek to contain human vulnerability by progressively shutting out those processes of life—eventually all life—that are too closely associated with the knowledge of death, become death-like and death-producing themselves. They are another expression of the perverse love of the inanimate, itself generated by the fear of death, that is a central element of *V.*. This is expressed in the narrator's passionate jeremiad against the System's founding of organic chemistry in which the idea that

> "the World is a closed thing, cyclical, resonant, eternally-returning," is to be delivered into a system whose only aim is to *violate* the Cycle. Taking and not giving back, demanding that "productivity" and "earnings" keep on increasing with time, the System removing from the rest of the World these vast quantities of energy to keep its own tiny desperate fraction showing a profit: and not only most of humanity—most of the World, animal, vegetable and mineral, is laid waste in the process" (V412/B480)

This process of destruction, this expression of the "order of Analysis and Death" (V722/B842), is stimulated not merely by a desire for profit but by the Firm's own suspicion of its inability to totally shut out the world that it fears. The Firm cannot completely ignore its residual awareness of the repressed but threatening world, and neither can it totally obscure its own fascination with death. The passion that motivates Jamf and the Nazis is grounded in the fears that they cannot extinguish. Fearing death, they become fixated by it. They, like Blicero, come to love the death that they create, preferring it to that which comes to them from beyond. Not all characters passively await the hand reaching down from the clouds announcing their death. Rather, knowing and fearing death, they attempt to master it, to use it to eliminate those who threaten them; they seek to become, with the Rocket, their tool, the secular version of the announcement that falls from the sky: "death in the service of the one species cursed with the knowledge that it will die" (V230/B267). Invariably, however, those who fear death the most and who attempt to use it become its submissive agents. Jamf seeks to be its voice, Brigadier Pudding its lover, Blicero its mystic votary. As he did in *V.*, Pynchon depicts the dark romanticism of those who in struggling against the reign of death come to acknowledge their ultimate failure, and who consequently prefer to embrace death and to bring down upon themselves and the world a triumphant, self-annihilating apocalypse.

Indeed, Pynchon ironically suggests, for the fearful there is no alternative to the escalation of fear and transgression. Once consciousness becomes aware of what threatens it, it can never—no matter how hard it tries—blot out the knowledge of its own limits. The paradox of language is that by naming, words always point beyond themselves toward what is named even as the name itself distances consciousness from what is named and creates the seemingly protective system of controlled articulation. So that although the Firm would prefer the movement away from the source of the name toward the self-contained system of meaning, their vision remains nonetheless fixed on what the word so comfortably placed within language systems invokes beyond them. A recurring metaphor in the novel, for example, is the small region of light cast by a solitary bulb that represents the equally narrow realm of security created by human consciousness. And always, just beyond the light lies darkness, and beyond self-consciousness, nonconsciousness. It is as if the light invoked its opposite, just as the mind believes in the immanence of what threatens it. The situation, as Pavlov noted, is that of paranoia: brain cells "being excited to the level where, through reciprocal induction, all the area around becomes inhibited. One bright, burning point, surrounded by darkness. Darkness it has, in a way, called up" (V90/B104; see also V299/B348, V647/B754).

Too great an awareness of one's words, of the names one gives to phenomena, and one is suddenly aware of the transitory and immaterial nature of language. And just beyond it, the untamed world. Blicero, that mystic in love with death, is particularly susceptible to the sensations of horror and stimulation evoked by Enzian's blasphemies. "Tonight he feels the potency of every word: words are only an eye-twitch away from the things they stand for" (V100/B116).

In Pynchon's novels, human consciousness is continuously beset by that which would annihilate it. At the same time, it both doubts its ability to master life and rushes headlong toward an incapacitating and death-producing rigidity. Once the System is accepted, the rage for order feeds upon itself. And because this rage for order manifests itself in all forms of human activity, the culture created by Jamf, Bland, Weissman, and others—the Firm in toto—becomes increasingly oppressive. Any ideal collective potential is transformed into a program of social exploitation. Language itself, the model for knowledge and control, is manipulated by the Firm for its own ends. For example, rather than a cybernetic society of effective communication among society's institutions and citizens being created, it is rumored that "the whole German Inflation was created deliberately, simply to drive young enthusiasts of the Cybernetic Tradition into Control work" (V238/B277).

The social order that is established operates according to the same principles as language, science, and technology to the detriment of the countless victims of that order. Just as the actions of language and consciousness result in a move from a forced fragmentation of existence to an imposed and ultimately repressive systemization, Pynchon's characters find their lives to be fragmented, and themselves to be but fragments of a much greater and finally oppressive social homogenization. The individuals living within the System dimly perceive themselves as isolated, impotent entities forced into patterns of behavior that they can only obscurely recognize. The world appears at one and the same time to be incredibly diverse and anarchic and also subject to unseen but all-powerful forces of control. What the Firm creates is a regimented but digressive complexity. The War, for example, is only one of the Firm's characteristic activities. "The War needs to divide this way, and to subdivide, though its propaganda will always stress unity, alliance, pulling together. The War does not appear to want a folk-consciousness, not even of the sort the Germans have engineered, ein Volk ein Führer—it wants a machine of many separate parts, not oneness, but a complexity" (V130–31/B152).

Within this complexity, the individual experiences life as confusion. Against personal values and perceptions, the Firm presses its own ideas and demands. It offers its own "reality," hoping to convince its citizen-victims that what is offered is as valid as the now diminishing world of nature. It is a choice offered Slothrop, himself a diminishing reality. It is a choice to treat Bianca and himself not as real people with responsibilities to each other, but instead to avoid the consequences of his rejection of her and his substitution of a "bureaucracy of departure" (V470/B549) for honest feeling. Instead of returning and saving her and perhaps himself, he is tempted by, and gives in to,

> how much easier just to leave her there . . . and have comfort enough to try only for a reasonable facsimile—"Why bring her back? Why try? It's only the difference between the real boxtop and the one you draw for Them." No. How can he believe that? It's what They want him to believe, but how can he? No difference between a boxtop and its image, all right, their whole economy's based on *that*...but she must be more than an image, a product, a promise to pay.... (V472/B551)

The overall result of the Firm's control is the constant victimization of its citizens. For the individuals, this means living in a state of constant paranoia. But rather than fearing the absence of systems of adequate language and meaning, Pynchon's figures fear the results of all systematization. They realize that the world humans have created to protect themselves is more threatening than what is shut out. All are aware of the limits of their own means of coping with the world and are fatefully conscious that they are surrounded by forces that, in seeking to control the world, seek to control them. Once they suspect the limits of their own attempts to comprehend and order experience, while at the same time recognizing the existence of other ordering systems, the characters can never be confident that their own perspective is not inferior to, controlled by, or subsumed into another's system. The environment in which Pynchon's creations live is one of barely disguised, if seemingly unfocused, aggression.

According to Pynchon, we are all living inside the System faced with the same dilemmas as Slothrop and the Preterite. And as he states, "living inside the System is like riding across the country in a bus driven by a maniac bent on suicide" (V412/B481). The relative peace and freedom that the liberal, corporate society allows us appear increasingly illusory as one inquires into the workings of what Pynchon can only call the Firm. And more frightening, perhaps, is the suggestion that the interconnections among the political, economic, technological, and military interests of the Firm only become evident as they reach the point of total control, a point at which any individual or even collective action may prove futile. It is as if society approaches its own critical mass, portending total oppression and/or self-destruction. "Here to say that critical mass cannot be ignored. Once the technical means of control have reached a certain size, a certain degree of *being connected* one to another, the chances for freedom are over for good" (V539/B627).

III

Is it possible to get off the bus, or to change the driver before the crash? For Pynchon, it seems, the question cannot be satisfactorily answered. There is no simple way to perceive the real structures of the System in this overdetermined world—a world in which all behavior, institutions, and beliefs appear to echo and support each other. It is difficult to seize upon any premise that may be said to be the generating force behind the cultural rage for order. And furthermore, when the world is so interconnected, it is difficult even to know what data or what experiences might signal the presence of a specific structure of intentional domination. In a paranoid society, everything appears "meaningful." And in Pynchon's totalized world, everything may indeed *be* meaningful. If we only knew how to accurately apprehend and interpret it.

The first challenge, Pynchon suggests, is, in fact, that of interpretation. The initial step toward freedom is to view all institutions and behavior as concealed languages, as systems of signification. It is necessary, in effect, to discover the ideology of everyday life, to recognize the patterns of control that we live by. What one needs to do is look closely at the behavior of the System, at the products it creates and supports itself by, in order to perceive the design of its needs. For the Preterite, those victims of the Elect's attempt to transcend life, the challenge is to interpret the silent language in the most mundane aspects of contemporary life.

> The rest of us, not chosen for enlightenment, left on the outside of Earth, at the mercy of a Gravity we have only begun to learn how to detect and measure, must go on blundering inside our front-brain faith in Kute Korrespondences, hoping that for each psi-synthetic taken from Earth's soul there is a molecule, secular, more or less ordinary and named, over here—kicking endlessly among the plastic trivia, finding in each Deeper Significance and trying to string them all together like terms of a power series hoping to zero in on the tremendous and secret Function whose name, like the permuted names of God, cannot be spoken...plastic saxophone reed *sounds of unnatural timbre*, shampoo bottle *ego-image*, Cracker Jack prize *one-shot amusement*, home appliance casing *fairing for winds of cognition*, baby bottles *tranquilization*, meat packages *disguise of slaughter*, dry-cleaning bags *infant strangulation*, garden hoses *feeding endlessly the desert*...but to bring them together, in their slick persistence and our preterition...to make sense out of, to find the meanest sharp sliver of truth in so much replication, so much waste.... (V590/B688)

But the interpreter must also learn the lessons of meaning systems. Against these systems, against the System, what response is valid? The quandary that Pynchon places his characters in—from the Whole Sick Crew of *V.* and the various subcultures of dropouts in *The Crying of Lot 49* to the Counterforce in *Gravity's Rainbow*—is that any alternative to the System is itself a system. And though he speaks of a few rebels going over to the Titans every day (V720/B840), in effect most of the Preterite are unable to live in the extrahuman world, whether it appear to be the void or the chaos of undifferentiated existence. The problem is explicitly raised in *The Crying of Lot 49* when Oedipa ponders the many subcultures that communicate by the WASTE system. "It was calculated withdrawal, from the life of the Republic, from its machinery. Whatever else was being denied them out of hate, indifference to the power of their vote, loopholes, simple ignorance, this withdrawal was their own, unpublicized, private. Since they could not have withdrawn into a vacuum (could they?), there had to exist the separate, silent, unsuspected world."[2]

Could they? This final question lingers, tantalizingly. Can one drop out beyond culture, beyond systems, in essence beyond language and rational consciousness, to exist with the Titans or the void? The question is posed intriguingly by Slothrop, who, in the first stages of his dismantling, is disturbed by his developing antiparanoia, "where nothing is connected to anything, a condition not many of us can bear for long. . . . Either They have put him here for a reason, or he's just here. He isn't sure that he wouldn't, actually, rather have that *reason*...." (V434/B506). And if finally Slothrop slips over into the world beyond human systems, language, and consciousness—at the price of individual identity while regaining "naturalness" (V626/B729)—the rest of the Preterite are left behind to form the Counterforce. The situation of Slothrop is unique and seems to offer an instance of ambiguous myth. His questionable fate recalls to us the narrator's self-deprecating nostalgia for the world of the Titans and his effort to imagine creation before human consciousness. Slothrop's condition can only be suggested, not articulated. Pynchon and the Counterforce must remain within that human, and basically romantic, dilemma: to strive to overcome through language and consciousness the state of alienation from existence that is the product of language and consciousness. Finally, as much as Pynchon's critique of the System is based on a theory of transgression by consciousness against the natural order, there is no sustained suggestion that a return is possible. It is not an ideal reality, a primal and pure existence, that is being offered, but more a nostalgic vision that sets the present decadence and victimization in relief.

In order to do war with the System, the Counterforce must itself be a system of sorts, a "We-system" against a "They-system" (V638/B743). But the danger of any system, as the Counterforce knows at least initially, is its own bureaucratization, its solipsistic tendency to deny whatever it defends itself against. It can survive as a counter-system only so long as it tempers its tendency toward systemization. Connections are made, but not codified. Instead of "interlocking" in as coherent a manner as the System attempts, the Counterforce promises randomness and improvisation. *"They're* the rational ones. We piss on Their rational arrangements" (V639/

B744). Indeed, all the positive characters in the novel cultivate improvisation—the temporary assumption of a seemingly effective order suitable only for a particular moment. The magic that Geli Tripping practices is exemplary. Rather than a codified system of "spells, witch-rivalries, coven politics," hers is an emotive force based on love, for which " 'technique is just a substitute for when you get older.' . . . You either come to the Brocken-complex with a bureaucratic career in mind, or you leave it, and choose the world. There are the two distinct sorts of witch, and Geli is the World-choosing sort" (V718/B837–38).

To choose the World—this is the goal of the Counterforce. But the world can never be experienced naïvely. Consciousness, language, and socialized behavior will always assert themselves. No matter how much nostalgia for the Titans permeates the book, there is no unmediated vision. The only alternative Pynchon offers is the refusal of stultifying codification and the warning that one should not become enmeshed in one's own system of paranoia. It is a lesson Slothrop hears from Geli. " 'It's an arrangement,' she tells him. 'It's so unorganized out here. There have to be arrangements. You'll find out.' Indeed he will. . . . Slothrop, though he doesn't know it yet, is as properly constituted a state as any other in the Zone these days. Not paranoia. Just how it is. Temporary alliances, knit and undone" (V290–91/B338). Temporary, self-conscious arrangements, these are the only patterns of meaning one can trust. Rather than codification, Pynchon suggests, we need improvisation, an active and creative association of disconnected parts. If, indeed, the creation of imaginary unities out of fragments lies at the base of the restrictive systems of the Firm, the only thing that differentiates the Counterforce (and Pynchon's own mammoth work) from the System is the self-consciousness of their venture—the full awareness of the origin of the linguistic principle of systems. Instead of the seductive delusion of causality, Pynchon offers the more suggestive, if basically fictitious, principle of analogy. Or, as Leni argues, " 'Not produce,' she tried, 'not cause. It all goes along together. Parallel, not series. Metaphor. Signs and symptoms. Mapping on to different coordinate systems. I don't know...' She didn't know, all she was trying to do was reach" (V159/B186).

This attempt to reach, to extend one's awareness beyond one's confinement within the rigid and arbitrary structures of our culture, characterizes Pynchon's works, as well as, one should add, the writings of most postmodernists. At the heart of their venture is a self-reflexive questioning of the nature of meaning, specifically of the patterns of linguistic association—analogy and metaphor. Metaphor—this "thrust at truth and a lie,"[3] the "Great Lie"[4]—is a constant concern of Pynchon's novels. Metaphor and the principle of analogy allow both a truth and a lie. They both create meaning and are, in essence, fictions. Yet, as Pynchon suggests, all human meaning systems are organized according to their principles. The world we know is constituted out of differentiated, analyzed, and *named* fragments of existence placed in suggestive associations. Metaphor represents the fusion of two disjunctive elements in order to create a new reality—a new image. It is the forceful joining of separate identities and, consequently, their individual obliteration. The belief that these creations, these meaning systems, are self-justifying or inherently valid is the basis of culture, but in excess it leads to the delusions that characterize the Firm.

The poet's responsibility, Pynchon implies, is to reveal the tentative and transitory base of all meaning systems. His challenge is to allow himself the freedom of dismantling his own creation in the very act of creating anew. He calls attention to the unstable base of the work as it playfully unfolds itself. This self-conscious, or rather self-reflexive, creation offers itself in the works of Pynchon and the postmodernists as a paradigm of cultural freedom. Rather than acquiescing to the inherited meaning systems imposed by society, one is offered the possibility of self-consciously creating one's own system of reference while demystifying society's.

Gravity's Rainbow is a vast edifice built out of an intricate and self-supporting system of metaphors and analogies, all of which ultimately point to their extreme tenuousness, their necessary artificiality, their suggestive truth. It is a significant panorama of cultural complexity, yet its own parts barely hold together. It sustains a narrative for more than seven hundred pages, yet constantly dismantles all emerging plot lines. Ultimately, the book offers at once an insightful and "realistic" portrait of the interconnecting systems of meaning and meaning-making in our overdetermined society, and a grotesque parody of that world. Its goal is to unmask and mock its culture. Rather than denying the rage for order that dominates contemporary society, Pynchon parodies its excess. His comedy is that of the overdetermination, the profusion and chaos that result from uncontrolled systemization. Rather than stability and restrictiveness, his world engenders discontinuity and a surreal self-destructiveness. Where Jamf desires to seize and join antagonistic electrons to create a mineral reality, Pynchon shows us not the absoluteness of any new reality but its disjunctive base.

It is the disparateness of the terms of any metaphor that he focuses on, and it is the silence, the void between the terms, that he accents. Thus in every attempt at an order, Pynchon offers us its potential insubstantiality—the chaos at the heart of meaning, not meaning's legitimization.

Whether the System that Pynchon describes will achieve its absolute and death-producing connectedness or whether it will fall apart under the weight of its own internal conflicts and the anarchy of the Counterforce remains to be seen. At times Pynchon suggests that any system, based on such absurd efforts to instill order among the fragments it has created, is doomed to the comic absurdity of surrealism. For example, when he hears a Jamaican black man sing a German Renaissance hymn during a Christmas service in wartime England, Mexico perceives "these are not heresies so much as imperial outcomes, necessary as the black man's presence, from acts of minor surrealism—which, taken in the mass, are an act of suicide, but which in its pathology, in its dreamless version of the real, the Empire commits by the thousands every day, completely unaware of what it's doing" (V129/B150–51).

Pynchon's method is to make that surrealism evident, and to suggest the fragmenting madness and liberating vision it may allow. For in surrealism is not only a deconstructive cultural politics but a principle of anarchic creative action. The surrealists' basic technique was to find both a marvelous, "convulsive" beauty and a freedom from domination by quotidian reality in their startling metaphors that brought together widely disparate images to create new and amazing visions. This anarchic and surreal impulse is basic to most postmodern literature, especially in the United States. The spirit of rebellion and liberation of vision in the works of Vonnegut, Coover, Barthelme, Sukenick, Brautigan, Reed, Burroughs, and Charles Wright, for example, thrives on the absurd and comic juxtaposition of fragmentary images ripped free from their cultural context. These writers cultivate the "mindless pleasures" (V270/B314, V681/B794) that, in their life-affirming antics, are threats to unquestioned order.

But unlike the surrealists, there is no primal alternative reality for the postmodernists. The marvelous does not lead to a vision of the creative primacy of the subconscious or of the achievement of a super-real realm of experience. Instead, postmodern playfulness must turn the deconstructive process back upon itself as well, even if this process implicitly raises deeply troubling questions about its ultimate value. As Pynchon knows, these "antisocial and mindless pleasures" also ravage the brain (V681/B794). A life that denies causality, that revels in the shifting and temporary alliances of chance events, threatens itself with its own ultimate dissolution. The self that can be defined only as a transitory locus of immediate perceptions and self-conscious fictions has no promise of stability or continuity. One may reject, as does Slothrop, the compulsion to constantly judge one's life or to incessantly seek the meaning of every event (V204/B238), but one might then also be avoiding those real responsibilities that are placed on oneself, as is Slothrop in his fatal disengagement from Bianca (V470/B549). And like Slothrop, destined to be present at his own and his time's assembly, one might find oneself "being broken down instead and scattered" (V738/B861).

The problem that the Counterforce, Pynchon, and many postmodern writers face is that of the viability of what amounts to an anarchic response to social totalization. Their alternative systems are threatened, on the one hand, by all the dangers inherent in systemization—such as Enzian's and the Counterforce's tendency to create their own bureaucracies (V525/B612, V738/B861)—or, on the other hand, by complete disintegration into mindless and destructive pleasures. The anarchy of the Counterforce is in danger of becoming more like the System the more it focuses on its opposition to the System. But the more it engages in its own pleasures and self-reflexive playfulness, the more impotent it will appear and the more fragmentary will be its works. This is the quandary posed to Mexico when he realizes that the War wants division, or when he wonders which is better, "living on as Their pet, or death?" (V713/B831). The fragmentation of contemporary life and the apparent individualistic freedom that liberal-corporate society offers us are corollary aspects of the individual's relative lack of a critical and effective means of action. One accepts one's impotence as the necessary price of one's freedom. The work of Pynchon and the postmodernists may stress the demystification of cultural codes of ideology and behavior, but they are unable to offer any response other than the continuous process of self-reflexive assertion and the dismantling of private alternate visions.

Pynchon's mammoth work, more than any other recent book, presents us with a comprehensive picture of the nature of contemporary social reality—the interconnections of politics, economics, technology, the social sciences, and ideology. It treats the ambiguous and threatening relationship of individual and collective interests. But at the heart of the book is an essential paradox that ultimately suggests the limits of the postmodern vision. Pynchon's work here, as in *V.*, is based on an analysis of the historical development of this repressive totalized culture, but its central message is the denial of history, the denial of the possibility of significant change. History is presented only as the record by which we read the progressive dehumanization of culture and the increasing growth of a death wish that seems to govern society. There appears to be a natural law of history, as of all systems—that of a diabolic entropy. All systems tend toward decay and death. Human creations seem to participate in their own collapse. Up to now, the process has only been nearly as strong as the anti-entropic forces of life (V720/B840), but the balance may have been tipped with the Rocket, and the constellations of real and potential *Brennschluss* points that dot the sky above us bode our immanent destruction (V302/B351–52).

According to Pynchon, history is only a construct that one reads in hindsight. The authorities define it as meaningful and progressive (V682/B795), whereas Pynchon shows it to be destructive. But the life processes, and anarchic play, have no history, no pattern of necessary development. One cannot presume to see and act by a theory of history. That is the temptation that Tchitcherine faces, that allows one to enlist for a cause, that convinces one to die for potential life, and that is ultimately only another form of the System (V701/B818, V704/B821). According to Pynchon, perhaps all one can say is, "History's changes *are* inevitable" (V701/B818). But they have no predetermined shape. Therefore, action is meaningless if it presumes to offer specific results that extend any further than its mere immediate focus of personal desires and responses.

History is a false construct, Pynchon implies, because it depends on a belief in cause and effect, and thus on the continuity of identifiable and controllable forces. At one point, the narrative voice states, "All talk of cause and effect is secular history, and secular history is a diversionary tactic" (V167/B195). Indeed, if history exists for Pynchon, ironically it is a version of religious history—the history of the Fall. The progressive decline of humanity, the accelerating self-destruction of the modern world—these are the historical visions of Thomas Pynchon. It is an organic record that he traces, our ambiguous role in the struggle of life against death. And it is to the organic in us that he appeals. If Pynchon recommends a sustained course of action, it is that of uncovering and interpreting the systems of death that surround us and of searching for the remaining fragments of life that we can cling to. The faith that the book expresses is merely that the life processes are still stronger than the death process. "But in each of these streets, some vestige of humanity, of Earth, has to remain. No matter what has been done to it, no matter what it's been used for.... . . . At least one moment of passage, one it will hurt to lose, ought to be found for every street now indifferently gray with commerce, with war, with repression...finding it, learning to cherish what was lost, mightn't we find some way back?" (V693/B807–8). But the lesson of the book is that there is no way back. Slothrop will never return to America; Tchitcherine will never be allowed to regain the Center; Enzian will continue to follow his destiny northward. We are all within the System—on the Street, the same street that Benny Profane found himself wandering down in *V*.. The only possibility is to protect and cultivate the residual life that is left to us.

The power of *Gravity's Rainbow*—its verbal and conceptual intricacy and suggestiveness, its inventiveness and humanity—testifies to Pynchon's faith that such life might flourish, however minimally. But there is no imaging of what recovered life may be like. No unified vision of an alternative world is possible, or permissable, in the postmodern aesthetic. Rather, Pynchon offers us a massive system of analogies of decay and destruction, of repression and fragmentation, analogies that may only fall apart as does the book in its final section. And out of this dismantling—a promise? The art of fragments—whether they portend death or revitalization—this is the final gift of Pynchon. It is an anarchic vision that promises either freedom or impotence, creation or mindless pleasures.

1. Norman O. Brown, *Love's Body* (New York: Random House, 1966), p. 247.
2. Thomas Pynchon, *The Crying of Lot 49* (New York: Bantam, 1966), p. 92.
3. Ibid., p. 95.
4. Thomas Pynchon, *V.* (New York: Bantam, 1963), p. 305.

The Morning and the Evening Funnies: Comedy in *Gravity's Rainbow*

By Roger B. Henkle

There is nothing humorous about death in the morning. Especially when one is hung over and filthy, as Pirate Prentice is on the morning that opens *Gravity's Rainbow*. Just before waking, Pirate had dreamed of a darkened railway carriage full of "drunks, old veterans still in shock . . . hustlers in city clothes, derelicts, exhausted women with more children than it seems could belong to anyone" (V3/B3). He comes to in an apartment draped with the drinking companions of the night before: snoring, hacking, smelling of booze, sweat, and semen. "How awful. How bloody awful." Pirate climbs out onto his roof garden and looks East, and there, a white vapor trail on the horizon, is Death on its way to London, possibly to Pirate. Another German rocket arches along its silent, nearly invisible ballistic path.

But almost immediately, Pynchon's comic powers go to work on morning death. Pirate Prentice whips up his outrageous banana breakfast: banana omlets, mashed bananas molded in the shape of a British lion rampant, banana croissants and banana mead and banana flambé. "Now there grows among all the rooms, replacing the night's old smoke, alcohol and sweat, the fragile, musaceous odor of Breakfast: flowery, permeating, surprising, more than the color of winter sunlight. . . . It is not often Death is told so clearly to fuck off" (V10/B11).

The banana, itself a parody of the rocket. The banana, arching as if in its own parabolic flight away from its branch, ending in its own *Brennschluss*. The banana, another classic phallic symbol as is the German rocket in all its imagery in *Gravity's Rainbow*. A rich and natural thing, however; nutritious, fragrant, contributing to man's health and not his destruction. Therein lies the working of Pynchon's comedy—the metaphorical reduction of the fearful into the playful. Control of the ominous by converting it imaginatively into a subject for ludicrous parody of all its elements. Metaphorical transformation has been Pynchon's chief comic method since *V.*; it is not only the source of some of his most brilliant set pieces, but is, as Fausto Maijstral observed in *V.*, the poet's chief way of keeping alive humane illusions in the face of depersonalization.

The metaphorical process of comic imitation and variation preserves the balance between Pynchon's seriousness about paranoia and the control mechanisms of modern corporate existence, and the objectivity he must have, as an artist, in order not to be victimized by his own material. Seriousness is deadly in Pynchon's universe; only those like Roger Mexico and Tyrone Slothrop who can maintain the capacity to laugh at themselves escape the obsessional. Take the case of the humorless, arch-conspirator Pointsman, for instance, who callously manipulates people in the service of dehumanization, and who is incapable of acquiring a humorous perspective—thus unable to see how ludicrous is the ultimate nightmare of the Pavlovian experimenter with dogs: a confrontation with the

> stalking Reichssieger von Thanatz Alpdrucken, that most elusive of Nazi hounds, champion Weimaraner for 1941 . . . his liver-gray shape receding, loping at twilit canalsides strewn with debris of war, rocket blasts each time missing . . . [until at last] the gray dog can turn and the amber eyes gaze into Ned Pointsman's own.... (V142–43/B166–67)

Pointsman is doomed to live within his obsessions until they grow surreastically supernatural and devour him. Pynchon, however, maintains a constant poise through the comic involution of his own most cherished and worked ideas—as in, for instance, the comic scene in which Slothrop is obliged to go through the Disgusting English Candy Drill, by sampling Mrs. Quoad's hoarded English candy "delights": pepsin-flavored nougats with chewy camphor gum centers, hard sour gooseberries with powdered cloves inside, eucalyptus-flavored fondants with grape gum arabic cores. More than a take-off on the notoriously eccentric English sweet tooth, it is also a metaphoric reduction of the joined Pynchon images of war and sex. One particularly debilitating English bonbon is shaped after a six-ton earthquake bomb, and it (or another in Mrs. Quoad's arsenal) detonates in Slothrop's mouth like an explosive charge, deadening the nerves, sending "freezing frosty-grape alveolar clusters" into his lungs, and giving him a momentary floating feeling (V116–19/B135–38). The sensation is not unlike that of sexual climax, also, and in the next paragraph we encounter Slothrop, limp and exhausted from intercourse.

The connection between the transformative powers of art and the workings of comedy have been made by several of the major theoreticians of comedy. Freud describes it as a process of "wit-work" by which a joke-teller or comic writer must rework the animosity in any comic attack into a manner of presentation that is socially acceptable and, in some cases, aesthetically pleasing. Arthur Koestler also notes the tendency of comic invention to shade into the creative—to move beyond pure attack or reductiveness into new combinations or elaborations.[1] Ernst Kris, a follower of Freud's, advances an analysis that is particularly relevant to comedy in modern Western societies, where, as in *Gravity's Rainbow*, the humor must deal not so much with a specific comic target, such as an authority figure, but with the vaguer paranoias and neuroses that characterize our existence in a world whose operations of evil are diffused and impersonal. Kris suggests that the comic probes along the edge of the comic writer's submerged anxieties. It parries our fears, and constantly advances to what Pynchon might call the "interface" with psychic disequilibrium.[2]

In the comedy of *Gravity's Rainbow*, that darker edge is never far removed. When Pynchon charges up for sustained comic narrative, he is snappy, brusque, and a bit nervous.

> [Pirate] will then actually *skip* to and fro, with his knees high and twirling a walking stick with W. C. Fields' head, nose, top hat, and all, for its knob, and surely capable of magic, while the band plays a second chorus. Accompanying will be a phantasmagoria, a real one, rushing toward the screen, in over the heads of the audiences, on little tracks of an elegant Victorian cross section resembling the profile of a chess knight conceived fancifully but not vulgarly so— . . .
>
> In 1935 he had his first episode *outside* any condition of known sleep— it was during his Kipling Period, beastly Fuzzy-Wuzzies far as eye could see, dracunculiasis and Oriental sore rampant among the troops, no beer for a month, wireless being jammed by other Powers who would be masters of these horrid blacks, God knows why, and all folklore broken down, no Cary Grant larking in and out slipping elephant medicine in the punchbowls out here. . . . (V12–13/B14–15)

A dazzling performance of tripping fast talk, of the quick allusion, the sketchy detail, the exotic reference. An ornate patina of near-vaudevillian mannerism, old bits, fill and patter develops into a kind of routine. Comedy saves us through such rituals of language and quick change; we pass off the horrors by distracting ourselves from them. It is fixation, after all, that stultifies; it is the devotion of time and attention to a thing that imbues it with intolerable significance.

Yet we sense at times an uneasiness in such frenetic comic virtuosity. Too much quick change, hinting, as comedy often does, that it is a dangerously thin cover, and, sure enough, the tricks do not turn fast enough on the narrative surface of *Gravity's Rainbow* to keep the book itself from being obsessive. The Rocket, and death, and conspiracy-theory lurk behind all the comedy. Pynchon undoubtedly wants a certain amount of such tension—it is a darkly comic vision—but he betrays also the perilousness of his enterprise, the difficulty in keeping the comic method from being a quirky, troubled, almost reflexive operation.

The metaphoric character of his writing harbors similar perils. For the repetition in another form, even if in a ludicrously reductive one, of the motifs of the novel tends to keep those motifs constantly in mind. No matter how many times one transmogrifies the image of explosion—into orgasm, into eating, into defecation—it lingers in our consciousness, constantly receding, perhaps, but still wavering into view, a red image on the mind's fatigued retina. For, as I have argued elsewhere,[3] Pynchon's commitment to a metaphoric reconstitution may signify an inability to achieve a total imaginative transmutation of his material. The "ghost of Walter Rathenau" defines the problem in a cynical way: " 'But this is all the impersonation of life. The real movement is not from death to any rebirth. It is from death to death-transfigured. The best you can do is to polymerize a few dead molecules. But polymerizing is not resurrection' " (V166/B194). On the imaginative level, the book struggles with the same difficulties, of getting beyond what is largely reconversion and into a different creative frame, in which the old lines of connection, the familiar realizations of desires and anxieties, are replaced with a new vision.

Pynchon's use of comedy suggests, in fact, that Western man finds himself more and more caught up in the analogies of his own discoveries in physics and his technology. The episode of Byron the Bulb involutes the problems of the human characters in the novel. Byron represents the human tendency to anthropomorphize inanimate objects and give them a mock human consciousness. Byron yearns for immortality; he tries to organize an insurrection among light bulbs to break away from the "grid." The humor in this episode recalls Charles Dickens's comic responses to the onset of the dehumanization of modern urban life: his tendency to play with the idea of an interchange of psychic forces between the animate and the inanimate. In Dickens, chimney stacks grinned and peered maliciously, walls ominously creaked, clothes and furniture mimicked human beings. Conversely, the victimized little people and the fanatic villains of the London underworld took on queerly inanimate qualities, often becoming projections of their function in a bureaucratic, technical world. Dickens's crucial observation was that the last desperate act of men and women who find themselves becoming dehumanized is to entertain the idea that a common energy permeates all things; in this manner, they can project into inert objects some of the vitality and "personality" that is being denied or stifled in *them*. The people in *Gravity's Rainbow* constantly engage in the same practice: Blicero's imprisonment of Gottfried in the final German rocket is his ultimate, insane attempt to fuse together the two things into which he had projected his own unsatisfying love: the boy and the machine. Similarly, we are told that Franz Pökler became an "extension" of the Rocket long before it was ever built because Leni had denied him love. Technology becomes the Great Substitution for what is missing on the human level; the laws of physics replace what used to be mysteries of human behavior.

As Joseph Slade and Edward Mendelson have pointed out,[4] Pynchon's ideas in *Gravity's Rainbow* have been influenced by the writings of Max Weber. Part of Weber's thesis holds that post-Reformation man has cultivated the notion of "objectivity" as a means of establishing his individuality and freedom. Gradually, however, this has produced alienation, and then forms of nearly mechanistic dehumanization. In what is described as "more Ouspenskian nonsense," a medium working for the White Visitation describes the process: " 'Putting the control inside was ratifying what de facto had happened—that you had dispensed with God. But you had taken on a greater, and more harmful, illusion. The illusion of control. That A could do B. But that was false. Completely. No one can *do*. Things only happen . . . ' " (V30/B34). The first illusion, following on the progress that Weber describes, is that human will can effect changes—the illusion (which we will discuss later) of cause and effect. As the society becomes less responsive to individual will, and as man's confidence in rational control over his destiny wanes, essentially toward the end of the nineteenth century, then one loses the conviction that individual intention will achieve its goals. One becomes increasingly a "victim" of circumstances; the twentieth-century comedy of the victim, the "little man," the non-hero in the absurd universe, gathers imaginative force. A theory of comedy—Henri Bergson's[5]—emerges in 1900 that adequately captures this impression, arguing that comedy is a response to our awareness that we often behave mechanistically. We laugh at what has become automoton-like in the presumably human; comedy, with its transmogrifying powers, attempts to reassert human flexibility and self-control. In part this progression explains why comedy has become such a prevalent mode in twentieth-century literary expression; it explains, perhaps, why Pynchon writes comic novels about the present condition. For comedy is the most appropriate means of registering our internalized disquiet over the uneasy relationship that we have toward our increasingly mechanized existence, and our futile projections in response to it.

It is interesting to note also that the avant garde artistic movements at the turn of the century were, in a large sense, a variation on the process that Weber describes. The tendency toward objectification, in a movement like cubism, and the abstractions of surrealism were both prompted by the determination of a generation of artists to assert their *individuality* in the face of bourgeois conformity. But the expression of that individuality often took the form of conscious dehumanization; in an effort to avoid the sentimentalist, conformably rationalistic, and habitual qualities of bourgeois "realism," a major group of artists developed an agonistic vein of expression that had the effect of continuing the comic interplay of the human and the inanimate. Much of Pynchon's writing toward the end of *Gravity's Rainbow* is consciously surrealistic—an involuted configuration of the pattern that seeks to "control" dehumanization through comic play with some of the forms that dehumanization has taken.

A corollary to this problem emerges in the dilemma that Pökler faces. Each year the German government grants him a brief furlough, which he spends with his daughter Ilse, who has become a prisoner of the state and implicitly a hostage for Pökler's loyalty. Seeing his daughter so rarely, Pökler harbors the uneasy notion that perhaps he is not being given the same child each time (and, indeed, that may be the case). "So it has gone for the six years since. A daughter a year, each one about a year older, each time taking up nearly from scratch. The only continuity has been her name . . . and Pökler's love—love something like the persistence of vision, for They have used it to create for him the moving image of a daughter, flashing him only these summertime frames of her, leaving it to him to build the illusion of a single child . . . " (V422/B492). Here, metamorphosis itself is in question; perhaps it is not a real change, but the illusion of transformation. The issue penetrates to the very nature of the comic power itself: is that too simply a series of temporary displacements, and not really a transforming continuity? Can art exceed the limitations of its material if it must necessarily build on fractions of time and situation? Are we condemned to a series of quick projections of essentially formulaic reworkings of mundane material?

The issue of the powers of comedy to transform its subject matter is further complicated by an essential paradox in comedy itself. We have been speaking of comedy as if it were an expression of the human instinct for freedom and flexibility. We have noted its reliance upon the transformative powers of art. We are familiar with its changeableness, its irreverence. When George Santayana or Suzanne Langer or Henri Bergson or Northrop Frye[6] speak of comedy, they all emphasize its vitalistic spirit; it is organic, transformative, free-wheeling. And that surely is how it works in much of *Gravity's Rainbow*, when Pynchon's metaphors compare rockets and bananas, when his narrative language takes off on one of its buck-and-wings. But comedy has also been associated with stasis. It has been a means of escaping time as well as of riding the crest of time's flux. Indeed, comedy in the last two hundred years has enjoyed a kind of double status; it has been both a means, an approach or point of view (as when we speak of a comic rendering of reality, or a comic play with it), and it has also been, for many artists, a separate plane of existence. Northrop Frye describes comedic expression in terms of a mythos, and postulates various phases of the mythos in which characteristic actions occur and a characteristic mood prevails.[7] In some of these phases, the world is enchanted and still, a "green world" in which the vicissitudes of normal existence are suspended and an aura of innocence, freedom, and delight envelops everything. Dickens was intrigued with such an alternative mode of human existence, and he associated it, in the writings of his *David Copperfield* period, with the fairy tale. It was a respite from the hard demands of the competitive adult world of modern life, a marvelously frozen imaginative realm in which nothing aged or corrupted or disintegrated. This curiously inconsistent yet enduring attitude toward the comic lies at the heart of Pynchon's vision of the Zone in part three of *Gravity's Rainbow*. For the Zone belongs neither to the Germans nor the Allies; it has no government, no body of conspiratorial forces governing it. Slothrop thinks that "maybe that anarchist he met in Zürich was right, maybe for a little while all the fences are down, one road as good as another, the whole space of the Zone cleared, depolarized . . . without even nationality to fuck it up...." (V556/B648). Comedy and change thrive in the Zone, and part three of the book represents an extended series of metamorphosizing, anarchic episodes. And it offers the illusion of being temporarily outside of time—that is, outside of the "official" measurements of time, for it is at the end of one war and before the corporate forces can get the program organized for another.

For romantic appeal of the comic paradox of vitality and stasis enriches what is surely one of the comic high points of *Gravity's Rainbow*: the aerial battle between Slothrop and Major Marvy's men. In a wild Katzenjammer chase, Marvy and his besotted troops have pursued Slothrop through the labyrinths of the Mittelwerke, and now are bearing down upon Slothrop as he tries to escape in Herr Schnorp's balloon. Singing "another verse that's worse than the other verse" of the German version of an old fraternity drinking song, "In Prussia they never eat pussy," Marvy's men buzz Slothrop's balloon with their plane. Slothrop and Schnorp hurl custard pies, the ultimate comic prop: "He flings it, perfect shot, the plane peeling slowly past and *blop* gets Marvy right in the face. Yeah. Gloved hands paw at the mess. The Major's pink tongue appears. Custard drips into the wind, yellow droplets fall in long arcs toward earth" (V334/B389). Suddenly the balloon drifts into a gigantic cloud, and the anarchic, uproarious action of the comic chase is muffled, suspended. A scream of "Oh, fuck!" signifies that a well-aimed custard pie has hit the engine cowling; there are a few frantic shots from Marvy's crew, a sputtering of the plane's engine, and one vein of comedy has been superseded by another. In a memorable piece of description, the triumphant Slothrop and Schnorp float above the green of German fields, the clouds pink and broken up with the setting sun, and they watch the shadow of the earth race across Germany at 650 miles an hour. For a moment they are in the ecstasy of removal, sailing miles above time's darkening, speeding effects.

But as the image of a suspended interlude suggests, the green world in which comedy's imagination resides is a temporary respite. It is an illusion, just as is the false sense of freedom in the German Zone. History, politics—the "normal" measures of time—will reassume their sway and force men back into their mechanistic roles. Indeed, what we came in the 1960s to call the "military-industrial complex" had always been bent toward the spoliation of the comic vision. The horrible little triangle of Blicero and Gottfried and Katja enacting Hansel and Gretel had been Blicero's parodic debasement of the charm of enchantment. The mock fairy-tale kingdom of Zwölfkinder, with its Glass Mountain twinkling rose and white, its elf king and queen, its soda water fountains, was a cynical German charade. The legacy of World War II was the despoiling of the children.

And beyond that, Western culture, in its orientation toward time and function, has never been able to integrate its dream of a comic-imaginative green world into its mode of consciousness. In English Victorian culture, where the idea thrived, it followed a steady decline into puerility. From the vitalistic, energetic embodiment of it in Dickens's Mr. Pickwick, it evolved into the passive retreats of Dickens's own fairy tale vision, then into Carroll's Wonderland of talking creatures, and then into the heavily sentimental Peter Pan. From its essentially pastoral origins, in which it offered a critique of, and a commentary on, the "real" world of adults, the green world, heavily charged with post-Romantic childhood worship, declined into anti-adult retreat. The American version of it, which was ostensibly more activist and rebellious, nonetheless has proved to be an equally inadequate alternative. One of the chief distinctions between American and European versions has been the anti-intellectualism of our expression. Pynchon's comedy often situates itself in an anti-intellectualism, and there is no denying that it has had a certain appeal for him. From the very first scenes of *V.*, Pynchon has taken a particular fancy to the boyish high jinks of fraternity parties and sailors' shore leaves. Pig Bodine appears as a comic "hero" in both novels, and his particular brand of humor is the gross-out. At times, indeed, "comic" life in the Zone can best be described by the single word "raunchy." In addition, Pynchon favors a comic-strip humor. Major Marvy's bloated face can almost be envisioned leering out of a Sunday funnies frame, colored florid red, and in the next panel his gang of baddies lurching out of the cockpit and side windows of his little plane, waving their arms. It is "Pirate" Prentice, and it is Rocketman; Slothrop in his green cape and dehorned helmet, legs spread, fists on hips, straddling the body-strewn scene yelling, "Fickt nicht mit der Raketemensch!" *Gravity's Rainbow* seems at times like an old "Terry and the Pirates"—or more likely, "Steve Canyon," who was very big in the fifties. And the version of human life—and more important, the version of history—is distressingly like that of those funny-paper staples. For it is a Daddy Warbucks romanticization of the military-industrial complex. It looks upon modern human affairs with much the same simplistic point of view that characterizes the non-intellectualism of aspects of American popular culture. And it, as much as Peter Pan, refuses to take a complexly "adult" outlook on human events.

To be fair, we must acknowledge that Pynchon is conscious of the orientation of this material. For instance, the various images of idealized golden girlhood that constitute an ingredient of the American popular culture's formula gather together in the nymphet Bianca, late in part three. She is, explicitly, an embodiment of all the despoiled children—the Ilses and Katjes—of the novel; and when Slothrop witnesses the grotesque spontaneous orgy that erupts as she is spanked by Margherita (shortly after Bianca did her Shirley Temple imitation), and when Slothrop himself makes love to her, Slothrop realizes that he is participating in the debauching of a cultural icon. Specifically, she is the American golden-haired girl, whom you saw out of the windows of the passing Greyhound bus, whom you watched Lindy Hop, whom the comic strips glorified, and he is not sure that she was ever real— "she must be more than an image, a product, a promise to pay . . ." (V472/B551). Pynchon is aware that this version of The Girl Next Door, The Girl Back Home, The Girl That I Marry, is a nostalgically blurred concept, fraught with the urge to return to preadult innocence of vision. Yet we perceive that a part of that worship of the golden girl was the desire to despoil her. Even the supposedly simplistic formulas of the comic-strip culture do not come clean; they are confused with lust and a nostalgia for innocence. And yet this should be no surprise; for, just as the green world of the imagination has been a repository for all the desires and feelings that hardpaced everyday life cannot seem to accommodate, it has also harbored that other dimension of human life for which the open and dominant cultural expression has had no mode of presentation: sex. In so much of English and American culture, sex has been an outlawed or tabooed subject; thus it has been driven into other, oblique forms of expression—forms that were often either highly sanitized and romanticized in a fairy-tale manner, or were pornographic. In *Gravity's Rainbow*, we are frequently conscious of an uneasy slippage into perverse forms of sexuality, as if the characters were incapable of defining love in any other way. But that slippage had always been a thinly disguised background to "green world" idealizations of love and of innocence; we all know about Lewis Carroll's supposedly illicit feelings toward little girls; we all understand what Shirley Temple's fetching little dance steps aroused.

Slippage—signifying the instability of values and attitudes—is. what ultimately proves the bane of the comically "free" existence.

The age-old charge against comedy—particularly favored in the Puritan ethos that Max Weber chronicles—centered upon its potentiality for chaos. Comedy's origins lay in the saturnalia, interludes of celebrative disarray that vented the anxieties and tensions of the normally ordered and hierarchical cultures. The belief lingered well into the nineteenth century that if the spirit of comedy, with its irreverence, its amorphousness, its changeableness, were allowed to prevail in a society, or a pocket of society, the consequence would be anarchy, immorality, and finally disintegration. Comedy (especially in its imaginary green worlds) was a nice place to visit, but nobody wanted to live there long. And this proves to be the case with the comically oriented Zone in *Gravity's Rainbow*. Because life in the Zone is by its very nature ad hoc—"Temporary alliances, knit and undone"—and because the previous American and British cultural visions of comic interludes have been so elusive and ingenuous in their orientations, existence in the Zone proves to be dangerously unstable. In a bewildering series of episodes, the "plot" lines ravel and unravel, characters wander the countryside and the rubble of the cities, meet and part, connect and miss connections. Underneath it all lurks the danger of psychic breakdown. For with no values to sanctify, with disillusionment the legacy of war, and with cultural heritage discredited, an individual has precious few concepts on which to reconstruct himself.

An early metaphoric excursion illustrates the potential hazards of giving way completely to subjective flux. Slothrop, in a drug-induced fantasy, yields to all the anti-social, comically free-wheeling impulses that he suppresses in ordinary contexts. He imagines that he has fallen into a toilet bowl and is floating through the sewer system. His is the "excremental vision" familiar to Western satire and comedy, the vision of Jonathan Swift, or of Samuel Beckett when he says that "the way down is the way out." Slothrop serves as a manic commentator on the waste of a gorged society because he is able, for a moment, to indulge himself in all his perverse fascinations. Slothrop releases himself from the inhibitions that constrict him. But the content that emerges from the unconscious is unsettling. It exposes not only the normal human inclination toward the scatalogical, to befoul oneself, but it also reveals unexpectedly strong animosities toward blacks, in particular. Fear of being buggered by a black triggers the fantasy. It is almost as if tolerance toward blacks and other minorities were something that is maintained in Slothrop only under the constraints of the superego. Once these constraints vanish, a disturbing discharge of race-hatred, violence, perversion—random fecal matter of hate and fear and self-loathing—tumbles out. And it warns the reader that once all the socially dictated conformities are broken down, even if in the comic flux, we are vulnerable to irrational tendencies that we could not imagine that we harbored.

Thus, in the Zone, Slothrop discovers himself frequently on the verge of self-disintegrating indulgence. In order to love Margherita, he must torture her, and in a vivid instant he realizes that sadism contains a perverse fascination for him. "Whatever it is with her, he's catching it. Out in the ruins he sees darkness now at the edges of all the broken shapes, *showing from behind them.* . . . Across the façade of the Titaniapalast, in red neon through a mist one night he saw DIE, SLOTHROP. One Sunday . . . a crowd of little kids in soldier hats folded from old army maps plotted to drown and sacrifice him" (V446/B520). He is on the edge of psychic death.

Too often comedy breaks out in mayhem, and too often there are willing victims to every random bit of violence, every sadism, every perversion. Pynchon has long been intrigued by the mentality of subject peoples. The Hereros, a doomed race, fulfill a confusing role in Nazi Germany; like lemmings they have streamed into the homeland of their torturers to attend upon the German's casual whims of sadism. "They calculate no cycles, no returns, they are in love with the glamour of a whole people's suicide—the pose, the stoicism, and the bravery. . . . The Empty Ones can guarantee a day when the last Zone-Herero will die, a final zero to a collective history fully lived. It has appeal" (V318/B369–70). As the name of the people suggests, they are hero-zero, the anti-heroes of the twentieth century, symbolic carriers of the widespread disease of passivity, of impotence. The society that Pynchon depicts is under the control of no man; its institutions seem to be entropic in their self-sustaining quality. Hence the modern sense of powerlessness, of the inability to control events, to work one's will.

The comic literature of the last fifty years has placed particular emphasis upon this perspective; we have a rich tradition of the comic victim, the Chaplinesque clown, the little man who is buffeted by the whims of Fortune, abused by venal "authority figures" and who yet preserves the essential human decencies. Such a little man has been the staple of our situation comedies. He is Buster Keaton, Red Skelton, Laurel and Hardy, and even, in his cheeky way, W. C. Fields. He is Kingsley Amis's Lucky Jim, John Hawkes's Skipper, James Joyce's Leopold Bloom. The rise and survival of such a cultural figure suggests that comic expression has seized upon a felt quality of modern life. Since comedy is the "open" mode, since it is, as Suzanne Langer says, the mode of Fortune, and tragedy is the mode of Fate, it has been the natural vehicle for this feeling. And, intriguingly enough, the advent of this particular comic vision—of the little man victim rolling with the punches—has corresponded with the critique of the notions of human intentionality and its workings, and of cause and effect, at the end of the nineteenth century. In particular, Henri Bergson, in *Time and Free Will*, and Friedrich Nietzsche, in *The Will to Power* (and, in a different way, Arthur Schopenhauer in several writings), raised the first questions about Western man's long-hallowed way of looking at human intention and human activity. They both argue that the notion of causality is an illusion; we *surmise* cause and intention from the "schema of the effects." As so often happens, a social observation begins to correlate with philosophical theorizing to form the background for a perspective on life that literature begins to express in more and more explicit terms.

There can be little doubt that Pynchon is probing, in *Gravity's Rainbow*, the implications of this possible change in our way of thinking about human behavior. The vast majority of characters in the novel do, of course, cling to the idea that human will can operate in the way that we have been accustomed to believe that it does—that one makes choices, forms intentions, and acts from those intentions, and that what happens politically and socially in the world is a result of individuals engaged in this process. But there are some individuals, notably Roger Mexico, who argue that we must " 'junk cause-and-effect entirely, and strike off at some other angle' " (V89/B103). Leni argues the same thing against Franz Pökler, although she is not quite sure how to articulate it": "He was the cause-and-effect man. . . . 'There is no way for changes out there to produce changes here.' 'Not produce,' she tried, 'not cause. It all goes along together. Parallel, not series. Metaphor. Signs and symptoms. Mapping on to different coordinate systems. I don't know...' She didn't know, all she was trying to do was reach" (V159/B186). Mexico is more specific; it is a principle of randomness that governs our existence. And little does he know, but he has an unlikely coconspirator, the German film-maker von Göll, busily at work, producing "under the carpet" motion pictures that ridicule cause and effect: "a reverse world whose agents run around with guns which are like vacuum cleaners operating in the direction of life—pull the trigger and bullets are sucked back out of the recently dead into the barrel, and the Great Irreversible is actually reversed as the corpse comes to life to the accompaniment of a backwards gunshot . . . " (V745/B870).

I am indebted to Joseph Slade's book *Thomas Pynchon* for an insight into the significance of this idea for Pynchon. Slade suggests that it comes from exploratory work by the psychologist C. G. Jung and the physicist Wolfgang Pauli on the notion of coincidence and noncausal phenomena.[8] Jung and Pauli raise the possibility that we deceive ourselves in assuming that the operative pattern in many incidents and happenings is causality, and that we must open ourselves up to other ways of looking at physical behavior. We must entertain the idea of randomness and chance as an operative principle in the unfolding of human events. I touch upon this subject in writing about comedy in Pynchon because it seems to me that Pynchon is toying with a world view that has been essential to the comic in the last fifty years. Opposed in *Gravity's Rainbow* is, on the one hand, the noncomic orientation that has governed Western thought for hundreds of years—an orientation that attaches *consequences* to things, that suggests we are responsible for the shape of our societies and our lives, that all action has meaning, and derives from some form of intentionality—and, on the other hand, the comic orientation, which suggests that we trust to luck, ride the crest, develop an anarchic, free-wheeling attitude toward life. If the latter is truer to the physical and psychic actualities of our condition, then the comic literature that portrays man as essentially a victim of circumstances is the genuinely prophetic mode—or at least the apter mode.

Pynchon probes the frontiers of this concept in *Gravity's Rainbow*, but goes no further because it is a heady realm nearly impossible to navigate in the narrative prose of a cause-and-effect tradition. Arthur Koestler points out that Jung found it difficult to proceed on the terms he had suggested, and ended up postulating a concept of synchronicity that showed "the apparently insurmountable difficulties of breaking away from our ingrained habits of thinking in terms of cause and effect."[9] Koestler says that whenever earlier Western philosophers developed a similar line of thought, they almost invariably attempted to reconcile randomness with cause and effect by returning to the idea of an omniscient, God-like intelligence that unified everything. Lyle Bland in *Gravity's Rainbow* appears to have been pursuing such a course. In his advanced stages of Masonic mysticism, Bland claimed to be journeying (while lying on his back on the couch in his study) "underneath history: [he imagines] that history is Earth's mind, and that there are layers, set very deep, layers of history analogous to layers of coal and oil in Earth's body" (V589/B687). Bland, as comic a voyager into philosophical netherlands as one could conceive, does finally, after settling his affairs ("One night he called his whole family together around the davenport in the study. Lyle, Jr. came in from Houston. . . . Clara drove down from Bennington and Buddy rode the MTA in from Cambridge" [V590–91/B688]), depart his physical chains altogether. He abandons all contexts, even the couch, for his ultimate trip into Randomness.

Few others are able to abandon their human contexts so completely. And, in fact, the "charm" of world war had been the total context that it supplied for those involved in it. We are told of a

> long-time schiz . . . who believes that *he* is World War II. He gets no newspapers, refuses to listen to the wireless, but still, the day of the Normandy invasion somehow his temperature shot up to 104°. Now, as the pincers east and west continue their slow reflex contraction, he speaks of darkness invading his mind, of an attrition of self.... The Rundstedt offensive perked him up though, gave him a new lease on life. . . . (V131/B152)

More people than the long-time schiz relied on the war for focus and direction. Slothrop disappears from the coordinates of other people's concern, and thus, in a way, from existence, because of the end of the German campaign. Mexico's love for Jessica is only a creature of the War. Hence it is problematic that a noncausal world view could ever gain acceptance for Western peoples, who are so reliant upon historicity and upon control theories for the contexts of their lives.

Indeed, Pynchon suggests that everything we do and think about is programmed in some way by our social and cultural contexts, and that ultimately all we will be able to do, even in a comically open world view, is rehearse a wider variety of programs. This plight comes to the surface at the time of what is presumably Slothrop's first disorientation. At the beginning of part two, we see him at the rest and recreation spa, Casino Hermann Goering. His first time out on the beach, he espies a gigantic octopus grasping a lovely blonde in its tentacles, about to pull her out to sea. Slothrop rushes to her rescue, not yet aware of what a fanciful parody it is on the themes of his situation: the octopus a fitting analogue to the many-tentacled corporate conspiracy; the blonde a symbol for all the cultural values the Allies are fighting for (including both purity and sexuality); and Slothrop's action a splendid, comic-book illustration of heroism, taking control of one's situation, and so on. Unfortu-

nately, the octopus is Grigori, the Fabulous Octopus of the Pointsman lab's Pavlovian experiments, the girl is Katje Borgesius in the
employ of the White Visitation, and the entire episode has been
staged. Slothrop recognizes all this in short order—"What th' fuck's
going on?" (V187/B218)—and immediately contracts paranoia.
Subliminally, we as readers make the connection between the state
of paranoia and staged effects, and we are haunted with the implication that every mental state, even so devastating as the pattern of
this one, is a schema. As we progress through the novel, we perceive more and more that the historical and psychohistorical aspects
of Pynchon's version of the world are highly theatrical. Constantly
the text shifts us from "actual events" to cinematic, comic-strip, or
fictional analogues to them. The interpenetration is so intense in
Gravity's Rainbow that one must conclude that there is *nothing* that
people do or think about that is not fit somehow into a scheme.
Fatality and suffering, love—everything—has its repertoire of
scenarios that we unconsciously apply to every situation. We cannot act without our texts, even in a contingent, random world (for
comedy has supplied us with many texts for chaos, and pornography and psychological literature with many texts for psychic
disorientation).

If anything, Pynchon seems to emphasize this fact more and
more. The reminders are interlaced in narrative description: "The
story here tonight is a typical WW II intrigue . . . " (V247/B287) or
"It's a Sunday-funnies dawn, very blue sky with gaudy pink clouds
in it" (V295/B343). Human life in the Zone is a patchwork of scenarios and frantic roles. The Argentine gaucho-anarchist Squalidozzi turns to the German movie-maker Gerhardt von Göll in the
hope that von Göll will be able to script an appropriate actuality for
him and his men. Von Göll is heady with the recent success of his
"invention" of the Schwarzkommando, whom he had conjured up
as a devious Allied trick and then found out later that they existed.
" 'It is my mission,' he announces to Squalidozzi, with the profound
humility that only a German movie director can summon, 'to sow in
the Zone seeds of reality. The historical moment demands this, and
I can only be its servant. My images, somehow, have been chosen
for incarnation. What I can do for the Schwarzkommando I can do
for your dream of pampas and sky . . . ' " (V388/B451). A new
scenario is needed for the Argentines, since they do not seem to be
able to get their act together:

> The crew that hijacked the U-boat are here out of all kinds of Argen-
> tine manias. El Ñato goes around talking in 19th-century gaucho slang—

cigarettes are "pitos," butts are "puchos," it isn't caña he drinks but "la tacuara," and when he's drunk he's "mamao." Sometimes Felipe has to translate for him. Felipe is a difficult young poet with any number of un-pleasant enthusiasms, among them romantic and unreal notions about the gauchos. He is always sucking up to El Ñato. . . . Luz is currently with Felipe, though she's supposed to be Squalidozzi's girl—after Squalidozzi disappeared on his trip to Zürich she took up with the poet on the basis of a poignant recitation of Lugones's "Pavos Reales," one balmy night lying off Matosinhos. For this crew, nostalgia is like sea-sickness: only the hope of dying from it is keeping them alive. (V383–84/B446)

Everyone in the Zone, and in the wake of the War, is having trouble keeping his act together. The characters, and the narrative vision itself, rely more frequently on comic-strip, literary formulas and on cinematic schemes for organizing and interpreting the episodes of their lives. When Von Göll (in the role of Springer) abandons his faithful companion Närrisch, surrounded by trigger-happy Russian troops and apparently doomed, Slothrop criticizes him for the treachery. Von Göll is unconcerned; Närrisch, like the Asp or Punjab or any number of characters from the comic strips, has been last seen on many occasions in apparently hopeless cir-cumstances, only to reappear again. " 'But what if they *did* shoot him?' " Slothrop asks. " 'No. They weren't supposed to,' " von Göll answers. " 'Springer, this ain't the fuckin' *movies* now, come on.' " " 'Not yet. Maybe not quite yet' " (V527/B614). By the end of the novel, it *is* the movies. Major Marvy is arrested, mistaken for Slothrop, and castrated—a poetic revenge that will bring the entire theater audience to delighted applause. Roger Mexico wreaks his vengeance on Pointsman and the Corporate Conspiracy by break-ing into their board meeting, jumping on the board table, whipping out his cock, and pissing on the shiny table, the papers, the ashtrays. As security police dash into the room, Mexico dives under the table, the men colliding and butting heads as they grapple for him, and then begins the escape: " . . . Aficionados of the chase scene, those who cannot look at the Taj Mahal, the Uffizi, the Statue of Liberty without thinking chase scene, chase scene, wow yeah Douglas Fairbanks scampering across that moon minaret there—these en-thusiasts may find interest in the following . . . " (V637/B742).

As such a passage suggests, the narrative of *Gravity's Rainbow* becomes more and more self-conscious as the contexts of the War and the plots that circulated within it break down and randomness prevails. The comic narrative method of the last phases of the novel is not that of the earlier phases, in which metaphor was used to dis-charge the tensions of a rigid, inhumane world order. Rather, we have now *improvisation* in the face of manic disorder. Part four is largely made up of spliced stories, comic routines, skits, film clips, vignettes. One senses the strain in a narrative mode that had its origins and its greatest successes in approaching its materials from the point of view of cause and effect, now struggling to dominate a fragmented, random world view. That "conventional" novelistic mode can only summon up its old schemata, but even these are briefer, less cohesive—and gradually more remote, as in the final pages, Pynchon deals out his material through tarot cards— signifiers of the mysteries of the random. *Gravity's Rainbow* charts some sort of ritual passage in the uses and the outlook of comedy. Initially the comedy serves to vent the anxieties and pressures of a hardened world. Then, in the long section dealing with life in the Zone, the comedy is an excursion into flux and freedom, a working through of its own "green world" and pop culture manifestations, and a penetration deep into its own perverse shadows—across that dark "interface" that Ernst Kris speaks of. Finally comedy engages in a kind of frenetic improvisation, an exhibition of virtuosity, as it flashes rapidly through scenarios and quasi-cultural schemata in an attempt to cope with the challenges of randomness. And at the end of *Gravity's Rainbow*, we are invited to follow the bouncing ball—an almost parodic analogue of the novelistic mode's dogged struggle to master an emerging new comic vision.

1. Sigmund Freud, *Jokes and Their Relation to the Unconscious*, trans. James Strachey (1905; rpt. New York: Atheneum, 1966); Arthur Koestler, *The Act of Creation* (New York: Macmillan, 1964).

2. Ernst Kris, *Psychoanalytic Explorations in Art* (1952; rpt. New York: Schocken Books, 1964), pp. 173–216.

3. Roger B. Henkle, "Pynchon's Tapestries on the Western Wall," *Modern Fiction Studies* 17 (1971): 207–20.

4. Joseph Slade, *Thomas Pynchon* (New York: Warner Books, 1974); Edward Mendelson, "Gravity's Encyclopedia," in George Levine and David Leverenz, eds., *Mindful Pleasures: Essays on Thomas Pynchon* (Boston: Little, Brown, 1976), pp. 161–96.

5. Henri Bergson, "Laughter" (1900), reprinted in *Comedy* (Garden City, N.Y.: Doubleday, 1956).

6. George Santayana, "Carnival," in *Soliloquies in England and Later Soliloquies* (New York: Charles Scribner's Sons, 1922); Suzanne Langer, *Feeling and Form* (New York: Charles Scribner's Sons, 1953); Bergson, "Laughter"; Northrop Frye, *Anatomy of Criticism* (Princeton: Princeton University Press, 1957).

7. Frye, pp. 163–86.

8. Slade, pp. 214, 215, 236. The essays by Pauli and Jung appear in *Naturerklärung und Psyche. Studien aus dem C. G. Jung-Institut*, No. 4 (1952).

9. Arthur Koestler, *The Roots of Coincidence* (New York: Random House, 1972), pp. 97–98.

Notes on the Contributors

KHACHIG TOLOLYAN received his B.A. in molecular biology, then studied oceanography and English literature for some years before earning his doctorate in comparative literature. He is now associate professor of English at Wesleyan University in Middletown, Connecticut. His interests in science and literature led him to Pynchon's work, on which he has published several articles. He is also the author of essays on John Barth and Jorge Luis Borges, and is writing a book on cosmographic narrative ranging from the *Iliad* to *Gravity's Rainbow*. He has coedited *Pynchon Notes* since its inception in 1979.

ALAN J. FRIEDMAN is an associate research educator and the director of astronomy and physics education at the Lawrence Hall of Science, University of California, Berkeley. His research is primarily concerned with understanding the relations among science, technology, and the culture at large. He has published articles, often with coauthors from other disciplines, in *Contemporary Literature, Journal of College Science Teaching, Sky and Telescope, Physics Education, Trema,* and the *San Francisco Review of Books.*

CHARLES CLERC is professor of English and chairman of the department at the University of the Pacific, Stockton, California. He is a winner of the Spanos Award for Distinguished Teaching at UOP. During 1980–81 he served as Distinguished Visiting Professor at the U.S. Air Force Academy. He is coeditor of *Seven Contemporary Short Novels* (3d ed., 1982), and editor of *Fifty Great Short-Short Stories* (1982). His play *The Pillar* was produced in 1973, and his articles and stories have appeared in *Modern Fiction Studies, Midwest*

Quarterly, Satire Newsletter, Western Humanities Review, English Journal, and other periodicals.

JOSEPH W. SLADE is professor of English, director of the Communications Center, and chairman of the Media Arts Department at Long Island University, the Brooklyn Center. He was the first critic to write a book-length study of Pynchon (1974), and he has also published three articles on his work. In addition, he is the author of two dozen articles on subjects ranging from literature to film to contemporary society. Since 1968, he has served as editor of the *Markham Review,* an interdisciplinary quarterly. Recently he was the recipient of a year-long NEH Fellowship in Technology at the University of Chicago.

RAYMOND M. OLDERMAN resigned as an associate professor of English at the University of Wisconsin at Madison. Before he left the academic profession, he won awards for outstanding teaching. His book *Beyond The Waste Land: A Study of the American Novel in the Nineteen-Sixties* (1972) won the Eighteenth Annual Explicator Award. He is presently awash in the pleasures of preterite life.

JAMES W. EARL is assistant professor of English at Fordham University. He has written numerous articles on Anglo-Saxon and other medieval literature.

CHARLES RUSSELL is an assistant professor of English at Rutgers University in Newark. He formerly taught at the University of Virginia and also served as research specialist at the Center for Twentieth Century Studies at the University of Wisconsin—Milwaukee. His book, *The Avant-garde Today: An International Anthology* was published in 1981, and his articles on contemporary literature and the avant-garde have appeared in *Modern Fiction Studies, Diacritics, Modern Language Notes,* and elsewhere. He is executive editor of the *American Book Review,* and is now at work on a book on the theory and history of avant-garde literature.

ROGER B. HENKLE is professor of English at Brown University. He is the author of *Comedy and Culture: England 1820–1900* (1980), which deals with the uses of comedy by the middle class to express its social and cultural concerns, and *Reading the Novel: An Introduction to the Techniques of Interpreting Fiction* (1977). He is managing editor of *Novel: A Forum on Fiction;* and has published articles on comedy and comedy theory in the *Virginia Quarterly Review, Sewanee Review, Critical Quarterly,* and *Mosaic.* An earlier essay on Pynchon appeared in *Modern Fiction Studies,* and is reprinted in the Twentieth Century Views collection, *Pynchon.*

Index

Index